BASIC ECONOMIC CONCEPTS
Macroeconomics

BASIC ECONOMIC CONCEPTS
Macroeconomics

Second Edition

Werner Sichel
Western Michigan University

Peter Eckstein
formerly of Western Michigan University

Rand McNally College Publishing Company/Chicago

A companion volume, *Microeconomics,* and
a complete single-volume edition are available

77 78 79 10 9 8 7 6 5 4 3 2 1

To our parents:

Lilly and Joseph Sichel
Virginia and Charles Eckstein

Acknowledgments

In a very real sense this book has been a joint effort, with both of us actively involved in the development of every chapter. Some division of labor should be noted, however.

The chapters on General Economic Concepts and Supply and Demand, as well as the four chapters embracing Microeconomics and Industrial Organization, were the primary responsibility of Werner Sichel. Peter Eckstein assumed basic responsibility for the three chapters on Macroeconomics and the chapters on Public Finance, Economic Inequality, International Trade, and Economic Development. The idea for an introductory economics book divided into concepts was Sichel's.

Several persons helped greatly in bringing this work to fruition. Rand McNally Acquisition Editor Bob Erhart urged and egged us on from the beginning. Manuscript editor Charlotte Iglarsh made thousands of changes in order to make the manuscript intelligible to people as well as to economists. Ralph Beals and Rod Peterson helped render the manuscript intelligible to economists as well as to people. Adrienne Malley provided the indispensable viewpoint of a beginning student of economics by telling us whenever we weren't getting through.

The revision of our book for its second edition was greatly facilitated by our colleagues around the United States and Canada who were kind enough either to fill out and make comments on opinion cards furnished by Rand McNally or to write us personally expressing opinions and offering suggestions. To these more than 100 persons—too many to mention by name—we wish to express our deep appreciation. We are especially grateful to three professors, Rod Peterson of Colorado State University, and Phillip Caruso and Raymond Zelder of Western Michigan University, who critically reviewed our first edition for this revision.

We met our editorial deadlines only through the patience, secretarial skills, and expert organizing of Em Hollingshead and Cress Strand, and the added help of Jill Hollingshead and Gretchen Tarchinski. Christine Truckey was of great assistance in preparing the second edition.

Those for whose patience we are most grateful, however, are our wives and children—Beatrice, Larry, and Linda Sichel, and Janet and Anne Eckstein.

W.S.
P.E.

Kalamazoo, Michigan
Summer, 1976

CONTENTS

To the Instructor

This book is designed to introduce the most important concepts in elementary economics. Each one is defined and explained—briefly, carefully and simply—with enough illustrations or applications to the real world to make them interesting and intelligible. In the course of introducing 90 major concepts, a large number of additional concepts are also introduced and defined. For example, in the discussion of *Opportunity Cost*—a major concept—we introduce and explain the idea of production possibility, just as important an idea, but less suited to being treated independently.

While it can be used as a basic reference work, the main purpose of the book is to serve as a core textbook for an introductory course in economics. To promote this purpose the 90 major concepts are not arranged alphabetically but are organized into thirteen chapters designed to facilitate the flow of ideas.

The book has three different incarnations: a complete single volume and two partial volumes, one emphasizing microeconomic concepts, the other emphasizing macroeconomic and international concepts. Both of the split volumes contain the introductory two chapters—General Economic Concepts and Supply and Demand—to accommodate courses that begin either with micro or macro. Both also include the chapter on Public Finance to accommodate courses that join this area either to micro or macro.

The hallmark of the book is flexibility. The material has been carefully organized and presented in a way that maximizes flexibility—flexibility in the kind of course that can be built around it and flexibility in the order in which the material is introduced.

Several features of the book provide maximum flexibility in the kind of course that the instructor chooses to offer. The entire book is only 331 pages long, and an abbreviated assignment list for a short macro course (described on pp. xv–xvi) would cover only 238 pages. The reading load required to cover fundamental principles, then, is light enough for most instructors to feel free to assign additional materials, making the course as timely and relevant as possible.

For example, in a course stressing microeconomics the instructor might use this book in conjunction with such works as: North and Miller, *The Economics of Public Issues,* 3d edition (Harper and Row, 1976); Tucker, *Current Economic Issues and Problems* (Rand McNally, 1976); Lee and McNown, *Economics in Our Time* (Science Research Associates, 1975); Phillips and Votey, *Economic Analysis of Pressing Social Problems,* 2d edition (Rand McNally, 1977); or Schachter and Dale, *The Economist Looks at Society* (Xerox Publishing, 1973).

In a course stressing macroeconomics the book might be used along with such works as: Friedman, *Inflation, A Growing World-Wide Disaster* (Anchor Books, 1975); Lerner, *Flation* (Penguin, 1974); McNown and Lee, *Economics in Our Time, Macro Issues* (Science Research Associates, 1976); Bach, *The New Inflation* (Prentice Hall, 1972); or Okun, *The Battle Against Unemployment,* revised edition (Norton, 1972). Another useful supplement might be the latest *Economic Report of the President,* including the report of the Council of Economic Advisers.

In a course covering both microeconomics and macroeconomics, this book might be used together with such works as Puth, ed., *Current Issues in the American Economy* (D. C. Heath & Co., 1976); Rosen, ed., *Economic Power Failure* (McGraw-Hill, 1975); Mermelstein, *Economics: Mainstream Readings and Radical Critiques,* 3d edition (Random House, 1976); or Hailstones and Mastrianna, *Contemporary Economic Problems and Issues,* 4th edition (South-Western, 1976).

Furthermore, the organization of the book is flexible enough so that those materials can be woven into the course sequence in a wide variety of ways. Our hope is that many instructors will be able—perhaps for the first time—to create their own kind of economics course without being bound to the coverage of a standard textbook.

To provide maximum flexibility in the order of presentation, we have discussed each concept as a self-contained unit. The 90 concepts are presented in an order that we think makes sense for an introductory course. The instructor, however, can choose from a variety of sequences in assigning particular chapters or the discussions of concepts within each chapter. The instructor need not assign all of the concepts in a chapter. For example, many teachers of elementary courses prefer not to introduce *Indifference Analysis* or isoquants and isocost lines as used in *Best Factor Combination.* These may easily be left out without losing continuity or necessary prerequisites for further material. Yet instructors who wish to include such concepts in their courses are able to do so. In examining individual concepts, we have not struggled unduly to avoid repeating ourselves. Indeed, some points are emphasized several times when we felt this would enable the individual discussions to stand on their own feet. At the same time, there are obviously some practical limits on how independent we could make the coverage of each concept. Such basic terms as "function," "real income," and "variable" are not repeatedly defined. Rather, in the introductory message "To the Student," we have introduced these all at once in the section called "Some Basic Terms." Students using the book should be advised to read that message first. The first two chapters of the book—General Economic Concepts and Supply and Demand—also lay the groundwork for future work. Not every discussion in these chapters, however, is essential for understanding all of the chapters that follow. For example, the discussion of *Money* in Chapter 1 is useful but not necessary for understanding some of the microeconomic concepts covered in later chapters. It is, however, important for understanding the process of *Money Creation* described in the chapter on macroeconomic behavior. Inevitably, some of the discussions of individual concepts must build on earlier ones. For example, in the micro chapter on market types it is difficult to understand *Monopoly* except by way of contrast with *Pure Competition,* which is discussed earlier in the same chapter. Likewise, there is some progression of ideas as the student moves through the three macroeconomic chapters. In particular, the discussion of *Equilibrium Income with Money* builds on the discussion of *Equilibrium Income with Government,* which in turn builds on the theoretical framework developed in *Equilibrium Income.* These discussions do not, however, rely in any way on the detailed discussions of the *Consumption Function* and the *Investment Function.*

To minimize unnecessary duplication, and to facilitate the work of the student, we have established a complete system of cross-references to other discussions. The student who feels confident of the groundwork can safely ignore these; the student who is unsure should be encouraged to go back and read or reread.

We feel this book represents an important new approach to the teaching of elementary economics, one well suited to the needs of the contemporary classroom. We wrote in the first edition that "We hope that instructors and students using the book will agree; certainly they will have many ideas of their own as to how the book can be used and how it can be improved. We would greatly appreciate hearing how the book is working out in the classroom." Our hopes have been realized. Tens of thousands of students have used our book during the past two years. Our students at Western Michigan University have generally been very complementary. So have the more than 100 instructors who have taken the time to fill out opinion cards or write letters to us. We have nonetheless made substantial additions and changes in the second edition.

One general effort we made was to introduce more tools to help the student evaluate economic phenomena. We have added a discussion of *Equity,* and the *Efficiency* concept has been simplified and expanded to include a section on long-run growth, which may be seen as efficiency over time. This permits an instructor early in the course to introduce a framework of three overriding goals of economic policy—efficiency, equity, and growth—and some of the tradeoffs among them. That framework can be applied repeatedly during the discussion of specific policy questions. Alternatively, those two concepts may simply be omitted, as an understanding of the subsequent portions of the book does not require them. But we think they can be used to add an important new dimension to the course.

In addition, we have added evaluative sections to our discussion of *Unemployment of Labor, Inflation,* and *Balance of Payments.* Chapter 1 has been enlarged—and, we believe, improved—by the addition of two more new concepts: *Opportunity Cost* and *Discounting the Future.* Instructors will be able, then, to refer back to these important concepts whenever they arise later in the course. We have also rewritten several other concepts that were included in the first edition. *Production Possibility* has been deleted from the micro chapter on factors of production and incorporated in the *Opportunity Cost* concept. A new concept on *Human Capital* has been added to the chapter on factors of production, and one on the *Cartel* has been added to the industrial organization chapter. A new concept on *Equilibrium Income with Money* has been added to the macroeconomic policy chapter. It relates the single demand function introduced in the revised discussion of *Demand for Money* to the $C + I + G$ diagram introduced in *Equilibrium Income with Government* and shows the important role of money in determining a macroeconomic equilibrium. The other new concept in the same chapter is *Planning for Full Employment.* This discussion can serve as a capstone to the three chapters on macroeconomics—and does so in a way that brings the student to the frontier of the policy debates of the late 1970s. The discussion goes further than most parts of the book in presenting a specific point of view, but it should serve to stimulate active classroom discussion. A number of concepts throughout the book have been substantially rewritten, and all have been updated. In particular, the book incorporates the 1976 changes made by the Department of Commerce in presenting data—both in the *National Income Accounts* and especially in the *Balance of Payments.*

We hope that you will agree that our second edition is much improved. We once again solicit your comments and suggestions.

SUGGESTED SHORT COURSE OUTLINES

Microeconomics

A Note To the Student

General Economic Concepts
    Scarcity
    Marginal Analysis
    Opportunity Cost
    Efficiency
    Equity
    Economic Theory
    Economic Rationality
    Equilibrium

Supply and Demand
    Market
    Demand
    Supply
    Supply and Demand Analysis

Factors of Production
    Capital
    Land
    Labor
    Diminishing Returns
    Division of Labor
    Economies and Diseconomies
      of Scale

Price Theory
    Cost
    Profit Maximization
    Utility Analysis
    Elasticity of Supply
    Elasticity of Demand

Market Types
    Pure Competition
    Pure Monopoly
    Monopolistic Competition
    Oligopoly

Macroeconomics

A Note To the Student

General Economic Concepts
    Scarcity
    Opportunity Cost
    Efficiency
    Equity
    Economic Theory
    Equilibrium
    Money

Supply and Demand
    Market
    Demand
    Supply
    Supply and Demand Analysis

Framework for Macroeconomics
    Aggregate Demand
    Unemployment of Labor
    Inflation
    Phillips Curve
    Economic Growth

Macroeconomic Behavior
    The Propensity to Consume
    Equilibrium Income
    The Investment Multiplier
    The Demand for Money
    Money Creation

Macroeconomic Policy
    Equilibrium Income with
      Government
    Fiscal Policy
    Monetary Policy
    Monetarism
    Public Debt
    Planning for Full Employment

Total Number of Pages: 200   Total Number of Pages: 238

Total Pages for a Short Course Combining Micro and Macro: 438

To the Student

Every year nearly a million students in the United States enter a course in the principles of economics. Very few of them do it because they hope to become professional economists; most do it because they would like to understand better the world in which they live. They want to operate more intelligently as they purchase products, read newspapers, operate businesses, pay taxes, and vote for candidates for public office.

We live in a world of recessions and inflations, of changing values for the dollar on world currency markets, of environmental abuse and energy crisis. The daily papers are full of headlines about government policy toward the economy—taxes, expenditures, controls, welfare programs, antitrust actions, public utility regulation, tariffs, import quotas, and the growth of the money supply. Such policies affect each of us as individuals, but they also dominate much of our political life and our relationships with other nations. This book is designed to provide you with a set of tools for better understanding these problems and policies.

The most important tools of economics are a set of basic concepts. Most introductory textbooks try to hide these concepts in a maze of narrative, in the hope of making these ideas seem as painless as possible to learn. This book uses the opposite approach: it lays out the most important concepts in as straightforward a manner as possible. Our experience is that the way students can master these concepts painlessly is to face them directly and in the process to see clearly how they relate to one another and how they apply to problems in the real world.

The book contains discussions of 90 major concepts grouped together in thirteen chapters. Each of the major concepts is listed in the Table of Contents, and each chapter begins with a short introduction suggesting how the concepts within the chapter fit together. Each individual discussion of major concepts introduces some additional terms that we have called "subconcepts." Each of the subconcepts is underlined where it is first introduced and defined.

The index at the end of the book plays an important role, since it lists all of the concepts and subconcepts (as well as other names and terms) in alphabetical order. The index lists all the pages on which a term is mentioned, with heavy type (boldface) used to indicate the page on which a particular concept or subconcept is introduced and defined.

As far as possible the discussion of each of the individual concepts is designed to stand on its own feet, to be understandable to you even if you have not read and mastered all that has gone before. Inevitably, however, some concepts within a chapter do build on those that have preceded it. Where one discussion relies on something that has gone before, we have tried to indicate this with a reference. For example, the discussion of *Tax Incidence* includes the reference: (see *Supply and Demand Analysis,* pp. 63–68). If you feel you already understand the basic ideas of supply and demand analysis as described on those pages, you need not look back. If, however, you do not remember the basic tools introduced there, refer back to the pages indicated; they will help you in understanding the problem of who actually pays a tax like the sales tax.

This book by itself is not designed to provide all the answers to the pressing economic problems of the day. We have deliberately kept it shorter than most of the introductory economics textbooks. We see it as a springboard, enabling you to understand better other books and articles you will read on immediate economic problems and issues. Your instructor may assign some of these materials along with this book. Or you may want to read on your own some of the books listed on page xii. An understanding of the basic economic concepts described in this book should provide you with important insights into current economic issues, and reading about those issues should add depth to your understanding of the basic concepts. The two together should give you a meaningful—and, we hope, fascinating—introduction to the world of economics.

SOME BASIC TERMS

Economics, like any science, has a large technical vocabulary. Fortunately, not all of it needs to be learned in an introductory course, but some of it is necessary. Some of the words you probably already know, but in economics they may take on a more specific meaning—words like capital, investment, and rent. Others you may not have heard before—words like oligopoly, elasticity, and production function. These and other terms are among the concepts and subconcepts described in the book. Here some basic terms are introduced that will be used many times throughout the book. You should become familiar with them before reading further.

Economics, like any social or physical science, is concerned with the behavior of variables—things that may take on different values over time as conditions change. The supply of money, the price of tea, and the unemployment rate are a few examples of economic variables. Often the economist seeks to express the relationship among variables in terms of a function—a statement of how one variable depends on other variables. For example, one variable—the quantity of tea consumed in Boston in a week—may be a function of such other variables as the price of tea, the income of Boston families, and the price of coffee. When one variable is being described as a function of other variables we call it the dependent variable, while the variables upon which it depends are called the independent variables. Thus when we consider the function describing the demand for tea, the dependent variable is the quantity of tea consumed, while the independent variables are the price of tea, the incomes of families, and the price of coffee. If we were considering another function, however, the classification of variables might change. For example, the incomes of Boston families might be treated as a function of such variables as the rate of unemployment in Boston, the education and skills of the income-earning members of Boston families, and the wealth held by those families. Family income would then be the dependent variable in this functional relationship.

One of the most basic distinctions in economics is between a stock and a flow. A stock is a quantity defined at a particular point in time—$155 in a bank vault on Wednesday, seven eggs in the refrigerator at noon. A flow is a quantity defined over a particular period of time. It is often described by the rate at which the flow is occurring—$5 being added to the bank account every month, two eggs being eaten per day. An easy stock-flow relationship to see is provided by a bathtub. At exactly 7:15 on a Saturday night the bathtub might have contained 13 gallons of water—a stock of water. At the same time, the water might have been pouring into the tub at the rate of two gallons per minute—a flow of water. The flow, of course, would be changing the stock, so that by 7:17 the bathtub might contain a stock of 17 gallons.

The stock-flow distinction is central to understanding two important economic variables—wealth and income. Wealth is a stock—the value of property owned at any particular time. <u>Income</u> is a flow—measured by the rate at which money is being earned or received. By setting aside some income—by saving it rather than consuming it—a family or a nation can add to its wealth. Thus the flow of savings out of income can add to the stock of wealth.

In describing how income and wealth vary over time, it is important in a world of changing prices to make the distinction between real and nominal values. Assume that the wealth of a family consists largely of the house it owns, which was worth $30,000 at the beginning of the year. Assume, too, that prices in the economy have generally gone up by 10 percent during the year, so that the house is worth $33,000 at the end of the year. The <u>nominal value</u>—or money value—of the house has increased by 10 percent. But the <u>real value</u> of the house—its value adjusted for changes in purchasing power—has not increased at all. Likewise, suppose that the dollar amount of family earnings increased by 10 percent in that year—say, from $10,000 to $11,000. We would then say that <u>nominal income</u> had increased by 10 percent, but <u>real income</u> had not increased at all, since the higher money income after prices went up was not able to buy any more goods and services for the family.

Another distinction is important in thinking about the flow of income and product in an economy—the distinction among raw materials, intermediate goods, and final goods. <u>Raw materials</u> are unprocessed goods, and <u>intermediate goods</u> are partly processed goods. Both types of goods are completely transformed or used up in the course of current production. By contrast, <u>final goods</u> are ones that are used directly for consumption or investment purposes. Raw materials would include wheat and iron ore, while intermediate goods would include flour destined for bakeries or steel sheets to be stamped into automobile bodies. The final goods, of course, would be the bread produced by the bakeries or the automobiles sold to the public.

THE USE OF DIAGRAMS

Students sometimes anticipate that working with the lines and curves in diagrams will be confusing or difficult. Actually, however, diagrams are often the best—and the easiest—way to understand a concept and to see the relationships among variables. Once you overcome any initial fear, you will find that a diagram can help you to understand the ideas being discussed.

For practice with diagrams, look at Figure 1. Like most diagrams in this book, it begins with a zero point, or origin. The line that goes straight up from the origin is the vertical axis, and the line going straight off to the right is the horizontal axis. These two axes are scaled—marked off with numbers—to show varying amounts of the variable being measured along the axis.

Figure 1 describes how the production of corn might increase on a hypothetical (or imaginary) 50-acre farm as more and more workers are employed on the farm. The amount of corn produced is measured on the vertical axis, while the number of workers is measured on the horizontal axis. The diagram is really a picture of a function—the function that shows how the production of corn (the dependent variable) depends on the number of workers employed (the independent variable).

Figure 1   Corn Production on a 50-acre Farm (hypothetical data)

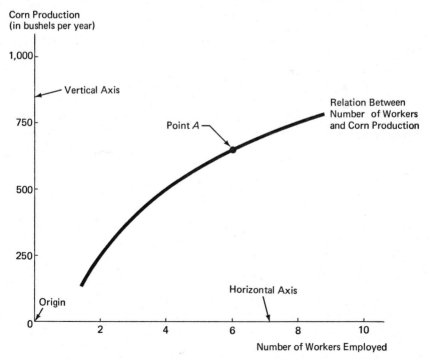

Each point on the curve provides one piece of information. To read the information from a point—like Point *A*—draw two straight lines (one vertical, the other horizontal) from the point itself to each of the two axes. When this is done, as in Figure 2, we can read the information off the two axes. Point *A* says that if 6 workers are employed (as read off the horizontal axis), they will be able to produce 650 bushels of corn (as read off the vertical axis). A curve like this can also be used to tell how many workers would be required to produce 750 bushels of corn (8 workers, as read off the horizontal axis) or how many bushels of corn 4 workers could produce (500 bushels, as read off the vertical axis). The diagram, then, is a quick way of summarizing all we know about the relationship between production and employment on our imaginary farm.

The number of farm workers and the number of bushels of corn produced tend to go up or down together. In a case like this we say there is a positive relationship between the two variables. A curve like the one depicted in Figures 1 and 2, which depicts a positive relationship between variables, is always upward sloping—that is, the height of the curve increases from left to right. In other cases, of course, there is a negative relationship between two economic variables—for example, the higher the

Figure 2   Relating Corn Production and the Number of Workers

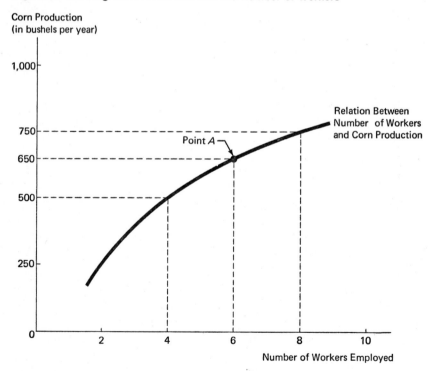

price of tickets to a particular football game, the fewer tickets the promoters are likely to sell. A curve relating the number of tickets sold to the price of tickets would be <u>downward sloping</u>—that is, the height of the curve declines as it goes from left to right. This is illustrated in Figure 3.

Once you understand how to read diagrams like Figures 1, 2, and 3, you will be ready to tackle the rest of the diagrams in this book. While some may appear to be more complicated, because they include more than a single curve, all of the diagrams follow these basic principles.

Figure 3   Relating the Price of Football Tickets and the Number of Tickets Sold

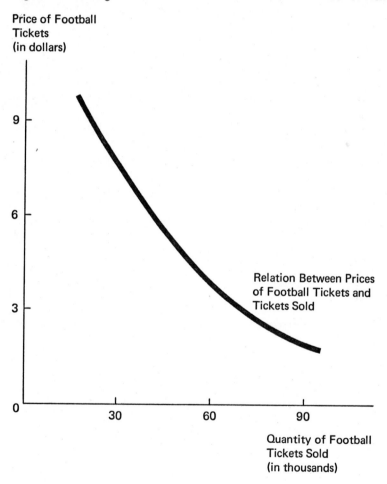

Price of Football
Tickets
(in dollars)

Relation Between Prices
of Football Tickets and
Tickets Sold

Quantity of Football
Tickets Sold
(in thousands)

1
General Economic Concepts

The general economic concepts discussed in this chapter provide some tools that economists use in pursuing the answers to economic problems. The central concern of economics is expressed in the concept of **Scarcity**. It recognizes that human wants are virtually infinite but that resources—labor, land and natural resources, and machines—are limited. This is the essence of "the economic problem." It gives rise to three major decisions that must be made in any economic system: which goods and services to produce, how to produce them, and who shall receive them.

Most economic decisions are not of an all-or-nothing variety. The use of **Marginal Analysis** makes it possible to reach conclusions about very small changes in economic behavior. **Opportunity Cost** is that which we must give up because we have decided to obtain something else, for example, the goods and services we cannot have because we use our resources to produce some other goods and services. Limited resources allow only limited production.

Efficiency provides a standard for judging whether a society is doing as well as it can to solve the economic problem. It raises such questions as: Do business firms use resources well, and can any shift in the use of resources make some individual better off without making someone else worse off? Efficiency, however, is only one criterion for judging an economic system. We must also ask whether output is growing at a satisfactory rate and whether our economic system provides for **Equity**—a just and fair distribution of burdens and benefits.

Basic generalizations about economic behavior are known as **Economic Theory**. Most theories that economists use to predict economic behavior are based on a central assumption—**Economic Rationality**—that is, the idea that people behave in a fashion consistent with their own self-interest.

Economic variables often tend towards **Equilibrium**—a state of balance in which the forces for change offset each other. Economists try to identify and analyze these forces in order to be able to predict the direction of change.

The final two concepts discussed in this chapter are basic to the functioning of a modern economy. **Money** is generalized purchasing power that gives a person the ability to buy the full range of goods and services for sale in an economy. **Discounting the Future** is a process that recognizes that the value of a given sum of money or bundle of goods is less if we receive it in the distant future than if we receive it now.

SCARCITY

Scarcity refers to the limitations that exist in attaining all the goods and services that people want. Webster defines scarce as "deficient in quantity or number compared with the demand." The economist uses scarcity in much the same way, but only if the term "demand" is understood to refer to demand at a price of zero. For example, if 1,000 units of a particular good are available at $5 per unit and only 50 are demanded at that price, the good would not be considered scarce, using Webster's definition of the term. However, the economist recognizes that price is a device that limits the quantity of goods demanded. At prices below $5 per unit more than 50 units will probably be demanded. If, indeed, any units are demanded at any positive price (including a price of zero), the economist would consider the good scarce. Whenever people want more of a good than is available to them "free of charge," the economist refers to that good as scarce.

The concept of scarcity in economics recognizes the limitations of the physical world. In fact, it is precisely these limitations that give rise to economic problems and justify the existence of the discipline of economics. Economics is basically a study of scarcity and all the difficulties that arise as its consequence.

Scarce Factors of Production

Goods and services are scarce because they must be produced by the use of scarce resources. These scarce resources—or factors of production, as they are sometimes called—may be thought of as the basic inputs used to produce goods and services. We may conveniently separate resources into two broad categories: (1) human resources and (2) nonhuman resources. Human resources include all forms of labor, from the least skilled factory or agricultural worker to the most highly skilled manager or professional. Nonhuman resources may be further broken down into land and capital. Land refers to all "gifts of nature" that can be used in production, such as the ground itself, the minerals in the ground, the vegetation that grows without anyone planting it, and the undomesticated animals that are found in the wild. Capital goods are man-made factors of production, such as the factory buildings or machines and equipment that are used to produce goods and services.

At any particular time the quantity of resources is fixed. Over time, their quantity and quality may change, but they are still limited. We must, therefore, decide to which of many alternative uses they are to be put. This is basically what economics is all about. A frequently used definition of economics is "the optimum allocation of scarce resources." The economist is concerned with putting our scarce resources to use in the very best way.

Economic Goods and Free Goods

Goods and services may be classified as either free or economic. Most are economic, that is, scarce, but a few goods are more plentiful than the demand for them at a price of zero. These are referred to as free goods. Examples of free goods include the air above the Canadian prairie provinces, the water in the Indian Ocean, and the sand on a nearly isolated beach along the coast of Africa. Free goods may also be much less desirable than these; for example, the polluted air or body of water in an area where nothing is being done to combat pollution. Goods of this kind—both the more desirable and less desirable ones—are not scarce because they are plentiful in relation to demand for them and because they are not produced through the use of scarce resources (factors of production). They are, therefore, outside of the concern of the economist. Most goods and services are brought forth via scarce resources in order to meet a demand. They are found in limited quantity relative to demand at a zero price; therefore, they demand a positive price. Such goods are called economic goods, and it is with these that the economist is concerned. Thousands of examples of economic goods and services could be listed with little difficulty. Such a list might include shoes, haircuts, and pencils. Free goods can become economic goods if scarce resources are used to move them or to alter their condition so that they can be more useful. The air in an air-conditioned office, the water in a stream that has been purified due to its previously polluted condition, and the sand in a sandbox are all economic goods.

Decisions That Confront a Society

If the factors of production were in unlimited supply, everyone would be able to have as much of everything (goods and services) as they wished, and therefore there would be no economic decisions for a society to make. Since such a utopia does not exist, societies are confronted with at least three major decisions: (1) which goods and services to produce and in what quantities; (2) how goods and services are to be produced; and (3) who shall receive the goods and services that are allocated to consumers out of the total amount produced.

The first question is based on the realization that choices have to be made between alternative uses of scarce resources, both now and in the future. Shall we produce telephones or shall we produce toothpaste? The answer is probably that we should produce both, and the crucial question is, how many of each? Rather than occupying all our resources in the production of goods and services to be consumed now, we may want to divert some of them into factory buildings and machines, or into conservation programs, or into research so that we will have more in the future.

Once the first question is answered, we are confronted with the decision of what particular resources to use in production. There is almost always the possibility of substituting one factor for another, such as a machine (capital) for some labor, or a more elaborate machine for two less elaborate ones. Certainly in the case of an economy that finds itself with a large supply of labor and a small supply of capital equipment, this question would be answered differently than for an economy that was experiencing the opposite situation.

The final question deals with the problem of distribution. This involves both how large a bundle of goods and services each consumer will get and what particular ones go into each consumer's bundle. Once we have decided to produce a particular list of goods and services, in particular amounts, and in a particular fashion, we must still decide how much should be offered to final consumers, in what combinations, and who will be allowed to enjoy these goods and services. Shall they go to "those who need them most," or to "the highest bidder," or to "those who got there first"?

All economies—large or small, rich or poor, benevolent or malevolent— are confronted with these questions and called upon to provide answers. Different economic systems will offer different solutions. These run the gamut from the extreme cases of an economy in which goods are allocated and distributed only by the market to an economy in which the government directly allocates all the available goods. A market economy depends entirely on prices set by the conditions of supply and demand, while a directed economy relies on planners (government officials) to make the determination. In between lie the many combinations or mixtures that economies actually choose among and adopt.

While no nation strictly conforms to the market economy model, it is instructive to see how such an economy would answer the three questions that we posed. The first question was, which goods and services—and how many of each—will be produced? This would be determined by the buying response of consumers to the offerings of sellers. For example, if a business person is willing to sell 10,000 units per month of a certain good at $2 per unit, consumers will respond by buying less than 10,000 per month, by buying 10,000 in less than a month, or coincidentally by buying just exactly 10,000 per month. Each of these responses acts as a signal to the seller. In the case where the seller is disappointed by less than expected sales, he may offer a lower quantity the next time around or decide to take the good off the market entirely. If he sells out before the month is up, he may be motivated to produce more in the future. In the coincidental case where perfect matching occurs, the seller is likely to continue to offer the same quantity again.

The second question, how goods and services are to be produced, is determined largely by the existing competition among firms. For example, one firm in an industry may use some elaborate machines and a few skilled workers to produce a certain good at a cost of $1.50 per unit while another firm uses somewhat less elaborate machines and more workers to produce the same good at $2.00 per unit. It is obvious that the first firm is able to outcompete the second firm. The first firm could sell the good at $1.95 and make a 45¢ per unit profit, while if the second firm would match the $1.95 price it would incur a 5¢ per unit loss. Therefore the high cost firm is expected either to switch its method of production to that of the low-cost firm or to go out of business. In either case, the good will henceforth be produced only with the more elaborate machines and the few skilled workers.

The answer to the final question, who shall receive the goods and services that are produced, is determined by which persons have more money to spend and which persons want some goods more than others. If each good and service is offered at a particular price, then those who are willing and able to buy them will do so. Poor people may buy a lot of bread, but very little steak. Mink coats and yachts will be bought by a relatively few very wealthy people. To fully answer this question, however, we would have to deal with why some people can afford certain goods while others cannot. This will depend upon how goods and services are priced and what determines differences in income and wealth among consumers.

MARGINAL ANALYSIS

Marginal analysis is an approach frequently used by economists to predict or evaluate the outcome of economic decisions. Since economic decision making is what the whole field of economics is about, an understanding of marginal analysis is central to understanding economic theory. The term marginal means extra or additional. It refers to either the last unit that has been added or the next unit that may be added. The marginal unit of a product that an individual considers is the last one he bought, or the next one that he might buy. Being "on the margin" means deciding between alternatives. The little child standing in front of a candy counter with 15¢ in her hand is on the margin among various kinds of candy. She may consume one more Hershey bar, one more roll of Lifesavers, or one more Milky Way.

Marginal analysis recognizes that economic decisions are only rarely of an all-or-nothing nature. Business firms are not usually trying to decide whether to produce or not to produce. Rather, they are more often concerned with how much of particular products to produce this week or this year. Individuals, likewise, must decide how much to buy of particular goods and services. It is rarely a question of whether food, clothing, or shelter should be purchased, but instead, what combination of these will best serve the individual. Should a little more food be purchased and thus a little less clothing, or more of both at the expense of a somewhat inferior apartment? Individuals also face marginal decisions in regard to the amount of work they wish to do. Students typically do not think in terms of studying versus not studying at all; rather they must decide how much time to devote to study and therefore how much to leisure activities or to outside jobs. Should a third hour be devoted to studying for an exam, or should that hour be spent relaxing?

The Use of Marginal Analysis in Functional Relationships

Marginal analysis is widely used in economics. Economists are very interested in functional relationships—in which one variable depends on one or more other variables. For example, consumption is said to be a function of income; at higher income levels individuals consume more goods and services, and at lower income levels they consume less. We are concerned with how much one variable changes as another variable on which it depends also changes. This is marginal analysis. How much more will an individual spend for consumption purposes (as opposed to saving) if his income is increased by a certain amount? He may receive an increase in salary from $10,000 per year to $11,000, so that the marginal change in his income is $1,000 per year. If he spends an extra $900 for consumption purposes (above what he spent before) and saves an extra $100, then his marginal consumption expenditure was 90 percent or .9. Information of this kind may be considerably more useful than averages that pertain to people's total incomes. If the government is contemplating an income tax hike or cut, the consequences of such a move are determined at the margin. What will be the expected decrease in consumption expenditures resulting from an income tax increase, or what is the expected increase in consumption expenditures resulting from a tax decrease?

The Relationship Between Marginal, Average, and Total

Many theories in economics make use of marginal, average, and total measures. It is important to recognize how they differ and how they are related. The <u>total</u> is the whole of whatever variable we are measuring. The <u>marginal</u> is what we add to the total or subtract from it in any one step. The <u>average</u> is the total divided by the number of units dealt with. For example, a student may have gone to the movies 25 times this year and paid $2 each time. His total expenditure on movies is $50, his average expenditure is $2 ($50/25), and his marginal expenditure is also $2, the price of the last movie. The total amount is always the sum of all the marginal amounts—25 movies at $2 per movie add up to $50. If the student were to go once more to the movies and find that the price had suddenly increased to $3, the marginal expenditure (on the 26th movie) would be $3, the new total expenditure $53, and the new average expenditure about $2.04 ($53/26 = $2.04). Note that the increased marginal expenditure caused an increase in the average expenditure. Whenever a marginal amount is higher than an average amount, the average amount must be increasing over time. Likewise, whenever a marginal amount is below an average amount, the average amount must be decreasing. Therefore, only when the marginal amount is neither higher than nor lower than the average amount—that is, when marginal equals average, as in our case before the price of movies increased—is the average amount neither increasing nor decreasing. This relationship will always hold because the marginal amount causes the average amount to either rise, fall, or remain the same.

Marginal Cost and Marginal Benefit

Many significant economic theories predict by comparing marginal cost with marginal benefit. People are expected to act so as to maximize their well-being, and this will normally occur when they equate their marginal cost with their marginal benefit.

Suppose you are out camping in the woods and come across an area where wild blueberries are growing. You reach down and pick a small handful growing at your feet. Since you were hungry, the blueberries provide you with a good deal of benefit for very little cost in personal effort. You see more berries growing nearby and walk over and pick those as well. The satisfaction of eating fresh blueberries is still well worth a little bit of extra effort. After you have spent twenty minutes or so eating blueberries, you are no longer as hungry as you were, but still you derive some satisfaction from eating more blueberries. The longer you pick and eat, however, the harder it is to find berries that are conveniently located. Some of them are up on a hill, others are guarded by thistles, and still others are perilously close to what looks like poison ivy. The longer you keep picking blueberries, then, the greater is the cost of picking more, since it requires more trouble to get to them. At the same time, the longer you go on eating blueberries, the less satisfaction each additional handful provides. After half an hour or so you reach the point where the benefit to you from eating another handful of blueberries is just equal to the cost in inconvenience of picking another handful. After this, you stop picking blueberries and continue with your hike. Any additional berries you might pick would be more trouble than they would be worth. Thus, consciously or not, you have used marginal analysis to reach an optimal level of blueberry picking and eating. You have continued up to the point at which the marginal benefit of eating blueberries is equal to the marginal cost of picking blueberries, and after that you have stopped.

We may see the above example more clearly through the use of a diagram. Figure 1–1 includes a positively sloped curve showing the marginal

Figure 1–1 The Marginal Benefit and Marginal Cost of Picking and Eating Blueberries

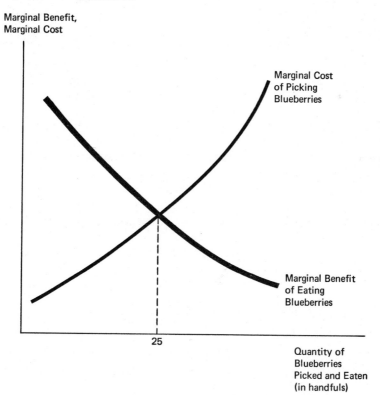

Marginal Benefit,
Marginal Cost

Marginal Cost
of Picking
Blueberries

Marginal Benefit
of Eating
Blueberries

25

Quantity of
Blueberries
Picked and Eaten
(in handfuls)

cost of picking blueberries. It also includes a negatively sloped curve showing the marginal benefit from eating blueberries. Note that on the far left portion of the diagram the marginal benefit far exceeds the marginal cost (you're very hungry and the blueberries are very easy to reach). On the far right portion the marginal cost greatly exceeds the marginal benefit (your hunger is pretty well satisfied and the blueberries are relatively hard to reach). Anywhere to the left of the intersection of the two curves (less than 25 handfuls of blueberries), the marginal benefit exceeds the marginal cost and it pays to continue picking. Anywhere to the right of the intersection of the two curves (more than 25 handfuls of blueberries) the marginal cost exceeds the marginal benefit and it is unwise to be picking. Therefore, we expect you to pick and eat exactly 25 handfuls of blueberries, your optimal level of blueberry picking and eating.

This simple story illustrates a technique that can be applied to a great variety of economic problems. When marginal benefits are high but declining and marginal costs are low but rising, it is generally true that an individual or an organization will reach an optimum point by equating marginal cost and marginal benefit. A worker may use this technique in deciding how many hours of overtime he wants to put in. A family may use it in deciding how big a car it wants to buy. A firm may use it in deciding how much output to produce or how many workers to hire. And a government may use it in deciding how many missiles to install, how many job-training programs to operate or how many tax dodgers to prosecute. By equating marginal benefits and marginal costs, each is able to determine how far it wants to carry a particular economic activity. Equating marginal benefit and marginal cost, then, is the essence of the economic theory of choice.

Criticism of Marginal Analysis

The marginalist technique is not every economist's "cup of tea." Since the turn of the century, the "institutionalist school" of American economists has argued that economic choice can only be understood in the framework of history and the contemporary economic laws, customs, and attitudes. In recent years, another school of economists—most frequently referred to as radical political economists—has taken great issue with marginalism. They argue that it deliberately abstracts from history and present institutions and centers its sights upon the mechanics of choice. Furthermore, they contend, it inevitably diverts attention from the important issues—income distribution, freedom of consumer choice, economic growth and the environment—that should receive the economist's attention. Many economists agree that to some extent they have been too preoccupied with the trees to give much thought to the forest. But to most economists the validity of marginal analysis as a tool can be separated from any particular ideology. Marginalism can be useful in changing existing institutions as well as in preventing their change.

OPPORTUNITY COST

The opportunity cost of doing something is the benefit that could have been obtained doing the next best thing with the same resources. Opportunity cost can be seen as the true cost of choosing one alternative over another. For example, in the area of production the next best good or service that could have been produced is the opportunity cost of what actually is produced. Whenever resources are scarce, the decision to do something involves an opportunity cost. With limited resources we cannot "have our cake and eat it too." Particular resources cannot be employed to produce certain things and still produce everything else that people want. Opportunity cost describes the fact that when we employ resources in a particular way, we are not merely making a decision to produce those goods; we are also deciding not to produce some other goods or services. That which we implicitly decide not to produce is the opportunity cost of what we do produce.

Consumers likewise encounter opportunity cost. Since people have only so much income and hold a limited amount of wealth, they are continually confronted with buying decisions. When consumers decide to spend their dollars for one item, those dollars are not available for some other item that they might have bought. The opportunity cost of ordering a pizza in a restaurant might be the spaghetti and meat balls that were therefore not ordered. Going on a trip to the Caribbean might mean foregoing a new car.

People also face opportunity costs in terms of their time and sometimes their effort. If a particular Saturday night offers a college student both a party and a basketball game, the event that she doesn't attend is the opportunity cost of the one she decides to attend. Finally, a college student who decides to attend a summer session experiences two kinds of opportunity costs: (1) the goods he forgoes so that he can pay for tuition and books, and (2) the goods he could have bought with the money he would have earned had he spent his summer in gainful employment.

Government is also confronted with opportunity costs. At first blush it may seem that government is exempted because it can tax people, borrow money, or even print money if it wishes to undertake more programs. On closer examination, however, we discover that when government draws additional resources from the private sector of the economy, the opportunity costs are the private goods that must be forgone. For example, if a country becomes apprehensive about its neighbors, it might raise taxes to buy more military equipment. The opportunity cost of the defense buildup would be the consumer goods that the taxpayers could no longer afford to buy. Within the expenditure bounds that are set by a government, the opportunity cost of one government program is that of another program. A state legislature may have to decide between funding a mass transportation program or building additional prisons.

Production Possibility

The opportunity cost of production is sometimes expressed as a trade-off—how much of one good or service must be traded off or given up to gain a certain quantity of another good or service. The notion of tradeoff is incorporated in the concept of production possibility, which describes the limited number of goods and services that societies can produce during any given time period.

The production possibilities for a nation are too diverse to express in tabular form or to represent in a diagram. Goods and services can, however, be grouped into two categories—say, goods versus services—in order to illustrate the meaning of this concept.

A Production Possibilities Schedule

Table 1–1 represents a production possibilities schedule for the fictitious nation of Yano. Note that all possible production has been divided into the two categories of goods and services. Furthermore, note the assumption that there is a common unit of measure for each category. For example, a haircut may be 1 service unit, while an examination by a physician is 30 service units. A potholder may be 1 good unit, while a pound of hamburger is 5 good units. Imagine that in this fashion we have tabulated the production possibilities for Yano during a particular year—1977. The numbers are calculated on the basis of Yano's resource base and state of technological development in 1977. That is, in 1977 Yano has a population of a certain size and age distribution, a certain stock of capital, and a certain amount and quality of land, including known natural resources. Also, in 1977 Yano possesses a particular level of technological ability concerning the use and combination of resources.

The numbers in Table 1–1 disclose that there is no way for Yano to produce more than 10,000 billion units of goods and that there is no way to produce more than 4,000 billion units of services. In fact, the only way to produce such high levels of one category is to produce none of the other. In

Table 1–1 Production Possibilities: The Nation of Yano, 1977

Goods (in billions of units)	Services (in billions of units)
10,000	0
9,800	500
9,400	1,000
8,800	1,500
8,000	2,000
7,000	2,500
5,800	3,000
4,400	3,500
0	4,000

between these all-of-one and none-of-the-other alternatives there are many possible combinations of goods and services for Yano to produce. Seven examples are provided in the table (such as 9,800 billion units of goods plus 500 billion units of services, or 7,000 billion units of goods plus 2,500 billion units of services), but surely there are countless others. It follows from the data presented that if Yano decides, for example, that its population must have 2,000 billion units of services in 1977, then no more than 8,000 billion units of goods can be produced. Alternatively, if Yano decides that it must have 9,400 billion units of goods, it can have no more than 1,000 billion units of services.

Increasing Marginal Opportunity Costs

Notice that the tradeoff between goods and services changes as we move up or down Table 1–1. If we begin with the combination of 10,000 billion units of goods and zero services, we see that 500 billion units of services can be gained by giving up only 200 billion units of goods (we might say that the opportunity cost of 500 billion units of services is 200 billion units of goods). However, Yano must give up 400 billion units of goods to get the next 500 billion units of services. This pattern continues—larger and larger amounts of goods must be given up in order to gain additional blocks of 500 billion units of services—as we move down Table 1–1. Comparing the last two lines in the table we see that the opportunity cost of the last 500 billion units of services is 4,400 billion units of goods.

Likewise, the opportunity cost of goods in terms of services can be seen to increase as we move up Table 1–1. Going from the combination of zero goods plus 4,000 billion units of services to the next highest combination, the opportunity cost of 4,400 billion units of goods is only 500 billion units of services. Moving up one more combination in the table, Yano gains only 1,400 billion units of goods at an opportunity cost of 500 billion units of services. Finally, when we compare the top two lines in the table, the opportunity cost of only 200 billion units of goods is 500 billion units of services.

Why should we expect to find increasing marginal opportunity costs? Why is it that the more goods or the more services that Yano has, the higher is the opportunity cost of gaining additional ones in terms of the other category? The answer is that all of Yano's resources are not equally adept at producing both goods and services. Some are much more productive in producing goods, while others are much better at producing services. Workers skilled at performing appendectomies might be unsuited for coal mining. Land well suited for growing wheat might be a poor location for a barbershop. And a factory building used for manufacturing steel may be poorly suited as a dental clinic.

At some combination in the middle of Table 1–1 (say 8,000 billion units of goods plus 2,000 billion units of services), we would expect to find most resources employed in the field for which they are best suited. As we move from that combination—either up or down the table—resources are shifted to tasks at which they are less productive. Toward the very top of the table, only the resources best suited to the production of services will be left producing services, making it very expensive in terms of services foregone to produce any more goods. Likewise, toward the very bottom of the table, only the resources best suited to the production of goods will be left producing goods, making it very expensive in terms of goods foregone to produce any more services.

A Production Possibilities Curve

Figure 1–2 plots the data in our production possibilities schedule (Table 1–1) on a set of axes in order to obtain a production possibilities curve. Note

Figure 1–2   Production Possibilities Curve for the Nation of Yano, 1977

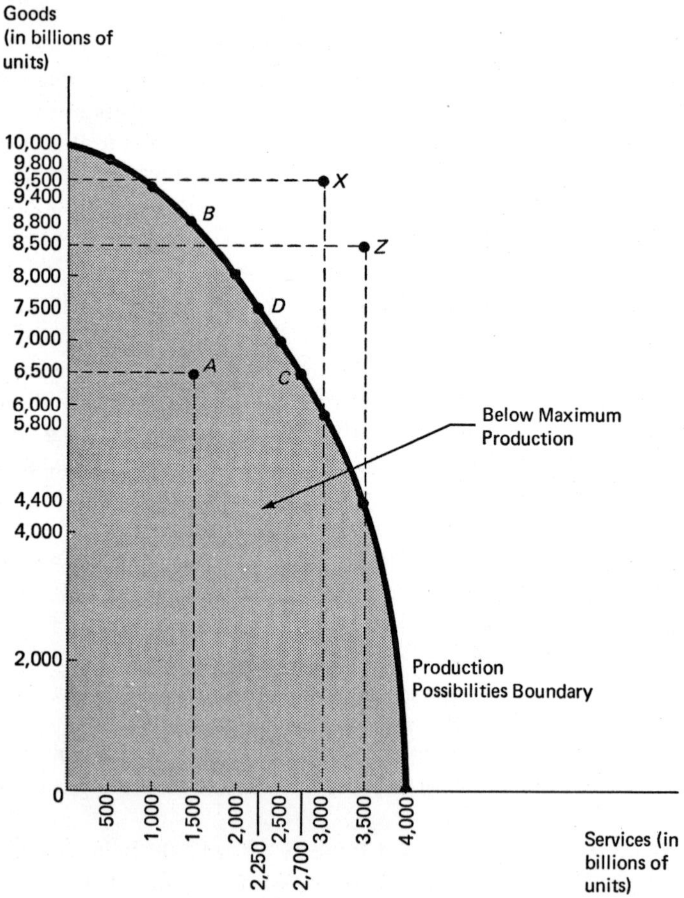

that the plotted points are joined, enabling us to find all of the possible combinations of goods and services that Yano can produce in 1977.

The curve in Figure 1–2—sometimes called the production possibilities boundary or frontier—represents the maximum amounts that can be produced. Production levels such as X (combination of 9,500 billion units of goods plus 3,000 billion units of services) or Z (combination of 8,500 billion units of goods plus 3,500 billion units of services) are impossible for Yano to achieve. However, the entire shaded area is made up of combinations of goods and services that are attainable. For example, point A (combination of 6,500 billion units of goods plus 1,500 billion units of services) is an attainable combination for Yano. But, given its resources and known-how, Yano can do better than point A by producing more goods, or more services, or more of both. Instead of 6,500 billion units of goods, it could produce 8,800 billion (which would place it at point B), with no reduction in the services produced. Or, instead of 1,500 billion units of services, it could produce 2,700 billion (which would place it at point C) with no reduction in the goods produced. Finally, it could produce more of both and move to a point such as D (7,500 billion units of goods plus 2,250 billion units of services).

Suppose that Yano is producing at point A in Figure 1–2. Suppose also that Yano would like to produce as much as possible—to raise the standard of living of the population—and that there are no environmental reasons for limiting maximum production. What does this tell us about the Yano economy? One or both of two circumstances are indicated: (1) unemployment of resources, and (2) inefficient use of resources. Point A production may be the result of some resources being idle. For example, certain skilled or unskilled workers may not be able to find jobs, particular mineral deposits may not be mined because of a fear that additional supply would depress prices, or machines to stamp out automobile bodies may not be in operation because not enough cars are being sold. The other circumstance that gives rise to producing below the production possibilities boundary is inefficient use of resources. This could be due to outright waste—for example, not permitting qualified and healthy people over the age of sixty-five to hold jobs. Alternatively, it could be due to combining resources in a less than optimal way. If, for instance, each individual Chevrolet fender were cut out by hand instead of stamped out by a press, the cost of production would be substantially increased. Whenever goods or services are produced at higher cost than could be achieved by using an alternative combination of resources, production is not efficient (see Efficiency, pp. 18–23).

Point A production—or some other point below the production possibilities boundary—is a very likely combination for Yano to be producing in 1977. In fact, Yano would be a very rare nation indeed if it did not experience some unemployment of resources and some production inefficiencies. It is important to understand, however, that a nation producing below its production possibilities boundary is able to improve—in Yano's case, to produce more goods or more services, or more of both—without an expansion of its resource base or its technological knowledge, both of which take a long time to achieve. By contrast, if Yano were producing on its production possibilities boundary, it could increase its production of goods in the short run only by decreasing its production of services. Alternatively, Yano could increase its production of services only by decreasing its production of goods.

Shifts in Production Possibilities Curves

What would the production possibilities boundary for Yano be expected to look like in 1980? Recalling that the 1977 boundary was limited by Yano's resource base and technological knowledge, it would be very surprising if the boundary had not shifted out to the right by 1980. Figure 1–3 illustrates such a shift. The 1980 production possibilities boundary is everywhere above the 1977 boundary because Yano has increased its resources and technological knowledge related to both goods and services during those three years. Population has probably grown (more working-age people), the stock of capital increased (with saving and investment), and new natural resources discovered. Also it is probable that the "state of the arts" in many industries advanced, so that more output of goods and services would have become possible in 1980 even if Yano's resource base had not increased.

Figure 1–3 shows the same output points, *B*, *D*, and *C*—maximum output combinations in 1977—to be less than maximum output combinations in 1980. Point *Z*, which was unattainable in 1977, is on the new production possibilities boundary and therefore attainable in 1980. But point *X*, which was impossible to produce in 1977, is still unattainable, though not by nearly so much.

Production possibilities boundaries are expected to shift upwards over time, but there is no guarantee; they could remain stable or actually shift downward. It is difficult to imagine a decrease in the technological knowledge of a society in the absence of an H-bomb explosion or other major catastrophe. It is not so difficult, however, to imagine a decrease in a nation's resource base. Population—especially working-age population—could drop. A decrease in capital goods could take place if saving and investment lag behind the depreciation of the capital stock. And natural resources may be used up faster than new discoveries are made.

Figure 1–3   Shift of Production Possibilities Curve for the Nation of Yano, 1977 to 1980

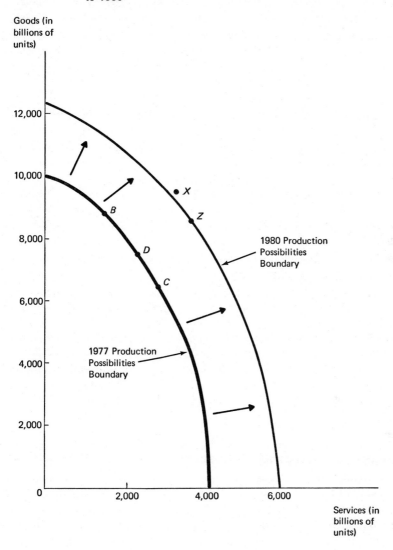

EFFICIENCY

Economists use the term "efficiency" in two ways. First, there is the efficiency of production. A plant may be said to be efficient if all its resources (land, labor, and capital) are used well. This would imply that a given level of output is being produced with the least resource cost, or, looking at it another way, that given productive resources are being used to produce output with a maximum value.

Second, there is the efficiency of an economic system. An economic system is efficient if it can't do more for one person without doing less for someone else. That is, the system is efficient if it uses resources and distributes commodities and services so well that it is impossible to make anyone in the system better off without making someone else worse off. This concept of efficiency was developed early in the twentieth century by the Italian economist Vilfredo Pareto, and it is sometimes known as Pareto-efficiency. Of course, an economic system cannot be efficient unless there is efficiency of production in the plants that are providing its commodities and services. For example, the cook in the West Side Pizzeria may always forget to put the cheese back in the refrigerator, so that it spoils by the end of the day. As a result of this productive inefficiency, some customers are not able to enjoy cheese on their pizza. The inefficiency could be corrected if the cook would just remember to keep the cheese cold. In this case the customers would be better off without anyone else being worse off. But the efficiency of an economy, or Pareto-efficiency, goes beyond the efficiency of production. It also takes into account who does the work and how the goods are distributed. It is necessary, then, to take a longer look at both concepts.

The Efficiency of Production

Efficiency in production can be described in two ways—technical efficiency and economic efficiency. The technical efficiency of production is a purely physical concept. It describes the physical inputs required for production, such as worker time, machine time, land, raw materials, and parts, without asking how much any of these may cost. A production process is technically efficient if it doesn't waste any of those inputs. For example, if two workers are building a boat and decide to use two hammers instead of just one, this decision will be efficient only if it permits them to use less of some other kind of input—like their own labor. Using the extra hammer would not be efficient if they would still have to work as long—and use just as much wood, as many nails, and as many other tools—to complete the boat. But if the extra hammer would permit them to spend fewer hours finishing the job, then using it would be technically efficient.

Obviously, many different ways of building the boat would be technically efficient, but some ways might be a good deal more expensive than others.

Thus, we must raise the question of the <u>economic efficiency</u> of production—whether it is being carried out at the least possible cost. To answer this we must know the costs of hiring workers and of buying or renting hammers and just how much worker time would be saved by having the extra hammer. If the workers' time was worth $5 an hour and if the extra hammer would save them both an hour, then the cost of not having the hammer would be $10. A simple hammer might cost only $3 to buy, so that it would be worth buying even if it had to be thrown away at the end of the job. On the other hand, if the required tool were a jackhammer that would cost $30 to rent, then it would make more sense to spend $10 for the extra labor time than $30 for the extra hammer. Technically—in the absence of any information about prices—there may be a wide range of ways to build a boat that could be considered efficient. Economically—in full knowledge of the wages that must be paid to workers and the rental prices of capital goods—usually only one of the many technically efficient ways will prove to be the cheapest.

The Efficiency of an Economic System

The second broad sense in which economists use the term efficiency relates to the efficiency of a whole economy or economic system. When we ask whether one person can be made better off without making anyone else worse off, we raise questions as to how efficiently individual plants are operating. But we also raise questions as to how the operations of all plants relate to one another, how goods are distributed to consumers, and how intensively the factors of production (land, labor, and capital) are used.

To illustrate how some of these questions can be answered efficiently or inefficiently, let us again consider the pizza industry. On the production side, pizza eaters may agree that the best pizzas are made with a combination of mozzarella and provolone cheeses. A wholesaler may, however, supply only provolone to the West Side Pizzeria and only mozzarella to the East Side Pizzeria. Under those conditions, both pizzerias may make the best pizza that can be made with only one kind of cheese. In other words, each of the plants—the two pizzerias—may display efficiency of production, given the resources they have available. But the economic system as a whole is not operating efficiently. Customers in both pizzerias could be made better off—and no one would be made worse off—if some of the mozzarella cheese were sent to the West Side Pizzeria and some of the provolone were sent to the East Side Pizzeria.

Efficiency can also be influenced by the ability of consumers to choose freely the goods they want to consume. If a pizzeria sells only a 16-inch pizza, then this will force inefficiencies in consumption. For example, the following sequence would be possible: A poor customer comes in to the West Side Pizzeria, hungry for a 10-inch pizza. Seeing that only the 16-inch size is available, he decides not to buy and goes away hungry. Soon afterwards a rich customer comes in and also wants only a 10-inch pizza.

Faced with a choice between no pizza and a 16-inch pizza, he buys it. But he eats only half and throws the other half away. Neither customer is very happy about the situation. If the pizzeria had been prepared to sell 10-inch pizzas, it would have sold just as much—since two 10-inch pizzas are about equal to one 16-inch pizza. Thus, the business would have been no worse off. But both customers would have been better off. The poor customer would have been able to buy the pizza he wanted, and the rich one would not have had to pay for more pizza than he wanted. By arbitrarily denying its customers the right to buy just the amount of pizza they want, the pizzeria is forcing inefficiency in consumption.

Efficiency can also be influenced by how intensively the factors of production are used. Assume that Agnes is a pizza chef at the East Side Pizzeria and is paid $100 a week for a 40-hour week, or an average of $2.50 an hour. Assume, however, that Agnes values her leisure time highly. After she has worked 30 hours and earned $75, she has enough money to meet her needs for the week. She would be happy to work the next 10 hours only if she were paid $5 an hour rather than $2.50. Unfortunately, the pizzeria owner insists that she work the full 40 hours. Agnes needs the job, so she works all 40 hours. At the same time, Mildred, who is also an experienced pizza chef, would like to work at $2.50 an hour but cannot find a job that pays that well. An efficient solution would be for the pizzeria owner to let Agnes stop working after 30 hours a week and offer Mildred $25 to work the remaining 10 hours. Mildred would be better off earning some money, and Agnes would be better off with more time to herself. Only the stubbornness of the pizzeria owner prevents an efficient solution.

It is useful to note that the inefficiencies we have described are not necessary outcomes. Indeed, there will often be strong market pressures in the pizza business to operate on a more efficient basis. A wholesaler who repeatedly sent only mozzarella to one pizzeria and only provolone to another would not stay in business long if both pizzerias were asking for both kinds of cheeses. They would turn to another wholesaler who would send them what they wanted. By the same token, if the West Side Pizzeria is selling only the 16-inch size of pizza, then the East Side Pizzeria may try to lure customers away from it by offering a wide range of pizza sizes. Before long, if business began to fall off, the West Side Pizzeria might get the message and also offer more sizes. Likewise, the West Side Pizzeria might learn of Agnes's dissatisfaction and offer her a job at $75 for 30 hours. She might then threaten to quit the East Side Pizzeria, where she is obliged to work a full 40 hours. Faced with the prospect of losing a good chef, the owner of the East Side Pizzeria might relent and let Agnes work the 30-hour week she prefers.

In general, more flexible economic arrangements are more likely to be more efficient. When pizzerias can get just the combinations of cheeses they want, when customers can buy just the size pizzas they want, and when pizza chefs can work just the number of hours they want, the economy is less likely to have situations in which it is possible to make one person better off without making any other person worse off. There are, of course, real limitations to how flexible economic arrangements can be. Substantial cost savings can be made by using a machine that puts 20 cigarettes in each pack rather than having a sales clerk count out and wrap up just the number of cigarettes a customer wants. It is difficult to run an assembly line if each worker is perfectly free each week to decide the days and hours he wants to work. More flexible arrangements might make some persons better off—like the customer who wants only 14 cigarettes or the riveter who wants to go fishing on Wednesday. The result, however, would not be greater efficiency if the cost of production were raised, thereby making others worse off.

The Inefficiency of Price Discrimination

Another general rule to remember is that an economic system is *always* inefficient if the same good costs more in one place than another, or if the same good costs more to one buyer than another—unless, of course, the difference is justified by the cost of transporting the good.

Such inefficiency can be illustrated by the following example. Assume that a motorcycle company sets up retail stores to sell a limited number of cycles in each of two towns, Squaresville and Dullsville. The company lets the local store managers set whatever price they want to charge, so long as each sells only to residents of his own town. The manager in Squaresville decides that people in his town are rich enough to pay $1,000 for a cycle, while the manager in Dullsville decides that his town is too poor for him to get away with charging more than $800. Let us see how inefficient this situation is. Assume that a customer in Dullsville feels that a cycle would be worth $850 to him, so he buys one for $800. A traveling shoe salesman passes through Dullsville and offers the customer $900 for the cycle he has just bought for $800. The customer decides to sell, since the cycle was worth $850 to him but not $900. The salesman then rides the cycle over to Squaresville. There he meets a resident who would have paid $950 for a motorcycle but couldn't quite bring himself to spend the $1,000 that was being charged in Squaresville. The salesman offers to sell the cycle he just bought in Dullsville for the $900 he paid for it, and the Squaresville resident readily agrees.

Note that everyone is now better off as a result of these two transactions. The Dullsville resident has made himself a quick $100. The Squaresville resident has bought a motorcycle that was worth $950 to him but for which he had to pay only $900. And the traveling salesman got a free ride. Thus, charging $1,000 in one town and $800 in another town for the same product clearly resulted in an inefficient situation—as shown by the improvement that the salesman was able to bring about without making anyone worse off.

This example illustrates the general rule that *economic efficiency is possible only if there is a single price charged for identical goods.* Where price differences are not justified by differences in transportation costs, it will always be possible to arrange some exchange that can make two parties better off without making anyone else worse off. Usually it will take the form of a transfer of the good from someone who was just willing to buy it at the low price (like the cyclist in Dullsville) to someone who was just discouraged from buying it at the high price (like the cyclist in Squaresville). The transfer will take place at a price (like $900) somewhere between the high and the low.

Questions of Growth and Equity

Efficiency is not an ultimate standard by which an economic system should be judged. It is really not enough just to know that a system has allocated existing resources so as to maximize the production derived from them or that it has distributed the goods produced so as to provide maximum consumer welfare (given the incomes and preferences of households). There are at least two other important goals of an economic system that must be considered: growth and equity. Even the most efficient economic arrangement might be considered inadequate if it provided no growth—if there were no ability to increase production over time. Likewise, it would surely be considered inadequate if it were not equitable—if there were not a fair distribution of the tasks to be done and the rewards to be received. The next section will discuss the important goal of fairness, or *Equity* (see pp. 24–29). Here we will deal briefly with the goal of growth and how it relates to the goal of efficiency.

Economic Growth—Efficiency over Time

In recent years economic growth has become a controversial goal. It has been too readily associated with the depletion of our natural resources and the destruction of our environment. Some of the side-effects of production and its growth will be discussed later in this book (see *Externalities,* pp. 254–58). For the moment, let us simply note that not all forms of growth have negative side-effects. For example, in 1966 an automatic calculator was a large and noisy desk-top machine consisting of 50 pounds of metal and wire and costing $800. By 1976 the same calculations—adding, subtracting, multiplying, and dividing—could be performed by a completely silent machine small enough to fit into a shirt pocket and costing as little as $5. As a result, many more persons could do more calculations faster, without noise, and with far smaller demands on the world's resources of metal. Economic growth—with all its potential problems—is still the only way we know to permit one generation of men and women to enjoy a higher level of living than did their fathers and mothers.

At its best—and stripped of its negative side-effects—some rate of economic growth can be seen as the attainment of efficiency over time.

Consider the case of a corn farmer who last year planted 10 bushels of corn as seed and was able to grow several hundred bushels. After selling some of the corn to cover his costs of production, he was able to keep 100 bushels of the corn he had grown. This year the farmer can eat all 100 bushels (or sell it to buy other consumption goods), or he can again plant some of the corn and use it to grow more corn to enjoy next year. He has already decided to plant at least 10 bushels, from which he should again be able to realize (after costs) 100 bushels next year. He is thinking about also planting an eleventh bushel. As he examines his own preferences, he knows that he would not be willing to give up another bushel of corn this year if it would get him only 1 more bushel next year, but he would be willing to give up 1 more bushel this year if he could get at least 2 more bushels next year. He examines production conditions, and he estimates that one more bushel planted this year will actually get him (after costs) 6 additional bushels next year. This is 4 more bushels than the 2 that would be needed to persuade him to give up the eleventh bushel from this year's crop. Thus, he decides to plant at least 11 bushels this year in order to increase his next corn crop from 100 bushels to 106.

Was this an efficient decision? The farmer has certainly made himself worse off this year (by giving up an extra bushel of corn) in order to make himself better off next year (by getting 6 more bushels of corn). Since he would rather have the 6 bushels next year than the 1 bushel this year, he has clearly made himself better off in the long run. Thus, the farmer's decision to promote economic growth has increased the efficiency of the economic system over time, since he has made himself better off in the long run without making anyone else worse off.

Obviously, not all economic growth is efficient. It would not be efficient for our farmer to plant so much corn that the last bushel planted only increased his output by 1.01 bushels. That would make him worse off in the long run since his own tastes are such that it would take 2 bushels next year to persuade him to give up 1 bushel this year. Likewise, it would not be efficient if the farmer could grow 6 more bushels only by adding more fertilizer that ran off his land in the rainy season and polluted a valuable fishing lake. That would make the farmer better off only by making some fishermen worse off.

Few economists would argue, however, that the U.S. economy in the 1970s has run out of areas in which it can grow rapidly enough to satisfy individual preferences and safely enough to avoid hurting the environment. Along with equity and short-run economic efficiency, real long-run economic growth remains an important goal of our economic system.

EQUITY

Equity is fairness, or justice. It is not enough to ask whether an economic policy contributes to the efficiency of an economic system or to the growth of that system (see *Efficiency,* pp. 18–23). Any policy must also be judged on whether it contributes to the basic equity of a system. The goal of equity raises the questions of how fairly an economy distributes its burdens and its benefits. The burdens include work, unpleasant working conditions, and undesirable living conditions. The benefits include income, wealth, job satisfaction, and a pleasant living environment.

To see why both equity and efficiency are important, consider two economies with the same productive resources per person. One economy may operate efficiently, but the vast majority of workers may be forced into arduous labor in order to produce gourmet foods, fine clothing, and luxurious homes for a few parasitic rulers. The workers may be paid meagerly for their efforts, and those unable to work may be left to starve. In another economy, operating with some inefficiency, arduous tasks may be equally shared among all the workers. There may be no one allowed to starve and no one paid enough to live in opulence. Clearly, the efficient-but-exploitative system will generate a great deal less economic welfare for the average citizen than the wasteful-but-equitable system.

Equity is more a philosophical concept than a scientific one. Certainly scientific theories and objective findings can be used to illuminate the equity—or the inequity—of particular economic arrangements. For example, the articles and photographs by Jacob Riis in the 1890s did much to reveal the dreadful living and working conditions among the poor of New York City. A book on *The Other America* by Michael Harrington did much to awaken the nation in the 1960s to the persistent problems of poverty. But ultimately each person must judge a particular economic system or policy by applying his or her own sense of justice to the facts at hand.

In the business world the word "equity" is often used for another purpose—to describe an ownership share in a business. In this book, however, we will generally avoid the business use of the term.

Equity and the Inequality of Income

The most critical question of equity is, How unequal—or how equal—should be the incomes of different families in an economy? Let us examine three possible standards for judging income inequality—the standard of the marketplace, the standard of full equality, and the standard of equality of opportunity.

The income generated in a pure market economy (see pp. 5–6) is necessarily highly unequal. For example, a skilled inventor may be able to sell his or her services for millions of dollars, while there may be no jobs at all available to someone who has been badly mangled in an automobile accident. The nineteenth-century British sociologist Herbert Spencer argued that this was desirable:

> The command 'if any would not work neither should he eat' is simply a Christian enunciation of that universal law of nature under which life has reached its present height—the law that a creature not energetic enough to maintain itself must die.

By contrast, almost all Americans today would feel that it was not equitable to permit the inventor to live in luxury while the accident victim starved to death. They would want to see some governmental or private charitable agency intervene to provide some income to the accident victim. For this to happen, money that the rich inventor (and others) had earned in the marketplace would have to be taxed away or donated so that the accident victim could live—and perhaps even enjoy life a little.

Note, however, that if the accident victim had permanently lost his capacity to work, then there would be nothing inefficient about letting him die. He could be made better off only by making the inventor and others worse off—that is, without improving the efficiency of the system. Results that are perfectly efficient, then, may be terribly inequitable. It would be a cold-hearted economist indeed who would judge an economic arrangement purely on the basis of its efficiency.

At the other extreme, a few economists—but only a few—would contend that the ideal of full equity can be realized only through complete equality of income. The problems with this approach are numerous. First of all, the unit must be defined. Does equity require complete equality of income for each family, for each person, or for each worker? Second, the needs of each family or person are not equal. Some families are smaller than others, and some persons are healthier, or younger, or older than others. The nineteenth-century German economist Karl Marx defined the ideal of communism not as perfect income equality but by the rule: "From each according to his ability, to each according to his need." Third, not every worker works as long, or as hard, or as well as every other worker. It may not be fair to pay two workers the same amount of money if one is prompt and diligent, while the other one arrives at work late, fools around on the job, and then leaves early. Fourth, some jobs—like airline pilot or brain surgeon—require a great deal of preparation, often including a long and expensive education. It does not seem fair to deny any additional rewards to those persons who have sacrificed time and money to learn to do their jobs well. Fifth, defining equity as equality of money income ignores many other elements of work and the work situation that may generate pleasure or pain. Running a large corporation or taking photographs for *Playboy* (or *Playgirl*) magazine may offer more job satisfaction than digging tunnels or washing dishes. Economists use the term <u>psychic income</u> to describe those satisfactions from a job or life situation that are not received through payments of money or physical commodities. Some small part of the existing inequality of income is due to differences in money incomes used to offset differences in psychic income—like the extra pay a movie stuntman receives for risking his life by riding a motorcycle off a cliff.

Some would go further and add a sixth reason why pure equality of income is not equitable. They argue that it is only fair that those who are born talented—with strong scientific abilities or with beautiful singing voices—are entitled to extra rewards for doing better work than those who are less gifted. Others would question, however, whether there is anything inherently fair in rewarding someone for a talent acquired by the luck of birth rather than as the result of effort and sacrifice.

There is another possible standard of equity, somewhere between the standard of full equality and the standard of the marketplace—equality of opportunity. The idea is that government should intervene in the race for incomes in the marketplace but only to insure that everyone has a fair chance—not to insure that everyone comes out equally. Laws that prevent job discrimination against women or racial minorities are examples of an effort to achieve equality of opportunity. Such measures are often steps in the right direction, but by themselves they cannot achieve full equity.

One major problem is that the real race often begins well before the contestants are at the post. A person's ability to earn is heavily determined long before he or she ever begins looking for a job. Many influences are important—including prenatal nutrition, childhood health care, the stimulation of the home environment, formal education, family contacts with potential employers, and the inheritance of wealth. As President Lyndon Johnson said in 1965:

> You do not take a person who, for years, has been hobbled by chains and liberate him, bring him up to the starting line of a race and then say, 'you are free to compete with all the others' and still justly believe that you have been completely fair. It is not enough to open the gates of opportunity. All our citizens must have the ability to walk through those gates.

A second problem is that the standard of equality of opportunity fails to deal with those who can't make it. Some persons—through no fault of their own—are born with too many handicaps or too little natural ability to earn a decent living.

A third problem is that equality of opportunity fails to deal with those who simply don't make it. A man may be born and raised with a full share of the advantages of life but may be diverted from economic pursuits by wine, women, or song—or some combination of the three. Just because it was—in some sense—his own fault, do we just let him drink himself to death in some skid row gutter? If he is the sole breadwinner for his family, do we stand by and let them starve?

For most Americans, we suspect, "equality of opportunity" is too weak a measure of equity. While they might reject full equality of incomes as the standard, they would at least like to see some floor—some basic level of living—placed under the existence of every member of the society. They might want to go further and eliminate the extremes of luxury at the other end of the income scale. In broad terms they might agree with the ideal stated by the British economist R. H. Tawney: "Differences of remuneration between different individuals might remain; contrasts between the civilizations of different classes would vanish."

Equity, Efficiency, and Growth

Thus far we have dealt with equity as a philosophical concept, asking the question, How much equality is fair? The philosophical question, however, is complicated in the real world by the existence of two other goals of an economy—short-run efficiency and long-run growth. A high measure of efficiency is needed if the economy is to come close to realizing its present potential for producing the things that individuals want. Some measure of growth will be realized whenever the economy usefully exploits its most attractive opportunities for increasing that potential for production. We must also ask the practical question, How can we best reconcile these three goals?

It may help to see the economic goods of the world as a gigantic pie. The capacity of the economy to produce is the pie pan, and it may become larger as economic growth occurs. Whether the pie is as large as the pie pan—that is, whether the economy is producing all the goods that it can at any given time—will be determined by how efficiently the economy is functioning. How fairly the pie will be cut up—whether some persons will get pieces that are too big, while others will get pieces that are too small—is the issue of equity.

Some economic policies may contribute to two—or even three—goals at once. Sometimes, for example, a policy to carve the economic pie more fairly will also increase the size of the pie—or the pie pan. All too often, however, it becomes necessary to choose among the three goals. Many policies that are well designed to move the economy closer to one of the three goals would also move it further away from one—or both—of the others. Let us briefly examine, then, some ways in which these three goals may reinforce each other or may be in conflict.

Sometimes the goal of equity is compatible with efficiency. For example, both goals may be advanced by the overthrow of a parasitic ruling class (like the eighteenth-century French aristocracy) or by ending barriers to letting the best-qualified person obtain a job (like the tradition of keeping women and blacks out of top management positions).

All too often, however, the goals of efficiency and equity are in conflict. If in the name of equity all corporation executives are required to spend four hours a day emptying waste baskets and sweeping floors, it may prevent them from obtaining enough information about market conditions to make efficient managerial decisions. Moreover, if equity considerations are carried to the point where the pilot flying the plane cannot be paid any more than the steward serving the drinks, young people may not bother to train to become skilled pilots—resulting in lower air safety as well as in economic inefficiency.

Sometimes there is enough of a conflict between these two goals to alter the conclusions we might reach by considering one of the goals in isolation. For example, a rich patient might have to pay a surgeon three times as much for a particular operation—say, an appendectomy—as a poor patient would have to pay. Charging different prices for the same commodity or service violates one of the first rules of *Efficiency* (see especially pp. 21–22). But this practice may be far more equitable than if the surgeon were to earn the same living by charging all patients the same rate for appendectomies. Likewise, it may or may not be fair for Barbra Streisand to earn more money than another singer just because she was born with a better voice. But it will be more efficient—and lovers of music will be better served—if Streisand is offered enough money to lure her to sing in movies and concerts before large audiences, while a less-talented singer only sings before the small audiences at supper clubs.

In other words, there is often an important tradeoff between these two goals. In many situations some efficiency must be given up to obtain more equity, or some equity must be sacrificed to obtain more efficiency. Arthur Okun, a Brookings Institution economist, emphasized the importance of this tendency throughout our economic life when he wrote a book entitled *Equality and Efficiency: The Big Tradeoff.*

When we look at another pair of goals—equity and growth—we again see that the two sometimes reinforce each other, but more often they suggest different policies. If banks tend to discriminate against women and blacks in the granting of business loans, then outlawing that discrimination may do more than promote equity. It may also encourage some important growth-producing forms of investment that white businessmen would have overlooked. By contrast, advocates of greater growth sometimes argue that large reductions in the federal tax on the profits of corporations would encourage more investment and growth. Opponents of such reductions argue that high taxes on corporations are needed to promote equity by indirectly taxing the incomes of the corporate shareholders, who tend to be wealthier than the average citizen.

When we look at the last pair of goals—growth and efficiency—we find that they are often compatible. Generally speaking, an efficient and productive economy is better able to set aside a larger share of its production to invest in future growth. But these two goals may also be in conflict. For example, an economy made up entirely of small competitive firms may be highly efficient at using the resources at hand. At the same time, none of these very small firms may be engaging in research and development activities. The potential benefits to any one small firm (out of hundreds producing the same kind of good) may seem too small to justify the cost of research, and the growth of the economy may suffer.

The issues we have raised in this section are among the most perplexing in economics. We cannot answer them definitively in this section or even in this book as a whole. They are, however, issues that students of economics should think about as they examine specific concepts and policy proposals in the field of economics. True economic wisdom consists of skill in finding ways to advance all three goals. This is seldom done through a single policy, but it may be achieved through a combination of policies. Each element of that combination must be chosen so as to advance at least one of the goals substantially, while doing a minimum of damage to the other two.

ECONOMIC THEORY

A theory is an abstraction that enables us to better understand reality and to more accurately predict what will happen. It is an analytical device that serves as a focus for logical analysis and for empirical investigation into actual situations. Theory guides research.

Economic theories are frequently referred to as models. A model is a formal statement of a theory—a simplified view of how some part of the economy is assumed to operate. A simple model of total consumption, for example, might describe it as dependent only on current income, while a more sophisticated model might describe other influences, like wealth or expected future income.

When studying problems in economics, we search for relationships that occur between different economic variables—for example, the price of a good and the quantity demanded of this good. Theory, however, is more than a mere description of particular relationships. It is an effort to generalize about relationships that occur regularly, not about coincidental happenings. If we observe that a particular relationship between two variables frequently occurs, we may predict that it will occur again in the future.

Theory and Assumptions

A theory need not fit all the facts. This often bothers beginning students of economics. It should not. Assuming away real world phenomena does not connote naiveté. Rather it expresses a realization that in order to see and comprehend relationships between particular variables it is necessary to simplify and to isolate. We must abstract from the multitude of economic and other data in the real world. For example, in particular cases we may assume that firms seek only to maximize their profits, that government does not exist (or has no influence on the variables being considered), or that the underlying causes of economic behavior do not change while their effects are being worked out.

Often we need these unrealistic assumptions in order to simplify and in order to develop theories that yield reliable and meaningful predictions about phenomena not yet observed.

Testing Economic Theory

Economics is a social science. Generally speaking, the social sciences are less exact than the natural or physical sciences. The social scientist must often be satisfied in predicting direction instead of amount. The natural scientist deals with molecules and cells and is concerned with people in an anatomical or physiological sense, while the social scientist is concerned with people's behavior. Therefore the social scientist is not able to use the "scientific method" (the controlled experiment) as effectively as can the natural scientist. If, for example, a chemist wants to determine the color reaction of chemical A with chemical B, he can place in two identical and sterile test tubes the same measured quantity of chemical B and then add a particular quantity of chemical A to one of the two test tubes. If he now observes a change in color in the test tube to which he added chemical A but observes no change in color in the other test tube, the color change may clearly be attributed to the reaction of chemicals A and B. If this experiment were performed hundreds of times, we would expect the same results to occur each time.

Contrast a simple experiment in economics. We want to find out by means of a controlled experiment what effect a one-shot $1,000 increase in income will have on people's spending and saving patterns. One hundred people are chosen for Group A and an additional 100 people for Group B. These people are selected because they have certain similar characteristics. They are not chosen at random. All have annual incomes of $12,000, all are thirty years of age, all have three dependents, and all live in the same section of the same city. Each person in Group A is given $1,000 (we give nothing to the people in Group B) and the difference in spending patterns of the two groups is observed. Let us assume that our findings are that Group A spends more than Group B—specifically that Group A members spend an average of $738.50 more per person than do members of Group B. How much faith do you have in this experiment? Would you expect that if the $1,000 had been given to the people in Group B instead of Group A, they, too, would have spent $738.50 more per person than those of Group A? Chances are that the figure would be at least slightly different—perhaps it would be quite different. Why? Because we are dealing with people, and people do not all behave in the same way. While this experiment may allow us to predict that a one-shot increase in income will cause people to spend more, it does not allow us to predict that they will spend 73.85 percent of their additional income.

The techniques used in testing economic theory are many and varied, but they generally fall into two categories: the logical and the empirical. In both categories the use of mathematics is very important. Mathematics helps to express conclusions that are clear, consistent, and that can test the validity of the theory. The use of mathematics and statistics to formulate and then test economic theory is referred to as <u>econometrics</u>.

Proving a Theory

We cannot prove that a theory about economic behavior is correct. We simply see that it is not contradicted. It is not like proving a theorem from certain stated axioms, as is done in euclidean geometry. What we derive from theories are expectations about facts. For example, a theory that has often been substantiated, and as far as is known never contradicted, is that when a tree falls to the ground it makes a crash or a thud. However, if we are told about a particular tree in an uninhabited forest that has fallen without making a crash or a thud, we are unable to prove that the claim is false.

Using Economic Theory

The most important requisite of a theory is that it be useful. Most economists are not interested in theorizing for its own sake. Man is a curious creature who wants to know what makes things "tick," but more important, man has problems. Things are very often not the way he would like them to be—he may not have enough, he may have too much. He wants to know what will bring about the desirable result, and the answers lie in the utilization of present theories or theories not yet devised.

Positive and Normative Economics

John Neville Keynes (father of the more renowned John Maynard Keynes), writing in 1891, distinguished between positive and normative economics. He cautioned against the confusion among their methods, a warning still needed today. Positive economics deals with what is; normative with what ought to be. Normative economics is based upon value judgments, while positive economics is essentially void of value judgments. For example, a front-page newspaper article on the facts and causes of inflation would be described as positive economics. By contrast, the same newspaper's editorial telling what ought to be done to control inflation is an example of normative economics.

ECONOMIC RATIONALITY

Economic rationality refers to a basic assumption made by economists about the economic behavior of human beings; that is, they are motivated by self-interest and therefore want as much of "good things" as they can get. It is assumed that individuals appraise the alternative courses of action with which they are confronted and then choose that particular one that promises the greatest net gains.

Rational behavior need not be totally selfish. "Good things" come in many different packages and have to be appraised very carefully. While it is rational for Sally to prefer two new dresses to only one new dress, it may also be rational for her to prefer to buy her brother a basketball for his birthday than to buy herself the second new dress. If a rich old uncle wishes to be well remembered after he departs from this world and feels a sense of responsibility to his relatives, it is rational for him to leave $500,000 to his favorite niece. Furthermore, it is rational to give to one's favorite charity. Self-interest, then, is used more broadly in economics than in common usage. People not only consider themselves better off when they add to their stock of material goods but also feel more fortunate when they believe that they have done the right thing.

The rationality assumption enables economists to make predictions concerning economic behavior. In the absence of this assumption, most economic theory would lose its predictive power. If people were indifferent between becoming better off and becoming worse off, their actions would not be predictable.

Few would assert that the assumption of economic rationality is completely accurate. Actually, most individuals base economic decisions on social, political, and ethical considerations as well as on personal gain. Economists adhering to the "institutionalist" school of thought suggest that economic activity is based heavily on habit, custom, tradition, and the technological process. They argue that self-interest is not innate, and that the way people express self-interest is culturally determined. Most American economists today are of the "neoclassical" school. They do not deny the importance of institutions, but they feel that it is not necessary to understand why people are motivated by self-interest in order to analyze the implications of such behavior. Every society weaves a fabric of institutions—laws, organizations, and customs—that guide its economic behavior. The impact of such institutions may be analyzed even when their origins are not understood. Whether self-interest is institutionally determined or whether it is part of the basic makeup of man is an imponderable that few economists feel qualified to explore. Instead they merely recognize that the assumption of self-interest as the prime mover is very useful. It is a simplifying assumption on which important economic theories can be built.

The economic units whose behavior concerns us can conveniently be divided into four groups: (1) consumers; (2) business decision makers; (3) owners of land, capital, and labor; (4) government.

The Rational Consumer

The rational consumer is defined as one who seeks to maximize his satisfaction. In order to derive the greatest possible value from his income he deliberately buys those things he wants most rather than things that he considers less attractive. This definition implies that the rational consumer is consistent and that he can calculate. If he prefers A to B and B to C, then he must prefer A to C. We need not say that the consumer is maximizing his satisfaction under perfect conditions, but only that he is doing so with the limited information he possesses. If he is disappointed after he makes a purchase, he will alter his purchases the next time he shops.

The Rational Business Decision Maker

The rational entrepreneur—the business decision maker—is defined as one who seeks maximum profits and uses the best possible production techniques available to him. He will therefore be willing to produce additional output only so long as his expected additional income is greater than his expected additional cost. Likewise, he will be willing to curtail his output if he expects that such action will result in a greater decrease in cost than in revenue. In this way he can increase his profits—or reduce his losses.

The Rational Capitalist, Landowner, and Laborer

The rational owner of capital, land, and labor attempts to maximize his return in much the same manner as the rational entrepreneur. The rational capitalist seeks the maximum interest rate; the rational landowner seeks maximum rent; the rational laborer seeks the maximum wage rate. If, for example, a man is offered employment as a train conductor on the XYZ Railroad at a wage rate of $5.50 per hour, he would not be a rational laborer if he would accept the same job under similar working conditions at the nearby ABC Railroad at a wage rate of only $5.40 per hour.

Rational Government

The groups discussed so far are all primarily concerned with maximizing their own incomes or satisfactions. Clearly, however, this is not the function that governments are supposed to perform.

We need not always face the subtle philosophical question of what it is that a rational government should attempt to maximize. An economist can take the easy way out and simply describe the workings of the private economy, using the results to point out to policymakers the impact of certain governmental policy, such as a tax cut or an antitrust suit. In this sense, the economist asserts merely that it is more rational for a policymaker to act in full knowledge of the consequences than in ignorance.

Sometimes an economist will choose to take governments as they are in attempting to predict their behavior. Predictions may be based entirely on past behavior. For example, a 1 percent increase in interest rates may have been found to cause local governments to reduce road expenditures by 2 percent. Therefore, future interest rate changes are assumed to result in like responses.

A second approach is for the economist to recognize that government is made up of individuals who have particular personal motives. Here the economist tries to predict government behavior on the assumption that government officials, just like private citizens, will direct their behavior toward ends that will serve their self-interest. Specifically, government officials are expected to attempt to maximize their own job security, income, and glory. In the case of elected officials, job security—to be reelected—is of prime importance. This may lead them to advocate "popular" policies or at least to appear to provide whatever the majority of their constituents favor. But all government officials, including those whose jobs are not dependent upon the voting public, are concerned with job maintenance, job promotion, and pleasant working conditions. Under this interpretation rational government action is any action that brings policymakers closer to these goals, however useless it may be to the public the government is supposed to serve.

A third approach is to define rationality in terms of the functions and services that governments should perform. Some present-day economists begin with the assumption that there are some goods—like national defense—that the market cannot be expected to provide adequately (see *Public Goods,* pp. 423–25). They define a "rational" government as one that can most accurately reflect the sum of individual preferences for such goods. Other economists define a rational government as one that will maximize social welfare (assuming that they can define social welfare), even if the policies required are not always popular. For example, the policymaker decides on the basis of a value judgment that the elderly widows of Spanish-American war veterans are more deserving of additional income than are wheat growers. Then it is "rational" to cut price supports for wheat and use the money to increase pensions for the widows even though the wheat growers may represent more votes than the widows. Rational government action can only be judged in the light of goals. Most economists would agree on one point. If some action can be taken that will increase the welfare of at least one person without reducing the welfare of any other person, then it is rational for government to take that action. When policies meet this criterion, economists praise them as "efficient" (see *Efficiency,* pp. 18–23).

EQUILIBRIUM

Equilibrium refers to a state of balance. It is a situation in which any forces for change within a system offset each other to the point that there are no internal tendencies for the system to change.

Suppose that there are three adjoining rooms in a building, each connected by a closed door. The one on the right is heavily heated, say to 90°. The one on the left is strongly air-conditioned, say to 30°. And the room in the middle is neither heated nor air-conditioned. If the doors between the rooms are opened, both warm air and cold air will rush into the middle room. After a while the temperature in the middle room will reach an equilibrium position—a state of balance.

Equilibrium positions may be stable or unstable. In our example it is likely that the temperature of the middle room will go to about 60° and stay there. This would be a stable equilibrium—one which tends to restore itself in the face of disturbances. If a large cake of ice were now placed in the middle room, it would cause the temperature to decline, say, to 50°. However, after a while the ice will melt and eventually the temperature in the room will return to 60°—the stable equilibrium.

Unstable equilibrium situations are also observed. Suppose that you stumbled across a drunken man lying on a sidewalk and you decided to pick him up and stand him on his feet. With some effort you might be successful in bringing him to an equilibrium upright position. However, one small step on his part or a slight shove from a passerby will cause him to fall. There will be no tendency for him to bounce back up and regain his previous equilibrium.

In economics we observe mostly stable equilibrium situations—positions of balance that will tend to be restored if they are temporarily upset. For example, if $1 is the price at which yo-yo producers want to sell the same quantity of yo-yos that consumers want to buy, $1 is the equilibrium price. At prices above $1, the supply of yo-yos will exceed the demand for them. This will tend to drive prices down, as firms find themselves unable to sell their whole supply of yo-yos at that high a price. At prices below $1, the demand for yo-yos will exceed the amount that producers are willing to sell. This will tend to drive prices up as consumers find themselves unable to buy all the yo-yos they want at this low price. If everything else remains the same (for example, people's tastes, people's incomes, the cost of producing yo-yos), a price of $1 will be maintained over time.

The economist is very much concerned with the concept of equilibrium, but only rarely is it actually attained. Usually disturbances appear that prevent equilibrium from actually being reached. If we can identify an equilibrium position, however, we can predict—or seek to influence—the direction in which economic changes will occur. For example, a nation may have an equilibrium national income of $1 trillion (even though at that moment it may actually be several billion dollars above or below). If it is considered desirable to raise national income by 10 percent, then policy can be introduced that will alter the variables so as to provide for a new equilibrium position at $1.1 trillion.

Statics, Comparative Statics, and Dynamics

The static approach is one in which a particular situation is analyzed with no time for the underlying conditions to change. In the realm of statics the economist tries to define equilibrium positions. Comparative statics, as the term implies, is the technique of comparing various static equilibrium positions. Equilibrium positions change as a result of changes in one or more underlying determinants of the variables. If the cost of producing yo-yos increases so that sellers raise the price they charge for any quantity of yo-yos that they offer, we may expect a decline in the equilibrium quantity bought and sold. Comparing this new equilibrium position with the original one is engaging in comparative statics.

By contrast, dynamics includes time as a continuous variable. Dynamic analysis does not concern itself with the definition of equilibrium positions but rather with the movement (the process of adjustment) of variables over time between two equilibrium positions. While a great deal of economic theory makes use of statics and comparative statics, mathematical tools are increasingly enabling economists to engage in dynamic analysis.

Partial Equilibrium vs. General Equilibrium

Partial equilibrium refers to the analysis of one economic unit at a time and assumes that all the others are unaffected. By contrast general equilibrium analysis takes into account nearly all the repercussions that are related to any specific economic disturbance which is being studied.

Partial equilibrium analysis is widely used in economics and can be justified by the need to simplify and handle as few variables as possible. This approach is proper for the handling of a wide range of economic problems. For example, in the automobile industry—one of the largest and most far-reaching industries in the United States—the use of partial equilibrium analysis is sometimes appropriate, while in other cases general equilibrium analysis is necessary. An increase in the hourly wage rate for auto workers will raise the costs of auto producers, thereby raising the equilibrium price and lowering the equilibrium quantity of automobiles. Partial equilibrium analysis would be confined to examining this immediate effect, which might be all that we were interested in. It is reasonable, however, to expect several other effects that could be examined in a general equilibrium framework. The increase in income of these auto workers will increase their effective demand for automobiles as well as all other goods and services. The higher price of automobiles may change the percentage of consumers' incomes spent on automobiles and, therefore, alter the demand for other goods and services. The decrease in the production of automobiles will decrease the demand for many inputs, such as steel, tires, or batteries. All of these effects could, in turn, feed back on the automobile market and, thus, on the price and quantity sold of automobiles. Partial equilibrium analysis abstracts from these repercussions, while general equilibrium takes account of them. In the automobile industry, where a wage hike may have a substantial impact on the demand for automobiles and other goods, the use of partial equilibrium will sometimes be insufficient. However, in smaller and less economically important industries, like the watchband industry or the golf cart industry, a wage hike would generate relatively minor repercussions, and the use of partial equilibrium would usually be sufficient.

MONEY

Money is generalized purchasing power. It is anything generally accepted as payment for commodities and services in an economy, especially that which the seller accepts in the expectation that he in turn can use it to make purchases of his own.

Over the ages the forms of money have changed considerably. Primitive economies typically use commodity money that has immediate value in use, such as cattle, tobacco, tools, beaver skins, cocoa beans, or dried fish. A slightly more sophisticated form of commodity money is precious metal—especially gold and silver—usually minted into coins of a standard size and weight. In both cases, however, the acceptability of the money is largely due to its inherent value.

The use of fiat money became common in Europe and America in the eighteenth century. This form of money does not have an inherent commodity value equal to its face value but is backed by the issuing agency (a government, or sometimes a bank). Thus, a coin may be minted from metals that have a much smaller inherent value than the face value of the coin itself. (A prime example is the Eisenhower dollar, which contains steel and a copper-nickel alloy worth about 3¢.) Paper currency is the ultimate in fiat money, since it makes no pretense of having any inherent value, and a dollar bill can be produced by the U.S. Bureau of Printing and Engraving for about a penny.

An even more sophisticated form is deposit money, which is nothing more tangible than a bookkeeping entry in the accounts of an established bank. Yet, by writing a check, a person is able to pay his laundry bill as effectively as if he paid with currency, gold coins, or a can of smoked herring. In the U.S. economy today, demand deposits—bank deposits that are payable on demand through the mere presentation of a check—represent approximately three-fourths of the total U.S. money supply.

What makes all these things money? In the case of coins and paper currency, it is the backing of the U.S. government. Fifty years ago this backing took the form of a willingness to exchange paper money for a commodity—gold or silver. It was easier to carry around a $100 bill called a "gold certificate" or a "silver certificate" than the larger bar of precious metal for which the bill could ultimately be exchanged. However, the government eventually came close to running out of the precious metals necessary to maintain this backing. The government stopped paying out gold for paper dollars in 1934, and it stopped paying out silver in 1968. Today, government backing for our currency merely takes the form of a declaration that it is "legal tender." This means that the courts will consider it appropriate for the payment of any private financial debt or obligation and that the government will accept it as appropriate for the payment of taxes.

By contrast, demand deposits are not "legal tender." They are money only because the seller of a commodity or service has confidence in the check that he accepts in payment. He must believe that the check is being issued by someone who has the funds to cover it deposited in the bank and that the bank will redeem the check—either with cash or with a check that some other bank will accept. The seller may be unwilling to accept the check in payment if the writer of the check is suspect (for example, if he cannot produce proper identification) or if the bank on which the check is written is suspect (for example, if its head cashier is three weeks late in getting back from a vacation in Brazil).

In general, we may say that a seller accepts a particular form of money in payment for goods because he expects that it will be accepted by others. Although paradoxical, it is true that the acceptability of a form of money is derived from its very acceptability. In the nineteenth century, hundreds of different commercial banks were in the practice of issuing their own "bank notes." Some sellers would not accept any of these bank notes in payment for goods, while others would refuse to accept the notes of a bank they held to be particularly shaky or suspect. This proved to be a very unsatisfactory form of money, and bank notes were eventually prohibited.

Liquidity

Assets or elements of wealth may be classified according to how rapidly and easily they may be transformed from their particular form into money itself—what we call their liquidity. Full-fledged money, generally accepted in exchange for the widest possible range of assets, is considered 100 percent liquid.

At the other extreme, consider a capital asset such as a factory, a farm, or an office building. Although the value of such an asset may be great, that value is difficult to ascertain precisely. To find a buyer willing to pay all that a particular factory or farm is really worth might take many months or even years. Other physical assets, like automobiles or stereo sets, are slightly more liquid. Because they are mobile, the buyer is not obliged to use them in the same physical location as the seller did, and they can be transported to a central market. They are also likely to have more standardized character- istics, so that they can be more readily described and advertised.

Financial assets are typically more liquid than physical assets, although there is a great deal of variation even among these. There is probably no continuous organized market for a highly individual financial asset, like a $1,000 bond issued at 3 percent to pay for the sewers in Kenosha, Wis- consin, and redeemable at face value in 1993. An asset becomes more liquid, however, if it is inexpensive to sell (for example, if broker's fees are low), if transaction times are short, and if there is a high certainty as to its cash value. Thus, a U.S. government "bill" (short-term debt instrument) paying 5 percent and due in two weeks can be translated into cash almost instantly at a price that will not vary significantly from its face value. Such an asset is sometimes called <u>near-money</u>, indicating that it is almost as liquid as money itself.

Aside from coins, paper currency, and demand deposits, the most liquid financial assets are probably savings deposits (sometimes called "time deposits") in banks, credit unions, or savings and loan associations. Legally, the bank or association may require that the holder of a savings account wait thirty days or even longer before converting his account to cash. In practice, however, it is usually possible to convert an account to cash through the personal presentation of a passbook during banking hours. Easy as this may be, it is still easier and faster to write a check on a demand deposit at any hour of the day or night and then use that check to make a payment. Thus, while economists today almost always include checking accounts in their definition of money, they sometimes exclude savings accounts as being somewhat less liquid and treat them instead as near-money.

Liquidity in an asset is desirable, but it often has a price—a lower rate of return on the asset. Coins, currency, and demand deposits earn no return, and the interest paid on savings accounts is typically lower than the return on longer term or riskier financial assets, including corporate stocks and bonds.

Roles of Money

Economists recognize four distinct roles for money in an economic system: as (1) a medium of exchange, (2) a store of wealth, (3) a standard of value, and (4) a unit of account.

Serving as a <u>medium of exchange</u> or means of payment is the distinguishing characteristic of money. This function is of central importance to a modern economy. Without a general medium of exchange an economy must either remain unspecialized (each household producing to meet its own needs in food, clothing, shelter, and recreation) or must engage in <u>barter</u> (the direct exchange of goods) in order to trade those goods that the household specializes in producing. For example, a farmer may raise chickens but not produce shirts; in the absence of money he must go out and look for some shirt makers who have a particular taste for chickens. This may be possible in a village society with rudimentary specialization. It would be extremely difficult, however, for an assembly-line worker who fits fenders onto Buicks to barter his services for the whole range of commodities and services his family requires. General Motors might pay him with one Buick Galaxy every three months, but it is hard to see how he could barter that car for just the right combination of housing, college education, hamburgers, and clean diapers that his family needs. One Buick might trade for 10,000 hamburgers—considerably more than his family can eat. Besides, the owner of the hamburger stand might already have a car and want to trade his next 10,000 hamburgers for an extra bedroom built onto his house.

Without a generally accepted medium of exchange, it would have been all but impossible to create the fine <u>division of labor</u> that is the basis of our modern-day, complex industrial civilization.

Insofar as money is not perishable—neither physically nor in value—a generalized medium of exchange can also serve as a very useful <u>store of wealth</u>. Few persons want to spend money on commodities and services the instant they receive it. In fact, some persons want to retain their ability to purchase for months, years, and even generations. The durability of gold and silver contributed to making them such highly attractive forms of commodity money. Paper currency and checking accounts are also both durable—at least so long as the currency doesn't burn or get eaten by termites, and so long as the banks stay solvent. Recall, however, that these forms of commodity and fiat money have one major disadvantage as a store of wealth—they do not earn any return. (Of all the forms of commodity money known to man, perhaps cattle are the most likely to earn a return for those who hold them, though their durability is uncertain.) Also, in times of severe inflation, paper currency and demand deposits both do become highly perishable, not in a physical sense, but because they lose their real value. One of the major costs of severe inflation is that it interferes with money's function as a store of wealth.

A third function of money is to serve as a <u>standard of value</u> of the flow of products in the economy. If the Gross National Product were seen as a hodgepodge of Buicks, chickens, shirts, and diaper services, we would have no way either of adding up the items into a meaningful total or of comparing the values of two items. For example, assume that the same worker could produce four Buicks or 400 shirts in the course of a year. Without money he would constantly have to investigate the ratio at which Buicks and shirts were being exchanged in order to tell whether his labors would be more fruitful doing one job or the other. In a money economy, however, he can measure his wages in a common unit—dollars per hour or dollars per year—and decide which form of employment he prefers.

A fourth function of money is to serve as a <u>unit of account</u>. When households, firms, or governments are trying to understand their financial positions or evaluate their debts, money serves as an indispensable basis for comparison. Only by keeping books in a standard denomination like the dollar is it possible to compare assets and liabilities in order to determine a net financial position.

Money as Wealth

The money holdings of an individual are obviously part of his personal wealth in that they give him a direct command over real commodities and services. But what is true of individuals is not necessarily true of the nation as a whole. The national wealth would not include money as such. It would include only real goods that directly provide satisfaction to consumers or have the capacity to produce other economic commodities or services. Food, clothing, houses, factories, machines, automobiles, and appliances are all part of the national wealth. Untapped natural resources should probably be included, and many economists would also include the productive skills (learned and unlearned) of the work force. We should also include all forms of commodity money and the commodity content of fiat money (like the copper value of the penny). But most of the money supply—the demand deposits and most of the value of the fiat money—is not part of the wealth of the nation as a whole. It would be absurd to think that by spending a few cents to print a $10,000 bill the government could thereby increase the national wealth by nearly $10,000. The printing of the bill would only be a way in which the government could create for itself a new claim on the existing wealth of the country.

DISCOUNTING THE FUTURE

Discounting the future is a process that determines what the value is at the present time of payments that are to be received in the future. It recognizes that money can earn money and that individuals are often impatient to receive it. It is therefore preferable to have a certain sum of money now than to be assured of the sum of money at a future date. For example, if money earns an interest rate of 8 percent per year, $1,000 today is worth $1,080 in one year. This statement can be turned around to say that $1,080 to be paid in one year is worth only $1,000 today. Or, as an economist might put it, the present value of $1,080 next year is $1,000.

When a person places his funds in a savings bank, in corporate bonds, in municipal bonds, in a real estate mortgage, or merely lends money to a business associate, these funds will bring him a certain monetary return. The interest rate—or annual rate of return—is the dollar return that he receives each year divided by the amount of dollars that he lent. Thus we have:

$$\frac{\text{annual dollar return}}{\text{amount of dollars lent}} = \text{interest rate}$$

$$\frac{\$80}{\$1,000} = .08 \text{ or } 8\%$$

Knowing the relationship among these three variables, we are always able to find the third one when we know the magnitudes of the other two. Thus in addition to the above formula we also have:

$$\text{the annual dollar return} = \frac{\text{the amount of}}{\text{dollars lent}} \times \frac{\text{the interest}}{\text{rate}}$$

$$\$80 = \$1,000 \times .08$$

and:

$$\frac{\text{the annual dollar return}}{\text{interest rate}} = \frac{\text{the amount of}}{\text{dollars lent}}$$

$$\frac{\$80}{.08} = \$1,000$$

The Interest Rate

At any given time and place, similar interest rates will tend to prevail for similar kinds of loans. For example, in San Diego on a particular date all the banks may be charging $9\frac{1}{2}$ percent for mortgage loans. The interest rate that a lender can charge will determine the amount of return that he can receive on a loan. Interest rates, however, are not uniform. Many different interest rates prevail at any one time and they also change over time. For example, savings and loan associations usually offer savers a variety of interest rates, depending upon the length of time that money has to be committed. During the first half of 1976 savings and loan associations typically offered immediate withdrawal accounts paying $5\frac{1}{4}$ percent interest and also four-year savings certificates which paid $7\frac{1}{2}$ percent interest. During this same period the U.S. Treasury was paying about 5 percent interest on "treasury bills" (very short-term bonds) that were due to mature—that is, to be paid off—in 13 weeks. Long-term treasury bonds—those maturing after 20 or more years—were paying a little over 8 percent interest. High-quality 30- to 40-year corporate bonds paid from 8 percent to 9 percent interest, while some corporations (that were considered somewhat less reliable) paid 10 percent interest. Even though this sample is very small, two important criteria for interest rates seem to emerge: (1) the length of time for which money must be committed and (2) the degree of risk that is being incurred.

The interest rates during the first half of 1976 were substantially below those of 1974, yet they were much higher than they were during the 1950s. The most important reason for the change in interest rates over time is a change in the degree of general price inflation—or, to be more precise, a change in peoples' expectations of future inflation. For example, if a lender expects inflation of 6 percent over the next year, he ordinarily will not accept less than 6 percent interest, since that is how much less the money will buy when it is paid back to him. He would be better off buying some good that he could store for a year—a bar of gold, or a carload of wheat—that he expects to go up in price by at least 6 percent.

The Price of Bonds

We may observe the discounting mechanism by examining the changing value of certain bonds that promise a fixed payment. For example, assume that in 1970 the prevailing rate of interest for corporate bonds was 8 percent. The ABC Corporation raised money in that year by selling Ms. Jones a $1,000 bond. It promised to pay $80 each year for 50 years to the current owner of the bond. It also promised to pay off the bond for $1,000 in 50 years (the year 2020), when the bond would "mature." We see that the ABC bond thus pays the 8 percent per year interest rate that prevailed on the bond markets in 1970.

By 1980, however, conditions may have changed. Assume that by then the prevailing market interest rate for such bonds has fallen to 4 percent. The XYZ Corporation might raise money that year by selling a $1,000 bond due to mature in 40 years (also in the year 2020). At an interest rate of 4 percent, it need only promise to pay $40 each year to the current owner of the bond and to pay off the bond for $1,000 in the year 2020.

In the bond market of 1980 a potential bond buyer like Mr. Smith should be willing to pay $1,000 for the XYZ bond because it will pay exactly the prevailing interest rate of 4 percent ($40/1000 = .04 = 4%). But Mr. Smith should be willing to pay much more than $1,000 if Ms. Jones would sell him one of the bonds she bought from the ABC Corporation 10 years earlier. Both bonds can be cashed in for $1,000 in 40 years. But in the meantime the ABC bond that Ms. Jones bought will be paying $80 for each of 40 years, while the XYZ bond will be paying $40 a year. The market value of the ABC bond Ms. Jones bought has gone up—to well above $1,000—because the market rate of interest has gone down. It will be worth exactly $1,000 in year 2020, when it can be cashed in to the ABC Corporation for that amount. But in the meantime, with an interest rate of only 4 percent a year, the payments of $80 a year make the bond worth more than $1,000.

On the other hand, interest rates may go up by 1980. If the prevailing interest rate were to go up to 12 percent, then the XYZ Corporation could sell a bond for $1,000 and promise to pay it off for $1,000 in the year 2020, but it would have to promise to pay out $120 a year to the current holder of the bond ($120/$1000 = .12 = 12%). In this case, the value of the ABC bond owned by Ms. Jones would be less than $1,000 in 1980. Mr. Smith would not pay her $1,000 for her old ABC bond paying $80 a year when he could buy a new bond paying $120 a year from the XYZ Corporation for $1,000. Ms. Jones could hold her ABC bond for 40 years and sell it for $1,000 in the year 2020. But if interest rates stayed high, she could not sell it to Mr. Smith or anyone else before the year 2020 unless she were prepared to take less than $1,000 for it.

The general rule is this: When interest rates fall, the market value of existing bonds goes up, and when interest rates rise, the market value of existing bonds goes down.

The Discounted Present Value

The discounted present value (usually just referred to as present value) is the term used to describe what the value is now of a future payment. If the payment is made in one year the formula is:

$$PV = \frac{X}{1 + i}$$

where PV is the present value, X is the total payment in one year, and i is the rate of interest. In our previous example, in which the rate of interest was 8 percent and $1,080 was to be paid in one year, the present value is $1,000:

$$1,000 = \frac{1,080}{1.08}$$

The same formula may be used to derive the present value of a sum of money that is to be paid further into the future:

$$PV = \frac{X}{(1 + i)^T}$$

where T is the number of years between the present time and the time that the payment will take place.

It is necessary to take the $1 + i$ in the denominator of the formula to the appropriate power—the number of years between the present time and the time that the payment will take place—because of the phenomenon of compound interest. Each year, after the first year, interest is earned not only on the principle amount of money but also on previously paid interest. Thus if $100.00 is placed in a saving bank at 5 percent interest it will be worth $110.25 after 2 years. The $110.25 is made up of the original $100.00 placed in the bank, $5.00 interest earned on the $100 during the first year, $5.00 interest earned on the $100.00 during the second year, and 25¢ interest earned during the second year on the $5.00 interest earned during the first year.

At 8 percent interest, the present value of $1,000 in 4 years is:

$$\frac{\$1,000}{(1.08)^4} = \frac{\$1,000}{(1.08)(1.08)(1.08)(1.08)} = \frac{\$1,000}{1.3605} = \$735.02$$

The above example may be read as: at 8 percent interest, $735.02 would have to be invested today in order to obtain $1,000.00 in 4 years. Or, alternatively, it may be read as: at 8 percent interest, the promise of $1,000.00, 4 years from today, is presently worth $735.02.

At lower rates of interest the present value is always higher. At 4 percent interest, for example, the present value of $1,000.00 in 4 years is $854.80. Similarly, the further away the payment date, the lower the present value. For example, at 4 percent interest, the present value of $1,000.00 in 12 years is $624.60.

2

Supply and Demand

In a free market economy prices are determined by the interaction of supply and demand. Eggs or toothpaste, appendectomies or massages, bonds or stocks, or even money itself—the prices of these goods and services are established in a market through the forces of supply and demand.

A **Market** is an organized interaction between buyers and sellers that enables them to engage in trade. **Demand** for a good is the set of quantities that buyers wish to purchase at various possible prices. At any particular moment we expect that the lower the price, the greater the quantity that will be demanded. **Supply** for a good is the set of quantities that sellers wish to offer at various possible prices. At any particular moment, we expect that the higher the price, the greater the quantity that will be supplied.

Supply and Demand Analysis brings together information concerning the supply and the demand of a good in the context of a market. Economists use this analysis to determine the equilibrium price of a good and the quantity that will be bought and sold.

MARKET

A market is an organized interaction of buyers and sellers that enables them to trade or exchange. To the buyer it is the place or means through which he can buy. To the seller it is the place or means through which he can sell.

Markets can vary significantly. There are markets for tangible goods or commodities like bananas or shoes, markets for services like massages or medical attention, and there are markets for factor inputs like construction workers or farm land. There are international markets like the world market for rare coins and local markets like the market for cleaning services in Paw Paw, Michigan. There are continuous markets such as the market for movie viewing in New York City and limited-time markets such as the market for bank services on nonholiday weekdays between 10 A.M. and 3 P.M. There are markets where the transactions between buyers and sellers are face to face, as in retail purchases of groceries or clothing, and there are markets like the New York Stock Exchange where buyers and sellers of securities transact through a network of middlemen (called brokers) without even knowing of each other's existence. There are markets that involve very well-defined and nearly homogeneous products, such as twelve-pill containers of Bayer aspirin, and there are markets for heterogeneous factor inputs like unskilled labor.

The Importance of Markets

We can imagine at least two sorts of economic systems that do not require markets. First, a system where each family unit is virtually self-sufficient. In such a society, each family provides all of the goods and services that it consumes and goes without those that it does not produce. Second, a system where a central agency determines all production and distribution. The government decides which resources (human and nonhuman) will produce what goods and services—and who will ultimately consume them. Any system between these two requires markets.

Societies based on self-sufficient family units are very inefficient since they do not take advantage of the division of labor and other forms of specialization. Specialization requires markets in order to facilitate exchange. Adam Smith, often considered to be the founder of modern economics, persuasively argued in *The Wealth of Nations* (1776) that the division of labor and specialization make for tremendous gains in productive output. He wrote of a pin factory that he visited where ten workers performing different tasks "could make among them upwards of forty-eight thousand pins in a day . . . But if they had all [worked] separately and independently . . . they certainly could not each of them make twenty, perhaps not one pin a day. . ." But man cannot live by pins alone. These ten men required markets in order to exchange their pins (or money, if they were employed and not paid in pins) for items of food, clothing, shelter, and amusement. The workers were too busy to provide these goods for themselves, since they were occupied in making pins.

The second marketless system—a directed economy—is completely devoid of freedom. Free choice cannot be exercised because government makes all of the allocative decisions. No such extreme form of planning has ever actually existed, but some societies do depend less on markets to allocate resources and goods and services than do others. Capitalism is often associated with markets and communism with the nonmarket (direct) allocation of resources, although these categories must not be drawn too stringently. Some communist societies depend upon markets as much as do capitalist societies. In communist countries, however, government is more apt to set prices in order to determine the market results. Markets are freer in capitalist countries. Buyers can usually buy and sellers can usually sell what they want, when they want, and where they want. The price in a free market is determined by these buyers and sellers alone.

Markets, Money, and Prices

Markets do not require money. Goods may be exchanged directly for other goods. This is referred to as barter. But barter has an inherent disadvantage. It requires individual A, who wishes to sell something, to find individual B who not only wants exactly what A has to sell but also wishes to sell exactly what A wants. Money eliminates this problem by functioning as a medium of exchange. Money is a commodity that everyone wants, because everyone knows that everyone else wants it. A farmer who has corn to sell and would like a bicycle does not have to look for someone who wants to trade a bicycle for corn. Rather he sells his corn in a corn market for money and then uses the money to buy a bicycle at a bicycle shop. In this way the use of money makes for better and less cumbersome markets. A monetary price can be negotiated by buyers and sellers to enable trades to be made.

Difficulty in Identifying Actual Markets

It is easier to understand the meaning of the market concept than to identify actual markets. For example, is there such a thing as a United States steel market? The answer is quite complicated. First, there are many different steel products—structural steel, cold rolled steel, tin plate, stainless steel, and wire, just to mention a few. Second, there exist several other materials that are more or less good substitutes for steel, depending upon its intended use. Aluminum, paper, plastic, and glass containers are substitutes for tin (steel) cans, reinforced concrete is a substitute for structural steel, and aluminum is a substitute for stainless steel. Third, locational differences may be important. Some structural steel products produced on the West Coast compete very little with identical products from the eastern part of the United States because the bulky nature of the material makes it expensive to transport. Certain steel products from Japan and West Germany, however, sometimes compete in U.S. markets because the price—even with transportation costs—is significantly below prices charged by U.S. firms. Locational differences may also affect delivery time, convenience, and the cost of obtaining information, all of which are factors that influence markets. We must conclude then, that there are many steel markets, expressed in terms of particular steel products in particular geographic locations. They may be quite different from each other, yet they are not wholly independent. Also, there are many product markets in which the steel product is only one of several that compete with one another. Even though markets are difficult to identify in particular cases, the market concept is central to economic analysis.

The Perfect Market

In this section we will overlook some of the turbulence of the real world and deal with each market as though it were a perfect market. A perfect market is one that works well. It has three characteristics. First, all the buyers and sellers in the market have perfect knowledge of the offers that are being made to buy and to sell. Second, all the buyers and sellers have full mobility—the ability to move around enough to take advantage of any attractive offers that may be made. Third, there is vigorous competition among sellers and buyers. This means that each seller is prepared to take customers away from other sellers, and each buyer is prepared to outbid other buyers, if this serves their own interests.

Collectively these characteristics imply that in a perfect market there is only one price prevailing at any given time. To see this, consider the case of a large trading village where farmers and merchants meet every Saturday in the village square to sell and buy corn. Assume that in one part of the square farmers were selling—and merchants were buying—large amounts of corn for $2 a bushel. If a farmer knew about those transactions and was able to get over to that part of the square, he would not be willing to sell his corn anywhere else in the square for less than $2 a bushel. Likewise, a knowledgeable, mobile, and competitive merchant would not be willing to buy corn anywhere else in the square for more than $2 a bushel. That single price of $2 would be the only one that could prevail at that particular time.

In the real world, most markets are not perfect. It may be difficult—and even expensive—to obtain information or to "shop around" for the best place to buy or to sell. Buyers and sellers may be unwilling—or even unable—to compete with each other. But enough markets come close enough to this ideal enough of the time that it is useful to develop a model of how markets would behave if they were operating perfectly.

DEMAND

Demand refers to the amount of a good or service that buyers are willing and able to purchase at a particular moment at each possible price. At that particular moment the analysis assumes that buyers have fixed tastes and constant incomes, and that they face unvarying prices for all related goods. Demand reflects more than a *desire* to purchase; it reflects the *ability* to purchase as well.

Demand Schedule

Given the static assumptions that tastes, income, and prices of related goods are all fixed, the demand schedule states the relationship between the two variables of price and quantity demanded. Think of the numbers in the demand schedule presented here as having been derived from interviews with consumers. Each individual is asked how many of this particular type of sport shirt he will purchase at a price of $10, of $8, of $6 and of $4. The answers presented in Table 2–1 are not surprising, since these individuals offered to buy more sport shirts at low prices and fewer at high prices.

Table 2–1   Demand Schedule for Sports Shirts, May 22, 1977

Price per Sport Shirt (in dollars)	Quantity of Sport Shirts Demanded per Year (in millions)
10	1
8	2
6	3
4	4

The Demand Curve

If we had continuous data for each possible price, the demand schedule could be plotted on a graph as a demand curve. The economist always places price on the vertical axis and quantity demanded on the horizontal axis. Price is the independent variable and quantity demanded is the dependent variable. Figure 2–1a includes precisely the same information (no more, no less) given in our demand schedule. In Figure 2–1b these four plotted points have been joined by drawing a line through them. This line adds an infinite number of price-quantity points. For example, we now see that at a price of $5, consumers are said to demand 3.5 million sport shirts. However, since our interviews did not include a question asking how many sport shirts would be bought at $5, we are only assuming that 3.5 million would have been the answer. We can see that all the points along the demand curve, except those few for which we have data, are based on the assumption that they will fall on the connecting line.

Figure 2–1 Demand

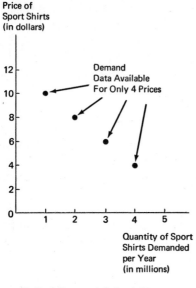

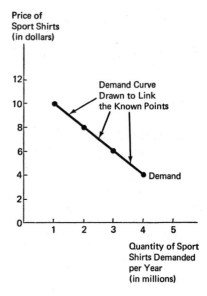

a Plotted Demand Schedule   **b** Demand Curve

Slope of the Demand Curve

In Figure 2–1b we drew the demand curve sloping downward from left to right. This curve has a negative slope, which means that the variables are going in opposite directions (as price decreases, the quantity demanded increases, and vice versa). There are two reasons why this is the usual case. The first reason is the income effect. Whenever a good or a service that a person buys goes up or down in price, it will affect that person's real income (his income in terms of purchasing power) and thus his well-being. If it goes up in price, his real income will go down and he will be worse off. Alternatively, if it goes down in price, his real income will go up and he will be better off. Suppose, for example, that a particular family spends $100 per month on meat out of its $1,000 after-tax monthly income. Suppose further that the price of meat suddenly doubles. This decreases the family's real income by somewhat less than 10 percent. The family has become poorer and must decrease its consumption. It may decide to eat as much meat as it did before the price rise by spending $200 on meat instead of $100 and spend $100 less on other foods, or clothing, or entertainment. More likely, however, the family will decide to buy less meat and less of other goods and services—all because of the decrease in its real income. Thus one effect of the increase of the price of meat is that the family decreases the quantity of meat demanded.

Had the opposite situation occurred—had the price of meat fallen in half—our hypothetical family's real income would have been raised (by 5 percent). The family would be richer. It would be able to buy the same amount of meat as before the price decrease and have $50 left over. This $50 could be spent on any other goods and services like beer, phonograph records, and movies, but also on meat. Thus the decrease in the price of meat raises the family's real income and therefore the quantity of meat it demands.

The income effect of a change in the price of meat can be substantial because a family typically spends a large share of its income on meat. The income effect of a change in the price of salt would be trivial, however, since most families spend a very small share of their incomes on salt. Even if a family could get all of its salt free of charge, it would not be noticeably richer.

The second reason why we expect the demand curve to slope downward is the <u>substitution effect</u>. Whenever the price of any good or service changes while other prices stay constant, relative prices are altered. Families will wish to substitute goods and services that became relatively cheaper for those that became relatively higher priced. For example, if the price of beef goes up, we may expect many families to substitute some pork, veal, lamb, poultry, or fish for some beef. Since the price of these other meats did not change, beef became relatively more expensive. A family that had been buying 25 pounds of beef and 5 pounds each of the other meats per month might buy only 20 pounds of beef and a pound more of each of the others. Had the opposite occurred (a decrease in the price of beef), we would expect substitution of beef for the other meats. Thus, because of the substitution effect, the demand for a good will increase when its price falls and decrease when its price rises.

We have treated the income effect and the substitution effect separately; in fact, they occur simultaneously. For most families a substantial rise in the price of beef lowers their real income *and* causes them to substitute other meats for beef. Both the income effect and the substitution effect explain the downward sloping demand curve.

At times and places exceptions to the downward sloping demand curve may occur. These unusual instances will be limited to a segment of the demand curve and not cover its entire range. There may be three reasons for an upward-sloping demand segment (positive relation between price and quantity demanded): (1) <u>Conspicuous consumption</u>. The good is demanded because of the enjoyment derived by its possessor from the knowledge (real or imagined) that other people envy him for owning this high-priced item. For example, some people contend that the most important reason why diamond rings are demanded is that they are very high priced. It is conjectured that if the price of diamond rings dropped to only a few dollars, the demand for them—given some time to get used to the idea—would decrease.

(2) Expectation of price changes. More of the good is demanded at a high price relative to a low price because the high price indicates to the buyer that the price will go up further. Less of the good is demanded at a low price relative to a high price because the low price indicates to the buyer that the price will go down further. For example, speculators who see the price of a share of IBM stock go up 10 points in a day may conclude that it is going to go up even more. Therefore the speculators may buy more of the stock. Likewise, if they see it go down 10 points, they may conclude that it will continue to fall and therefore not buy it. (3) Quality-price relationship. More of the good may be demanded at a higher price if buyers assume that higher priced goods are of a higher quality than are lower priced goods. People with very little information about a good sometimes use price as an index of quality. For example, many years ago a brand of ballpoint pens retailed for 39¢. Sales were disappointing, and it was discovered that most people were afraid to buy that cheap a pen. When the price was raised to $1.69 demand increased sharply.

Movement vs. Shift in Demand

We have already stated that at varying prices of a particular good, varying quantities will be demanded. Such a movement along the same demand curve is shown in Figure 2–2a. Here the price of sport shirts fell from $10 to $6, and as a result the quantity demanded increased from 1 million to 3 million per year. It is important to keep in mind that while this movement along the demand curve is occurring, tastes, incomes, and prices of related goods are assumed to be fixed. If any one or all of these static assumptions are allowed to vary, we may witness a shift of the demand curve. Figure 2–2b pictures an upward shift from the original demand curve to a higher one (to the right) or a downward shift from the original demand curve to a lower one (to the left). An upward shift means that more will be sold at any given price. Likewise, a downward shift means that less will be sold at any given price. Figure 2–2b shows that 3 million sport shirts were originally sold at $6 per shirt. After the upward shift 5 million were sold at that price and after the downward shift only 1 million were sold at $6.

First, an increase in *consumer taste* for a good will bring about an upward shift in demand and a decrease in taste will cause the demand curve to shift down. If businessmen decided to dress less formally—discarding their dress shirts in favor of sport shirts—the demand for sport shirts would shift up. If, instead, college students decided to wear more dress shirts to school, the demand for sport shirts would shift down.

Second, an increase in *consumers' incomes* will usually bring about an upward shift in demand, while a decrease in income usually causes the demand curve to shift down. Men can afford to buy more sport shirts when their income is higher and less when their income is lower. Only in rare instances will higher income cause people to demand less and lower

Figure 2–2 Increases and Decreases of Demand

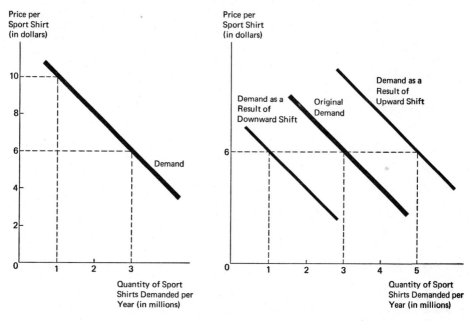

a Movement along Demand Curve   **b** Shift of Demand Curve

income to demand more. It is conceivable, however, that at considerably higher income levels some people will demand fewer hamburgers since they have switched to steak.

Third, shifts in demand also occur when *prices of related goods* change. Related goods may be grouped into two categories: substitutes and complements. Substitutes are goods that may be used instead of one another. Examples of good substitutes are beer and ale, briefcases and attaché cases, and vinyl kitchen flooring and kitchen carpeting. An increase in the price of a substitute good will bring about an upward shift in demand, and a decrease in the price of a substitute good causes a downward shift. If pullover knit shirts go up in price, many people will buy more sport shirts; likewise a decrease in the price of pullover knit shirts will undoubtedly decrease the demand for sport shirts. Complements are goods that are used in conjunction with each other. Examples include automobiles and gasoline, tea and sugar, and kites and string. An increase in the price of a complementary good will bring about a downward shift in demand, while a price decrease causes the demand curve to shift up. If slacks that match sport shirts increase in price so that the combination of slacks and sport shirts becomes more expensive, the demand for sport shirts will probably go down. Alternatively, if the price of slacks decreases, more sport shirts will be demanded.

SUPPLY

Supply describes the amounts of a good or service that sellers are willing and able to sell at a particular moment at each possible price. Because the supply curve describes conditions at a single moment, a number of things are assumed to remain fixed. These include the cost of inputs required for production, the state of technology (the know-how in the industry), sellers' price expectations of other goods and services, and sellers' goals or reasons for being in business.

The Supply Schedule

Given the above static assumptions, the supply schedule states the relationship between the price of a good and the quantity of it that will be supplied. To obtain a supply schedule for a particular type of dress shirt, spokesmen for shirt manufacturers might be interviewed and asked how many dress shirts they are willing to sell at a price of $4, of $6, of $8 and of $10. We would probably obtain a supply schedule like the one in Table 2-2, in which businessmen (sellers) offered to sell few dress shirts at low prices but more at high prices.

Table 2-2   Supply Schedule for Dress Shirts, June 18, 1977

Price of Dress Shirts (in dollars)	Quantity of Dress Shirts Supplied per Year (in millions)
4	1
6	2
8	3
10	4

The Supply Curve

If the data were continuous for each possible price, we could plot the supply schedule on the graph as a supply curve. The economist places price on the vertical axis and quantity supplied on the horizontal axis. Price is the independent variable, and quantity supplied is the dependent variable. The four points given in our supply schedule are plotted in Figure 2-3a. In Figure 2-3b these points are joined by drawing a continuous line through all of them. This line adds an infinite number of additional price-quantity points. We do not have any direct data for these points but can assume that they will fall on or very near the connecting line.

Slope of the Supply Curve

In Figure 2-3b the supply curve slopes upward from left to right. The positive slope of the curve means that the variables are going in the same

Figure 2–3   Supply

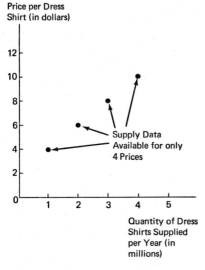

Price per Dress
Shirt (in dollars)

a   Plotted Supply Schedule

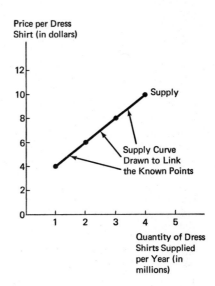

Price per Dress
Shirt (in dollars)

Supply

Supply Curve
Drawn to Link
the Known Points

b   Supply Curve

direction (as price increases, the quantity supplied increases, and vice versa). Supply curves are expected to look this way because profits are an important goal for businessmen (sellers). It will be profitable for shirt manufacturers to sell more dress shirts if their price is $8 than if their price is $6. At higher prices firms are willing and able to commit additional resources to production. For example, shirt manufacturers would be willing to use some of their older (higher production cost) equipment to produce additional dress shirts when their price reaches a certain high level. Likewise, at higher prices of dress shirts, these manufacturers might be willing to hire less experienced workers who were not considered productive enough to be hired when the price of dress shirts was low. Multiproduct firms—firms also manufacturing other products such as sport shirts, pajamas, and women's blouses—may also find that, at a higher price, it pays for them to shift more of their production facilities into dress shirts.

Only infrequently do we find exceptions to the rule that supply curves are positively sloped, and these exceptions are limited to segments of supply curves and do not cover their entire ranges. Sometimes we can observe the backward bending supply curve of labor. Consider for example, a student who is subsidized by his parents or other angels for his tuition, room, board, and books while attending college. He is on his own for any extras he desires—cokes, movies, a car—and, consequently, seeks employment. Table 2–3 presents the number of hours he is willing to work (supply his labor) at different hourly wage rates (prices). In Figure 2–4, we have plotted

Table 2–3
College Student's
Supply of Labor

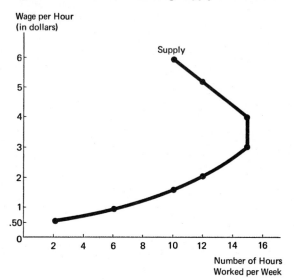

Figure 2–4 Backward-bending Supply Curve of Labor

Wage per Hour (in dollars)	Number of Hours Worked per Week
.50	2
1.00	6
2.00	10
3.00	15
4.00	15
5.00	12
6.00	10

this data and connected the points. At low wage rates—50¢ to $3—a normal, positively sloped supply curve may be observed. The student is willing to work only two hours per week for the paltry wage of 50¢ per hour, but at progressively higher rates—up to $3 per hour—he finds it worthwhile to give up additional hours of schoolwork and leisure. However, if the price goes up from $3 to $4 per hour, he will still only be willing to work 15 hours. He is able to increase his income from $45 to $60 per week, maintain his status in school, and retain some leisure time in which to enjoy his earnings. The same sort of reasoning lies behind his decision to work three less hours at $5 than at $4. His income remains the same ($60) whether he works 12 hours at $5 or 15 hours at $4, but he has more time to enjoy the cokes, movies, and car that he can already afford. What good is a car if you don't have time to drive it? At $6 he decides to work even less, while still not giving up income.

Movement vs. Shift in Supply

We have seen that at varying prices of a particular good, service, or factor of production, varying quantities will be supplied. Such a <u>movement</u> along the same supply curve is illustrated in Figure 2–5a. At the price of $10, a firm is willing to sell 4 million dress shirts, and at the lower price of $8 only 3 million will be offered for sale. Keep in mind that this movement along the supply curve merely reflects different possible responses by sellers to various prices at a particular point in time. Over time the cost of inputs may change,

Figure 2-5   Increases and Decreases of Supply

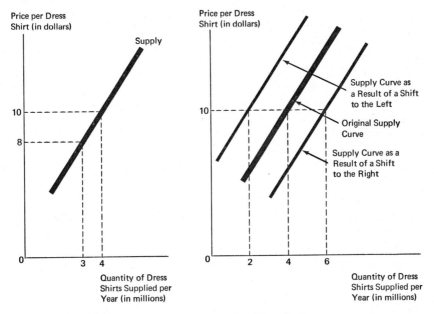

a   Movement along Supply Curve   b   Shift of Supply Curve

technological know-how may increase, price expectations about other goods may alter, and, indeed, the goals of the seller may change. Any one or a combination of these changes would likely <u>shift</u> the supply curve. Figure 2-5b pictures both a shift to the right and a shift to the left. A shift to the right means that more will be offered at any given price, and a shift to the left that less will be offered at any given price. Figure 2-5b shows that 4 million dress shirts were originally supplied at a price of $10 per shirt. After the shift to the right 6 million were supplied at that price, and after the shift to the left only 2 million were supplied at $10.

First, an increase in *input costs,* such as higher wages, higher material costs, or higher interest rates will cause a firm to want to sell less output at any given price (the supply curve shifts to the left) since profits will be lower. The firm will find it profitable to alter its product mix away from this product and in favor of other products that are now relatively more profitable. The reverse case—input costs decreasing—will cause the supply curve to shift to the right. More resources will be employed to produce this product. An advancement in technological know-how, such as new and more efficient machinery or a better managerial technique, is reflected as a decrease in cost. We would not expect a firm to adopt a new technology unless it resulted in lowered costs and therefore was profitable. In such cases the supply curve shifts to the right.

Second, the supply curve may also shift as a result of *price changes of other goods.* For example, a manufacturer of dress shirts who also produces sport shirts and pajamas will most likely determine his production mix among these products on the basis of price expectations. He will produce more dress shirts if he expects the price of sport shirts and pajamas to fall and fewer dress shirts if he expects those prices to rise. Hence, a firm's supply curve for one product has a tendency to shift to the right when prices of its other products fall and to shift to the left when prices of its other products rise.

Third, supply curves shift according to changes in the *motivations of sellers.* Throughout this discussion we have assumed that sellers are in business to make profits. If firms were indifferent to profits, the theory of supply would break down; firms would just as well sell more as less when the price is low. The assumption that firms prefer more profit to less profit does not, however, mean that no other motivation can play a role. Altruism—the desire to do good—may be a motivational factor. A toy firm may want to sell more educational toys, at least partially because "they are really good for the children." Security—concern over survival—is another motive upon which firms act. Firms may want to sell more of their products because they expect "bigness" to provide greater long-term security rather than because they expect larger profits. Firms may wish to avoid large risks—even if they might pay off handsomely—and decide not to commit themselves to producing certain products whose prices have temporarily gone up. Individual managers' goals—as distinct from the firm's goals—may also affect supply. The president of a firm may seek the prestige and salary that accrues to the president of a very large firm. Thus the supply curve would shift to the right as he would be willing to supply more at any given price. Alternatively, another firm's president may wish to decrease the size of his firm so that he can have a hand in every facet of the business. In that case the supply curve would shift to the left as he would supply less at any given price.

SUPPLY AND DEMAND ANALYSIS

Supply and demand analysis brings together all the supply and demand information about a good or a service for the purpose of determining the equilibrium point—the price and the quantity bought and sold. Supply and demand analysis is useful in dealing with all kinds of goods and services that are consumed as well as with resource inputs like a particular skill of labor or a certain kind of machine. It may also be applied to aggregates in the economy, such as aggregate demand and supply for all goods and services within a nation or the supply and demand for money.

An understanding of *Supply* (see pp. 58–62), *Demand* (see pp. 53–57), *Market* (see pp. 50–52), and *Equilibrium* (see pp. 36–38) is essential to a clear comprehension of supply and demand analysis. The supply concept specifies the (usually) positive relationship between prices and the amounts that will be offered for sale. The demand concept specifies the (usually) negative relationship between prices and the amounts that will be purchased. The market is the means by which the buyers (demanders) and sellers (suppliers) get together. And equilibrium is achieved when there is a balance—that is to say, at the price where the quantity supplied is equal to the quantity demanded.

Equilibrium Price and Quantity

Table 2–4 and Figure 2–6 show how supply and demand operate in a market to determine an equilibrium price and quantity. Table 2–4 presents the various quantities of leather coats that sellers are willing to supply at different prices and the quantities that consumers are willing to buy at those same prices during 1977 in City X. The higher the price, the more leather coats are offered for sale and the fewer are demanded. The lower the price, the fewer leather coats are offered for sale and the more consumers want to buy. This relationship is also seen in accompanying Figure 2–6. The supply and demand data from the table have been plotted and a continuous line drawn through the points so as to depict the supply and demand curves.

Consider first the price of $200 per leather coat. This is a price so high

Table 2–4   Supply and Demand for Leather Coats During 1977 in City X

Price per Leather Coat (in dollars)	Quantity Supplied during 1977 (in thousands)	Quantity Demanded during 1977 (in thousands)
200	110	40
160	100	50
120	70	70
80	40	110
40	1	190

Figure 2–6   Supply and Demand for Leather Coats During 1977 in City X

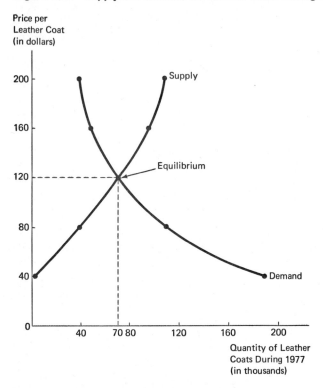

that sellers are willing to supply a total of 110,000 coats. Consumers, however, are only willing to buy 40,000 at this high price. At a price of $200 there is said to exist an excess supply of 70,000 leather coats (110,000 − 40,000 = 70,000). Sellers are frustrated in their efforts to sell coats at this price and will ultimately lower it. At a price of $160, there will be 10,000 more demanded and 10,000 less supplied (see Table 2–4). While this constitutes a movement in the right direction—alleviating the problem somewhat—an excess supply of 50,000 units still exists. The price was simply not lowered enough.

Alternatively, consider the very low price of $40 per leather coat. At this price sellers are willing to supply only 1,000 units, while 190,000 are demanded by consumers. This time we have a case of excess demand— 189,000 units. There are not enough to go around, and buyers, frustrated in their efforts to buy the coats, will have a tendency to bid up the price. A somewhat higher price, such as $80, will increase the supply by 39,000 and decrease the demand by 80,000 but will still leave an excess demand of 70,000 units (see Table 2–4). The price will be bid up again, reminiscent of an auction sale.

All of the prices thus far examined resulted in unstable situations—either supply exceeded demand or demand exceeded supply. At only one price

—$120 in our example—will supply be equal to demand and a stable situation exist. At the equilibrium price of $120 both excess demand and excess supply are zero, since sellers want to supply 70,000 leather coats and consumers wish to buy 70,000 as well. The quantity bought and sold at the equilibrium price is called the equilibrium quantity.

Reaching Equilibrium

Will equilibrium price and quantity always be reached? Not necessarily, for two reasons: (1) there may be inadequate competition, and (2) shifts in supply and demand may occur too frequently.

Whenever there is excess demand in a market (the quantity demanded is greater than the quantity supplied at a particular price), we expect an upward pressure on price. However, this expectation is based on a belief that buyers will adequately compete—that they will bid up the price. Likewise, whenever there is excess supply in a market (the quantity supplied is greater than the quantity supplied at a particular price), we expect an downward pressure on price. This expectation is based on the belief that sellers will adequately compete—that they will engage in competitive price cutting. If either the buyers in an excess demand case or the sellers in an excess supply case do not compete vigorously enough, an equilibrium price and quantity may never be reached.

In our discussion of demand shifts (see *Demand,* especially pp. 56–57) and supply shifts (see *Supply,* especially pp. 60–62), we offered several reasons why such shifts may occur. For example, demand may shift up (to the right) if consumers' incomes increase, if their taste for the good gets stronger, if prices of substitute goods increase, or if prices of complementary goods go down. Supply may shift as a result of changes in input costs, technological know-how, prices of other goods, and the motives to which businessmen respond. We expect fairly frequent changes in some of these variables. Every such change will bring about a shift, except for the coincidental case in which these changes exactly offset each other—for example, where income goes up at the same time that there is a compensating decrease in the price of a substitute good. Every shift will bring with it a new equilibrium price and/or quantity. But supply and demand may shift so fast that there is not enough time to adjust to any one equilibrium before a new one appears. In this case an equilibrium price and quantity will never be reached.

Whether or not there is enough competition and enough time between supply and demand shifts to reach equilibrium price and quantity, actual price and quantity tend to move toward equilibrium. We can expect that in most instances they will not be very far away for very long.

Surpluses and Shortages

The terms surplus and shortage are frequently used to express excess supply and excess demand situations. A surplus refers to the amount by which the quantity supplied exceeds the quantity demanded at the prevailing price. A shortage refers to the amount by which the quantity demanded exceeds the quantity supplied at the prevailing price. Under normal competitive circumstances surpluses and shortages will be reduced or eliminated by the ensuing price adjustments. However, government may intervene to cause a surplus or a shortage and to prevent adjustment toward equilibrium. There are many examples of such government action in the United States.

One example of a government action that brings about a surplus is the use of agricultural price supports. Small farmers in the United States have for some time been in a rather depressed situation. They have been unable to take advantage of the great technological advancements that have taken place in farming. The large (often corporate) farm has become quite efficient while the small family farm is steeped in inefficiency and struggles just to survive. Consequently, a great deal of political pressure has been brought to bear on government to do something to alleviate this. One important effort has taken the form of farm price supports—government guaranteeing farmers a higher than equilibrium price. Figure 2-7 illustrates a hypothetical case involving wheat. If competition in the market were allowed to determine

Figure 2-7   Supply and Demand for Wheat

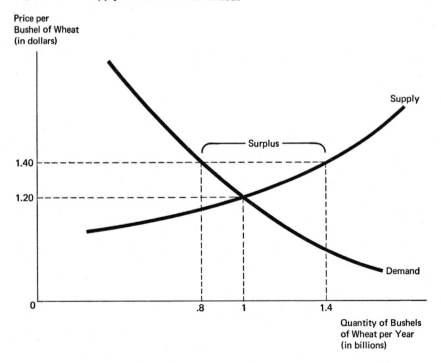

equilibrium price and quantity, the price would settle at $1.20 and the quantity bought and sold would be 1 billion bushels. If, instead, a farm subsidy in the form of a support price of $1.40 were introduced by the government, a surplus would be created. The amount of the surplus would be 0.6 billion bushels. At the artificial (support) price of $1.40, consumers would demand 0.2 billion bushels less and farmers would supply 0.4 billion bushels more than they would have supplied at the competitive price of $1.20. Government can maintain the support price only by purchasing the surplus.

Turn now to an example of a government-caused shortage—the imposition of ceiling prices. A ceiling price, as the term implies, is a restriction on raising price above a prescribed level. During World War II, ceiling prices were imposed by the U.S. government on a large number of commodities, including gasoline, tires, coffee, and sugar. The purpose was to prevent the prices of these goods from being bid up as a result of the increased demand associated with the war effort. In the early 1970s, ceiling prices were again imposed—this time the action was called a wage-price freeze—and again the purpose was to curtail inflation. Figure 2–8 illustrates a hypothetical case

Figure 2–8 Supply and Demand for Tires

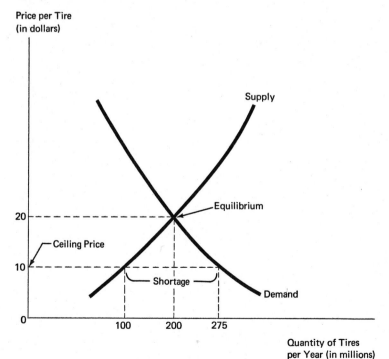

involving a ceiling price on tires. The competitive market equilibrium price for tires is $20, and at that price 200 million tires are sold. When a $10 ceiling price is imposed by the government, a shortage of 175 million tires results (the supply is decreased by 100 million and the demand is increased by 75 million). Given this shortage, some form of rationing must be used to determine who will be the "lucky customers" to get the tires. (Ration coupons, favoritism, bribery, and first-come–first-served are all possible methods of rationing.)

Persistent surpluses and shortages are caused by interference with the competitive market by preventing supply and demand adjustments. When government imposes the price rigidity or enacts minimum wage and rent controls, persistent surpluses and shortages can occur. Government is by no means the only source of market interference. Individual business firms and labor unions that possess a high degree of monopoly control can also bring about persistent surpluses and shortages. For example, they can set prices and wages above equilibrium levels, thereby creating a surplus.

3
Framework for Macroeconomics

"Macro" means "large," and macroeconomics, or national income theory, is the study of large totals or aggregates in the economy—national income, total consumption, total investment, and the nation's money supply. By contrast, "micro" means "small," and microeconomics is concerned with the behavior of individual units—households, factors of production, and firms. Macroeconomics at a policy level is concerned with the problems of maintaining overall price stability, high employment, and growth. Modern macroeconomics had its origins in the Great Depression of the 1930s. In 1936 a British economist, John Maynard Keynes, offered a new framework for understanding the problem of unemployment and the problem of inflation as well. His book *The General Theory of Employment, Interest, and Money* clearly described aggregate demand as the key to that understanding.

The central concept in modern macroeconomics is **Aggregate Demand**—the total demand for output in an economy exerted by consumers, investors, and government.

Aggregate demand and its components are measured within the statistical framework known as the **National Income Accounts**, compiled regularly to take the "temperature" of the economy. Gross National Product, National Income, and Personal Income are all part of these accounts. The fluctuations of aggregate demand can be reflected in the **Business Cycle**, which is a series of general ups and downs in total economic activity.

When aggregate demand falls below the ability of the economy to supply output, the result will be the **Unemployment of Labor** (as well as capital and land) and the failure of the economy to produce all the goods and services of which it is capable. When aggregate demand rises above the supply capability of the economy, the result will be **Inflation**—a general increase in the prices of commodities and services. The relationship between unemployment and inflation is described further in our discussion of the **Phillips Curve**.

While macroeconomics is primarily concerned with aggregate demand, the question of aggregate supply is also considered. Increases in the total supply capability of the economy are analyzed in the discussion of **Economic Growth**.

AGGREGATE DEMAND

Aggregate demand is the total amount spent on the commodities and services in an economy. It is expressed as a flow of dollars over a specified period of time, say $1,000 billion per year. In dollar terms aggregate demand will always end up being the equivalent of the total purchases in the economy.

Significance of the Aggregate Demand Concept

In 1932, in the depths of the Great Depression, unemployment in the United States had climbed to 25 percent, and real national product was down by as much. Yet few of the economic leaders of the nation or the world really understood why this calamity had occurred. Andrew Mellon, who had served as Secretary of the Treasury throughout the 1920s, admitted he did not have "any means of knowing when and how we shall emerge from the valley of depression." The Governor of the Bank of England said, "I approach this whole subject not only in ignorance but in humility. It is too great for me."

Today there is a remarkable consensus among economists on the importance of aggregate demand in explaining the high rates of unemployment that sometimes occur in the developed industrial economies of the world. There is also a consensus that aggregate demand can explain the high rates of inflation that sometimes occur. A college freshman today can more readily understand these problems than could the financial wizards of the 1920s.

The impact of aggregate demand depends on its relationship to another variable—the capacity of the economy to produce, which might also be called aggregate supply or full employment output. It is not necessarily a rigid value. Rather, it may increase in the short run if extra effort is applied, as in wartime, and it typically increases in the long run, as the labor force and capital stock grow or as production becomes more efficient. To simplify, however, assume that an economy has just enough workers in the labor force and just enough machines to produce a particular level of output—an aggregate supply—worth $1,200 billion at current prices. If aggregate demand is only $1,000 billion, then actual output will be only $5/6$ of capacity, and a considerable share of the work force and the machinery will be unemployed or not fully employed (underemployed). There may also be some tendency for prices to fall (deflation), since individual firms may try to increase their sales by cutting their prices.

By contrast, if aggregate supply is still $1,200 billion but aggregate demand is now as high as $1,400 billion, then more money will be bid for goods than there are goods available at current prices, which will cause prices to be bid up. As a first approximation, we might expect widespread inflation, with prices on the average increasing by $1/6$, so that goods that formerly sold for $1,200 billion would now sell for $1,400 billion. In summary, then, extensive unemployment (and possibly some deflation) will result from aggregate demand falling significantly below capacity, while extensive inflation will result from aggregate demand rising significantly above capacity.

Three Components of Aggregate Demand

Broadly speaking, there are three major domestic components of aggregate demand—consumption, investment, and government purchases.

<u>Consumption</u> is private expenditure on new commodities and services that meet current wants. Consumption occurs whenever a person buys a glass of beer, a suit of clothes, or admission to a movie.

<u>Investment</u> is private expenditure on new commodities to meet future wants. These commodities are called capital goods and can be used in the future to produce other commodities and services. <u>Capital goods</u> include plant (like factory or office buildings), equipment (like production machinery or office typewriters), and additions to inventories (like bicycles a factory has not yet sold or stationery on which a secretary has not yet typed letters). They also include houses and apartment buildings. Economists use the word *investment* specifically to describe purchases of new physical capital goods (like those mentioned above) rather than to describe payments for financial, or "paper," assets, like corporate stocks or bonds. For example, Smith may pay Jones $1,000 for the ten shares of General Electric common stock that Jones inherited from his grandfather. Then Smith has $1,000 less to spend on consumption, and Jones has $1,000 more. But in the economy as a whole, there has been no investment—no creation and purchase of new capital goods.

<u>Government puchases</u> include expenditures on services—including labor services—as well as expenditures on commodities. Thus they include payments to filing clerks in the Department of Agriculture as well as payments for nuclear submarines. Government purchases include some things, like food for soldiers, that in the private economy would be called consumption. They also include some things, like the construction of new post offices, that in the private economy would be called investment. However, government purchases do not include <u>transfer payments</u>—outlays to individuals to bolster their incomes rather than to reward them for current services to the government. Transfer payments for such things as Social Security, Medicare, or pensions of war veterans are a major portion of the outlays in the government budget. They help private individuals make consumption purchases, but from the standpoint of the government they should be seen as grants rather than purchases of current commodities or services.

Aggregate Demand and Circular Flow

We can visualize aggregate demand (see Figure 3–1) as a circular flow of purchasing power. On the right-hand side of the figure are shown the flow

Figure 3–1 Circular Flow of Demand (arrows show the direction in which expenditures flow)

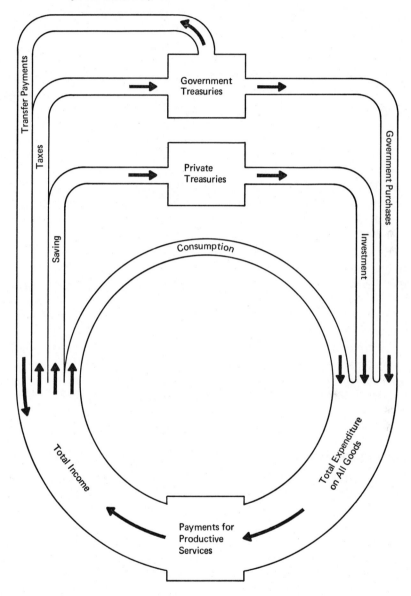

of expenditures on three components of total product—consumption, investment, and government purchases of commodities and services. In the box at the bottom we show the inflow of total expenditures on final goods that provides the dollars that are used to pay for productive services—the contribution to output of land, labor, and capital. These payments for productive services together with transfer payments from the government provide the total income of households and businesses that is shown on the left-hand side of the figure.

The flow of income branches off into the three ways that income may be allocated: for taxes, for consumption expenditure, or for saving. That portion of income that is allocated for consumption is immediately returned to the flow of expenditure in the form of demand for consumption goods, and to this extent the circular flow is exactly maintained. Saving and taxes, however, present a more complicated picture.

Saving can take many forms. A farmer or small businessperson may spend some of his income on a piece of equipment—a plow, or an adding machine. In this case the act of saving and the act of investment are simultaneous. The individual or household has through the same act both saved—withheld some of his income from consumption—and invested—purchased a piece of new capital. In most cases, however, the acts of saving and investment are undertaken separately, often by different persons at different times and places. Thus corporations save when they fail to pay out all their after-tax earnings in dividends; they may deposit the funds in a bank rather than use them to purchase new capital equipment. On the other hand, businesses are not limited by their own savings when they seek to invest. They frequently borrow from the banks, sell bonds, or even raise funds by issuing new shares of stock (ownership shares) in the company. Likewise, saving in the household sector need not be tied to investment. Households may save by stuffing money in a mattress or cookie jar, by putting money in a savings account, or by making payments on a retirement plan or life insurance policy. The money stuffed in the mattress is not available for investment. The money in banks, pension funds and insurance companies is available for investment, but there is no automatic guarantee that just because the funds are there, they actually will be invested.

These processes are represented on the upper part of Figure 3–1, where the middle loop shows savings pouring into a box called ''private treasuries,'' a shorthand expression for all of the places—from mattresses to banks to corporate treasuries—into which the savings of households and businesses may flow. Funds are also shown pouring out of that box as purchases of investment goods, but the box is used to represent the lack of an automatic mechanism to guarantee that all the funds that flow in will continue to flow out. Outflow from the box into the investment stream may also be the result of *Money Creation* (see pp. 167–72), a process that can occur within the banking system. It is entirely possible that the banks may be creating new money faster than individuals are hoarding it in mattresses and cookie jars.

A similar process takes place for taxes and government expenditure, shown in the top loop of the upper part of Figure 3–1. On the left-hand side, tax revenues are shown flowing into the treasuries of federal, state and local governments; on the right-hand side, government purchases of commodities and services are seen flowing out. Government transfer payments—payments to individuals to bolster their incomes rather than to reward them for current services to the government—are treated separately. They can be seen as a separate loop from the government treasuries, going off to the left and back down into the income stream. If governments as a whole are having a surplus, then the inflow of taxes will be greater than the outflow of purchases and transfer payments. If governments are running a deficit, the purchase and transfer outflow will exceed the tax inflow.

Figure 3–1 implies that the maintenance of a given level of aggregate demand is by no means certain. When we visualize the process as a circular flow, we can see that the flow has both leakages from it and injections into it. Leakages are the subtractions from the circular flow. In our diagram there are two forms of leakages. One is the taxes that individuals and businesses must pay to the government. The other is the saving of individuals and businesses from their after-tax incomes. In the real world we would also have to count a third form of leakage—expenditures on imports—since a payment for goods from other countries does not immediately or automatically return to the domestic expenditure stream. By contrast, injections are additions to the circular flow of expenditures. In our diagram there are two forms of injections. One is government outlays for purchases or for transfer payments. The other is investment in new capital goods. In the real world we would also recognize a third form of injection—demand for the nation's exports—since demand from other countries may stimulate aggregate demand within the domestic economy.

Thus six kinds of decisions become critical in determining whether aggregate demand will grow, remain constant, or shrink. On the leakage side, there is (1) the government decision to levy taxes, (2) the decision by individuals and businesses on how much to save, and (3) the decision by individuals, businesses, and government on how much to import from abroad. On the injection side, there is (4) the government decision on how much to lay out for purchases and transfer payments, (5) the decision by investors on how much to invest, and (6) the decision by foreigners on how much to spend on the goods that this country might export. Aggregate demand will grow if there is a tendency for governments, investors, and foreigners to add more to the expenditure stream than is being taken out in the form of saving, taxes, and imports. On the other hand, aggregate demand will shrink if there is a tendency for governments, investors, and foreigners to inject less into the circular flow than escapes through leakages from saving, taxes, and imports.

Government policies to curtail the growth of aggregate demand—to encourage leakages and discourage injections—are called restrictive policies. By contrast, policies to stimulate the growth of aggregate demand—to encourage injections and discourage leakages—are called expansionary.

Aggregate demand is vital in determining the rate of inflation and the level of unemployment. Thus economists—especially in the last four decades—have spent a great deal of time trying to understand better the decision by private individuals and firms concerning saving and investment and in prescribing the best policies for government to follow with respect to its total taxing and spending. The branch of economics known as macroeconomics is primarily concerned with the study of these significant forces in the economy—aggregate consumption, aggregate investment, and government expenditure—and the contribution they make to aggregate demand.

NATIONAL INCOME ACCOUNTS

The national income accounts are a framework for statistical data that present a comprehensive picture of the nation's economic life. They are essential for the study of long-term economic trends and business fluctuations and for the formulation of business and government economic policies.

The national income accounts provide a carefully integrated framework within which the current operations of the economy can be recorded. The accounts follow the same principle used by individual businesses when they use an income statement to record their annual operations. They measure the annual flow (as opposed to the stock at any point in time) of goods and services in our economy (see p. xix).

Aggregating the Data

Adding together millions of statistics from millions of individual enterprises is a cumbersome and time-consuming task. There are, however, some conceptual problems as well. Nothing should be counted twice, and everything should be counted once.

The problem of double-counting arises, for example, when bakery firm A buys semifinished products (like flour) from milling firm B. If the U.S. Department of Commerce included the value of the products of both firms, double-counting would result—the value of the flour would be included in both firms' reported figures. The double-counting pitfall can be avoided by distinguishing between final goods and unfinished goods (see p. xx). Final goods are bought for use in consumption and investment rather than for resale. By contrast unfinished goods—raw materials and intermediate goods—are bought by firms for transformation into more valuable goods and then resold in the new form. To avoid duplication, only the value of the final products is counted, and the unfinished ones are excluded. However, net additions to inventories are included as a form of investment.

The other problem is being sure that everything is counted once. Most producers sell their products or services, and we can measure the dollar value of their final sales to help build up the accounts. There is, however, a significant number of producers who do not sell their products or services but who should nevertheless be included. Some consume their own output (such as the farmer who grows part of the food that he and his family consume). Some receive income in kind—in the form of goods—such as the housekeeper who receives free room and board as part of her compensation. Finally, some give their services away (such as a commercial bank that offers free checking accounts in return for holding a depositor's money). In all these cases it is necessary to impute—to determine a charge for—the products provided.

The Accounts

Each of the accounts and their component parts (as defined by the Department of Commerce) are discussed below. We shall examine the relationships among them, working from the larger to the smaller-sized accounts.

Gross National Product.   GNP is the market value of the output of final goods and services produced by the nation's economy. It is "gross" because it does not deduct any charges for the depreciation of capital used up in the course of this production. However, all intermediate goods used up by business are excluded. GNP is made up of four components. They are:

1. *Personal consumption expenditures,* consisting of the market value of goods and services purchased by individuals and nonprofit institutions as well as the value of food, clothing, housing, and financial services received by them as income in kind.
2. *Gross private domestic investment,* consisting of newly produced capital goods—buildings and equipment—acquired by private business and nonprofit institutions, including the value of inventory changes and all new private houses, mobile homes, and apartment buildings. Gross investment can also be seen as consisting of two portions. One portion is necessary to replace the depreciation—or wearing out—of some of the existing stock of capital goods. The remaining portion is net investment and represents an addition to the size of the stock of capital goods.
3. *Government purchases of goods and services,* consisting of general government expenditures for compensation of employees, and net purchases from business and from abroad.
4. *Net exports of goods and services,* consisting of the amount of exports minus the amount of imports.

National Income.   NI is the total before-tax earnings of land, labor, and capital that arise from the current production of goods and services by the nation's economy. National Income is made up of five components. They are:

1. *Compensation of employees,* consisting of wages and salaries (including commissions, tips, bonuses, and payments in kind) and supplements to wages and salaries, such as employer contributions to government insurance programs (like Social Security) and to private pension, health and welfare funds.
2. *Proprietors' income,* consisting of the earnings from current business operations of sole proprietorships, partnerships, and producers' cooperatives.
3. *Rental income of persons,* consisting of the earnings of persons from the rental of real property, except for the earnings of persons primarily engaged in the real estate business.

4. *Corporate profits,* consisting of the earnings of corporations organized for profit that accrue to U.S. residents. These profits are measured before deducting taxes on corporate profits but after adjusting for the changing value of inventories.
5. *Net interest,* consisting of the excess of interest payments of the domestic business system over its interest receipts, plus net interest received from abroad. Interest paid by consumers and by government is excluded.

Personal Income.   PI is the current income received by persons from all sources. It includes transfer payments from government (such as Social Security payments) and business (such as corporate gifts to nonprofit institutions) but excludes transfers among persons. The term "persons" includes not only individuals (including owners of unincorporated enterprises), but also nonprofit institutions, private trust funds, and some private pension, health, and welfare funds.

Disposable Personal Income.   DPI is the income remaining to persons after deduction of personal taxes. Disposable Personal Income is made up of two components:

1. *Personal outlays,* consisting of the sum of personal consumption expenditures, interest paid by consumers to business, and personal transfer payments to foreigners.
2. *Personal savings,* consisting of the current savings of persons.

Relationship Among the Accounts.   One can go from any one of these accounts to any other by simply making certain additions and/or subtractions. Figure 3–2 shows how this is done, using the magnitudes for 1975.

Aggregate Demand—GNP or Final Sales?

Gross National Product is the best measure we have of total production in the economy, and it is the level of production that determines how many workers will be employed. As a first approximation, we may also see GNP as a measure of aggregate demand in the economy. It consists, after all, of the three domestic components of demand—consumption, investment, and government expenditures—plus any net export demand from foreign countries. But there is a complication. One part of Gross Private Domestic Investment is investment in inventories—the stocks of goods that businesses keep on hand. A women's clothing store will have substantial inventories of dresses it has not yet sold to its customers. A clothing factory will have two kinds of inventories—the finished dresses it has not yet sold to the stores and the cloth, thread, and buttons it has not yet made into dresses. Increases to such inventories are added when measuring private investment, and reductions in such inventories are subtracted.

Sometimes inventory investment is deliberate and should be seen as a part of aggregate demand, as when automobile dealers increase their

Figure 3–2 The National Income and Product Accounts: 1975 (all numbers are in billions of dollars)

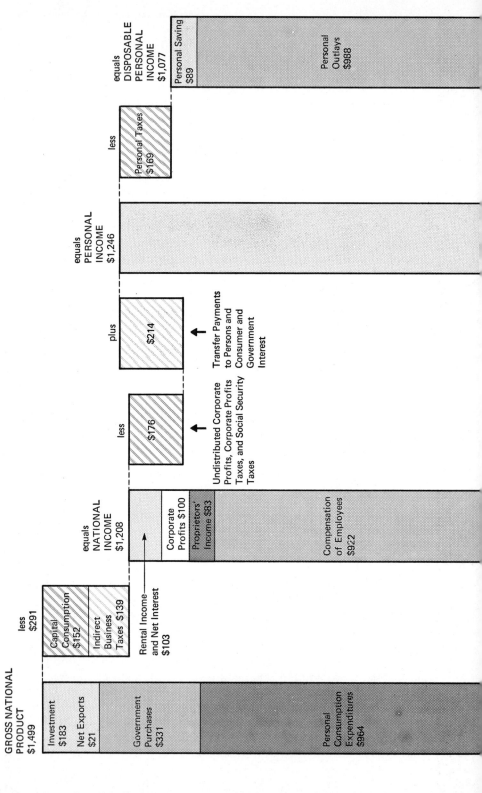

stocks of new cars because their business is increasing. At other times, however, inventory investment is unintentional, as when automobile sales fall off so quickly that dealers cannot sell all the cars that they had previously ordered from the factory. (In such times an economist may say ironically that a growing component of aggregate demand consists of all the cars that are piling up on the dealers' sales lots because no one wants to buy them.)

For this reason the Department of Commerce offers an alternative measure of aggregate demand—Final Sales. The Final Sales measure includes consumption expenditures, government purchases, net exports, and all forms of investment—in plant, equipment, and housing—except investment in inventories. It is simply GNP minus any increase in inventories that may have occurred.

BUSINESS CYCLES

Business cycle describes the ups and downs in general business activity that recur over time. If one expects to find a simple, regular pattern of these ups and downs, he will be disappointed. Economists cannot predict with any great degree of accuracy just when an upturn or a downturn will occur, but a study of such cycles does show that business activity tends to follow some kind of wavelike pattern and is not merely an assortment of random moves.

Lengths and Types of Business Cycles

Since the middle of the nineteenth century many different business cycles have been allegedly sighted, but like flying saucers, they often turn out to be elusive and difficult to identify. In the search for business cycles, economists have studied statistical series such as discount rates, bank balances, wholesale prices, interest rates, wage rates, foreign trade, aggregate production, retail sales, unemployment rates, profits, and stock prices. From these they have identified cycles of various lengths and complexities. One of the first business cycle theorists, Clement Juglar, claimed in 1889 to have identified a nine- to ten-year cycle. In the early 1930s Joseph Kitchen offered a forty-month cycle, and N. D. Kondratieff introduced a fifty- to sixty-year cycle. A few years later, Joseph Schumpeter attempted to integrate the Kitchen, Juglar, and Kondratieff cycles, arguing that the Kondratieff cycle was made up of six Juglar cycles, which in turn were composed of three Kitchen cycles. And so it has gone.

Identifying a cycle of particular length on the basis of some statistical series still leaves the question of causation unanswered. A theory that received a great deal of attention during the late nineteenth century was that cycles are a function of sunspots. The idea was that sunspots cause weather cycles, which create agricultural cycles, which in turn cause business cycles. Other, more plausible theories also explain cycles as a function of events external to the economic system—major technological innovations, political events and wars, rates of population growth, gold discoveries, and so forth. To rely on any of these external "causes" to explain business cycles is to oversimplify a complex phenomenon. But to combine some of these external influences with important internal reactions leads us to a more acceptable explanation of why some business cycles have occurred.

Since the mid-1930s most economists have agreed that business cycles reflect changes in *Aggregate Demand* (71–76). That is, economic activity goes up when aggregate demand goes up and goes down when aggregate demand goes down. Different components of aggregate demand have been stressed by different economists, however, as being most important in initiating change within the cycle.

A variable that many economists see as important in causing economic fluctuations is business investment—the purchase of capital goods like plant, equipment, and inventory. A few economists see changes in consumption behavior as important in generating changes in aggregate demand—both directly, and because businessmen will invest more when they expect consumption to grow rapidly. Government expenditure, the third major component of aggregate demand, has also been cited by some economists as important in initiating cycles.

Phases of the Business Cycle

Many different terms have been used to describe the various portions of the business cycle. Perhaps the most straightforward approach is to recognize four phases: trough, expansion, peak, and contraction. The <u>trough</u> is the lowest level of the cycle. It gives way to <u>expansion</u>, a period of increasing aggregate demand and business activity. This culminates in a <u>peak</u>, the highest level of the cycle. Eventually the peak gives way to <u>contraction</u>, a period of declining demand and business activity. This culminates in another trough, and the cycle can begin again.

Figure 3–3 illustrates these four phases. We begin with the dashed line representing the steady long-run growth trend in the economy. By contrast, the solid line represents the actual level of economic activity as it fluctuates around its long-run trend. While the phases of the business cycle must logically follow each other in this order, their length and actual shape will

Figure 3–3 Phases of the Business Cycle

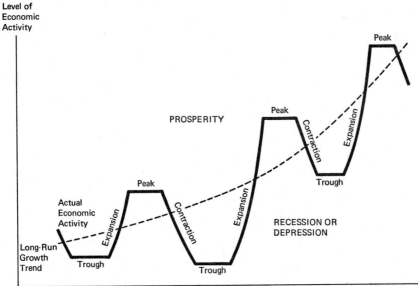

vary greatly from cycle to cycle. For example, the trough or peak of a cycle may last only a few weeks or—as implied in Figure 3-3—many months.

We show the region above the long-run trend as the broad area of prosperity, representing times of abnormally high aggregate demand and abnormally low unemployment. Likewise, the region below the long-run trend is labeled "recession or depression." Recession is a time when aggregate demand is abnormally low and unemployment abnormally high. Depression is a time when aggregate demand is severely low and unemployment severely high—for example, some have suggested 10 percent unemployment as the cutoff point between a recession and a depression. In Figure 3-3 the first and third troughs might be characterized as recessions, while the second might be characterized as a depression.

This use of the terms corresponds to the way most persons use these words. For example, it is often said: "When *you're* out of work it's a recession; when *I'm* out of work it's a depression." Obviously, the deeper the contraction of economic activity, the greater the likelihood that I'll be out of work as well as you.

Some economists use the terms *recession* to describe the contraction phase of the cycle and *recovery* to describe the expansion phase. Used this way, however, these terms can be misleading. The beginnings of a downturn or contraction may still be quite prosperous, and recession may seem an inappropriate description. Likewise, aggregate demand will still be near its lowest level when an expansion phase begins. To describe this as recovery may imply that the recovery is complete, when in fact it has only begun.

Over time there is typically *Economic Growth* (see pp. 113-18), or an increase in the capacity of the economy to produce. As a result there may be more real production and employment in a recession trough than there was during the peak of prosperity ten or fifteen years earlier. This is suggested in Figure 3-3, where the third trough represents a higher level of economic activity than the first peak that is shown.

Let us look at each of the phases of the business cycle in more detail. It may help us to see some of the internal mechanisms, as opposed to external events and government actions, that can help move the economy from phase to phase.

The trough phase is characterized by low aggregate demand that yields low output and low prices. It follows that unemployment is high, much of the nation's plant and equipment is idle, and inventory levels are low in line with low sales. Since aggregate demand is relatively low, an atmosphere of pessimism pervades the economy. There is a low demand for loanable funds for business investment, so banks have extra money to lend and are willing to charge low interest rates. An upturn in the economy will require some increase in expenditures. This may, of course, be initiated by the government or be caused by some other external factor, such as an important new technological discovery. Even in the absence of such external causes, however, there are important internal reasons why an increase in aggregate demand would eventually occur. Both capital goods (like machinery) and consumer durable goods (like automobiles and refrigerators) wear out, and businesses and consumers are forced either to repair or to replace them. At the same time prices are relatively low, and many goods are attractive buys.

Once a pickup in orders becomes evident, the stage is set for the expansion phase. Potential buyers now expect prices to go up and therefore wish to buy before prices rise. More jobs are created by the increased demand for goods, and personal income will rise as a result. This means more purchasing power and therefore still more buying. At some point a more optimistic outlook replaces the previous pessimism. Businessmen become more anxious to invest, banks become more willing to lend money, and consumers become more willing to buy. Gradually this optimism is reinforced by modest increases in output.

The continuation of this process leads to the peak phase. Prosperity is characterized by high aggregate demand and the virtual full employment of the economy's resources. As a result, prices are bid up by buyers who are willing and able to buy more than the economy is able to produce at current prices. Similarly, wages are bid up both in terms of hourly rates and the overtime work that is offered. Firms want to expand in order to satisfy the demand for the goods and services that they sell and are willing to pay more for the workers who will produce those goods and services. As they try to borrow more money, interest rates are bid up. Bad times are all but forgotten, and large debts are considered both prudent and reasonable.

Prosperity will continue until certain strains become evident. Some buyers may resist the relatively high prices, especially if they already own fairly new automobiles and appliances. Consumer credit payments must be met, leaving consumers with slightly less to spend on new purchases. As orders go down—even slightly—businessmen will cut production more, selling from inventories in order to satisfy demand. The contraction phase has thus set in. Bank loans go down, prices increase less quickly (or actually fall), and unemployment increases. Slowly but surely, a more pessimistic view sets in. Businesses that had intended to expand their operations or to modernize their plants decide to hold off, and investment falls sharply. Thus the cycle returns to the trough of recession or depression.

The Role of Government

Our description of the phases of the business cycle suggests that the private economy—if left to itself—can generate substantial swings in aggregate demand. But such self-generating cycles are not automatic. Today many economists prefer to speak of economic fluctuations rather than business cycles and to stress the important role of government in both offsetting and generating such fluctuations.

Since World War II a major objective of American economic policy has been to realize a gradual growth of output without substantial fluctuations around the growth path. *Built-in Stabilizers* (see pp. 198–203) help to advance this goal. In addition, the government uses both *Fiscal Policy* (see pp. 197–99) and *Monetary Policy* (see pp. 204–9) to accomplish this end. To some extent this policy has been successful. The severity of fluctuations in the business cycle has been greatly reduced since the 1930s. From 1929 to 1933—the low point of the Great Depression—Gross National Product dropped almost in half. Since then, no decrease of more than a couple of percentage points has occurred. Unemployment of labor rose from about 3 percent in 1929 to 25 percent in 1933 and then dropped to below 2 percent during World War II. By contrast, unemployment has fluctuated only between 3 and 9 percent since World War II. Our post–World War II economic policies have in large part prevented a swing as large as that of the Great Depression.

At the same time, government economic policies do not always contribute to the stability of the economy. For example, in 1966 and 1967 military expenditures increased with the escalation of the Vietnam war, but President Lyndon Johnson and the Congress were reluctant to cover these increases with higher taxes. Aggregate demand grew rapidly, and while unemployment fell to 3.6 percent, the rate of inflation increased from less than 2 percent in 1965 to nearly 5 percent in 1968. When Richard Nixon became president in 1969, he began to implement a "game plan" to reduce the rate of inflation by cutting the growth of aggregate demand. But inflation was slow to subside, and the major result was a decline in the growth of output and an increase in the rate of unemployment to 5.9 percent in 1971. Most economists attribute the ups and downs of that period to government policies rather than to any automatic operation of the business cycle.

UNEMPLOYMENT OF LABOR

Unemployment is the condition of being out of a job. Some persons may choose to be jobless because they are too old, too young, too busy getting an education, or too content to live off savings, inheritances, or welfare payments. Others are forced off the job market by mental or physical disabilities, by child labor laws, or by confinement to a prison or some other institution. But economists are primarily concerned with involuntary unemployment—the situation of those who want and are able to take suitable jobs but cannot find them.

In a modern industrial economy, high unemployment of labor is usually accompanied by the unemployment or underemployment—less than full use—of other resources, especially capital goods, including machinery, factories, and office building space. But the term *unemployment* almost always refers to the joblessness of labor.

Measurement of Unemployment

Involuntary unemployment in the United States is measured by the Bureau of Labor Statistics from a monthly survey of a carefully selected sample of households. The BLS seeks to define the unemployed more objectively than merely those who want jobs. The official unemployment total includes only those who are not working but have been actively seeking work. The total labor force is then defined as the sum of those working, plus those not working but actively seeking work. The rate of unemployment is the number of unemployed divided by the total labor force. The BLS reports monthly unemployment statistics in two ways—unadjusted and with a seasonal adjustment. Adjusting the numbers for seasonal variations can be useful because there are some months when unemployment is abnormally high (especially June, when students are looking for summer jobs) and some months when it is abnormally low (like December, when many temporary Christmas jobs become available).

Kinds of Unemployment

If, in a given month, there were 5 million men and women unemployed, it might seem that there were 5 million different causes of unemployment. But it is possible to distinguish—at least conceptually—among a few basic kinds of unemployment.

We begin with two grand totals: on the one hand, the labor force represents the supply of labor; on the other hand, the total number of available jobs represents the demand for labor. Even if the two totals were identical, significant amounts of unemployment could occur because of a mismatching of the supply of labor and the demand for it. Employers may be seeking persons with different skills, personal characteristics, or geographic locations than those of the job seekers. By the same token, the job seekers may be searching around for the best job available rather than simply accepting the first offer they receive. A short-run, temporary mismatching is called frictional unemployment; it covers those cases in which imperfections in mobility, information, or market organization prevent the job and the qualified job seeker from getting together immediately. In a changing economy, some workers are inevitably in the process of moving from one job to another.

By contrast, structural unemployment is attributable to a long-run mismatching between the nature of the supply of labor and the nature of the demand for it—that is, from relatively permanent discrepancies between the kinds of persons seeking jobs and the kinds of jobs that are available. Structural unemployment may occur because workers do not have the training and skills currently demanded in the labor market (high-school dropouts or harness makers). It may occur because employers discriminate against some categories of workers (nonwhites, women, long-hairs, or the elderly). It may occur because workers live in places that no longer have enough jobs (declining central cities or abandoned mining towns).

Often, however, the supply of workers in the labor force is greater than the total of jobs available, creating demand-deficiency unemployment. In this case total demand—or *Aggregate Demand* (see pp. 71–76)—for output in the economy is not enough to create a demand for all the workers who are available to produce that output. A further distinction can be made between two kinds of unemployment due to deficiencies in demand; cyclical and growth-gap unemployment. Cyclical unemployment is due to declines in demand during the recession or depression phase of a Business Cycle (see pp. 82–86). Growth-gap unemployment is due to a long-run failure of demand to expand sufficiently to cover the normal growth of the labor force and its increased productivity. (Economists sometimes use the term cyclical unemployment to describe demand-deficiency unemployment, but this is imprecise, since deficiencies in demand can steadily increase or decrease independently of the ups and downs of the business cycle.)

A fourth kind of unemployment is attributable to periodic deficiencies in demand within certain sectors but not aggregate demand. Seasonal unemployment results from expansions of supply (students seeking summer jobs) or contractions of demand (for example, the end of the harvest) that occur normally over the course of the year because of the weather, holidays, or customs.

These four basic kinds of unemployment—frictional, structural, demand-deficiency, and seasonal—are seldom estimated separately. They provide one useful way, however, of breaking down the total figure for unemployment as it is measured by the Department of Labor and announced each month.

Beyond these four kinds of officially measured unemployment there is a potentially large component of hidden unemployment. This consists of persons who might want to work if offered the opportunity but who are discouraged from seeking jobs because they have been unable to find work in the past or do not expect to be able to find it. Such persons, by definition, are outside the labor force and are not counted in the official BLS figure for unemployment. This can distort the figures, especially in times of high unemployment (like recessions or depressions) or in places of high unemployment (like black neighborhoods in many of the nation's largest cities). For this reason the BLS began in the mid-1970s to supplement the official unemployment figures with estimates of the hidden unemployment. The estimates show that in 1969, when official unemployment was at 3.5 percent, hidden unemployment was at 0.7 percent. By 1975, when official unemployment had risen to 8.5 percent, hidden unemployment had also risen—in this case to 1.2 percent.

In addition to unemployment, there is also a certain quantity of under-employment—employed workers who have not been able to find jobs that fully utilize their skills or who are employed for fewer hours per week than they would be willing to work. Underemployment is undoubtedly higher when the demand for labor is deficient and unemployment—both measured and hidden—is high.

Technological Unemployment

Economists sometimes speak of technological unemployment—the loss of jobs to new machinery or improved methods of production. Concerns over the problem go back at least to the first quarter of the nineteenth century, when groups of English workers—known as Luddites—set out to destroy the factory machines that they blamed for high rates of unemployment. In the last quarter of the twentieth century, there are still widespread fears that massive unemployment may result from automation—the mechanized transfer of parts through different stages of the production process under automatic controls.

Obviously, when production technology changes—just as when the pattern of demand changes—workers may lose their existing jobs. For example, the introduction of a cherry-picking machine will lower the demand for harvest workers. But the kind of unemployment that results will depend on the circumstances. If new technology displaces workers who are able to find new jobs within a few weeks, the unemployment would be called frictional. If the new technology creates a long-term pool of unemployed workers in similar circumstances—like workers with particular skills (or lack of skills), or workers in a particular area—the unemployment would be called structural.

We can also imagine technological change creating growth-gap unemployment. Over time, new machinery and techniques tend to increase the amount of goods the average worker can produce in an hour. Normally, this increased ability to produce is matched by an increased demand for goods in the economy. Increased production automatically generates increased income that can be spent—by workers for consumption, by businesses for investment, and by stockholders for consumption. If increased spending is inadequate, government can step in to stimulate aggregate demand. Furthermore, as workers become more productive they typically choose to realize some of the fruits of that increased productivity in increased leisure—a shorter work week or longer vacations—rather than entirely in the form of more material goods. There is no logical reason, then, why improved technology needs to cause persistent growth-gap unemployment.

Problems arise because technological progress is so uneven across the economy. In the twentieth century production per worker hour has increased much more rapidly in agriculture and manufacturing than in the service sectors. As a result, millions of workers have had to shift jobs— sometimes from one factory job to another, sometimes out of the farms and the factories and into such service lines as fast-food restaurants, insurance, and government. When we look at the economy as a whole, it is clear that new jobs can be created to replace old jobs—but not always for the same workers. If unskilled workers are displaced by a machine that can only be run by a trained engineer, then structural unemployment may be the result.

The Structure of Unemployment

Not all segments of the population or the economy are equally affected by unemployment. Figure 3–4 shows the unemployment rates for various groups during the relatively prosperous year of 1969 and the deep recession year of 1975. Overall, unemployment increased from 3.5 percent of the labor force in 1969 to 8.5 percent in 1975, and the rates for all the groups shown increased between those two years. But some of the differences between groups are striking. There is a persistent tendency for nonwhite (largely black) unemployment to be two times the rate for whites. The higher nonwhite rate reflects some combination of racial discrimination, lower average education and job skills, and low seniority in factory jobs where "the last to be hired are the first to be fired."

Unemployment is somewhat higher among adult women than among adult men, reflecting—in addition to problems of discrimination and low seniority—the difficulties that some women have in finding jobs when they return to the labor force after having raised their children.

Teenage unemployment rates are typically several times the rates for adults—reflecting the serious difficulties faced by new workers with low and untested job skills. Some economists argue that minimum wage laws that apply to teenagers and adults alike tend to price unskilled teenagers out of the job market.

Going beyond Figure 3–4, a prospective worker who is both nonwhite and a teenager faces the combined problems of both those groups. Black teenage unemployment was 24 percent in 1969 and an astronomical 37

Figure 3–4 Unemployment Rates for Selected Groups, 1969 and 1975

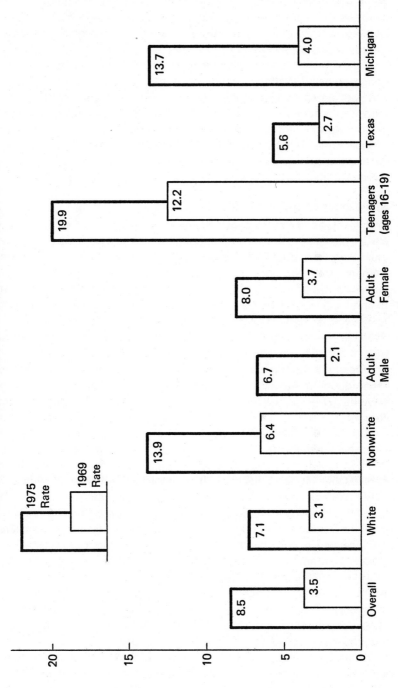

percent in 1975. These figures refer only to measured unemployment. If they included the hidden unemployment of those who were discouraged from seeking work by poor job prospects, the rates for the high-unemployment groups would be even higher.

Figure 3–4 also illustrates how unemployment can be concentrated geographically. Michigan, which produces so many automobiles, trucks, and appliances, had unemployment as low as 4 percent in the boom year of 1969. In the recession year of 1975, however, when businesses and consumers were postponing their purchases of these goods, Michigan unemployment reached 13.7 percent. By contrast Texas was able to sell such products as beef and oil in bad years as well as good. Its unemployment rate increased only from 2.7 percent in 1969 to 5.6 percent in 1975.

The Costs of Unemployment

High levels of unemployment inflict substantial costs on an economy. One simple measure is the loss of the commodities and services that the unemployed workers could have produced but didn't. The U.S. Department of Commerce measures this by comparing actual production each quarter of a year with the production that might have occurred if unemployment had been at 4 percent. For the severe recession year of 1975, when unemployment averaged 8.5 percent, the total loss of production by this measure was $230 billion—a full 15 percent of the production that actually occurred and an average of more than $1,000 for every adult and child in the country. Of course, the natural resources that might have been used up in producing those goods remained to be used later. But it was work effort that would have been the major source of the value of those goods—and that was lost forever.

The burden of this lost production is, of course, not shared equally by every person in the economy. One of the cruelties of unemployment is that it tends to fall most heavily on the poorer half of the economy—those families that can least afford it. The financial impact on an individual family may be cushioned by the availability of unemployment compensation. In effect this is a system whereby businesses and working families pay taxes to ease the burden on unemployed families. But that burden remains large. In 1974 weekly unemployment compensation benefits across the states ranged from 24 percent to 44 percent of the state's average weekly wage. Furthermore, by 1975 such benefits lasted a maximum of sixty-five weeks—and sometimes less—whether or not the unemployed worker had found a new job.

Beyond the loss of income to an unemployed family, personal and social stresses can greatly increase the personal costs of unemployment. When there are mass layoffs in an economy, it is not the fault of the individual workers who lose their jobs. Yet all too often they blame themselves, and sometimes other members of their families blame them, too. The jobless worker may lose status within his family, and the family may lose status and prestige within the community—and may tend to withdraw from its activities. When such personal strains are added to the economic ones, the results can be devastating. Based on past behavior, M. Harvey Brenner of Johns Hopkins University suggests that a serious recession is likely to be accompanied by increases of 15 percent or more in the rates of heart attacks, alcoholism, infant mortality, mental disorders, child abuse, and suicide.

Unemployment, then, redistributes the shares of the economic pie. But it does far more. It can also reduce the size of that pie substantially, creating personal as well as economic hardship for millions of families.

Policy Implications

Stimulating aggregate demand may be the most effective way to deal with demand-deficiency unemployment and its attendant hidden unemployment and underemployment. The ways in which aggregate demand is generated are discussed in Chapter 4 (Macroeconomic Behavior); the ways in which it may be manipulated are discussed in Chapter 5 (Macroeconomic Policy).

If, however, unemployment is primarily due to the mismatching of jobs and job seekers, policies to improve the match may produce more direct results. Thus frictional unemployment is best dealt with through improvements in the workings of the labor market—better information about job openings and greater mobility in getting potential workers to them. The more information an unemployed worker has, and the easier it is for that worker to reach a potential job, the less time the worker must spend in searching for a satisfactory job. Some economists argue that unemployment benefits—while necessary to reduce the financial burden of joblessness— may actually increase frictional unemployment by permitting the unemployed worker to spend more time looking for the right job. However, if the worker ends up finding a better job as a result of that longer search, that job may utilize the worker's skills more fully and provide him or her with more money or job satisfaction. Thus, in many cases the result of the longer search may justify the additional cost and effort.

Structural unemployment is a more difficult problem. Assume, for example, that there are 100,000 job vacancies for skilled engineers and 100,000 unskilled workers looking for jobs. Improvements in the functioning of the labor market would not put those workers in those jobs. This could be accomplished only through educational and training programs or through reductions in any discriminatory barriers to entering the engineering profession. Alternatively, over time there could develop an across-the-board downgrading of the skill requirements of many jobs so that unskilled laborers replace semiskilled laborers, who replace skilled laborers, who replace semiskilled engineers, who fill the jobs for which skilled engineers had been sought. As a third possibility, the problem might be alleviated by a shift in the underlying pattern of demand. Consumers might demand fewer changes in automobile styling and demand more lawn mowing. Or the government might demand fewer explorations into outer space and more street repairs, either because of a change in priorities among different kinds of public services or as a means of reducing unemployment in the ranks of unskilled labor.

Policies to stimulate aggregate demand are likely to be more inflationary when unemployment is structural than when it is of the demand-deficiency variety. For example, assume that the government cuts the income taxes that are paid by consumers. The increased consumer demand might create a need both for more skilled engineers and for more unskilled workers, thus bidding up the salaries of the engineers and the prices of the goods they help produce. Nonetheless, there are several ways in which increased aggregate demand can play a role in alleviating structural unemployment. First, it can directly provide jobs for some of the unskilled workers. Second, it can stimulate the downgrading of skill requirements; unskilled workers could more readily replace those who replace those who replace the engineers. Third, it would provide a climate in which educational and training programs could pay off in the form of new jobs for those acquiring new skills. All too often programs to provide job training for the unemployed have failed simply because aggregate demand in the economy was so low that the needed jobs simply did not exist. The problems of overcoming structural unemployment are discussed further in *Planning for Full Employment* (see pp. 229–37).

Full Employment

Economists frequently use the term full employment—or high employment—to designate a satisfactory level of employment. Full employment is typically less than 100 percent of the labor force, if only because some frictional and seasonal unemployment is inevitable. The term can be defined in two different ways. Some economists define it objectively as that level of employment at which total job vacancies just equal total job seekers—that is, the point at which demand-deficiency unemployment is zero. Other economists describe it more subjectively as the level of employment that can be increased only at the cost of generating inflationary pressures that are "intolerable"—either personally (from the viewpoint of the economist) or politically (from the viewpoint of the administration in power). During the administrations of Presidents Kennedy and Johnson, the Council of Economic Advisers tended to regard an unemployment rate of 4 percent as representing full employment. Under the administrations of Presidents Nixon and Ford, the council members tended to argue that structural unemployment had increased, so that an unemployment rate of 5 percent or more was closer to full employment. In large part this difference in definition reflects a difference in value judgments. Some economists are more willing to accept a higher level of unemployment in the hope that it will help to dampen inflationary pressure. Other economists are willing to risk a somewhat higher rate of inflation if that is the side-effect of policies to reduce unemployment.

INFLATION

Inflation is a rise in the general level of prices in an economy. An increase in the price of beef or the rent of an apartment does not, by itself, constitute inflation any more than one swallow makes a summer. Increases in some prices may well be offset by decreases in other prices, so that the general price level does not increase. Inflation occurs only when a great many prices increase together without a great many other prices going down. When this happens, the purchasing power of a dollar (or other unit of money) declines.

Inflation is usually measured through a price index—a summary of a whole range of prices in the economy, such as the Wholesale Price Index or the Consumer Price Index. For example, the Consumer Price Index is based on a "market basket" of goods consumed by a representative urban family in a particular year. The index measures how much change there has been in the total cost of that set of goods. When a general price index goes up significantly, we say that inflation has taken place. If—as happens less often—that index goes down, we say that deflation has occurred.

There are at least three reasons, however, why increases in a price index may exaggerate the loss of purchasing power of a dollar. First of all, a price index often ignores important improvements in the quality of goods—as when a new automobile provides greater fuel economy than last year's model. Second, a price index cannot measure the introduction of new goods that improve consumer welfare—like the antibiotic drug streptomycin that enabled many tuberculosis sufferers to avoid the rising price of a long stay in a sanitarium. Third, a price index is based on a fixed market basket, so that it cannot measure how consumers typically shift their purchases away from individual products that are becoming too expensive—for example, by switching to butter if the price of margarine is going up faster.

Inflation within a country may be caused internally by forces within the economy itself or externally by world economic events. Before considering the problem of externally caused inflation, let us examine the two major kinds of internal inflation in a modern industrial economy: (1) demand pull and (2) cost push. There is considerable debate among economists as to the relative importance of each cause in generating the inflation that actually occurs.

Demand-Pull Inflation

Demand-pull inflation occurs whenever increases in aggregate demand bid up the average price of goods in an economy. In order to see this, assume a situation in which there is equilibrium in all the markets for goods and for factors of production. Then something changes in the economy—an increase in the money supply, a new spurt of investment activity, or an increase in defense expenditure—so that the level of aggregate demand rises. At existing prices there will not be enough goods to satisfy the larger demand. Potential buyers will then bid up the prices of those goods until there is a new equilibrium in the various markets.

It is possible to think of this same problem in the aggregate with the help of Figure 3–5. The aggregate supply curve shows the different average price levels for final goods that would be required to induce producers to provide different quantities of final goods, given a certain initial set of wage rates and profit margins. Each aggregate demand curve shows the various combinations of price and quantity that are consistent with a given dollar volume of total demand. Thus, if we assume that the initial level of demand is $400 billion, this could be spent, for example, on 100 billion goods with an average price of $4 or on 40 billion goods with an average price of $10. Given the location of the aggregate supply curve, the system would reach equilibrium where the initial demand of $400 billion was spent buying 50 billion goods at an average price of $8 each.

Demand-pull inflation would occur if aggregate demand increased—that is, if the aggregate demand curve shifted to the right. The supply curve is

Figure 3–5   Demand-Pull Inflation

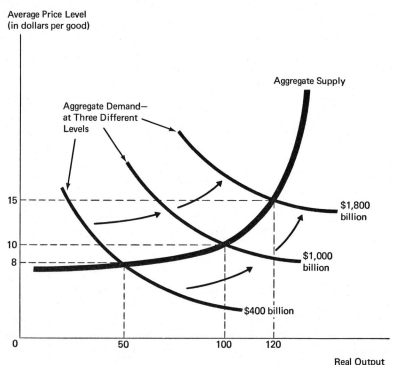

fairly flat on the left-hand side, where total output is far short of the levels that would be possible if the labor force and capital stock were fully employed. This means that if aggregate demand shifts to the right—from $400 to $1,000 billion—the increased demand will be largely expressed in higher levels of real output—not in higher price levels. Where most suppliers have a considerable amount of unused productive capacity, they are unlikely to raise prices and risk the loss of new business. This is especially so in manufacturing, where producers and retailers are accustomed to charging a relatively fixed price and varying the quantity sold as demand conditions change. (In agriculture, by contrast, producers usually grow what they can and let prices fluctuate in response to changes in demand.)

In the middle range the curve is shown sloping increasingly upward, suggesting that increases in output can only be obtained by bidding up the prices of goods to a higher level. Thus, a further increase in aggregate demand from $1,000 to $1,800 billion would have a greater impact on prices (be more inflationary) and do less to increase the level of total output. To the right of 120 billion goods, the supply curve becomes essentially vertical. This is because, with little or no capital or labor left unemployed, the economy has nearly reached its full capacity to produce. Since increased levels of output can be obtained in the short run only by making the existing capital and labor work harder, any further increases in aggregate demand will largely be translated into higher prices.

Cost-Push Inflation

Cost-push inflation describes a situation in which the average price level rises because suppliers of goods or productive services have taken the initiative to raise prices. Cost-push inflation may sometimes occur because the suppliers of final goods have themselves sought to increase their profit margins (the differences between the prices of the goods they sell and the costs of the materials and factors of production that they use). Alternatively, it may occur because producers are faced with cost-push elements in the markets for materials or factors of production. For example, if a powerful labor union is able to negotiate a substantial wage increase for its members, the firms paying the higher wages may attempt to pass them on to the consumer in the form of higher prices.

The idea of cost-push inflation is represented in Figure 7–6, which also employs the aggregate supply and aggregate demand curves used in Figure 3–5. Assume that the level of aggregate demand is $1,200 billion. The initial aggregate supply curve intersects the aggregate demand curve to give us an equilibrium average price level of $10 and quantity produced of 120 billion goods. Now consider the effect if producers take the initiative by insisting on a higher price for each quantity of goods they may sell. This can be represented as a shift to the left of the aggregate supply curve. If aggregate demand remains the same, the average price level will in-

Figure 3–6 Cost-Push Inflation

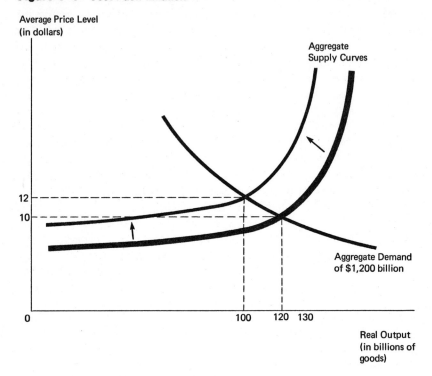

crease—in this case, to $12. There will be movement up the aggregate demand curve, and at the higher price buyers will demand only 100 billion goods.

There are real limits to how much inflation can be generated by cost push alone. First, in some sectors of the economy, firms cannot set the prices of things they sell and hence cannot engage in cost-push inflation. A gigantic firm in the American automobile market can raise its prices and expect the rest of the industry to follow. A Kansas wheat farmer, however, sends his crop to market and sells it at the current market price—a price that he cannot hope to influence by his own actions. Even the automobile firms have to keep one eye on foreign competition. Subcompact cars like Pinto and Vega may never be priced at much more than the small Volkswagen or the Toyota, though they may be priced at less.

Second, as Figure 3–6 makes clear, there are real risks in attempting cost-push inflation. The seller who attempts to raise prices without experiencing an upward shift in the demand curve for his product—or his factor service—runs the risk that the higher price will reduce the amount that he can sell. This places severe limits on how far any seller or group of sellers will want to go in imposing cost-push inflation on the economy. Repeated price hikes in the face of unchanging demand can be a formula for economic suicide.

It is doubtful, then, that cost push alone can be blamed for anything more than a mild inflation. Possibly, however, a continuing inflation might result from a combination of the forces of cost push and demand pull. Consider again the situation described by Figure 3–6. If sellers of products or factor services do succeed in driving up the average price level (from $10 to $12) and hence in driving down the quantity of output sold (from 120 to 100 billion goods), the result would be a sizable amount of unemployment of labor and capital. Government policymakers might look at the situation and conclude that aggregate demand was inadequate to maintain full employment at current price levels. They might attempt to expand aggregate demand through an expansive *Fiscal Policy* or *Monetary Policy* (see pp. 188–97 and pp. 204–9) in order to make it possible to sell the output of a fully employed economy at the higher price level. In our example, it would be necessary to increase aggregate demand from $1,200 billion to $1,440 billion for producers to be willing to sell the previous quantity of 120 billion goods at the higher average price of $12 ($12 $\times$ 120 billion = $1,440 billion). The increase in aggregate demand might make sellers again feel that they could attempt to raise their prices without substantially reducing the amount that they sell. Such an action by government is sometimes known as ratifying the inflation—letting it occur without creating declines in output and employment. The result could be a continuing inflation—alternately cost push and demand pull—with both parts of the process necessary to maintain the inflationary momentum.

Other Sources of Inflation

There are several other possible internal sources of inflation in a modern industrial economy.

First, a shift in the composition of aggregate demand may cause inflation in some sectors of the economy without causing deflation in others. For example, assume that both the steel and the aluminum industries have costs per ton of output that cannot be readily reduced. Their wage costs are set through contracts with the unions, and their materials costs are largely governed by prices on world markets for fuels and ores. If builders decide to use less steel and more aluminum, their decision might sufficiently increase the demand for aluminum enough for the price of that metal to go up substantially. But if steelmakers find it difficult to cut prices substantially, the reduced demand for steel might be reflected largely in a smaller quantity sold. Thus the shift in demand would cause one price (aluminum) to go up without causing the other price (steel) to go down. The average price level would rise even though aggregate demand had not increased.

Second, if productivity—output per worker—increases faster in some sectors of the economy than in others, the sectors with the slower growth of productivity may contribute to inflation. For example, in the United States productivity tends to increase faster in the manufacturing sector than in the service sector. Within the manufacturing sector, much of the rising productivity is typically paid to labor in the form of higher wages negotiated between employers and the labor unions. If productivity and wages should grow at exactly the same rate in all sectors, there would be no pressures on employers to charge higher prices for their output. The problem arises insofar as wages in manufacturing set a pattern for other sectors. Workers in the service sector may be able to obtain wage increases similar to those in manufacturing without realizing similar increases in productivity. There would then be pressures on employers in the service sector to pass on the higher wages to their customers in the form of higher prices. In fact, there is a long-run tendency in the U.S. economy for prices in the service sector to increase more rapidly than prices in manufacturing.

International Sources of Inflation

Thus far inflation has been described as though it always originated within the domestic economy. In fact, inflation in the United States may partly originate abroad for reasons that could also be classified as demand pull or cost push.

The United States is most vulnerable to demand-pull inflation from abroad if it has been buying more from other countries than it has been selling to them. As a result individuals, banks, and governments in other countries will have accumulated large quantities of American dollars. If buyers in those countries then decide they wish to purchase more American goods—for example, to buy American wheat to make up for a local crop failure—they can readily obtain the dollars with which to buy those goods. The decision to purchase more American goods may also be a response to an increase in the rate of inflation in their own countries.

To see how this might operate, consider the case in which another country, Germany, attempts to maintain a fixed *Exchange Rate* (see pp. 279–88) between its currency, the mark, and the American dollar. Assume that in recent years the United States has been buying $4 billion worth of Volkswagens from Germany and has been selling Germany only $2 billion worth of computers, so that German banks have been accumulating $2 billion a year of American money. Then assume that aggregate demand in Germany increases sharply and that all prices there rise by 50 percent. Both German and American consumers would find Volkswagens a good deal less attractive if they cost 50 percent more. As consumers sought to buy more American subcompact cars, the American automobile companies would be tempted to raise their prices. In the case of computers both German and American businesses would be less interested in buying German computers at the higher prices and more interested in buying American computers. The increased demand could cause American computer manufacturers to charge higher prices. Thus, prices in the United States—of both computers and subcompacts—would be increased by the inflation in Germany.

Consider next the case in which exchange rates are more flexible, and there is a regular or continuous adjustment between the values of the currency of one country in terms of the currency of another. For example, assume again that the United States has been selling $2 billion worth of computers to Germany, which has been selling $4 billion worth of Volkswagens to the United States. Assume that the Germans try to correct this situation by letting the value of the German mark rise from 25¢ to 50¢. Instead of giving 4 marks for every dollar they would now give only 2. This would mean that American computers at their original prices in dollars would cost Germans half as much (in marks) as before. Thus, a $10,000 computer would now cost 20,000 marks rather than 40,000 marks. German businesses would find it attractive to buy many more American computers than before, and the additional German demand might bid up the price of computers in the American market. The doubling of the dollar value of the mark would also mean that German Volkswagens at their original prices in marks would cost American consumers twice as much as before in dollars; a 6,000 mark VW would now cost $3,000 rather than $1,500. Not only would Americans buy fewer Volkswagens, but American manufacturers might produce more cars—and might well take advantage of the higher VW prices to raise the prices of competitive models like Vega and Pinto. Thus the decrease in the international value of the dollar would tend to raise American prices both for the kinds of goods it exports abroad (like computers) and for the kinds of goods it imports from abroad (like small automobiles). Both American and foreign demand for American goods would have increased. The increased demand would be concentrated in particular traded commodities, but the inflationary pressures might eventually spread to other commodities and to services.

Many economists attribute much of the inflation of the early 1970s—and particularly of 1973—to international causes. In that year world food and other commodity prices boomed due to crop failures in many parts of the world. Furthermore, the international value of the dollar fell about 15 percent in the three years following 1971, when many currencies ceased to be rigidly fixed in dollar terms. The result was an increased world demand for American goods and an upward pressure on the price level within the United States.

There can also be an international counterpart of cost-push inflation. If most of the countries exporting a particular commodity—like coffee, tin, or rubber—can organize to limit the total quantity supplied on the world market, they may succeed in driving up the world price. The most important recent example was the success of the Organization of Petroleum Exporting

Countries (OPEC), which in 1973 and 1974 raised the world price of oil to four times its 1972 level. The result was higher prices for petroleum products—and for many competing forms of energy—and higher costs for the thousands of commodities and services that require energy.

If a government is to deal intelligently with inflation, it must first understand the causes. If prices are rising primarily because of cost-push elements from abroad, a given amount of domestic aggregate demand will be able to purchase fewer goods, including fewer of the commodities and services produced at home. If the government interprets the inflation as primarily due to a high level of aggregate demand, it may act to curtail the growth of demand by raising taxes, cutting government expenditures, or slowing down the growth of the money supply. The result would be a further deficiency in demand for the output of the domestic economy and a substantial increase in the *Unemployment of Labor* (see especially pp. 87–89). For example, during 1974 the United States experienced its most severe inflation in twenty-five years—strongly led by the increases in fuel prices pushed up by the action of OPEC. The government responded by reducing the growth of the money supply to the lowest rate in five years. By May of 1975 unemployment had risen to 8.9 percent—the highest rate since the end of the Great Depression of the 1930s.

The Costs of Inflation

Some politicians and journalists are fond of comparing inflation to a thief who comes in the night and robs from the pocketbooks of rich and poor alike. Actually, moderate, internally caused inflation—like that realized in the United States during the 1950s and 1960s—does not notably reduce the amount of real income available in the economy. It can, however, redistribute some of that income from one group to another. The reason is simple: one person's costs are another person's income. If you pay more today for pork chops than you did a year ago, the extra money it costs you will find its way into the pockets of the grocer, the meatpacker, the hog farmer, or maybe even the corn farmer who grew the feed for the hogs. When prices generally go up, the revenues from sales at those higher prices are eventually expressed as higher incomes—wages, profits, or rents—for those who helped produce the more expensive goods. There is often an optical illusion in looking at inflation. People tend to feel that inflationary increases in the incomes they receive are well deserved and long overdue, while inflationary increases in the prices they pay are simply outrageous.

Of course, the redistribution of income due to inflation can be painful to some groups. First of all, inflation does not increase all incomes equally rapidly. Some workers are able to keep up with inflation fairly well because they have cost-of-living increases built into their contracts or because they are represented by unions strong enough to negotiate large wage increases into each new contract. Traditionally this was not true of white-collar workers, but by the 1970s many of them—especially government workers and teachers—belonged to aggressive unions that were able to keep their members' incomes growing faster than the cost of living.

Second, because inflation erodes the purchasing power of the dollar, it cuts into the real value of any asset that is fixed in money terms. A high rate of inflation helps debtors—those who owe fixed amounts of money—and it hurts creditors—those who are owed fixed amounts. For example, assume that this year you borrow $100 from the Friendly Loan Company at 10 percent interest, so that next year you must pay back $110. If prices go up 15 percent, the $110 you pay back will be worth less than the $100 you borrowed. You, as a debtor, will benefit from a higher rate of inflation, but the Friendly Loan Company, as a creditor, will be hurt by it. Most loan companies and banks will therefore try to charge interest rates that are higher than whatever rate of inflation they expect to occur.

There are many kinds of creditors and debtors in the economy. Creditors include the owner of a $1,000 bond, the holder of a $25,000 life insurance policy, or the recipient of a $4,000 a year pension. Debtors include the corporation or government that issued the bond, the life insurance company that issued the policy, and the company that has promised to pay the pension. A bank is a creditor when it issues a $30,000 mortgage, while the home buyer is a debtor. On the other hand, a bank is a debtor when a customer deposits $750 in a savings account, but the depositor is a creditor.

Retired persons can sometimes be the real victims of inflation, as many of them receive pension payments or interest payments that are fixed dollar amounts. However, Social Security payments to retired workers are not fixed in dollar terms. Over the 1950s and early 1960s the U.S. Congress acted from time to time to increase the size of these payments faster than the rise in the cost of living.

In 1963 Congress guaranteed that Social Security payments would automatically increase at least as fast as the level of prices. The threat to retired workers—and others living on fixed assets—could be reduced further if the U.S. government were to offer to sell inflation-proof bonds that would each year pay a rate of interest that was one or two percentage points above the current rate of inflation.

Inflation, like *Unemployment of Labor* (see especially pp. 92–93), can redistribute the shares of the nation's economic pie, usually arbitrarily and sometimes cruelly. But whereas unemployment always reduces the size of the pie, a moderate internal inflation need not. For example, even if the purchasing power of money declines by 1 percent a month—as it did during the near-record inflation of 1974—few persons will actually take time away from work to speculate in the purchase of commodities or to find ways to purchase goods faster.

Runaway inflation—or hyperinflation—can present a different picture. In the German inflation of 1923, customers who queued up to buy merchandise sometimes found that the price had doubled by the time they were halfway through the line and had quadrupled by the time they were able to buy. In such an atmosphere money no longer performs its important function as a store of wealth (see *Money*, especially pp. 41–42). The rational person spends less effort working at producing goods and more effort trying to spend money as quickly as possible—consuming by buying the goods needed for immediate use and saving by hoarding other commodities that may be expected to increase fastest in money value. Beyond this, hyperinflation creates a widespread demoralization, since all earlier savings that were fixed in money terms are virtually wiped out. Fortunately, the United States has never experienced this kind of inflation.

When inflation originates abroad, it also redistributes some of the real output of the U.S. economy—toward foreigners and away from those who live in the U.S. Consider an inflation due to demand pull based on dollars that had previously accumulated abroad. In this case, the redistribution may be justified. After all, foreigners accumulated all those dollars only because the U.S. economy had been buying more than it was selling and was paying for the difference in dollars rather than in real goods. Those dollars are now returning to permit foreigners their turn at obtaining some real goods for their dollars. Ordinarily, the dollars being spent from abroad will bid real goods away from American buyers. An exception would be a time when aggregate demand in the American economy would have otherwise been so low that the goods that foreigners are demanding can be produced with capital and labor that would otherwise have been idle.

In the case of cost-push inflation from abroad, a larger share of the U.S. economic pie also goes abroad, but it is much harder to presume that this advances the cause of justice. For example, in 1972—before OPEC drove up the world price of oil—the United States spent $4.6 billion for imports of oil. In 1974 we spent $26.1 billion. The quantity of oil imported went up by 28 percent, but the dollar cost went up by 467 percent. This form of inflation, then, involved a direct redistribution to the oil-producing countries of more than $20 billion dollars—much of which merely bought more luxuries for wealthy Arab sheiks.

Cost-push inflation from abroad poses a real challenge to U.S. policymakers. It is, as we have seen, the form of inflation that is least susceptible to control through reductions in the growth of aggregate demand, but it is also the form that is most costly to the U.S. economy as a whole. What are required are better methods for bargaining with an international price-raising cartel like OPEC—and greater conservation of imported materials.

PHILLIPS CURVE

The Phillips curve is an attempt to describe the tradeoff between the rate of price inflation and the rate of unemployment of labor. That is, for given conditions in the economy, it attempts to describe how much inflation must be tolerated if unemployment is to be reduced to a particular level.

Some description of the unemployment-inflation tradeoff is essential to gain a complete picture of the behavior of prices and output in the economy. A rising level of aggregate demand may cause an increase in the price level, an increase in the level of real output, or some combination of the two. Economists are still hotly debating the question of how increases in that demand are distributed between a higher price level and a higher level of real output. The Phillips curve is one effort to answer that question.

The Aggregate Supply Curve Relationship

An older view of the relationship between unemployment and inflation—the view advanced by J. M. Keynes in the 1930s—is represented by the aggregate supply curve described in our discussion of *Inflation* (see pp. 95–97). Such a curve shows producers willing to produce larger quantities of output at higher prices. If unemployment is high, so that there is considerable slack in the economy, then any increases in aggregate demand are likely to be expressed largely through increased output. At higher levels of aggregate demand, there is less idle capacity in the economy, and increases in aggregate demand are expressed more and more through increases in the average price level than through increases in the level of real output. If demand is so high that the economy is actually producing at full capacity, then further increases in demand can only be expressed through higher prices and not at all through increases in real output.

At the same time, a comparison of the level of aggregate demand with aggregate supply would lead us to expect a strong negative association between rates of inflation and rates of unemployment. If aggregate demand is higher than the full supply capability of the economy, we would expect unemployment to be low and prices to be bid up rapidly. By the same token, if aggregate demand is substantially lower than aggregate supply capacity, we would expect high levels of unemployment but very little inflationary pressure.

The Phillips Curve Relationship

A similar view of the relationship between unemployment and inflation was put forward in the late 1950s by the late New Zealand economist A. W. Phillips. Using data for Great Britain over the previous century, he found that wage increases tended to be much faster in years in which unemployment was low. He suggested that price inflation results when employers pass those wage increases on to their customers in the form of higher

prices. Thus a high employment situation appears to be inflationary regardless of movements in aggregate demand.

In Figure 3–7 we show a Phillips curve kind of relationship between price
inflation and unemployment. Low levels of unemployment are associated
with high rates of inflation. High levels of unemployment are associated with
low rates of inflation—or even some deflation if the unemployment is high
enough.

In order to understand why wages—and ultimately prices—might rise
faster in times of low unemployment, most economists would look to the
labor markets—especially ones in which workers are represented by active
unions. If the rate of overall unemployment in the economy is low, labor
markets are likely to be "tight"—that is, few workers are likely to be available
for the jobs that employers want to fill. Unions whose contracts are coming
up for negotiation can be more aggressive in pressing their wage demands
because higher wages would be less likely to generate widespread unemployment for their members. At the same time employers will be especially
interested in avoiding a strike since it would prevent them from meeting the
strong demand for the products of their firms. Even if the workers are not
represented by a union, however, employers may offer them higher wages.
If there is a strong demand for the products of an industry, some employers
may offer higher wages in order to bid workers away from other firms. Other
employers may have to raise wages defensively in order to prevent their

Figure 3–7   The General Form of the Phillips Curve

Rate of
Price Inflation

0

Rate of Unemployment of Labor

workers from being bid away. The result may be higher wages even for workers who are not organized to demand them.

By contrast, if aggregate demand is low and unemployment is high, wage increases can be expected to be more modest. Labor union leaders may hold off from making higher wage demands for fear that this could make some of their workers too expensive to hire, further aggravating the problem of unemployment. At the same time, a strike threat will be less effective in persuading employers to accept high wage demands. With low aggregate demand, employers may not even be sure of being able to sell all the output they plan to produce during the period of a potential strike. Likewise, employers in nonunion companies will not be interested in bidding workers away from other firms, nor will they have much reason to fear that other companies will try to bid workers away from them. If the occasional firm needs additional workers, there will be a large group of unemployed men and women to chose from.

This suggests, then, that both workers and employers might be expected to agree to larger wage increases in times of low unemployment than in times of high unemployment.

Experience in the American Economy

There have been some periods in the U.S. economy when the Phillips curve relationship has corresponded quite closely to actual experience. For example, Figure 3–8 shows the relationship from 1956 to 1970 between the annual rate of price inflation (growth from year to year in the Consumer Price Index) and unemployment in the previous year. The rate of price inflation seems more closely related to unemployment in the previous than to unemployment in the current year. There may be three reasons for this: (1) it takes time for employers and workers to adjust to current labor market conditions in negotiating wages; (2) it takes time for wages in the unionized sectors of the economy to be transmitted to the nonunionized sectors; (3) it takes time for some employers to translate wage increases into price increases.

Along with the dots in Figure 3–8 representing the experience of individual years we have sketched in a curve that seems to fit fairly well the experience from 1956 through 1970. No single year is exactly on the curve, but most of the points are clustered fairly closely to it.

Economists sometimes use a Phillips curve relationship to describe a "menu" of policy choices. That is to say, government policymakers can use *Fiscal Policy* and *Monetary Policy* (see pp. 188–97 and pp. 204–9) to expand aggregate demand. This should have the favorable effect of reducing unemployment along with the unfavorable effect of increasing inflation. Such an approach was used by Presidents Kennedy and Johnson in their efforts to bring the economy out of the recession that began in 1960. Alternatively, government can use fiscal and monetary policy to curtail the

Figure 3—8 An Actual Phillips Curve Relationship: 1956–1970 and Subsequent Years

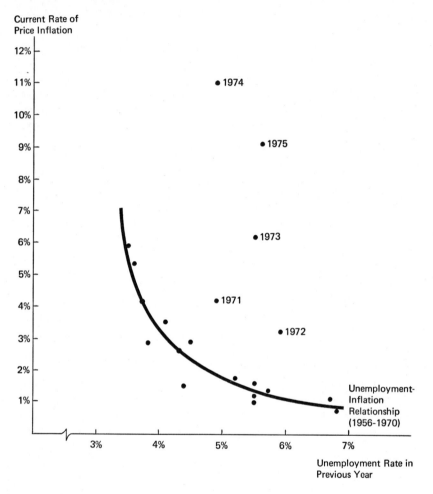

growth of aggregate demand—reducing inflation, but increasing unemployment. This was the approach used by President Nixon in 1969 and 1970 as he attempted to check the inflation of the late 1960s.

If the curve in Figure 3–8 describes the "menu," it suggests that an unemployment rate of 6 percent will be followed by an inflation rate of just over 1 percent and that an unemployment rate of 4 percent will be followed by an inflation rate of just under 4 percent. Thus, reducing unemployment by 2 percent—from 6 percent to 4 percent—would tend to increase the next year's inflation rate by more than 2 percent.

The most recent years (1971 to 1976) covered in Figure 3–8 do not appear to fit the curve at all. Indeed, the rate of inflation is 2 to 9 percent higher in those years than one would expect from the curve. Because of such disparities, the Phillips curve concept is coming under increasing attack. Some economists contend that there is no such thing as a Phillips curve relationship. Others argue that the broad relationship exists but that the location of the curve shifts somewhat from year to year. For example, a downward shift in the curve indicates a more favorable unemployment-inflation tradeoff; less inflation is associated with a given degree of unemployment. An upward shift in the curve, as may have occurred in the 1970s, suggests a less favorable tradeoff; more inflation can be expected to be associated with a particular level of unemployment.

Other Influences on Inflation

Economists have identified several other factors besides the unemployment rate that may influence the rate of inflation. Each may help somewhat in explaining why the Phillips curve of earlier years failed so badly at predicting the inflation experience of the 1970s. We will discuss five such influences: (1) the growth of productivity, (2) recent inflation, (3) the composition of unemployment, (4) employment and labor force participation, and (5) international influences.

Growth of Productivity. The growth of labor productivity—average output per hour worked—can be an important determinant of the tradeoff between unemployment and inflation. Productivity growth serves as a kind of buffer between the rate of increase in wages and the rate of increase in product prices. To see this, assume that hourly wages are growing at 3 percent per year. If labor productivity is also growing at 3 percent a year, then an employer with a given labor force can maintain his existing level of prices without reducing the ratio of profits to wages. This would be a case in which unit labor costs—the cost of paying the labor required to produce a unit of output—have not increased. Hourly wages have increased by 3 percent, but 3 percent more output is being produced in that hour. If, however, labor productivity is only growing at 2 percent a year, then wage increases of 3 percent would mean that unit wage costs are increasing by 1 percent (3 percent minus 2 percent). In this situation the employer must either raise prices by 1 percent or experience a decline in profits as a share of the firm's contribution to output. In the U.S. economy there is a long-run tendency for profits to take a fairly stable share of total output; therefore price increases tend to represent the difference between increases in the wage rate and increases in the productivity of labor.

The Phillips curve suggests that money wages increase most rapidly when aggregate demand is high. Consequently governments are sometimes tempted to sharply curtail the growth of aggregate demand in order to curb inflation—often with quite disappointing results. The disappointment may partly be due to the behavior of labor productivity. When aggregate demand is curtailed and firms are forced to lay off workers, there is often a sharp short-run decline in labor productivity. Consider the case of an automobile company. If it sells 10 percent fewer cars this year, it may be forced to lay off 10 percent of its production workers. But it cannot do much to cut back on many other kinds of employees—foremen, supervisors, purchasing agents, accountants, engineers, market analysts, executives, and salesmen. Assume that half of the company's employees are in these categories and that none of them can be laid off. Then the 10 percent decline in output will be associated with only a 5 percent decline in employment, and output per employee will decline by 5 percent. Even if wages were stable, the company's unit labor costs would increase by 5 percent that year.

The example may be exaggerated, but there is a tendency for productivity to decline and unit labor costs to increase whenever the economy moves into a recession. For example, unit labor costs rose sharply during 1973 and especially 1974 due partly to modest increases in the growth of wage rates but largely to sharp declines in productivity. In the short run, at least, a policy of restricting the growth of aggregate demand in order to increase unemployment and check inflation can prove to be self-defeating.

Recent Inflation.   It may seem ironic to describe inflation as a cause of more inflation. Still, it is not unreasonable to expect that wage demands will be greater—and more acceptable to employers—after a period of rapidly rising product prices. Workers will want their money wages to catch up with the recent inflation, and employers will be confident that they will be able to raise prices to cover their higher labor costs. In fact, the evidence indicates that the Phillips curve relationship will be higher—that more wage inflation will be associated with a given level of unemployment—when the economy has recently experienced high rates of price inflation.

The real issue is whether the situation is stable. Some economists argue that there can be a stable Phillips curve relationship. For example, assume a productivity growth rate of 3 percent. If the unemployment rate is 4 percent and if this generates wage increases of 7 percent each year, then price increases of 4 percent each year will follow. Real wages will go up only by 3 percent (7 percent increases in money wages less 4 percent price inflation). So long as workers and employers are prepared to continue on this basis, then the Phillips curve will be stable.

A few economists argue, however, that this situation will not persist. For example, assume that unemployment in the previous year was high, so that the current rate of price inflation is only 2 percent. If the unemployment rate is reduced to 4 percent and if this generates wage increases of 7 percent that year, then workers will be enjoying an increase in real income of 5 percent (the 7 percent wage increase minus the 2 percent rate of inflation). If the 7 percent wage increase forces employers to raise prices next year by 4 percent (the 7 percent wage increase minus the 3 percent increase in productivity), then workers may sooner or later recognize that their real wages are no longer growing by 5 percent but only by 3 percent. They may then insist on wage increases of 9 percent to maintain a real wage growth of 5 percent. If they are successful because of the tightness of labor markets, then employers will have to raise prices further; this in turn will cause workers to increase their wage demands further. The inflation will accelerate despite the fact that unemployment is constant at 4 percent. Such an interpretation of inflation denies that there is a stable Phillips curve at all. Its advocates deny that it is possible to maintain unemployment as low as 4 percent without initiating a spiral of accelerating inflation.

Whether or not this view is accepted, one can recognize that the location of the unemployment-inflation tradeoff in any year may be influenced by earlier experiences with inflation. In particular, the relatively high rates of inflation in 1969 and 1970 may help explain why inflation in subsequent years did not fall off as much as might have been expected from the high rates of unemployment in those years.

The Composition of Unemployment. There is also evidence that the location of the Phillips curve partly depends on which categories of labor are unemployed. Employers in manufacturing industries appear to be most interested in hiring men in the prime working ages between twenty-five and fifty-five. Rightly or wrongly, they generally prefer such workers to women, teenagers, or older men. Under these circumstances, a particular level of unemployment of, say, 4 percent may have very different implications for the manufacturing wage rate, depending on which group is unemployed. If all groups in the labor force are experiencing 4 percent unemployment, then manufacturing firms will have very little difficulty in finding men in the prime working ages, and there will be little upward pressure on wages. If, however, men between twenty-five and fifty-five are experiencing an unemployment rate of only 1.5 percent while women, young men, and older men are experiencing rates greater than 6 percent, then manufacturers will have a hard time finding the workers they most want. As a result, they may well be more receptive to granting larger wage increases.

Another way of looking at this is to use the concept of structural unemployment (see *Unemployment of Labor,* p. 88). If structural unemployment represents a larger share of total unemployment, it may be more difficult to reduce overall unemployment by expanding aggregate demand without at the same time increasing the rate of price inflation. Several economists have suggested that an increasing share of structural unemployment may have shifted the Phillips curve outward during the late 1960s and may account for the poorer unemployment-inflation tradeoff experienced during the early 1970s.

Employment and Labor Force Participation. Another suggestion is that the Phillips curve relationship may fail to hold because it attempts to explain inflation as a function of unemployment rather than employment. The unemployment rate is expressed as a share of the total labor force (see

Unemployment, especially pp. 87–89). But this ignores short-run and long-run movements in the rate of labor force participation—the share of the total population that is working or actively seeking work. In the short run, labor force participation responds positively to the availability of jobs—that is, potential workers are more likely to seek work actively when they think there are jobs available. In the long run, there has been a continuing increase in the rate at which women participate in the labor force (see *Economic Growth,* especially pp. 116–17). Some economists, then, have tried to use civilian employment (as a share of the adult population) as a measure of the level of aggregate demand and the tightness of labor markets.

Efforts to explain current inflation as a function of employment rather than unemployment are only moderately successful. The inflation rates associated with a particular level of employment are not clustered about a thin line but are within a fairly wide band. Nevertheless, the band does slope upward. That is to say, the inflation rates associated with a high level of employment are generally higher than those associated with a low level of employment. Furthermore, the inflation rates of 1971 through 1974 are not nearly so far out of line as they appear in the Phillips curve relationship. In particular the year 1974, which had the highest rate of inflation in twenty-five years, also had the highest percentage of the adult population employed—and 1973 was not far behind. The suggestion is that in these years the high rates of participation in the labor force meant that aggregate demand was higher than was indicated by the moderate-to-high rates of unemployment.

International Influences. Beyond these internal influences on inflation, we should recognize that there have been strong international pressures for inflation within the U.S. (see *Inflation,* especially pp. 100–102). Higher world food prices, the decline in the international value of the dollar, and the OPEC–induced skyrocketing of world oil prices—all these contributed to a high rate of world inflation that was fully reflected within the U.S., particularly in the years 1972 through 1974. The Phillips curve concept, which attributes inflation purely to domestic causes, is no help at all in predicting such influences.

Conclusion

Economists differ as to whether the many other influences on inflation invalidate the idea of an unemployment-inflation tradeoff or merely shift the location of that tradeoff from year to year. But few economists today would describe the Phillips curve as an iron law of economics. The events of the first half of the 1970s have clearly taught the pessimistic lesson that moderate-to-high rates of unemployment can be associated with more inflation than the Phillips curve predicted. The challenge to the future is to learn how to attain low rates of unemployment in ways that will generate less inflation than the Phillips curve predicts.

ECONOMIC GROWTH

Economic growth is an increase in the ability of the economy to produce commodities and services. Broadly speaking, economic growth occurs as the economy increases its human and material resources and learns how to employ them more productively. While some forms of production are wasteful and even harmful, a moderate rate of economic growth may be an efficient way for an economy to provide more of the commodities and services that people want (see *Efficiency,* especially pp. 22–23).

Economists use Gross National Products, or GNP (see *National Income Accounts,* pp. 78) as a measure of total production. Economic growth, however, cannot be equated strictly with the rate of growth of GNP. First of all, not all of the increase in GNP in a typical year is real (due to increases in the actual quantity of goods produced). Some—often a great deal—may be due to increases in the prices of those goods. Thus this inflationary factor needs to be excluded from the growth of GNP to obtain a measure of real economic growth. Real growth of GNP between 1976 and 1977, for example, might be described by using the prices of 1976 to compare the value of the goods produced in 1976 and 1977.

Second, it is often more useful to describe the growth of GNP in relation to the growth of population. Assume that GNP is growing at 3 percent in both the United States and Costa Rica, but population is growing at 1 percent in the United States and at 3 percent in Costa Rica. Then the average person in the United States has 2 percent more GNP at the end of the year, while the average Costa Rican doesn't realize any increase. In Costa Rica, therefore, GNP per capita (per person) has not risen at all, while it has increased in the United States.

Third, most economists would describe economic growth in terms of the capacity of the economy to produce rather than in terms of actual production. Using this approach, we can abstract from fluctuations in *Aggregate Demand* (see pp. 71–76) and look to the underlying potential of the economy to supply commodities and services. For instance, the President's Council of Economic Advisers has developed a measure of potential GNP—the volume of production that the economy could produce if it were operating with only 4 percent of the labor force unemployed. If aggregate demand in a particular year is so low that unemployment is actually at 8 percent, actual GNP will be far short of the potential. Then if, in the next year, aggregate demand increases enough to restore unemployment to the 4 percent level, the increase in actual GNP may be spectacular. Most of the increase, however, would be due to an increased utilization of productive capacity rather than to growth in capacity itself. Economists would describe it as an "unsustainable" expansion of GNP.

It is common to find economic growth expressed as simply the rate of growth of real GNP. A better measure, however, would be the per capita growth of the real level of potential GNP.

The Impact of Different Growth Rates

Small differences in growth rates, if they are sustained over many years, can make large differences in the productive potential of an economy. In 1975 the per capita GNP of the United States was about $7,000 and had been recently growing at a real rate of about 2½ percent. What would that growth rate mean if it were sustained for fifty years—to the time when today's college freshmen are beginning retirement? Figure 3–9 shows the growth of U.S. GNP per capita over fifty years under three different growth rates— 1½ percent, 2½ percent, and 3½ percent. At the 2½ percent growth rate, the per capita GNP would rise by the year 2025 to more than $24,000—or about 3½ times its initial value. By contrast, if the growth rate were down to 1½ percent per capita, GNP would rise to less than $15,000—slightly more than twice its initial value. And if the growth rate were as high as 3½ percent, GNP per capita would be a staggering $39,000—or more than 5½ times its initial value.

Differences in growth rates can also rapidly alter differences in the relative economic power of nations. Figure 3–10 illustrates what would

Figure 3–9   **Three Alternative Growth Paths for the U.S. Economy**

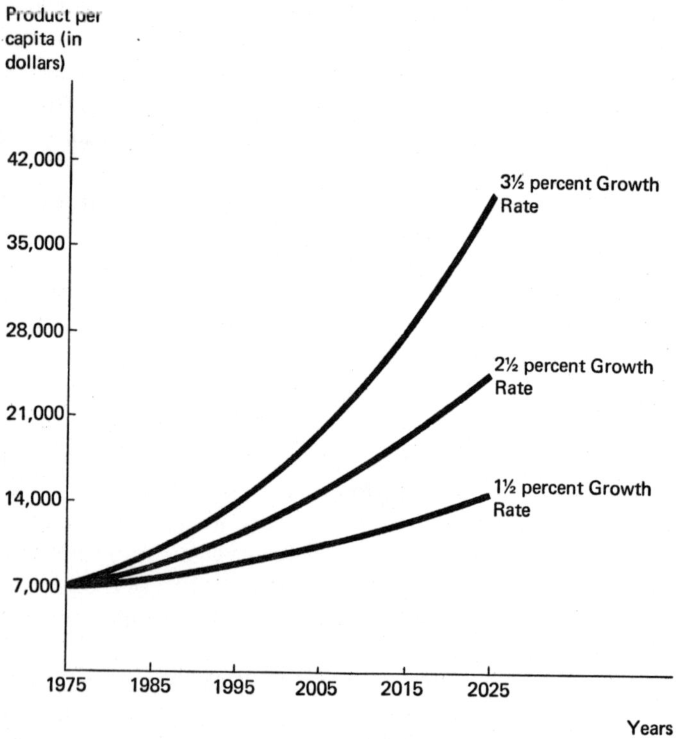

happen if the economy of Japan, which generated a GNP per capita of about $2,000 in 1970, were to continue to grow at the 7 percent rate it realized (or exceeded) during most of the 1950s and 1960s. If the United States continued to grow at only 2½ percent, the graph shows that within only twenty-one years the Japanese economy would equal the United States in GNP per capita and would be double that of the United States within thirty-seven years. These are mathematical projections of past trends—not predictions. But on the basis of such projections, some "futurologists"

Figure 3–10   The Future Implications of Different Growth Rates for the U.S. and Japanese Economies

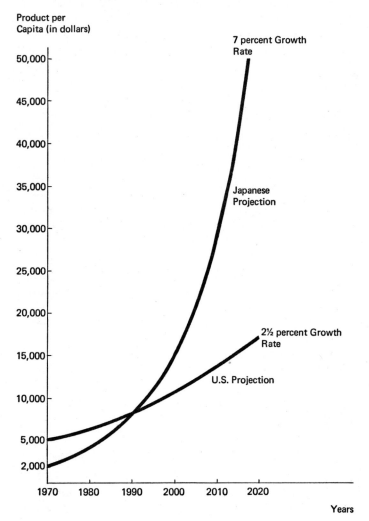

began to predict that the twenty-first century would find Japan as the world's dominant economic power. However, the worldwide increase in oil prices in 1973 sharply curtailed the Japanese growth rate—at least temporarily. It showed how vulnerable growth can be in an economy that—like Japan's—is almost totally dependent on foreign suppliers for its raw materials and fuels.

GNP as a Measure of Growth

Gross National Product—even the real level of potential GNP per capita—is often criticized as an inadequate measure of economic progress. In some ways the growth of potential GNP per capita understates long-run economic progress. For example, because GNP includes only output, it fails to take into account the increased leisure that workers have been able to enjoy in the form of shorter work weeks, longer vacations, and earlier retirements. In addition, the growth of GNP fails to take adequate account of improvements in product quality, so that a modern antibiotic might count for no more in the GNP accounts than an old-fashioned patent medicine selling for the same price.

In many other ways, however, the GNP measure exaggerates the rate of growth. GNP excludes the output of unpaid household labor, so if a housewife stops baking for her family to take a job in a commercial bakery, her efforts suddenly become recognized in the GNP statistics. The GNP measure takes no account of environmental costs, like resource depletion or pollution. The production of a ton of steel that sells for $250 is counted as contributing a full $250 to GNP even though its production may have depleted the country's national resources by $100 worth of iron ore and coal or generated air pollution that cost neighbors of the steel mill $50 in cleaning bills and medical care. In addition, an increasing number of commodities and services are included in the GNP as final goods, even though they are really only the costs of getting along in a complex industrial economy. Commuter trains and automobile rides, gray flannel business suits, banking services, government regulatory agencies, and protective hats bought by miners are all included in the GNP. However, they do not directly contribute to human welfare. Rather, they should be seen as a cost of doing business in a modern, urbanized economy. On balance, then, the rate of growth of real GNP per capita probably overestimates increases in the capacity of the U.S. economy to support economic welfare.

Sources of Economic Growth

During the seventy years from 1900 to 1970, the per capita capacity of the U.S. economy to produce real output increased by about 1.8 percent per year. In a logical sense there are only two possible sources of this economic growth: (1) increases in the number of labor hours that are worked per capita, and (2) increases in the productivity of labor during those working hours.

Hours Worked Per Capita. Output per capita can obviously increase if there is an increase in the number of hours worked per person in the country. This could occur either because a larger share of the total population joins the labor force or because the average member of the labor force works more hours each year.

From 1900 to 1970, an increasing share of the American population did participate in the labor force. One reason was that families had substantially fewer children in 1970 than in 1900, so that a larger share of the population consisted of persons of working age. Also, there has been a strong tendency for more women of working age to participate in the labor force. Families have fewer children to care for, household chores can be performed more quickly and easily with the aid of modern equipment, and traditional views of the role of women are breaking down. By contrast, men are staying in school longer and retiring earlier, so that working-age men are somewhat less likely to be in the labor force today than they were in 1900. The overall impact, however, has been for a higher overall rate of labor force participation.

A more important influence on the per capita labor input in the American economy has been the shortening of the work year. The average employed American worked about 30 percent fewer hours in the year 1970 than in 1900. This reflects the strong desire of workers to enjoy some of their increased earning power in the form of leisure as well as in increased money income. The reductions in the average working year have more than offset increases in labor force participation. Over those seventy years, then, the number of hours worked per person has shrunk at a rate of about .3 of 1 percent per year.

Thus any direct effect of hours worked has been to reduce rather than to increase the capacity of the economy to produce on a per capita basis. We cannot rule out the possibility, however, that the reduced work year has meant that when workers are on the job they are less fatigued by long hours. This may be one source of increase in worker productivity, to which we now turn our attention.

Productivity of Labor. If the hours worked per capita have declined in the United States during the twentieth century, then all the economic growth that has occurred must be due entirely to increases in the productivity of labor—the amount of output per hour worked. One important question is the extent to which productivity increases have been due to capital deepening (increased amounts of capital per worker) and the extent to which they have been due to the other causes.

From 1900 to 1970 the amount of capital per worker increased at nearly 2 percent per year. Economists have generally estimated that for the twentieth-century U.S. economy, a 2 percent increase in capital per worker alone should account for an increase in output per worker of about $\frac{1}{2}$ percent. In fact, however, labor productivity over the entire period increased at 2.1 percent per year. Thus less than one-fourth of the actual increase in output per worker can be explained by increases in the amount of capital per worker. The remaining increase of more than 1.5 percent per year must be explained by such causes as increasing returns to scale, improvements in the quality of capital and labor, and technological progress. Increasing returns to scale occur when a larger level of output permits the economy to take advantage of large-scale production techniques, including mass production. Improvements in the quality of capital include the use of more productive machinery, equipment, and buildings. Improvements in the quality of labor can result from increased education and training, better health care, and improved nutrition. Technological progress is the application of better scientific knowledge to the management, organization, and processes of production.

These results imply the importance for economic growth of improvements in the quality of the labor force and increased scientific and technological knowledge. Do the results also imply that capital investment is not very important to the process of economic growth? Not at all. A great deal of the important technological progress of the century could not stimulate economic growth until it had been embodied in new capital equipment. For example, the new technological knowledge gained from the invention of the basic oxygen process for steelmaking could not add to productivity until steel companies junked their old open hearth furnaces and invested in equipment that embodied the new oxygen method. Thus economists increasingly view capital investment not only as a means of increasing the amount of capital available to the worker but also as a means of updating the technology being employed.

4

Macroeconomic Behavior

To understand the behavior of aggregate demand in the economy, we must first look at some of its basic determinants in the private economy—the overall consumption and saving decisions of households, the investment decisions of businesses, and the supply and demand for money.

A basic tool of macroeconomic analysis, the **Propensity to Consume**, is used to summarize the tendency of households to consume or to save their incomes. The discussion of **Equilibrium Income** then provides an overall model for analyzing the impact of consumption and investment on aggregate demand. By using that model to analyze the effect of changes in the level of investment the **Investment Multiplier** can be derived. This refers to the tendency for an increase of one dollar in investment demand to cause an increase of several dollars in aggregate demand. The same model may be used to present the **Paradox of Thrift**—a surprising conclusion that increases in the tendency to save may not induce more saving in the economy as a whole.

Discussions of the **Consumption Function** and the **Investment Function** go beyond the simplified assumptions of the equilibrium income model and take a closer look at the determinants of these two important segments of aggregate demand.

Aggregate demand is expressed in money terms. Its behavior cannot be understood without an understanding of the **Demand for Money** by households and businesses and the role of the government and the banking system in the process of **Money Creation**. A theory that places special emphasis on the role of money in determining aggregate demand is the **Quantity Theory of Money**, which has been a formal part of economic thinking for nearly a century.

THE PROPENSITY TO CONSUME

The propensity to consume describes how households tend to divide their incomes between consumption and saving. The concept has played a central role in many macroeconomic models from the time it was introduced by John Maynard Keynes in 1936.

Keynes began by assuming that current consumption is primarily a function of—or dependent upon—current income. An economist who knew the propensity to consume and the income of the households in an economy could then readily calculate the amount of consumption expenditure in that economy.

Average and Marginal Propensities

It is important to distinguish between the average and the marginal propensities to consume. The average propensity to consume (APC) is the share of current income devoted to consumption. If we use Y to represent income, and C to represent consumption, then we have:

$$APC = \frac{C}{Y}$$

By contrast, we may also be interested in knowing what happens to consumption when income changes. The marginal propensity to consume (MPC) is the share of a change in income that will be reflected in a change in consumption. If we use the Greek letter Δ (Delta) to represent a change in a variable, then ΔY represents a change in income and ΔC represents a change in consumption. We then have:

$$MPC = \frac{\Delta C}{\Delta Y}$$

Keynes held that the marginal propensity to consume would normally be positive but less than 1—that is, increased income would cause households to increase their consumption, but not by as much as the increase in income.

The Propensity to Save

The propensity to save is the tendency of households to abstain from consuming a portion of their incomes. The average propensity to save (APS) is the share of income devoted to saving. If we use S to represent saving, then we have:

$$APS = \frac{S}{Y}$$

The marginal propensity to save (MPS) is the share of any change in income that is reflected in a change in saving. Using ΔS to represent the change in saving, we have:

$$MPS = \frac{\Delta S}{\Delta Y}$$

The propensities to save and to consume are obviously closely related. If by income (Y) we mean the disposable income or after-tax income of households, we can see that the household basically can do only two things with any portion of the income it receives. The household can consume—spend the income to meet its current needs—or it can save—set aside that income (as cash or as other assets) to meet future needs. These two uses of disposable income can be expressed in a simple equation:

$$C + S = Y$$

It follows, then, that the average propensity to consume and average propensity to save are defined so that they always add up to 1:

$$APC + APS = \frac{C}{Y} + \frac{S}{Y} = \frac{Y}{Y} = 1$$

For example, if disposable income is $100 billion, consumption is $80 billion, and saving is $20 billion, we would have:

$$APC = \frac{80}{100} = .80 \quad \text{and} \quad APS = \frac{20}{100} = .20$$

Then

$$APC + APS = .80 + .20 = 1$$

The marginal propensity to consume and marginal propensity to save are also defined so that they always add up to 1. Since consumption plus saving equals disposable income, any change in disposable income must be reflected entirely in a change in consumption plus a change in saving.

$$\Delta C + \Delta S = \Delta Y$$

By dividing each term by ΔY, we obtain:

$$\frac{\Delta C}{\Delta Y} + \frac{\Delta S}{\Delta Y} = \frac{\Delta Y}{\Delta Y} \quad \text{or:}$$

$$MPC + MPS = 1$$

If, as Keynes expected, the MPC is positive but less than 1, then the MPS will also be positive but less than 1. We might, for example, have MPC = .9 and MPS = .1, or we might have MPC = .85 and MPS = .15.

The relationship among the propensities appears more clearly in the hypothetical data in Table 4–1. The table shows income (in billions) increasing from $100 to $120 billion, consumption increasing from $80 to $90 billion, and saving increasing from $20 to $30 billion. We then have $\Delta Y = 20$, $\Delta C = 10$, and $\Delta S = 10$. Then:

$$MPC = \frac{10}{20} = .50$$

$$MPS = \frac{10}{20} = .50$$

$$MPC + MPS = .5 + .5 = 1$$

It is possible to see the same relationships graphically. Figure 4–1a shows a relationship between income and consumption that would generate the kind of data described in Table 4–1.

At an income level of zero, consumption would be 30, as households attempted to live off their accumulated wealth. For every additional dollar of income, the diagram shows consumption going up by half a dollar. Thus, at an income level of 100, consumption would be 80, or an increase of 50. Likewise, if income were to increase from 100 to 120, or a change of 20, consumption would increase from 80 to 90, or a change of 10. Thus, throughout the consumption line shown, the marginal propensity to consume is .5. In general, whenever the relationship between income and consumption can be represented by a straight line, the MPC will be constant.

Figure 4–1b shows the relationship between income and saving that is implied in Figure 4–1a. When consumption is greater than income, we say that households are dissaving—drawing upon their savings to pay for consumption. At an income of zero, Figure 4–1a shows a level of consumption of 30; Figure 4–1b, then, shows dissaving, or negative saving—a level of minus 30—at zero income. Likewise, at an income level of 100, at which consumption is 80, saving goes up by 50, from −30 to +20. Again, if income goes up from 100 to 120 (a change of 20) saving will increase from

Table 4–1   Average and Marginal Propensities

	Levels (In $ billions)			Average Propensities		Marginal Propensities	
	Y	C	S	APC	APS	MPC	MPS
1977 Level	100	80	20	.80	.20	—	—
1978 Level	120	90	30	.75	.25	—	—
Change (Δ)	+20	+10	+10	—	—	.50	.50

Figure 4-1   The Propensities to Consume and to Save

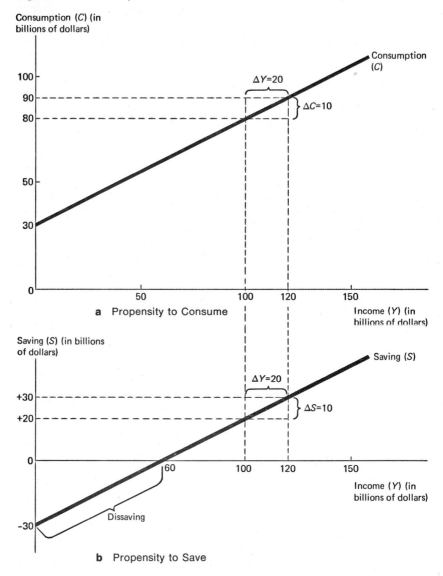

a   Propensity to Consume

b   Propensity to Save

20 to 30 (a change of 10). Thus, Figure 4-1b shows a constant marginal propensity to save of .5 throughout the straight line representing the relationship between income and saving. The MPC of .5 and the MPS of .5 add up to 1.

The simple tools of the propensities to consume and to save form an important part of the theory of determining *Equilibrium Income* (see pp. 125-34). More sophisticated views of what determines consumption are developed in our discussion of the *Consumption Function* (see pp. 149-53).

EQUILIBRIUM INCOME

Equilibrium income is that level at which aggregate demand tends to perpetuate itself. The equilibrium level of income is that level at which income recipients, taken as a whole, will tend to spend as much as they have earned. That spending, in turn, will generate an equal level of income. In equilibrium, the quantity of goods produced is exactly equal to the quantity desired.

Equilibrium income is a theoretical concept that is extremely useful in analyzing the direction in which an economy is moving. However, it is not a concept that we can readily observe or measure in the real world, since the economy is never actually in equilibrium. The underlying causes of the level of economic activity never stand still for very long. If the economy ever began to settle down to one equilibrium level, changing economic forces would soon shift it to a new equilibrium level.

In order to develop a model—or theoretical abstraction—of the economy, we must make certain simplifying assumptions. To make our job easier here, we will assume that there is no government expenditure or taxation, although we can later add these functions of government to a model of this sort (see *Equilibrium Income with Government,* pp. 179–87). Beyond this, simple Keynesian models of income determination—models named for the British economist John Maynard Keynes—typically make four additional assumptions: (1) The economy is operating at less than full capacity; that is, the level of *Aggregate Demand* (see pp. 71–76) is lower than the total supply potential of the economy. Thus increases or decreases in the level of income are determined by changes in the level of the aggregate demand rather than by changes in productive capacity. (2) Saving decisions and investment decisions are made independently of each other. Savers decide how much to save on the basis of the size of their incomes. Investors decide to invest on the basis of their estimates of future profitability. In these models there is no room for the idea that increased saving may make funds more available to investors—and probably available at lower interest rates—so that increased saving may itself stimulate investment. (3) The money supply responds passively to accommodate the forces of aggregate demand but does not itself influence those forces. For example, we assume that if some investors decide to borrow more money in order to invest more, then the banking system automatically expands the supply of money to accommodate those investors without raising interest rates or restricting the availability of credit in a way that would tend to discourage any other investors. We assume, in effect, that money is always readily available to be borrowed at a constant rate of interest. (4) The role of foreign trade can be ignored. We assume that no expenditure is injected into the domestic economy from foreign demand for the country's exports and that none is leaked away in the form of domestic demand for imports from abroad.

We make these assumptions so that we may construct a readily manageable model—not because we think they are realistic. Indeed, Keynes himself put forth his ideas in a book called *The General Theory of Employment, Interest, and Money*—and he saw interest rates and the money supply as playing a very active role in the determination of equilibrium income. In more complicated models of income determination it is possible—and important—to analyze the role of many of the influences that we are here temporarily assuming away (see *Equilibrium Income with Money*, pp. 210–17).

Expenditure Equals Income

Total expenditure (E) in the economy will always equal total income (Y), or $E = Y$. Looked at after the fact, this simply says that the economy's expenditures on final commodities and services (consumption goods, investment goods, and government purchases) all generate income. It may be the income of workers and managers, it may be the income of those who provided the necessary land or raw materials, or it may be the profit of those who organized the creation or the sale of the goods. Every penny of every dollar spent for the purchase of the final commodity or service eventually finds its way into someone's pocket as income.

For the economy to be at an equilibrium level of income, it is necessary that the circular flow of expenditure be maintained (see *Aggregate Demand*, especially pp. 72–76). This requires that people in the economy as a whole plan to spend an amount equal to total income in the economy. In other words, it is necessary that the level of actual income give rise to an equal amount of planned expenditure. In this sense, the equation $E = Y$ becomes a condition for equilibrium in the economy.

This relationship can be expressed graphically in a very simple way. A line is drawn in Figure 4–2 that traces all the points at which expenditure (measured on the vertical axis) equals income (measured on the horizontal axis). Note that it is a straight line through the origin of the graph forming an angle of 45°. If we pick any point on the line, like A, and trace that point back to the expenditure axis and the income axis, we can see that it indicates an equal amount of expenditure and income—in the case of Point A, $1,500 billion. This line can be used in two ways. First, although income (Y) is measured on the horizontal axis, the 45° line provides a vertical measure of the level of income. Second, since an equilibrium level of income must be one that gives rise to an equal level of expenditure, the equilibrium levels of E and Y will have to be somewhere on this line.

Determining Equilibrium Income

The simplest model of income determination is one in which we disregard the roles of government and international trade; government will be explicitly added to the model in our discussion of *Equilibrium Income with Government* (see 79–87). We assume, then, that expenditure (E) has only two broad components, total consumption (C) and total investment (I):

$$E = C + I$$

Figure 4–2   The 45° Line

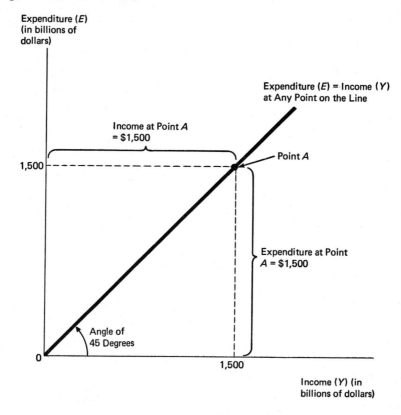

We assume that consumption is entirely determined by the level of income itself. Thus, if income is low, families will consume very little, while if income is high, they will consume a great deal. To simplify further, we assume that the amount of investment businesses wish to undertake is independent of the current level of income and the size of the capital stock that has resulted from earlier investment. Thus, at all levels of income, investment will be at the same level.

These assumptions are represented in Figure 4–3, which shows total expenditure (E) on the vertical axis and total income (Y) on the horizontal axis. The consumption line (C) shows an increasing level of consumption spending as total income in the economy increases. Note that the C line intersects the expenditure (E) axis at a positive point. This indicates that even if income were to fall temporarily to zero, people would still consume something—perhaps by living off their accumulated wealth. A uniform distance above the consumption line, there is another line representing consumption plus investment (C + I). The difference between them is the

Figure 4–3   Consumption and Investment Expenditure at Different Income Levels

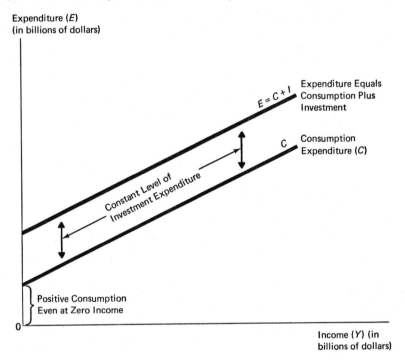

constant level of investment, *I*. The *E = C + I* line, then, shows a variety of possible combinations of total spending and total income in the economy.

At what level of income will the economy be in equilibrium? The answer can be seen when we put the two diagrams together, as in Figure 4–4. Equilibrium is indicated by the point at which the *E = C + I* line intersects the *E = Y* line (45° line). This is the only point at which the total expenditure generated by each alternative level of income (as given by the *E = C + I* line) equals the level of income (as given by the *E = Y* line). By tracing dashed lines from this point to the two axes of the graph, we can see the equilibrium level of income at $1,400 billion and the equilibrium level of expenditure (the sum of investment and consumption expenditures) also at $1,400 billion. Aggregate demand will maintain itself because an income of $1,400 billion will generate an equal amount of expenditure.

What happens if income is not at its equilibrium level? Figure 4–5 can help answer this question.

Consider first the case in which actual income is higher than the equilibrium level—for example, at $2,000 rather than $1,400 billion. If we follow the dashed line up from the income axis at $2,000 billion, we can see the *E = C + I* line, representing actual total expenditure, has reached only

Figure 4–4   Equilibrium Income where Expenditure Equals Income

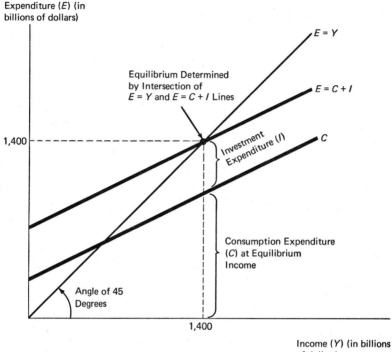

$1,700 billion, while the $E = Y$ line is at the full income level of $2,000 billion. Thus there is a gap (indicated by the brackets) of $300 billion, the amount by which the total consumption and investment expenditure generated at an income of $2,000 billion falls short of equaling that income. Such a level of income obviously cannot be maintained, since income will give rise to a smaller level of expenditure, and this in turn will only generate a smaller level of income. Aggregate demand will shrink and continue to shrink until income falls to the level of $1,400 billion, where it will generate an equal amount of expenditure.

Next we might look at an income level lower than the equilibrium, such as $1,000 billion. Note that the dashed line up from the income axis at $1,000 billion indicates an actual level of expenditure of $1,200 billion. (The distance of $200 billion by which the $E = C + I$ line exceeds the $E = Y$ line is indicated with brackets.) Income of $1,000 billion gives rise to expenditure of $1,200 billion, tending to increase the circular flow of demand and thus to increase income. This tendency will continue until income reaches the equilibrium level of $1,400 billion.

Therefore, whether we begin with a level of income greater or less than

Figure 4-5   Departures from Equilibrium Income

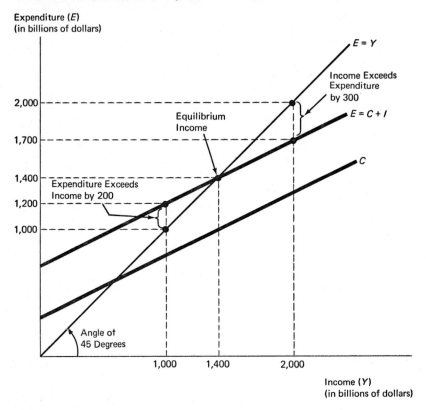

equilibrium, there will be a tendency for the economy to move toward equilibrium. Only at the equilibrium level of income, $1,400 billion in our diagram, does the total expenditure arising from income equal—and thus tend to maintain—the level of income.

An Alternative View

Equilibrium income can also be viewed as the level at which savers want to save just as much as investors want to invest. Remember that in a world without government the income the people receive (Y) will be allocated either to consumption (C) or to saving (S):

$$Y = C + S$$

We have already seen that Expenditure = Consumption + Investment:

$$E = C + I$$

For equilibrium to occur, the members of the economy as a whole must want to spend as much income as they receive:

$$E = Y$$

If we set the expression for expenditure equal to the expression for income, we have:

$$C + I = C + S$$

If C is subtracted from both sides of this equation, we have the equality of investment and saving:

$$I = S$$

Thus equilibrium implies that investors want to invest as much as savers want to save.

To present this graphically, we must first see how the savings line can be derived from the consumption line. Figure 4–6 shows the same consumption line (C) as do the previous figures and the same 45° line ($E = Y$) tracing the points at which expenditure equals income. Again, the $E = Y$ line provides a vertical measure of the level of income, so that we may use it and the consumption line to make vertical comparisons of income and consumption for any level of income. Saving is defined as income minus consumption ($S = Y - C$). Thus the vertical distance by which the $E = Y$ line exceeds the C line will be a measure of the level of saving. At the bottom of Figure 4–6 we show the levels of saving associated with each income level, as derived from the top part of the figure.

For an understanding of Figure 4–6, one point of departure is the point in the top half at which the two lines (C and $E = Y$) intersect at an income level of $600 billion. There is no vertical distance between the two at this point (both consumption and income are $600 billion), which means that saving is zero. This point is sometimes known as the break-even point, since households are consuming just as much as they are taking in. We may trace the income level of $600 billion down to the bottom half of Figure 4–6. We see that the saving line intersects the horizontal axis, which is another way of indicating that saving is zero at that level.

A second point of observation on Figure 4–6 is the zero level of income on the vertical axis. The top half of the diagram shows that at this point some $300 billion of consumption will take place. Thus, consumption will exceed income, a situation known as dissaving. It is represented in the lower part of Figure 4–6 by a negative level of saving—$300 billion below the zero point on the vertical axis at zero income.

A more normal situation occurs when income is at a level like $1,500

Figure 4-6   Relationship of Saving Behavior to Consumption Behavior

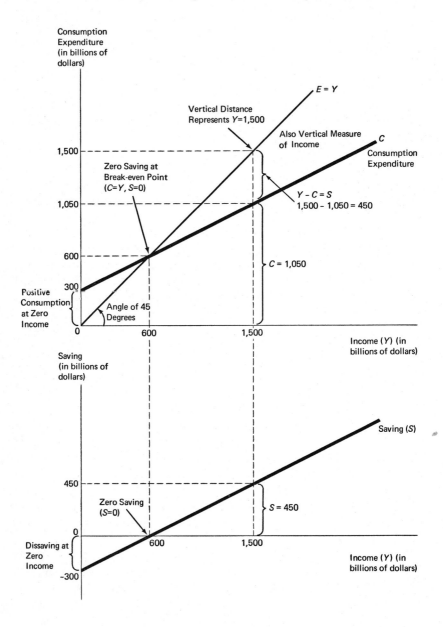

billion. The amount by which the $E = Y$ line exceeds the C line indicates the amount by which income of $1,500 billion exceeds consumption of $1,050 billion—and this represents $450 billion of saving. In the bottom part of the graph, the same amount of saving ($450 billion) is shown at an income level of $1,500 billion.

How equilibrium income is determined is shown in Figure 4–7. In the top part of the figure, equilibrium income is determined by the point at which the $E = Y$ line intersects the $E = C + I$ line. At the bottom of the figure, we show the saving line derived from the consumption line at the top. A horizontal line is also added showing the same level of investment as in the top part of the figure. (Note that the distance of $400 billion between the C line and the $C + I$ line at the top is the same as the $400 billion uniform height of the investment line at the bottom.) Equilibrium occurs in the bottom half of the figure at the point where the investment line intersects the saving line, indicating an equilibrium income level of $1,400 billion. Note that equilibrium in the top half of the diagram also occurs at $1,400 billion—and that at this point the $400 billion of saving generated just equals the level of investment (the distance between the C line and the $C + I$ line).

Thus we have found the equilibrium level of income, where savers want to save the same amount that investors want to invest. This is equivalent to finding an equilibrium level of income at the point where spenders want to spend just as much as income earners have earned. The two halves of Figure 4–7 represent alternative ways of using the same basic assumptions about the economy to reach the same conclusions about equilibrium income.

Figure 4–7   Equilibrium Income where Expenditure Equals Income and where Saving Equals Investment

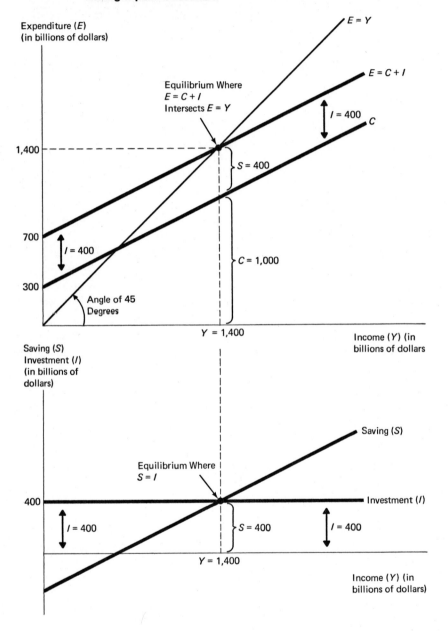

THE INVESTMENT MULTIPLIER

The investment multiplier describes the impact of a change in total investment upon total expenditure or income in the economy. It can be expressed numerically as the ratio of the change in income to the change in investment.

There are two types of investment multipliers. The equilibrium multiplier is used to describe the change in equilibrium income that results from a permanent change in the rate of investment in the economy. For example, we might ask about the effect on equilibrium income if annual investment permanently increases from $70 billion to $80 billion. The cumulative multiplier is used to describe the cumulative changes in income—in the present period and in all future periods—that result from a one-shot change in investment in the present period. For example, we might ask about the effects on income from 1978 to the end of the twentieth century of a decision to invest an extra $10 billion during 1978. In the first case, we are employing the tools of comparative statics (see *Equilibrium,* especially p. 37) to compare two equilibrium positions of the economy. In the second case, we are tracing out the impacts into the indefinite future of a single, one-shot change in investment.

The Equilibrium Multiplier

To see the impact on equilibrium income of raising the rate of investment in the economy, we must use some of the simplifying assumptions that were introduced in our discussion of *Equilibrium Income* (see pp. 125–34). In particular, we also begin by assuming that: (1) the economy is operating at less than full capacity; (2) saving and investment decisions are made independently of each other; (3) the supply of money in the economy responds passively to the expenditure demands in the economy; and (4) the roles of foreign trade and of government taxation and expenditure can be ignored, so that expenditure is seen as consisting only of private consumption and private investment expenditure. Furthermore, we again assume (5) consumption and saving are entirely determined by the level of income and (6) the amount of investment is independent of the current level of income and the size of the capital stock.

Figure 4–8 also uses some of the tools of our earlier discussion and shows equilibrium income at $1,500 billion, as determined by the intersection of the saving line (S) and the line showing the initial level of investment (I) at $400 billion. If the level of investment is permanently increased to $600 billion, the level of equilibrium income will increase to $2,100 billion. The change in investment (ΔI), equal to $200 billion ($600 − $400 billion), has led to a change in income (ΔY) equal to $600 billion ($2,100 − $1,500 billion). Thus the permanent increase in investment has led to a much larger increase—three times as great—in the level of equilibrium income. It is this

Figure 4-8   The Equilibrium Multiplier

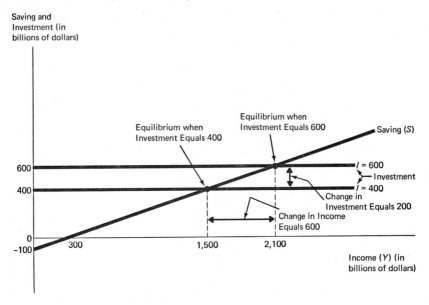

multiple relationship—an increase in equilibrium income greater than the permanent increase in the rate of investment—that gives the multiplier its name.

It is useful to examine the reason that an increase in investment should have this multiple effect. Why doesn't each increase of $1 in the rate of investment simply increase equilibrium income by $1? The answer is that total expenditure has two components (investment and consumption) and the consumption component is itself determined by the level of income. If income is higher because of increased investment expenditure, then consumption expenditure will also be higher. That higher consumption expenditure will itself generate additional income that can support even higher levels of consumption expenditure. This multiple effect would fail to occur only in an extreme case—if households saved 100 percent of every additional dollar of income and consumed nothing more in response to additional income. Here the increase in equilibrium income would be no greater than the increase in the rate of investment. In this highly improbable case, the multiplier—the change in income divided by the change in investment—would only be equal to 1.

We can see how the equilibrium investment multiplier depends on saving behavior in the economy. Figure 4-8 compares two different equilibrium income levels ($1,500 and $2,100 billion) corresponding to two different rates of investment ($400 and $600 billion). At both equilibrium levels of income the amount of investment that businesses wish to undertake is equal to the amount of saving that households wish to undertake. Thus, the change in saving (ΔS) between the two equilibrium points is equal to the change in investment (ΔI) involved:

$$\Delta I = \Delta S$$

We can compare these two values with the change in income (ΔY) by dividing both sides of the equation by ΔY:

$$\frac{\Delta I}{\Delta Y} = \frac{\Delta S}{\Delta Y}$$

Recall from the discussion of the *Propensity to Consume* (see pp. 121–24) that the share of additional income devoted to saving ($\Delta S \div \Delta Y$), is known as the marginal propensity to save (MPS). Therefore, we may substitute the term MPS for $\Delta S \div \Delta Y$ and obtain:

$$\frac{\Delta I}{\Delta Y} = MPS$$

The value we are really interested in, the expression for the multiplier, is the ratio of the change in income to the change in investment ($\Delta Y \div \Delta I$). To obtain this, we take reciprocals of both sides of the equation above—that is, we divide 1 by both sides of the equation:

$$\text{Equilibrium multiplier} = \frac{\Delta Y}{\Delta I} = \frac{1}{MPS}$$

This simply says that the equilibrium multiplier is equal to the reciprocal of (1 divided by) the marginal propensity to save. For example, if (as in Figure 4–8) households save $\frac{1}{3}$ and consume $\frac{2}{3}$ of their additional incomes, the MPS will be $\frac{1}{3}$ and the multiplier will be 3. If households only save $\frac{1}{10}$ and consume fully $\frac{9}{10}$ of their additional income, then the MPS will be $\frac{1}{10}$ and the multiplier will be 10. In general, the greater the tendency for households to spend additional income, the greater will be the impact on equilibrium income of increases in the rate of investment.

This can be shown graphically as well. In Figure 4–9a the marginal propensity to save is $\frac{1}{2}$, so that the saving line increases by $1 for every $2 of additional income. Here a permanent increase of $40 billion in investment generates an increase of $80 billion in the equilibrium income level. By contrast, in Figure 4–9b we have a marginal propensity to save of $\frac{1}{5}$, so that the saving line increases by $1 for every $5 of additional income. Here a permanent increase in the rate of investment of $40 billion generates an increase of $200 billion in the equilibrium income level.

Figure 4–9   The Equilibrium Multiplier with Different Marginal Propensities to Save

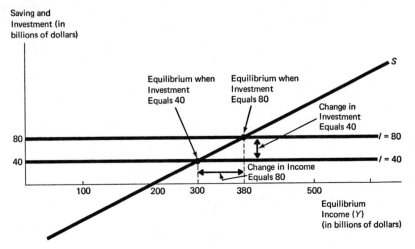

a   Marginal Propensity to Save of $\frac{1}{2}$ and Multiplier of 2

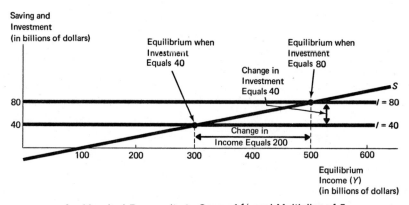

b   Marginal Propensity to Save of $\frac{1}{5}$ and Multiplier of 5

The Cumulative Multiplier

The cumulative investment multiplier describes the total impact into the future of a one-shot increase in investment in a particular year. For example, assume that in 1978 American oil companies decide to invest $10 billion in developing the oil reserves of the Alaskan North Slope. Assume further that the marginal propensity to save (MPS) is constant over time at a level of $\frac{1}{5}$. To simplify a bit, we shall take this to mean that consumers spend in one year $\frac{4}{5}$ of the income they received in the previous year. What will be the impact of the decision to invest in 1978 on expenditure in 1979 and in all subsequent years combined?

At first this may seem like an impossible question to answer. After all, those who receive the income from the investment—the construction workers, rigging manufacturers, and petroleum engineers—receive $10 billion in 1978. In 1979 they will spend $8 billion of the $10 billion on such goods as food, clothing, and television sets. In 1980 the farmers who grew the food and the workers and manufacturers who made the clothing and television sets will, in turn, spend $6.4 billion ($\frac{4}{5}$ of $8 billion) on consumption goods. Each year the additional consumption expenditure resulting from the initial, one-shot $10 billion in investment will be smaller and smaller, but each year it will be positive. (For example, it will be $5.12 billion in 1981, $1.07 billion in 1988, and $.11 billion in 1998.) If some increased consumption goes on forever, then won't the total into the indefinite future be infinitely great? Actually, it will not. In fact, a definable limit can be placed on the value of the cumulative multiplier—even if the chain of expenditure goes on forever.

In order to understand the limit on the cumulative multiplier, consider the analogy of an insect crawling across a room. Assume that on the first day it crawls halfway across the room, on the second day half of the remaining distance, and on the third day half of the distance still remaining. The insect may continue at this pace indefinitely. But if on any given day it never crawls more than halfway between its starting point and the end of the room, it will never quite make it to the other side. Every day it makes a little progress, but every day the rate of progress toward the target is less and less. There is a clear limit—the length of one room—beyond which the insect will never go.

Similarly, we can see a limit on how much total expenditure will be generated over time by the $10 billion in investment expenditure. The first addition to expenditure appears in 1978 and is equal to $10 billion in investment. Later increases in consumption expenditure can be described in terms of an ultimate target—in this case, $40 billion. The additional consumption expenditure in 1979 of $8 billion represents $\frac{1}{5}$ of the way between zero and $40 billion. This would leave $32 billion to go if total consumption expenditure is ever to reach the ultimate limit of $40 billion. Expenditure in 1980 is $6.4 billion—exactly $\frac{1}{5}$ of the remaining $32 billion. Thus we can see consumers—as they save $\frac{1}{5}$ of their additional incomes and consume $\frac{4}{5}$ of those incomes—moving each year towards spending $\frac{1}{5}$ of the difference between what they have already spent in the past and the elusive but fixed limit of $40 billion.

The cumulative multiplier is illustrated in Figure 4–10. An initial one-shot increase in investment expenditure of $10 billion in 1978 (darkly shaded area) generates a total of $36.57 billion in additional consumption by 1989 (lightly shaded area) for a total increase in expenditure of $46.57 billion. The limit on the total expenditure that would ultimately be generated by the $10 billion in investment is the $10 billion itself plus the limit of $40 billion in additional consumption expenditure, for a grand total of $50 billion. Note that this total of $50 billion is exactly five times the initial investment

Figure 4-10 The Cumulative Multiplier

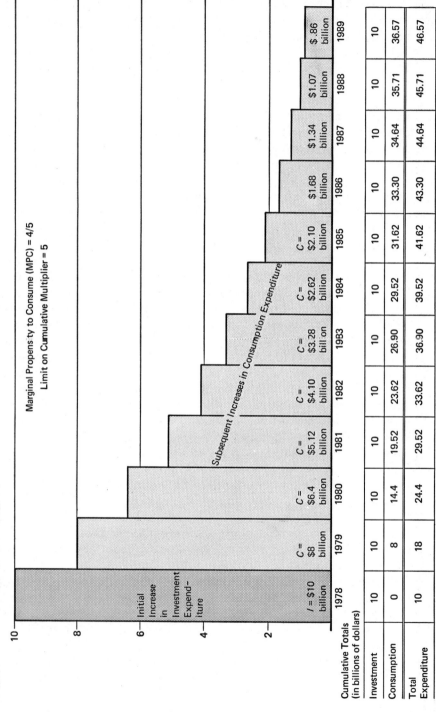

Marginal Propensity to Consume (MPC) = 4/5
Limit on Cumulative Multiplier = 5

Subsequent Increases in Consumption Expenditure

Initial Increase in Investment Expenditure

Cumulative Totals (in billions of dollars)	1978	1979	1980	1981	1982	1983	1984	1985	1986	1987	1988	1989
Investment	10	10	10	10	10	10	10	10	10	10	10	10
Consumption	0	8	14.4	19.52	23.62	26.90	29.52	31.62	33.30	34.64	35.71	36.57
Total Expenditure	10	18	24.4	29.52	33.62	36.90	39.52	41.62	43.30	44.64	45.71	46.57

expenditure of $10 billion. The cumulative multiplier in this case, then, is equal to 5—which is exactly equal to 1 divided by the marginal propensity to save. In fact, this relationship will always hold, so that we have:

$$\text{Cumulative multiplier} = \frac{1}{\text{MPS}}$$

Thus, if the MPS is $\frac{1}{3}$, the cumulative multiplier will be 3, which means that a single shot of $1 of initial investment will give rise to additional expenditure totaling the $1 of initial investment plus an ultimate total of $2 of additional consumption.

In the real world we may be less interested in the long-run impact of additional investment on income than in the impact over a limited period of time. For example, assume that the economy is in a recession, with aggregate demand $50 billion short of supply capacity, and this recession is expected to last two years. If the government wishes to give some encouragement to investment to help restore aggregate demand, it needs to know what impact additional investment this year will have on expenditure over the course of the next two years. Once the economy comes out of the recession, any additional expenditure attributable to this year's investment might only contribute to inflation rather than to a restoration of full employment and full capacity output. To estimate the impact of additional investment on expenditure for a limited number of years, we cannot use a simple relationship like 1 ÷ MPS. We can, however, describe the chain of expenditure from period to period resulting from each $1 of initial investment.

In the base period (period 0) the expenditure (in dollars) will be the initial investment of $1. In period 1 it will be equal to the marginal propensity to consume (MPC), since the MPC indicates the share of income (from the investment) that households will spend. In period 2, households will have received additional income (from the additional consumption in period 1) of MPC. They will spend that income multiplied by MPC, or:

$$\text{MPC} \times \text{MPC} = \text{MPC}^2$$

For example, if the MPC is .8, then: $.8 \times .8 = .64$

In period 3, households will have received additional income of MPC^2 and will spend MPC times that, or:

$$\text{MPC}^2 \times \text{MPC} = \text{MPC}^3$$

For example: $.64 \times .8 = .512$

In this manner the chain of expenditure continues. The total additional

Table 4–2   The Workings of the Cumulative Multiplier over Time

Time Period	0	1	2	3	4	5
Additional Expenditure	1	MPC	MPC^2	MPC^3	MPC^4	MPC^5
Kind of Expenditure	I	C	C	C	C	C
If MPC = .8	$1	$.80	$.64	$.512	$.410	$.328

expenditure over time that results from an initial $1 in investment is represented in Table 4–2.

Implications of Multiplier Analysis

Multiplier analysis has a certain simplicity—even beauty—and economists sometimes become intoxicated by the ability of multiplier models to yield clear-cut results. Keep in mind, however, that this analysis, like the *Equilibrium Income* analysis on which it is based (see pp. 125–34), makes a number of simplifying assumptions about the economy. If these assumptions are not met, the results will not be as precise as the multiplier models imply.

(1) If the economy does not permanently have excess capacity, then the increased investment and the resulting consumption expenditure will not be able to stimulate an increase in the quantity of goods produced. That is to say, increases in money income will be absorbed partly in higher prices. (2) If saving decisions are not made independently of investment decisions, the actual multiplier might be smaller than indicated. For example, the decision to increase investment might bid up the rate of interest somewhat, thus encouraging saving and discouraging consumption. This influence might partly offset the tendency for consumption to increase as additional investment generates additional income. (3) The money supply may not expand sufficiently to accommodate the increased investment and consumption expenditure described in these models. In this case, the increased investment and consumption could increase the demand for money and raise the interest rate, thereby choking off some investment that would otherwise have occurred. Thus, the full impact of the multiplier might not be realized. (4) The role of government taxation and expenditure can modify the multiplier considerably. When government increases its own level of expenditure—for example, on roads, schools, or submarines—it initiates a chain of consumption expenditure and raises the level of equilibrium income. And by taxing incomes, government reduces the share of additional income that households can spend on additional consumption. A multiplier analysis that takes account of the role of government can be found in our discussions of *Equilibrium Income with Government* (see pp. 179–87), *Fiscal Policy* (see pp. 188–97), and *Built-in Stabilizers* (see pp. 188–203).

A similar—but for the U.S. economy, smaller—effect can be expected if we include international trade in the model. This would introduce export demand from abroad as an injection and domestic spending on imports from abroad as a leakage that is not immediately returned to the domestic economy. (5) If consumption and saving are dependent on more than the level of income in a single year, multiplier analysis is not nearly so neat. For example, consumption may respond not just to this year's or last year's income but to some long-run level of expected average income (see *Consumption Function,* pp. 149–53). In this case the increased consumption generated by a short-run increase in income will not be so great, and the multiplier will be lower. (6) If investment is not entirely independent of the level of income and the size of the capital stock, an initial spurt of investment may have two kinds of complicating effects. On the one hand, it may build up the capital stock to the point where some of the investment that might otherwise take place later becomes unnecessary, so that investment one year takes place at the expense of investment in later years. On the other hand, if investment in one year stimulates consumption expenditure later, that consumption expenditure may itself create pressures for expansion of the capital stock in order to produce the goods that consumers want to buy. This, in turn, could stimulate investment later, setting off new multiplier consequences.

This kind of multiplier analysis, then, greatly oversimplifies the reaction of the economy to a change in investment. On the whole, one would expect much lower multipliers in the real world than the value of 1/MPS.

THE PARADOX OF THRIFT

The paradox of thrift states that, if everyone in the economy tries to increase the amount he saves, total saving will not go up—and may even decline. Individual efforts to increase saving may be successful, so that the Jones family, if it so desires, may save a larger share of its income. If, however, great numbers of families all attempt to increase their saving at the same time, aggregate demand will decline and total income in the community will fall. The amount subsequently saved out of the lower income may be no larger than the amount saved before the community tried to save more.

The paradox of thrift did not become a dominant idea in macroeconomics until the Great Depression and the analysis of John Maynard Keynes in the 1930s. For centuries, economists had considered thrift, or parsimony, an absolute virtue, because it permits resources to be invested rather than consumed. Hence it permits increases in the stock of capital (including plant and equipment) and helps provide employment and wealth. For example, Adam Smith, writing in 1776, argued that capital is "increased by parsimony, and diminished by prodigality and misconduct." The person who consumes more than he earns tends not only to impoverish himself but also to impoverish his country by depleting its capital stock. The act of saving did not reduce expenditure in the economy, Smith argued, because savings that are invested—or lent out to be invested—are consumed by "the laborers who produce the addition to the capital." Thus Smith and several generations of economists who succeeded him argued that saving merely represented the replacement of consumption expenditure by investment expenditure. The result, then, was not a reduction in aggregate demand but a diversion of resources from promoting present consumption to building up the capital stock of the country.

Quite different results follow, however, if we assume that saving and investment decisions are completely independent. Using the analytic tools developed in our discussion of *Equilibrium Income* (see pp. 125–34), with this and other simplifying assumptions, we can see how the paradox of thrift works.

The Paradox with Investment Independent of Income

Figure 4–11 shows investment (*I*) at a constant level of $400 billion—independent of the level of income and the level of saving. Equilibrium income is determined by the equality of investment and saving. Thus, let the line S_1 describe the amount of saving that individuals initially wish to do at each level of income. There is only one level of income, $1,600 billion, at which the savings intentions of individuals will equal the investment intentions of businesses, and this will determine the equilibrium of the economy.

Consider, however, what would happen if individuals decided that they would like to save more at each income level. This could be depicted by an upward shift in the saving line by $300 billion, from S_1 to S_2. The result

Figure 4–11   The Paradox of Thrift with a Constant Level of Investment

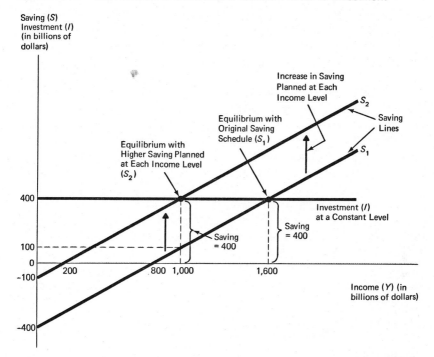

would be a shift in the equilibrium level of income from $1,600 down to $1,000 billion. Note what has happened to the level of saving in the economy. At the new level of income, $1,000 billion, the new saving line S_2 indicates that individuals are saving $400 billion. This is $300 billion more than the $100 billion they would have saved at that income level if they had continued to save according to the saving line S_1. Indeed, at any level of income, individuals are now saving $300 billion more than they would have if they had maintained the saving behavior described by the line S_1. But as a result of the shift in saving plans, the level of income has fallen to a point that leaves the actual quantity of saving unchanged. This result follows directly from our assumptions: investment is constant across all income levels, and equilibrium will occur at that income level at which saving equals investment. By increasing their saving plans, individuals have decided to consume less, and in the process they have reduced aggregate demand to that lower level of income at which saving still equals the constant level of investment.

The Paradox with Investment Dependent on Income

Alternatively, we might have assumed that the level of investment would *not* be constant across all income levels but would tend to be higher at higher levels of income. Since demand for goods is higher at higher income levels, a larger capital stock will be required, so that (at least temporarily) more investment might be expected to occur. Thus, in Figure 4–12, we show a level of investment which is low at low levels of income, but which rises gradually as income levels grow.

Assuming that savings intentions are described initially by the line S_1, an equilibrium of the economy occurs where S_1 intersects the investment line, indicating an income level of $1,600 billion and a level of saving and investment of $400 billion. If, however, individuals become more thrifty and decide to save more out of any level of income, there would be a shift in the saving line up to S_2. As before, this would reduce the level of consumption expenditure in the economy and lower aggregate demand. The level of equilibrium income would fall to $800 billion. In this case, however, a lower level of income will generate a lower level of investment expenditure. Thus, at the new equilibrium where both saving and investment must be equal, both will be $100 billion lower than before the increase in thrift. Again, there will be more saving at any particular income level than before, but the equilibrium level of income will be lower and, as a result, both investment and saving will be lower. In this case, then, the paradox of thrift indicates

Figure 4–12 The Paradox of Thrift with Induced Investment

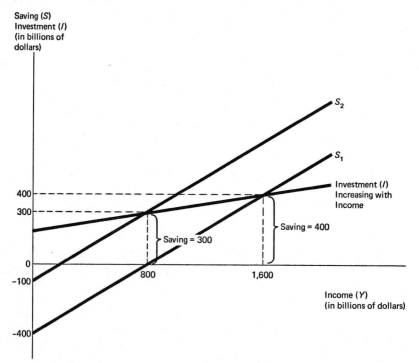

that an attempt to increase savings may lead to a *lower* level of savings in the economy as a whole.

Evaluation of the Paradox of Thrift

In one sense, the paradox of thrift is resolved when we consider that what is true for an individual may not be true for an economy as a whole. Thus a single farmer may sell more oats and increase his income because a few bushels more of oats do not have any observable effect on the nationwide price of oats. If all the oat farmers in the country tried to sell more oats, however, they might well drive down the price of oats far enough to offset the increased income realized from selling a larger quantity. So it is with the paradox of thrift. If Mr. Jones is a worker earning $14,000 a year in a Chevrolet plant and the Jones family decides to try to save more out of his wages, this decision is unlikely to have an appreciable effect on aggregate demand. It is especially unlikely to cause any reduction in Mr. Jones's earnings. Even if the family went so far as to reduce consumption and increase saving by not buying a new automobile and even if the automobile they passed up were a Chevrolet, it is unlikely that Jones himself would then work fewer hours on the assembly line. But if a great many families in the country decided to save appreciably more, the result would be different. Aggregate demand would decline, and families across the country would find their incomes reduced and their savings plans scaled down to the new lower level of income.

However, the paradox of thrift makes some very strong assumptions about the independence of saving and investment. Adam Smith would have asked why those additional savings were not being invested so as to increase the capital stock of the country. Later classical economists would have argued that an increased supply of savings would surely operate to drive down the rate of interest and make investment more attractive. In this way, an increased supply of savings would itself tend to stimulate the level of investment. This classical argument tends to ignore the possibility that some of the saving might be hoarded—stuffed into mattresses and cookie jars— and hence not be available for investment. But even Keynes—while propounding the paradox of thrift—conceded that lower interest rates might induce enough additional investment to partially offset the tendency for total expenditures to fall as families reduce their consumption. When we allow for this possibility of greater investment, it becomes less clear that total saving will in fact fall as families attempt to save more. Most economists would agree, however, that there would at least be some tendency for equilibrium income to fall—even though it might not fall as dramatically as depicted in Figures 4–11 and 4–12.

Going beyond the simple models and considering the role of government, it is possible to see thrift in still a different light. At the present time virtually every government in the world is committed to pursuing an active

Fiscal Policy and *Monetary Policy* (see pp. 188–97 and 204–9) to prevent aggregate demand from falling too far below full employment. In this context, increased thrift can again be seen as increasing the opportunities for growth in the economy. If the government is going to assume responsibility for maintaining aggregate demand at adequate levels, a tendency for individuals to save more means that the government has the opportunity to invest more itself or to encourage more private investment. For example, it might expand the money supply faster in order to make credit more available to investors. Thus, even if the spontaneous responses of private investors are not vigorous enough to restore aggregate demand, the government response may contribute to the accumulation of capital and economic growth of the economy.

THE CONSUMPTION FUNCTION

The consumption function is a statement of those conditions that determine the level of consumption in the economy. Personal consumption is the largest component of aggregate demand, amounting to about two-thirds of GNP in the U.S. economy. Economists sometimes make statistical estimates of the consumption function in order to be able to predict the course of demand over the next few months or years.

Current income is included as a major influence on consumption in all modern statements of the consumption function. Other variables that are sometimes included are previous levels of income or consumption, "permanent" or "lifetime" income, assets, and the interest rate. Each of these variables will be examined in turn.

Consumption as a Function of Current Income

No modern consumption function is able to ignore the important role of current income—or, more precisely, current disposable personal income, which is the after-tax income of persons. It is at the core of the rather simple theory of consumption described by the *Propensity to Consume* (see pp. 121–24). Figure 4–13 suggests the importance of current income. It shows how current consumption (shown on the vertical axis) over the years 1946–75 compares with current disposable personal income for those years. The relationship is very close to that of a straight line, but with some deviations in particular years.

Figure 4–13, however, may not be the best way of looking at the data, since the variables being compared—total consumption and total income—are so large that a difference as great as $10 billion is hardly noticed. In Figure 4–14 we show variations over time in the ratio of consumption to disposable personal income. Consumption was unusually low during World War II, when production was diverted to the war effort and civilian goods were rationed. But since the end of the Korean war in 1953, the annual consumption ratio has varied only between 89 percent and 93 percent. Consider that disposable income in 1975 was $1,077 billion. Thus a difference of 1 percent in the consumption ratio would represent a difference in aggregate consumption—and hence aggregate demand—of nearly $11 billion. A difference of 4 percent in the consumption ratio can represent a difference in aggregate demand of $43 billion.

Consumption as a Function of Previous Income

Many economists have argued that it is important to go beyond current income in explaining current consumption and to look at previous levels of income or consumption as an influence on current behavior. The contention is simply that a person becomes accustomed to a particular level of living and does not easily shift to a new level even when his or her income

Figure 4–13   U.S. Consumption Behavior (1946–1975)

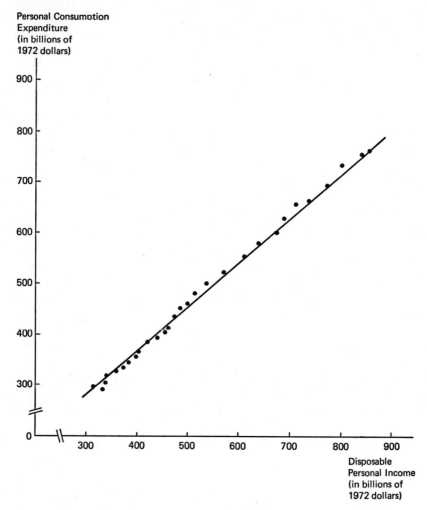

Source: *Economic Report of the President* (Washington, D.C.: U.S. Government Printing Office, January 1976), p. 191.

changes. A woman whose income suddenly increases may have become so accustomed to her past standard of living that she does not immediately increase her consumption of "the better things in life" nearly as much as she can afford to. Likewise, if her income declines, she may be extremely reluctant to give up the consumption goods that she has habitually enjoyed. She may feel forced to deplete her savings—or to borrow or sell her jewelry—to maintain her consumption standard in the face of the decline in income.

Figure 4–14 Consumption as a Percentage of Disposable Personal Income

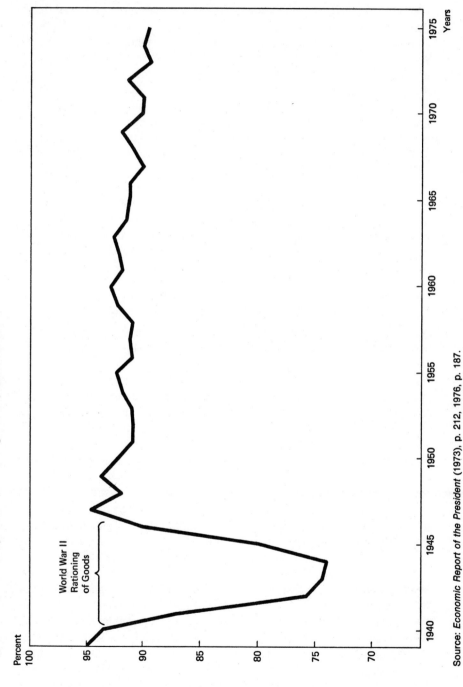

Source: *Economic Report of the President* (1973), p. 212, 1976, p. 187.

To apply this approach to consumption theory properly, we must distinguish between "consumption" and "consumption purchases." Most consumption goods are consumed at about the same time—or at least within a year of the time—that they are purchased. Most foods, some clothing items, and most personal services are clearly within this category. By contrast, most durable (or long-lasting) consumer goods, such as automobiles, refrigerators, and vacuum cleaners, are enjoyed—and may be said to be consumed—over a period of several years after the time of purchase. The distinction can be illustrated this way: A season ticketholder for the professional football season in 1976 was probably in the habit of watching football games and was likely to buy a ticket in 1977. By contrast, the purchaser of a home freezer in 1976 would be able to indulge his habit of keeping and freezing food at home without making another purchase for many years. In general, then, past consumption stimulates present consumption, but existing stocks of consumer durable goods—reflecting the income and purchases of previous years—inhibit rather than stimulate the current year's purchases of those goods.

Consumption as a Function of Permanent Income

Another approach argues that consumption is influenced not so much by the current year's income as by permanent income—the normal or average income that a household may expect to receive over its lifetime. A promising medical student may spend several thousand dollars more than his current income—perhaps going deeply into debt in the process—because he is confident that his future income will be considerably higher. By the same token, consider a family that has received an unexpected, "windfall" addition to its current income—a winning ticket in the Irish Sweepstakes, perhaps, or a legacy from a forgotten relative. The family may not immediately spend very much of that additional income, but it may try to spread out the enjoyment of the windfall over many years.

One implication of the "permanent income" approach to understanding consumption is that government policy to influence aggregate demand may or may not be effective, depending on how consumers interpret it. For example, assume the government cuts this year's taxes by $10 billion in an effort to stimulate private consumption. Advocates of the "permanent income" theory argue that the crucial point is whether consumers feel that this is a permanent shift to a lower level of taxes, or is a one-shot program designed to give a temporary boost to the economy this year but to be followed by higher taxes again next year. A one-shot tax reduction might be treated as an addition to the basic wealth of the family—just like the windfall gain from the Irish Sweepstakes—and most of it might not be immediately consumed. Tax reduction viewed as permanent would permit the family to permanently raise its consumption standard—by moving to a more expensive apartment, for example—and most of the money might be spent immediately.

Other Influences On Consumption

Current income is the major indicator of the ability to consume, and past consumption and "permanent income" are measures of the strength of the desire to consume rather than to save. Sometimes consumers also have the ability to supplement their consumption by drawing on past savings or by borrowing. Therefore, economists sometimes include measures of past savings and the ability to borrow in their descriptions of the consumption function.

Past savings are usually represented by some measure of the financial assets available to consumers, especially those which are most liquid, or most readily converted into money. A consumer who has $10,000 in a savings account may be more likely to draw on that for consumption purposes than a consumer who owns $10,000 worth of a small family firm that would be forced to close if he withdrew his share.

During World War II consumption opportunities were limited, due to the diversion of production to war purposes, and many consumers accumulated high levels of liquid assets, including U.S. war bonds and savings accounts. When the war ended and the capacity to produce civilian goods greatly increased, consumers were able to use those liquid assets to buy goods like automobiles and refrigerators that had long been unavailable.

The greater the ability of consumers to borrow, the greater their ability to go beyond current income in the purchase of consumer goods. Thus some economists argue that the consumption function should contain measures of the ease of borrowing. A full statement of these measures would include: (1) the cost of credit, usually represented by an interest rate; (2) the terms on which credit is available, including the required size of the down payment and the number of months over which the loan may be repaid; and (3) the availability of credit, or some measure of whether banks and other lending institutions are readily lending money at the interest rates and terms that currently prevail.

Measures of the ability to borrow would be especially important in the case of purchases for which consumers typically go into debt. Indeed, researchers have found that automobile purchases fluctuate partly in response to changes in the terms on car loans. For the U.S. economy as a whole, in which interest rates have shifted only gradually and over a fairly narrow range, few economic researchers have found changing interest rates to have a significant impact on aggregate consumption. However, there is increasing evidence from less developed countries—in which interest rates have sometimes shifted by as much as 15 percent in a few months—that higher interest rates can stimulate saving and hence curtail consumption.

THE INVESTMENT FUNCTION

The investment function is a statement of those conditions in the economy that have an important impact on the total level of private investment activity. Investment in the U.S. economy typically accounts for a smaller share of aggregate demand—about 15 percent—than either consumption or government expenditure. However, it is a crucial portion of that demand, since it is subject to severe short-run fluctuations.

Private investment consists of three components: (1) business investment in plant and equipment; (2) housing investment; and (3) investment in inventories of unfinished or unsold goods. Figure 4–15 shows the performance of these three components of investment over the past few years. Note that investment in plant and equipment is by far the largest of these three components, but it is also the most stable, following a gradual growth trend. Although housing investment and inventory investment are much smaller components, their annual dollar variations are typically greater than the dollar variations in plant and equipment investment. Since most home buyers pay for their houses by taking out a mortgage, housing investment is very responsive to changes in the availability of mortgage money and the interest rates. As for investment in inventories, this is the one component of aggregate demand that can actually become negative. Inventory investment is positive if producers and sellers are adding to their inventories of raw materials or finished goods. But inventory investment can go negative—as it did in the recession years of 1954, 1958, and 1975—whenever businesses as a whole deplete their inventories by selling off more goods than they are buying.

A snarp decline in private investment helped bring on the deep recession of 1975. But investment in plant and equipment actually increased slightly, at least in dollar terms, in 1975 over 1974. Investment in housing declined by $6 billion, and investment in inventories fell by a whopping $24 billion—from a positive $10 billion in 1974 to a negative $14 billion in 1975. When businesses decided that their sales prospects were gloomy, they stopped adding to their inventories and let their stocks of goods on hand run down. Thus, while economists often describe investment as the most volatile element of aggregate demand, this applies much more to housing and inventory investment than to investment in plant and equipment.

There are three major theories of the investment function: (1) as a function of the rate of interest; (2) as a function of the "acceleration" of the economy; and (3) as a function of the availability of funds within firms.

Investment as a Function of the Rate of Interest

Nearly every investment project is undertaken in the hope that it will yield a positive rate of return. A business firm incurs certain present costs such as building a plant, buying some machinery, or stocking up on inventories. This

Figure 4–15 Components of Investment

Billions of Dollars

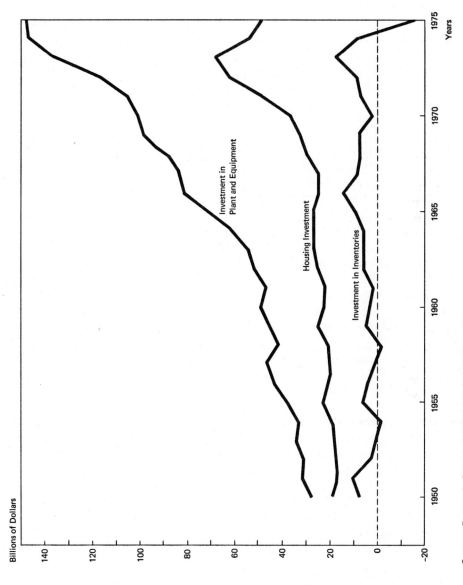

Investment in
Plant and Equipment

Housing Investment

Investment in Inventories

Years

Source: *Economic Report of the President* (1976), p. 181.

investment is rational only if the future income of the firm will be increased by more than the amount of those costs. For example, no firm would invest $100 if that amount would only increase its earnings by $25 in each of the succeeding four years. If, however, the firm could invest $100 and permanently increase its earnings by $25 a year, it would realize a yield of 25 percent on its investment. Such an investment would be the equivalent of buying a $100 bond that paid an interest rate of 25 percent indefinitely. (See *Discounting the Future*, pp. 44–47.)

Some investment opportunities are available that may yield a very high rate of return, such as the automobile industry in 1905 or the computer industry in 1955. Other investments in the economy may yield more modest returns but may still be profitable so long as those returns are greater than the interest rate.

Consider the case of Major Hartburn's chain of fried chicken takeout shops. Assume that the Major holds options to buy three parcels of land— one in the crowded city, one in the more sparsely settled suburbs, and one in the fairly isolated countryside. Market studies show that building a shop in the city will yield 25 percent per year, a shop in the suburbs 15 percent a year, and a shop in the country only 5 percent a year. Assume, too, that there is a single rate of interest (10 percent) at which the firm is able to borrow or lend money. The firm would then be justified in borrowing in order to invest in the city shop yielding 25 percent and in the suburban shop yielding 15 percent. It would not, however, be justified in borrowing in order to invest in the country shop, since the yield of 5 percent would be less than the interest cost of 10 percent. Similarly, if the firm had its own funds available for investment, such funds would be invested in the city shop and the suburban shop, but not in the country shop. The return of 5 percent would be less than the 10 percent the firm could earn by lending out its money at the current interest rate. A very simple rule of investment applies here: If there is a single interest rate at which funds are available in the economy, then a firm should invest in those projects that are expected to yield more than the current rate of interest. It should forego those projects that are expected to yield less than the current rate.

If all firms follow this rule, we can describe an investment function for the economy as a whole. Figure 4–16 shows a downward sloping curve representing the rate of return on all of the potential investments in the economy. The vertical axis measures the rate of return, and the horizontal axis shows the dollar volume of investment that has a yield at least that high. For example, the graph indicates that $10 billion worth of investment has a rate of return at the margin of 20 percent or more, while $30 billion of investment has a rate of return of 10 percent or more.

What will be the actual dollar volume of investment? That depends entirely on the rate of interest. If the rate of interest at which firms lend and borrow is 6 percent, then Figure 4–16 shows that some $42 billion worth of

Figure 4–16   Investment Expenditure as Determined by the Rate of Interest

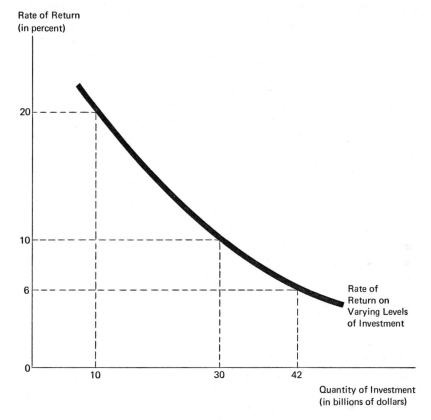

investment will be undertaken. Any investment beyond this will earn less than the 6 percent that it costs to borrow funds.

Note that the curve representing the rate of return on investment can be viewed as a downward sloping demand curve for investment funds. The lower the cost of the funds, as given by the market rate of interest, the more will be borrowed and used for investment purposes.

If the schedule showing the rate of return on investment projects is fairly stable—that is, if the same volume of investment will have the same yield from year to year—then we can use the rate of return schedule to predict the total level of investment demand in the economy. If, however, the rate of return is volatile—that is, subject to rapid shifts depending on economic conditions—then we will have to expand our view of the investment function.

Investment as a Function of the Acceleration of Demand

The accelerator principle holds that investment will be largely governed by the rate of growth of demand. This may seem paradoxical, since it is more natural to imagine that the level of demand—not its rate of change—will influence investment activity. On reflection, however, this paradox can be resolved.

The accelerator theory of investment begins with the notion of a quite rigid relationship between the level of output and the capital stock needed to produce that output. For example, in the computer industry it may take $300 worth of plant and equipment to produce $100 worth of computers every year. That is to say, the capital-output ratio in the computer industry is 3. If the computer industry is, in fact, producing and selling $1 worth of computers for every $3 of capital stock, and if the level of output is stable, then there is no need to increase the capital stock.

In discussing investment, it is important to distinguish between net investment and gross investment. Net investment is that which adds to the size of capital stock. Gross investment is total investment—net investment plus investment to cover depreciation (using up) of the capital stock. When output is stable, the computer industry may engage in some gross investment to cover depreciation, but it need not engage in any net investment. If, however, the level of demand for computers suddenly grows, this will put pressure on the capacity of the industry to produce. It may then be necessary to engage in net investment—to add $3 worth of plant and equipment to the capital stock in order to produce an additional $1 worth of computers. A relatively small percentage increase in the level of output can create the need for an equal percentage increase in the capital stock, but this may represent a much larger increase in the rate of investment.

In order to see the accelerator principle at work, consider the numerical example set out in Table 4–3. Assume that for many years the computer industry has been producing $10 billion worth of computers using a capital stock of $30 billion. Assume further that depreciation amounts to $3 billion every year to replace the $3 billion worth of capital that was bought ten years earlier and is now wearing out. Thus, Table 4–3 shows that for the first three years—in which the level of output is assumed to be stable—a capital stock of $30 billion is used to produce $10 billion worth of goods, and no net investment is required to increase the capital stock. Gross investment,

Table 4–3 Accelerator Principle and Investment in the Computer Industry (all figures in billions of dollars)

Year	Capital Stock	Output	Net Investment	Depre-ciation	Gross Investment
1	$30	$10	$0	$3	$3
2	30	10	0	3	3
3	30	10	0	3	3
4	33	11	$3	3	6
5	36	12	3	3	6
6	36	12	0	3	3

however, is $3 billion, due to the $3 billion worth of depreciation. Assume that in the fourth year the demand for computers increases to $11 billion, so that it becomes necessary for the industry to create the capacity to produce another $1 billion worth of computers. To increase output by 10 percent, it is necessary to increase the capital stock by 10 percent, from $30 billion to $33 billion. This means that net investment must go up from zero to $3 billion, which means that gross investment must go up from the $3 billion required to cover depreciation, to $6 billion. Thus, a 10 percent increase in output elicits a 100 percent increase in the level of gross investment. In the fifth year, the demand for computers may increase by another $1 billion. This will require a capital stock of $36 billion and another $3 billion worth of net investment. Gross investment will again be equal to $6 billion, the $3 billion worth of net investment plus the $3 billion of investment to cover depreciation. Thus a continuing increase in the level of output is required simply to induce a constant level of gross investment. To see this point further, consider what happens in the sixth year, when the level of output stops growing. In order to produce $12 billion worth of computers, we still only need a capital stock of $36 billion; no net investment is now required to attain this level. Gross investment now amounts only to the $3 billion required to cover depreciation. In general, the accelerator theory holds that when the rate of growth of output accelerates, the level of net investment increases; when output stops growing, net investment falls to zero.

Actual investment, of course, does not behave quite so mechanically. In the real world, firms may only gradually adjust the size of the capital stock to a new level of output. For example, producers will not respond to a 10 percent increase in output by increasing the capital stock by 10 percent unless they expect that higher level of output to be fairly permanent. Instead, they may decide simply to work their capital equipment overtime or to increase their backlog of unfilled orders.

Investment as a Function of Internal Funds

In recent years economists have come to feel that the rate of interest is not an adequate measure of the cost of investment to a firm. They argue that many firms act as though it is easier to invest the firm's own money, or internal funds, than to obtain money from outside the firm by borrowing from banks, or by selling bonds or new stock shares to the public. Borrowing may subject the firm to outside control by large creditors, or it may make the firm's financial structure appear fragile. The firm's internal funds come from two sources: money set aside to cover depreciation, and retained earnings. Retained earnings are that portion of the firm's profits that it does not pay out either in taxes to the government or as dividends to the shareholders. If a corporation follows a policy of maintaining its dividend payments at a fairly constant level, then high profits in a particular year will mean a large availability of internal funds. Corporate officers might be much more tempted to undertake investment projects that year than in a year in which internal funds were scarce.

Comparison of Three Approaches

It is possible to adopt a view of the investment function which takes account of all three approaches. For example, we might interpret the accelerator theory to mean that business investments in plant and equipment will have a higher rate of return when demand for output is high or growing—when there is pressure to produce more than the capacity of the existing plant and equipment. We might see firms as responding more favorably to these higher rates of return when the cost of investing seems low—either because interest rates are low or because internal funds are plentiful.

In fact, statistical studies of investment behavior in the United States do find all three influences at work, at least for some categories of business investment. Inventories of unfinished or unsold goods are often accumulated according to an accelerator principle. As we have seen, a leveling off of demand can cause businesses to stop accumulating inventories very abruptly. Manufacturing firms tend to invest more in plant and equipment when capacity is fully utilized and when internal funds are plentiful. Interest rates are especially important in influencing investment decisions by firms, like electric power companies, in which the plant and equipment are expected to last for several decades, so that small differences in interest charges can amount to substantial amounts of money over the years. In addition, private investment in housing responds sharply to the availability and cost of borrowing mortgage money. Each of the three approaches to the investment function, then, can be useful in explaining some forms of investment behavior.

THE DEMAND FOR MONEY

The demand for money describes the level of money balances that the public will choose to hold under varying conditions. It is sometimes tempting to say that the demand for money is unlimited—since just about everybody would like to have some more of it. But at any given time each household owns only a limited amount of wealth. Given its wealth, each household must decide the form in which it wants to hold that wealth. It may wish to hold some portion in the form of money—coins, currency, and checking accounts. (Some definitions of money would also include savings accounts as part of the money supply. See *Money,* pp. 39–43.) But the more of its wealth the household keeps in the form of money, the less it will be able to keep in the form of other assets—such as gold and silver bars, other commodities, real estate, shares of stocks, or bonds issued by government agencies or by corporations. In this context it is meaningless to say that the demand for money is unlimited, since holding money means giving up the opportunity to hold other kinds of assets. For example, a speculator might become firmly convinced that carloads of soybeans or shares of stock in the Hot Shot Rocket Company are going to double in value within a month. As a result, he might virtually empty his checking account to buy soybeans or shares of Hot Shot. The expected high rate of return on other assets would cause him to reduce drastically his demand for money as such.

In thinking about money, we should recognize that, like any other good in the economy, it has both a supply and a demand. The supply is usually determined by government policy in interaction with the banks and the public (see *Money Creation,* pp. 167–72, and *Monetary Policy,* pp. 204–9). At any time, the demand equals the supply, because all the money is held by someone. As with any other good, the supply and demand for money may not be in equilibrium. Some holders of money may feel that under prevailing conditions they are holding too much or too little money in relation to other assets. And, as with any other good, we can describe a schedule of demand for money—the conditions under which varying amounts of money would be demanded.

There is only one supply of money in the economy. For example, in September 1976, the money supply—coins, currency, and demand deposits in the hands of the public—was about $306 billion. Likewise, there is only one total level of demand for money. It is useful to think of that demand as resulting from a balance between two considerations—the reasons for holding money and the costs of holding it.

Reasons for Holding Money

There are two major motives for persons and businesses to hold money rather than other assets—the transactions motive and the precautionary motive.

The transactions motive arises from the need of households and firms to keep on hand enough money to conduct their normal business. Firms must have enough money in the form of cash or checking accounts to pay their suppliers and their workers. Households must have enough money available to buy the groceries and to pay the bills that are expected to come due before the next paycheck comes in. Other things being equal, the strength of the transactions motive for holding money will be closely related to the level of money income in the economy. The more that we are all earning and spending, the greater our need to have the money to spend. Economists have estimated that households and businesses on the average hold enough money to carry them through about four weeks of normal transactions.

Sometimes the economy develops new ways to economize on cash holdings—like the credit card, which enables a large number of persons to draw on the money holdings of a single bank or credit-card company. Such a development may cause a gradual shift in the relationship between the transactions motive and the level of income, so that less money is needed to transact a given level of money demand.

Beyond this there is the precautionary motive—the need to keep money on hand to make unplanned expenditures or to meet uncertain situations. Everyone likes to have a little extra available to be able to make unplanned expenditures—to buy the coat that is on sale at half the normal price, or to pay the doctor for stitching up a cut. In times of great uncertainty—for example, when people fear unemployment or fear inflation in the prices of things on which they cannot stock up—they are likely to increase their demand for money. During the early years of the Great Depression of the 1930s, when hundreds of banks were driven out of business, many depositors engaged in the hoarding of money—withdrawing it from the banks to hold it as cash.

The Cost of Holding Money

However strong the motives for holding money, a person or a business must weigh them against the cost of doing so. For the potential borrower, the interest rate is a real price that must be paid in order to obtain some amount of money. For any holder of money, however, the interest rate represents the *Opportunity Cost* (see pp. 11–17) of holding money, rather than lending it out or using it to buy an asset such as a bond. Consider the alternative of buying a bond, for example, that sells for $1,000 today and that the government will redeem for $1,000 ten years from today. If the bond yields an interest rate of 9 percent, then anyone who is holding $1,000 in money rather than using that money to buy the bond is foregoing the opportunity to earn $90 per year. However, if the interest rate is only 2 percent, the opportunity cost of holding $1,000 in money is much less—only $20 per year.

Speculators—those who attempt to buy at a low price and sell at a high price—will have even more reason to buy bonds (rather than hold money) when interest rates are high. Potential buyers of bonds have to choose between money and bonds not only on the basis of current earnings on bonds but also on anticipated changes in their prices. The government may issue a bond at a price of $1,000, and it may promise to redeem the bond for $1,000 ten years later, but in the meantime the price of the bond is determined entirely by the bond market. And if the government's credit is perfectly good, the current market price for a given bond is determined entirely by the current rate of interest. Consider the case of a bond on which the last interest payment has been made and which can be redeemed in a year for $1,000. If the current interest rate is 1 percent, the market should value that bond at $990.10. (The increase in the value of the bond over one year will be $9.90, or 1 percent of $990.10.) By contrast, if the current interest rate is 10 percent, the market should value that bond at $909.09. (The increase in value over one year will be $90.91, or about 10 percent of $909.09.) The iron rule of the bond market is that when interest rates go up, the prices of existing bonds go down—and vice versa.

This means that if interest rates go abnormally high (say, to 12 percent), prices of existing bonds will be abnormally low. An experienced speculator may expect interest rates to fall and bond prices to rise; accordingly, he may be very interested in using large amounts of his available money to buy bonds at "bargain" prices. Likewise, if interest rates fall abnormally low (say, to 2 percent), prices of existing bonds will rise. This may persuade speculators to avoid buying bonds because of the high risk that they will decline in value between the time of purchase and the time that they are redeemed. Thus money will be a more attractive holding when interest rates are low for two reasons: first, current interest earnings from bonds are not attractive, and second, there is a high risk that interest rates will rise and bonds will decline in market value.

Depicting the Demand for Money

In Figure 4–17 we show how the demand for money may be influenced by both the rate of interest and the level of money income in the economy. Just as the quantity demanded of any good normally increases as the price declines, so that quantity of money demanded will go up as its cost—the interest rate—goes down. But Figure 4–17 also shows that the entire demand curve for money should shift to the right if there is an increase in the level of income (in money terms). Thus, if the level of income is $1,500 billion, the public will want to hold more money at any particular interest rate—like 8 percent—than if the level of income is only $1,000 billion.

The two curves in the figure are drawn on the assumption that the precautionary motive has the same strength in both cases. On the other hand, if the public were to become more cautious—for example, because many workers expected to lose their jobs soon—then the demand curve for money would shift to the right.

Of course, it is not possible to describe the exact shape or location of the

Figure 4-17   The Demand for Money

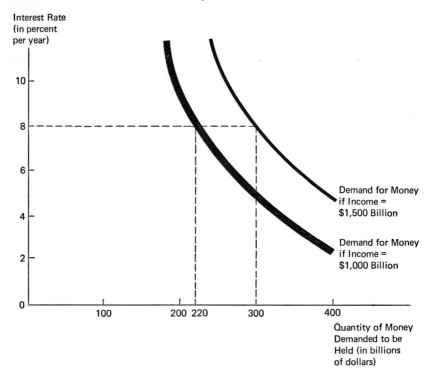

demand-for-money curve, Figure 4-17 is not intended as an actual representation of that curve at any given moment. Nevertheless, dozens of statistical studies have verified that, other things equal, the quantity of money demanded will increase as the rate of interest decreases and as the level of money income in the economy increases.

Obviously, the average working family does not sharply alter its patterns of holding money simply because of small changes in the rate of interest. Keep in mind, however, that most of the money in the economy is not held by such families but rather by wealthy individuals, mutual funds, foundations, trust companies, pension funds, and life insurance companies. For them, small changes in the rate of interest can represent large numbers of dollars. For example, General Motors may have set aside a few million dollars to pay a parts supplier next month. If the interest rate goes high enough, General Motors may decide to put the money into a short-term interest-bearing bond until it is needed to pay the supplier. What began as money held for transactions purposes may become money used (at least temporarily) to purchase a financial asset.

Furthermore, the demand for money is more complicated than has been described. There is not just a single interest rate in the economy, but many interest rates for bonds of varying degrees of risk and dates of maturity. The expected yield on shares of stock—the rates at which they are paying dividends, and whether their prices are expected to rise or fall—will also influence the demand for money. But the simplified view of a demand dependent on the level of money income and on the interest rate can serve us well in understanding some important features of the economy.

The Effects of Inflation

Economists find increasing importance in the distinction between the nominal interest rate and the real interest rate. The nominal interest rate is the rate actually paid; for example, a bond selling for $1,000 may pay $80 a year, representing a nominal interest rate of 8 percent. The real interest rate is one that expresses the real return on lending money by subtracting out the expected future rate of inflation. Assume, for example, that a bond is purchased for $1,000 with the expectation that the general price level will increase next year by 5 percent. That means the real value of the $1,000 is expected to decline over the year by $50. To calculate the real interest rate that will be earned, deduct the $50 from the $80 interest payment. This indicates a real gain of only $30 on the $1,000 bond—or a real interest rate of only 3 percent.

Which interest rate—nominal or real—represents the opportunity cost of holding cash? Clearly, it is the nominal rate. If the market price of the bond stays stable, next year the bond plus the interest earned will total $1,080, while money held idle will still total $1,000. Choosing to buy the bond rather than to hold the money will give the buyer more money next year, whether or not the purchasing power of money sharply declines.

Note, however, that in time of rapid inflation neither cash nor an 8 percent bond represents a very good way to hold wealth. In the 1960s and 1970s, several South American countries experienced persistent rates of inflation of 100 percent or more per year. If the rate of inflation is expected to be 100 percent, then an 80 percent nominal interest rate represents a real interest rate of minus 20 percent. This is a little better than holding money, which can be expected to decline in real value by 100 percent, but it is still no bargain.

If everyone has a common expectation that the rate of inflation will be 100 percent, then the nominal interest rate could adjust. That is to say, bond buyers who hope to earn a real rate of 4 percent might insist on being paid a nominal interest rate of 104 percent. Money would continue to be a very foolish way to try to hold wealth, but 104 percent bonds could be attractive. Thus, the quantity of money demand would be very low.

When rates of inflation get out of hand, financial markets often break down. Government regulations sometimes prevent nominal interest rates from rising to the 104 percent required to maintain positive real rates of return. Other times, buyers and sellers find it impossible to agree on the rate of inflation that should reasonably be expected over the coming year. In either case, nominal interest rates may no longer fully reflect inflationary expectations. The demand for money then may become largely dependent on the inflationary expectations themselves. Economists have done some serious studies of "galloping inflation" or hyperinflation, like that experienced by the Confederate States of America during the Civil War, when so much "Confederate money" was printed. These studies confirm the observation that the more rapid the inflation that people anticipate, the more they are inclined to run from the payroll line to the shops in order to get rid of their money to convert it into some commodity that will maintain its real value. If money is expected to lose its real value by the hour, the demand for money can be brought to a minimum. In the process, the velocity of money—the speed at which it changes hands—rises sharply. (See *Quantity Theory of Money,* pp. 173–76.)

MONEY CREATION

Money creation is the process by which the government and banking system increase the stock of money in the economy. *Money* (see pp. 39–43) does include cash—coins and currency—in the hands of the public, but the largest part consists of <u>demand deposits</u>—funds held by the public in checking accounts. The simplest part of money creation occurs whenever the mints in Denver and Philadelphia stamp strips of metal into coins, and when the Bureau of Printing and Engraving prints sheets of paper into dollar bills. What requires some understanding, however, is the expansion of the total volume of money held in checking accounts. In this process, both private commercial banks and the central bank—the Federal Reserve System—play an active role.

Money creation is not the same thing as "making money." We "make money" whenever we engage in some economic activity that earns wages, salaries, or profits. By contrast, money creation occurs only when there is an addition to the stock of currency or checking accounts within the total economy. A farmer may "make money"—that is, earn income—by discovering oil on his property and selling it to an oil company. In this case, the oil company writes the farmer a check, and the money is transferred from the oil company's account to the farmer's account. Money changes hands; the farmer is richer; but the money supply remains the same. The only private individuals who engage in money creation while making money are counterfeiters—and their activities are strictly illegal.

The Federal Reserve System

Much of the money creation in the U.S. economy results from the actions of the commercial banks and the Federal Reserve System. <u>Commercial banks</u>—those offering checking accounts—are privately owned institutions that accept funds from depositors and earn money by lending out a large portion of those funds. Watching over this process is the Federal Reserve System—a <u>central bank</u>, or a bank for bankers, that was created by the U.S. Congress in 1913. It regulates the availability of money and credit in the economy, both by issuing cash itself—in the form of Federal Reserve notes—and by supervising the actions of several thousand <u>member banks</u>—those that belong to the system. Only about half of the commercial banks in the country actually belong, but all the large ones do—and together member banks account for about 80 percent of the checking account and savings account deposits in the country.

Policy in the system is set by the seven-member board of governors, appointed by the President (subject to confirmation by the Senate) for terms of fourteen years. The system includes a staff and committees directly under the Board of Governors, and twelve Federal Reserve Banks located in each of twelve districts throughout the country.

A Federal Reserve Bank serves a commercial bank in much the same way that a commercial bank serves the public. Just as you may go into your local bank and make a deposit or try to take out a loan, so a member bank may make a deposit or attempt to borrow funds at the Federal Reserve Bank in its district. You can choose to hold your money as cash or in a checking account at your local bank. Likewise, a commercial bank may hold its own funds either in its vault or on deposit with its district Federal Reserve Bank. Either way, these funds constitute the <u>reserves</u> of the commercial bank. These reserves are not counted as part of the nation's money supply—not even the cash in the vault, since it is held by the bank and not the public. But such reserves are like money from the standpoint of the bank, and they can be rapidly converted into a part of the money supply, as when the bank takes cash from its vault and pays it out to a customer who cashes a check.

Money Creation by Commercial Banks

Banks have not always been able to create money. In the Middle Ages primitive banks were merely warehouses for storing money—usually in the form of gold or gold coins—that was brought to the bank for safekeeping and was credited to the account of the depositor. The gold was kept on hand, so that when the depositor requested it, he could obtain the gold that he had deposited—or an equivalent amount of gold that someone else had deposited. Over the years, however, commercial banks have found that in normal times very few depositors ever appear on a particular day to withdraw gold, coins, or currency from their accounts. Thus the banks can meet the normal withdrawal needs of depositors from the funds added by other depositors that day and from a limited supply of cash stored in vaults. This leaves the banks free to make loans or buy bonds with the money on deposit and to earn interest in the process. In the United States today this perfectly valid business practice is ratified by the Federal Reserve System requirement that member banks need to back up their deposits with reserves representing only a fraction of total deposits. Under law this fraction may range from 7 percent to 22 percent, depending on such things as the nature of the bank and the current policy of the Board of Governors of the Federal Reserve System. It is this ability to back up demand deposits with only partial reserves—in cash or on account with the Federal Reserve—that permits the banking system to engage in money creation. Basically, the idea is that if the reserve requirement is 20 percent, then $1 of cash in the vault (or other reserves) can be used by the commercial bank to support $5 in demand deposits. While the $1 in cash held in bank vaults is not counted as part of the money supply, the whole $5 in demand deposits held by the public is part of the money supply.

An Example of Money Creation by the Banks

To see the role of the banks in money creation more clearly, let us examine the accounts of two banks, the First National Bank and the Second National

Bank. Assume that these two banks are the only banks in a particular city, so that most people in the city have accounts in one or the other. Following the conventions of the accounting profession, we shall draw up balance sheets showing both the <u>assets</u> of the bank (everything the bank owns, or its claims against others) and its <u>liabilities</u> (the claims of others against the bank). To begin the process, assume that a realtor in town has $500 of cash that she decides to deposit in the First National Bank. The bank records this in two ways. It shows the asset it has acquired—the $500 in cash—in the asset column. It also records the realtor's checking account—a demand deposit of $500—in the liabilities column, since this is money owed to her. The bank now has reserves amounting to 100 percent of its demand deposits. Only $100 of the cash represents <u>required reserves</u>, those legally needed to support deposits; $400 represents <u>excess reserves</u>, the excess of actual reserves over required reserves, and can be used to earn interest.

First National Bank

Assets		Liabilities	
Cash reserves	$500	Demand deposits:	
		Realtor	$500

Assume next that a storekeeper in town comes along and wants to borrow $400 to buy a used car. The First National Bank makes the loan, drawing down its cash assets from $500 to $100, but acquiring a new asset—the promise of the storekeeper to repay the loan—which it lists as an "outstanding loan" of $400. (In working out this example, we ignore the interest payments the storekeeper would eventually have to make on the loan.) The storekeeper takes the $400 to a used-car dealer and buys the car, and the dealer deposits the money in his account in the Second National Bank. Thus, the Second National Bank acquires an asset of $400 in cash and incurs a liability of $400, represented by the checking account of the used-car dealer.

First National Bank

Assets		Liabilities	
Cash reserves	$100	Demand deposits:	
Loan outstanding:		Realtor	$500
Storekeeper	$400		

Second National Bank

Assets		Liabilities	
Cash reserves	$400	Demand deposits:	
		Car Dealer	$400

What has happened as a result of these perfectly straightforward transactions? We began with the $500 that the realtor had carried around in her purse. As a result of her deposit, the loan to the storekeeper, and the deposit by the used-car dealer, the money supply now equals $900:$500 in demand deposits at the First National Bank and $400 in deposits at the Second National Bank. (None of the cash is now counted as part of the money supply, since it is held in the vaults of the two banks rather than by the public.)

Now let us assume that a housewife comes along and wants to borrow $320 to buy a hi-fi set. She goes to the First National Bank first, but they turn her down because they have no excess reserves (those in excess of legal requirements) that they can lend her. She then goes to the Second National Bank, and they are happy to make her the loan. They have $400 in cash, but they need only $80 to support their demand deposits of $400. The housewife takes the $320 to an appliance store in town, buys the hi-fi, and gives the appliance dealer the $320; he in turn deposits the $320 in his account at the First National Bank. The balance sheets of the two banks are both altered by these new transactions. In the case of the Second National Bank, the assets of $400 in cash have now been replaced with only $80 in cash and $320 in the loan outstanding to the housewife. In the case of the First National Bank, the amount of cash on hand has gone up from $100 to $420, and the additional cash of $320 from the appliance dealer is balanced by an additional liability of the $320 in his checking account.

First National Bank

Assets		Liabilities	
Cash reserves	$420	Demand deposits:	
Loans outstanding:		Realtor	$500
Storekeeper	$400	Appliance dealer	$320
	$820		$820

Second National Bank

Assets		Liabilities	
Cash reserves	$ 80	Demand deposits:	
Loans outstanding:		Car dealer	$400
Housewife	$320		
	$400		$400

Thus, the money supply accounted for by the two banks consists of $820 in the demand deposits at the First National Bank and $400 in the demand deposit of the Second National Bank, for a total of $1,220. As a result of only two loan transactions and subsequent deposits, the money supply has expanded from $500 in cash to $1,220 in demand deposits. Furthermore, since the First National Bank now has on hand more cash ($420) than the $164 it is legally required to hold as reserves to support its demand deposits ($820 ÷ 5 = $164), it is now in a position to make additional loans.

The process of money creation can continue through many steps, but it cannot continue indefinitely. Some of the money that the banks lend out may not be returned to the banking system but may be held by the public as cash. Some banks may not lend out all of their available funds—either because they want to hold excess reserves or because they cannot find customers interested in borrowing. But even if the whole $500 in cash is used by the banks as reserves to back up new demand deposits, a 20 percent reserve requirement means that $500 in cash reserves can ultimately support no more than $2,500 of demand deposits ($500 = 20 percent of $2,500).

Expansion Potential of the System

We have seen how a 20 percent reserve requirement permits the banking system to take $1 in bank reserves (cash or deposits with the Federal Reserve Bank) and expand it to support $5 in demand deposits. Note, however, that there is nothing automatic about this process. Banks are not required to lend out the full amount of their reserves in excess of the legal requirement. It may prove profitable for the banks to do so if interest rates are high and if credit-worthy borrowers can be found. But if businesses and individuals are not interested in spending more money and in borrowing to obtain it, the process of money creation will stop cold.

Note, too, that the process of expansion of $1 in cash to $5 in demand deposits assumes that the cash is always returned to the banking system, so that it continues to serve as bank reserves. In the process of money expansion, the housewife who took out the bank loan or the appliance dealer to whom she paid the money might have decided to hold that money in the form of cash. If so, the chain of expansion would have abruptly stopped. Likewise, the realtor who made the initial bank deposit might suddenly decide that she would prefer to hold her money as cash in a sugar bowl rather than in a checking account. The banking system would then lose all the reserves that permitted it to expand demand deposits and, if it had no excess reserves, would be forced to contract the money supply.

Thus, while the system has the potential to expand the money supply to five times the amount of any new reserves, there is nothing to guarantee that this expansion will actually take place. Likewise, the loss of reserves can force the system to contract the money supply by five times the loss.

Money Creation by the Federal Reserve System

The Federal Reserve System itself also has the power to create money, and it need not worry about whether it has enough reserves. Put simply, the system can buy assets that are not money (bonds) and provide money in exchange. For example, the FRS may buy government bonds from the U.S. Treasury Department. In return, the Federal Reserve may increase the Treasury's checking account at a Federal Reserve Bank, or it may exercise its right to print money and provide the Treasury with $1,000 in crisp new Federal Reserve Notes. (Students are often surprised to see how many of the dollar bills they are carrying turn out to be Federal Reserve Notes.) Either way, the government can spend the new money and put it into circulation in the economy.

The Federal Reserve may also buy U.S. bonds from a private individual—a dealer in bonds for example. It will pay the dealer with a check drawn on the particular Federal Reserve Bank that receives the bonds. The bond dealer will then deposit the check in his own commercial bank account and have "money in the bank" rather than bonds. He will then be able to use that money for his own consumption or to purchase the bonds of private corporations—thus helping to finance new investment expenditure in the economy. Federal Reserve purchases and sales of bonds—known as open market operations—are an important instrument of *Monetary Policy* (see pages 204–9).

QUANTITY THEORY OF MONEY

The quantity theory of money takes two forms. On the one hand, it provides an <u>analytical framework</u> for macroeconomics—an equation saying that the quantity of money times its average velocity equals the quantity of output times its average price. On the other hand, it offers a <u>theoretical statement</u> about macroeconomic behavior—that there is a direct and proportional relationship between the quantity of money and the price level. Both forms require further explanation.

Analytical Framework

The quantity theory equation relates four variables in the economy:

M = The stock of money
V = the velocity of money, or the number of times per year that the average dollar turns over in the purchase of final goods
P = the price of the average final good
Q = the quantity of real output, or the number of final goods produced in the economy

The basic statement of the quantity theory is a straightforward equation

$$M \times V = P \times Q$$

which says that the stock of money times its velocity equals the average price of final goods times the quantity of such goods. Note that $P \times Q$ is the dollar level of income or expenditure in the economy—what we have been calling Y or E in this chapter.

The quantity theory equation is a definitional statement. In actual practice, we do not directly observe velocity, or V. We obtain direct measures for the money supply, M, and the dollar volume of final sales, $P \times Q$. We use these measures to define velocity:

$$V = \frac{P \times Q}{M}$$

Thus, if we knew that there were final transactions of $600 billion and a money stock of $200 billion, we could calculate the velocity:

$$V = \frac{\$600 \text{ billion}}{\$200 \text{ billion}} = 3$$

Note the logic of the basic equation. On the left-hand side is money times velocity ($M \times V$), which equals the annual dollar volume of final purchases in the economy. For example, if a money stock of $200 billion turns over an average of three times, this means that money has been used to make $600 billion worth of final purchases. On the right-hand side of the equation is final goods times price ($P \times Q$), which equals the annual dollar volume of final sales. For example, if 100 billion final goods were sold at an average price of $6, this means that these sales have totaled $600 billion. One person's purchases are another person's sales, and the two values must always be equal.

$$\$200 \text{ billion} \times 3 = \$6 \times 100 \text{ billion}$$
$$\$600 \text{ billion} = \$600 \text{ billion}$$

Because the quantity theory equation is definitional, it is meaningless to ask whether it is correct or not. It is true by definition because we define V so as to make it true.

The real question is whether the quantity theory equation is useful as an analytical framework. Does it isolate the macroeconomic variables that are important to look at? Both classical and modern quantity theorists would answer emphatically yes. They both use the analytical framework of the equation to make empirical statements about the behavior of the economy.

Theoretical Statement

The classical quantity theory was widely advocated in the late nineteenth and early twentieth centuries, most notably by English economists at Cambridge University and by Irving Fisher of Yale. The classical theorists made three important behavioral assumptions about V, P, and Q, respectively, while treating the money supply, M, as a policy variable under the direct control of the government.

First, they assumed that velocity, V, was relatively constant in the short run, determined by the banking institutions and payments patterns of the economy. Money was assumed to have no value as such, so that it would be irrational to hold money—rather than put it to work earning interest or profits—any longer than necessary to meet the demands of normal transactions. Velocity might drift upward or downward over time as habits or technology changed; for example, more efficient communications and transportation might permit faster payments on checks and hence cause velocity to gradually accelerate. But velocity was believed to be independent of short-run changes in the quantity of money or in economic conditions.

Second, the classical quantity theorists assumed that prices and wages in the economy were fully flexible, responding rapidly to short-run changes in supply and demand.

Third, the quantity theorists assumed that the quantity of real output, Q, was determined entirely independently of monetary considerations. They saw flexible prices and wages as assuring full employment—a labor market equilibrium in which the supply of labor just equaled the demand for labor. Labor productivity—as determined by the stock of capital and resources and by the level of technology—indicated how much real output the fully employed labor force would produce.

These three behavioral assumptions combined to dictate a simple, logical conclusion. If V and Q are both assumed to be fixed in the short run, while P is flexible, then any change in M will be accompanied by an equal percentage change in P. For example, assume that the initial money supply is \$200 billion, velocity is fixed at 3, and the fully employed labor force can produce 100 billion goods selling at an average price of \$6. If the money supply goes up by 50 percent to \$300 billion, then prices must also go up by 50 percent, from \$6 to \$9. The equations would be:

Quantity theory equation: $M \times V = P \times Q.$
Before monetary expansion: \$200 billion $\times$ 3 = \$6 $\times$ 100 billion.
After monetary expansion: \$300 billion $\times$ 3 = \$9 $\times$ 100 billion.

Thus the theory indicates that expansion or contraction of the money supply will have no effect on real output or employment. The only effect will be an expansion or contraction of the price level in the same proportion. Fisher asserted confidently that it was "nothing less than a scandal in Economic Science that there should be any ground for dispute on so fundamental a proposition."

Hence, inflation has only one cause—monetary expansion; deflation has only one cause—monetary contraction. Neither has any influence on real output or employment.

More Recent Developments

The onset of the Great Depression undercut much of the credibility of the quantity theory. Between 1929 and 1933 the U.S. money supply fell by 26 percent and the price level by 31 percent. While these figures alone might seem to be fairly close to the quantity theory prediction, the velocity of money was not constant; it declined by 27 percent. Likewise, the level of real output was not constant at the full employment level; it declined by 22 percent, and millions of men and women were thrown out of work.

Consequently, changes in money could no longer be seen as the only cause of changes in total purchases and sales, since velocity could swiftly change with changing economic conditions. Also, the optimistic assumptions concerning employment and the simplistic conclusions concerning inflation were both untenable in the face of the sharp departure of output from its full employment level.

From 1936 onward, the ideas of English economist John Maynard Keynes came gradually to replace those of the classical theorists as the dominant force in macroeconomic thinking. Keynes argued that real output, as well as prices, could respond to changes in demand when workers and other resources were not fully employed. He also argued that people did sometimes hold money for its own sake as a hedge against uncertain economic conditions. He concluded that the velocity of money could vary in the short run as people chose to hold more or less money idle. For example, if interest rates were high, it would be costly not to put money to work earning interest, and velocity would be high. If interest rates were low, there would be little cost in holding money idle, and velocity would be low.

Put another way, we can see the original quantity theory as based on a limited view of the *Demand for Money* (see pp. 161–66). Velocity will be constant in the short run if individuals and businesses have only one motive for holding money—the transactions motive—and if there are no changes in the cost of holding money. Then the need to hold money would go up directly with the volume of transactions and income in the economy. In our discussion of the demand for money, however, we have recognized another motive—the precautionary motive—for holding money. We have also recognized that the rate of interest—or the expected rate of inflation, if it is larger—is an important cost of holding money. Changes in these variables can all affect the demand for money. Hence, they can also affect velocity, since it is merely the ratio of the volume of final transactions to the stock of money. (For some examples of how velocity might change, see *Equilibrium Income with Money*, pp. 210–17.)

Even Keynes allowed, however, that the quantity theory might roughly describe the impact of monetary expansion in the long run, over which differences in unemployment of resources and precautionary holdings of money might average out.

Since the 1950s the American economist, Milton Friedman, has spearheaded the movement known as *Monetarism* (see pp. 218–23) in a revival of interest in the quantity theory. While Friedman reaffirms the usefulness of the analytical framework, he does not insist on the universal validity of all its empirical assumptions or conclusions. For instance, Friedman acknowledges that the quantity of real output, as well as prices, may be affected by changes in total purchases ($M \times V$). He also recognizes that velocity is not a short-run constant, but he argues that it is a stable function of other variables, including interest rates and the expected rate of inflation. If, for example, holders of money expect rapid inflation—so that the value of money will deteriorate noticeably in a few weeks or days—they will try to pass it on like a "hot potato," and the velocity of money will be high. In this form the quantity theory has proven useful in explaining several historical cases of very rapid price increases, or hyperinflation.

5

Macroeconomic Policy

National governments have three major goals of macroeconomic policy—low rates of unemployment, low rates of inflation, and high rates of economic growth. They attempt to advance these goals primarily by using fiscal and monetary policy to influence the level and composition of aggregate demand.

In the discussion of **Equilibrium Income with Government** our model of aggregate demand is extended to include the role of government expenditure and taxation. **Fiscal Policy** is the use of the government budget to help regulate the level of aggregate demand. Government attempts this through discretionary fiscal policy, which consists of deliberate changes in tax rates or expenditure programs. By contrast, **Built-in Stabilizers** include the automatic responses of tax collections and expenditure levels that help to offset changes in aggregate demand. **Monetary Policy** refers to government efforts to change the size of the money supply or the terms at which credit is available in the economy. In our discussion of **Equilibrium Income with**

Money, we finally extend our model of aggregate demand to include an active role for money. This enables us to obtain a richer perspective on the impact on the economy of changes in both fiscal policy and monetary policy.

The school of macroeconomics known as **Monetarism** stresses the effectiveness of monetary policy. Our discussion of this concept considers some of the differences between monetarists and those economists who stress the effectiveness of fiscal policy in regulating aggregate demand.

Fiscal policy determines whether the **Public Debt** is increased or decreased; monetary policy helps determine whether that debt is held by the public or by government agencies. Establishing a long-run framework for fiscal, monetary, and other policies to reduce unemployment is known as **Planning for Full Employment**.

EQUILIBRIUM INCOME WITH GOVERNMENT

Equilibrium Income (see pp. 125–34) is that level at which aggregate demand just tends to perpetuate itself. By including government in our model of the economy, we are able to see the role of government expenditures and taxes in determining equilibrium income.

As in our earlier models of the economy (without government), we make certain simplifying assumptions: (1) that the level of aggregate demand is lower than the capacity of the economy to produce, (2) that saving and investment decisions are made independently of one another, and (3) that the money supply responds passively to the forces of aggregate demand, (4) that the role of foreign trade can be ignored, and (5) that the amount of investment is independent of the level of income and the size of the capital stock. When we introduce government, a sixth assumption must be added—that government taxation and expenditure decisions are made independently of one another. This means that there is no automatic tendency to spend more when tax revenues are high and no tendency to tax more heavily when government expenditures are high. Such an assumption will be more realistic for the U.S. federal government than for state and local governments, since the federal government has more legal flexibility to run surpluses and deficits than do many states and municipalities.

With government in the model, our assumption concerning money implies that the government finances any deficit by creating money (for example, by printing it) and responds to any surplus by retiring some money from circulation. This ignores the very real possibility that government will cover a deficit by borrowing from the public or use a surplus to retire some of its debt (see, for example, *Monetary Policy,* pp. 204–9, and *Monetarism,* pp. 218–23).

Equilibrium Viewed from the Expenditure Side

Equilibrium income with government included can again be defined (see pp. 125–26) as that level of income that gives rise to an equal level of expenditure, so that the planned expenditure (E) equals the level of income (Y):

$$E = Y$$

When we include government, however, we arrive at a more complete definition of the ways in which expenditures are made and income is allocated.

Thus, there are three kinds of expenditures in the economy that serve as the sources of income. They include not only private consumption (C) and private investment (I) but also government purchases of commodities and services (G). The expenditure equation then becomes:

$$E = C + I + G$$

Graphs may also be used to describe the equilibrium level of income with government included. Figure 5–1 shows the different levels of expenditure that would arise at different income levels. The consumption line (C) slopes upward, showing that households will consume more as their incomes rise. We assume that investment is constant at $500 billion regardless of the level of income, and we show the consumption plus investment line (C + I) as being above the consumption line by a uniform distance of $500 billion. Here we also assume that government expenditure is constant at $300 billion. This is represented by showing the line for consumption plus investment plus government (C + I + G) as being above the C + I line by a uniform distance of $300 billion.

   The requirement for equilibrium is that expenditure equals income. In

Figure 5–1   **Total Expenditure at Various Levels of Income**

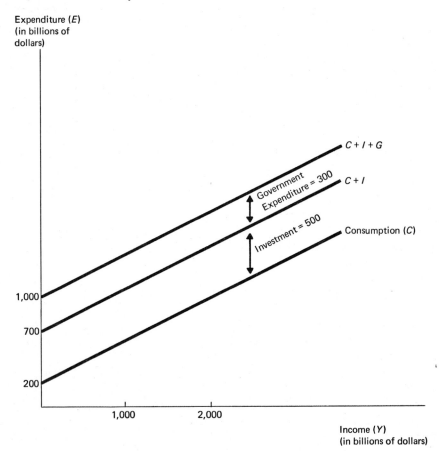

Figure 5–2   Equilibrium Where Total Expenditure Equals Total Income

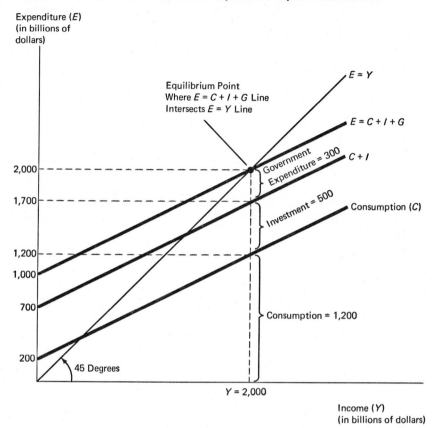

Figure 5–2 all the possible points meeting this requirement are traced out by the $E = Y$ line, the diagonal line coming out of the origin at a slope of 45°. The intersection of the $E = Y$ line with the $C + I + G$ line is the only point at which total expenditure equals the income that gave rise to that expenditure. The intersection indicates an equilibrium income of $2,000 billion and an equal level of expenditure—consisting of consumption of $1,200 billion, investment of $500 billion, and government expenditure of $300 billion.

Looking at income determination with government purely from the expenditure side can—within the overall limitations of the model—give us accurate results. It does, however, tend to disguise the role of one important variable—taxation. In Figures 5–1 and 5–2 the consumption line will be lower if the government is taxing incomes more, since households will have less money at their disposal to spend. Likewise, the consumption line will be higher if the government is taxing less, since households will have more money at their disposal. But rather than represent taxes indirectly, it is often more useful to show explicitly how taxation helps determine the equilibrium level of income.

Transfer Payments and Net Taxes

When we turn to models that explicitly include taxes, it becomes helpful to separate out two kinds of governmental outlays. The symbol G represents final expenditures made by the government for its purposes—that is, all of the actual purchases of goods and services. Expenditures on aircraft carriers, agricultural research, highway construction, and the salaries of government workers would all fall within this broad category. In addition, however, the government lays out large sums for what are called transfer payments—payments that are not made for goods or services currently provided to the government. Transfer payments include Social Security checks, veterans' bonuses, welfare payments, pensions to retired government workers, and unemployment compensation payments. The money is paid out by the government but used to purchase goods and services by the recipients of the transfer payment. By paying out a $450 Social Security check to a retired couple, the government does not itself use $450 in economic resources. Rather, the $450 is spent by the couple themselves for food, clothing, rent and electricity—all of which constitute private consumption. By contrast, if the government pays $450 to a Pentagon file clerk, a real economic resource has been used for a governmental purpose; the labor services of the clerk have been used to keep order in the files of the Pentagon.

Transfer payments do not bring economic resources into the government sector; they increase the ability of private individuals to command more resources. In this sense they are exactly the opposite of taxes paid to the government, which reduce the ability of the payers to command resources. The retired couple may own so many shares of stock that they have to pay $450 a month in income taxes on their dividends. In this case, the government gives with one hand (the Social Security Administration) and takes away with the other (the Internal Revenue Service). The Social Security payments operate like negative taxes—in this case just offsetting the $450 in income taxes the couple must pay.

When we introduce taxes into our analysis of equilibrium income, it is useful to refer to net taxes (T) rather than gross taxes. Gross taxes would be all of the revenues and fees collected by the government. Net taxes would be those same taxes less the transfer payments made by the government.

Equilibrium With Taxation Made Explicit

Equilibrium level of income can be viewed another way. In models that exclude government, equilibrium income occurs where planned saving equals planned investment. That is to say, there is equilibrium where savers wish to take out of the circular flow of aggregate demand the same amount that investors wish to add to that flow. In models that include government, we must also consider that net taxes represent funds removed from the circular flow, while government expenditure represents funds added to that flow.

We now have an expenditure equation that includes government purchases (G):

$$E = C + I + G$$

We also must recognize that households earning income allocate some of that income to net taxes (T) as well as to consumption (C) and saving (S). The income equation then becomes:

$$Y = C + S + T$$

Since equilibrium requires that planned expenditure equal income ($E = Y$), we may set the terms of the income equation equal to the terms of the expenditure equation:

$$C + S + T = C + I + G$$

Since consumption appears on both sides of this equation, we may subtract C from both sides and obtain:

$$S + T = I + G$$

Thus, income is in equilibrium when it gives rise to a total of saving (S) and net taxes (T) that is just equal to the total of investment (I) and government expenditure (G).

Figure 5–3 shows how the total of saving and net taxes is related to consumption expenditure. In the top part of the figure we show the same consumption line as in Figures 5–1 and 5–2 along with the 45° line ($E = Y$) showing the points at which expenditure (measured vertically) equals income (measured horizontally). The 45° line is useful in providing us with a vertical measure of income. That is to say, at any point on the line (like point A), income may be represented either as the horizontal distance of the point from the vertical axis or as the vertical distance of the point from the horizontal axis. It follows that for any income level the vertical distance between the 45° line and the consumption line represents the difference between income and consumption. Since income can be allocated to one of three uses—consumption, net taxes, or saving—the difference between income and consumption must be the sum of saving and net taxes. Thus the top of Figure 5–3 shows that an income (Y) of $1,500 billion would generate

Figure 5–3   Relationship of Saving and Taxes to Consumption

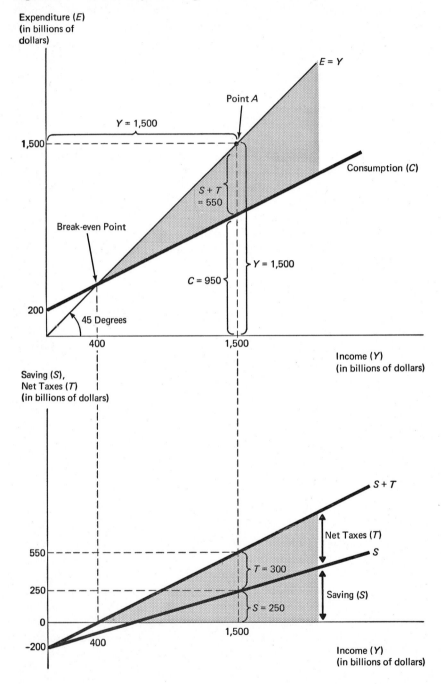

consumption (C) of $950 billion, leaving $550 billion for the sum of saving and net taxes (S + T). The bottom part of Figure 5–3 shows how the sum would be broken down at each income level; at an income level of $1,500 billion, there would be $250 billion saved and $300 billion paid in net taxes.

As a point of departure in looking at Figure 5–3, consider the "break-even point" at which consumption just equals income, which implies that the sum of saving and net taxes is zero. This is represented in the top half of the figure by the intersection of the consumption line (C) with the 45° line at an income level of $400 billion. In the bottom part of the figure it is represented by the point at which the S + T line intersects the horizontal axis, indicating a zero level for saving plus net taxes. At levels of income below $400 billion, the consumption line at the top of the figure is above the 45° line, indicating that consumption is greater than income. This means that "dissaving" is occurring, as households live off their accumulated wealth and their transfer payments. It is represented at the bottom of the figure by an S + T line that is below the horizontal axis, indicating a negative total for saving and net taxes. At levels of income above $400 billion, the consumption line is below the 45° line, indicating that income is greater than consumption, so that some of it is being devoted to saving and net taxes. In the bottom part of the figure, this is reflected in an S + T line that is above the horizontal axis, indicating positive amounts of saving plus net taxes.

We have seen above that the equilibrium income level will be at that level at which the sum of saving (S) and net taxes (T) equals the sum of investment (I) and government expenditure (G). Figure 9–4 adds to the S and the

Figure 5–4 **Equilibrium Where Investment plus Government Expenditure Equals Savings plus Taxes**

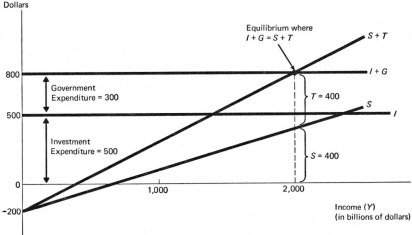

$S + T$ lines (like those at the bottom of Figure 5–3) two horizontal lines representing the two expenditure categories, I and G.

The I line represents investment expenditure, assumed here to be at the same level ($500 billion) regardless of the level of income. If government expenditure is also assumed to be independent of the level of income, then the $G + I$ line—representing the sum of government and investment expenditures—is a uniform distance ($300 billion) above the I line. That distance, of course, represents the level of government expenditures.

Equilibrium is indicated by the intersection of the $S + T$ line with the $I + G$ line. It is at this point that withdrawals from the expenditure stream (in the forms of saving and net taxation) just equal the additions to the expenditure stream (in the forms of investment and government expenditure). Figure 5–4 shows equilibrium at an income level of $2,000 billion and indicates (with brackets) the equilibrium levels of saving ($400 billion) and taxes ($400 billion). Note that in Figure 5–4 the government runs a surplus when income is at equilibrium. That is to say, net taxes of $400 billion are greater than government expenditures of $300 billion by an amount of $100 billion. At the same time, within the private sector, investment of $500 billion is greater than saving of $400 billion by an equal amount. The government is taking $100 billion more out of the expenditure stream than it is adding to it, but the private sector is adding $100 billion more to the expenditure stream than it is taking out.

This reflects a general condition in macroeconomics, which we can see in the equation expressing the equilibrium condition:

$$S + T = I + G$$

By subtracting G from both sides of the equation, and then S from both sides of the equation, we have:

$$T - G = I - S$$

This says that if the government is running a surplus ($T - G$ is positive), then private investment must always be greater than private saving by the amount of the surplus. The private sector must be adding to the expenditure stream as much as the government sector is taking out. Likewise, if the government is running a deficit, the situation could be expressed by multiplying every term in our equation by -1. Thus, we would have:

$$G - T = S - I$$

This says that if the government is running a deficit ($G - T$ is positive), then private saving must always exceed private investment by the amount of the deficit. What the public sector adds to the expenditure stream (through a deficit), the private sector must be taking out (through saving in excess of investment).

Implications

The foregoing analysis suggests that a large government has several powerful tools with which to influence aggregate demand and the level of equilibrium income. For example, it can stimulate consumption demand by reducing net taxes—either by increasing transfer payments or lowering tax rates. It can also stimulate demand directly by increasing the level of its own expenditures. These possibilities are explored further in the discussions of *Fiscal Policy* (see pp. 188–97) and *Built-in Stabilizers* (see pp. 198–203). Our discussions of *Monetary Policy* (see pp. 204–9) and *Monetarism* (see pp. 218–23) also explore some of the implications of introducing an active role for money.

FISCAL POLICY

Fiscal policy is the use of the government budget—tax rates and levels of expenditure—to promote full employment and control inflation by regulating the level of demand in the economy. An expansionary fiscal policy consists of some combination of lower tax rates, larger transfer payments, and increased government expenditures to stimulate the growth of aggregate demand and thereby to reduce unemployment. A restrictive fiscal policy consists of some combination of increased tax rates, smaller transfer payments, or reduced government expenditures to curtail the growth of aggregate demand and thereby to curb inflation.

Of course, budgetary policy also serves to allocate resources between the government and private sectors. Increased government expenditure and taxation will draw more resources into the government sector, while reduced government expenditure and taxation will permit more resources to be used for consumption and investment in the private sector. Here we will be primarily concerned, however, with the impact of the government budget on the level of aggregate demand.

The Impact of Fiscal Policy

To illustrate the role of fiscal policy, consider an economy in which current equilibrium income is substantially less than full employment income. Using the tools developed in the discussions of *Equilibrium Income* (see pp. 125–34), and *Equilibrium Income with Government* (see pp. 179–87), we can depict such an economy in Figure 5–5. Equilibrium income occurs where the sum of the withdrawals from the expenditure stream—saving (S) and net taxes (T)—equals the sum of the additions to the expenditure stream—investment (I) and government expenditure (G). Thus the intersection of the upward sloping $S + T$ line with the horizontal $I + G$ line indicates an equilibrium income of $875 billion, which is substantially short of the full employment level of $1,250 billion. The economy must generate considerably more aggregate demand if the full employment level of income is to be reached.

The government has two basic strategies of fiscal policy available: (1) It can seek to increase consumption expenditures by reducing net taxes (T)—that is, by reducing tax rates or by increasing the level of transfer payments to households; or (2) it can increase government expenditures on goods and services (G). Each of these strategies will be described.

Figure 5–6 shows an initial equilibrium level of income at $875 billion also, as determined by the intersection of the $S + T_0$ line with the $I + G$ line. Then a reduction in net taxes is introduced—reflecting either a reduction in tax rates or an increase in transfer payments. This pushes the total of saving and net taxes down to the levels shown by the $S + T_1$ line. The new $S + T$ line intersects the $I + G$ line at the full employment income level, $1,250

Figure 5–5   Equilibrium Income at Less than Full Employment

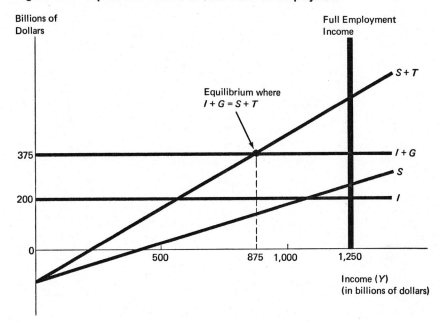

Figure 5–6   Effect of a Tax Cut on Equilibrium Income

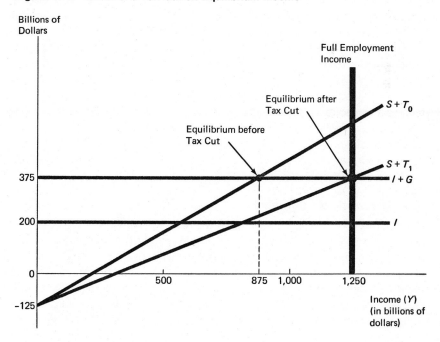

Figure 5–7   Effect of Increased Government Expenditure on Equilibrium Income

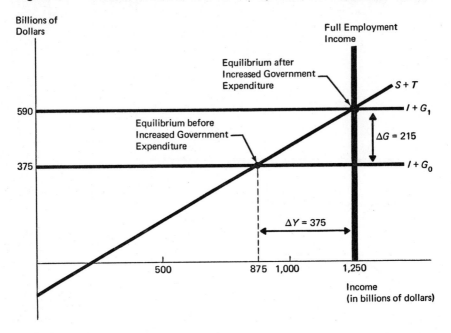

billion. Thus, reductions in net taxes can succeed in stimulating private consumption—and hence aggregate demand—enough to raise equilibrium income to the full employment level.

The alternative strategy is to move to full employment by increasing government expenditures. Figure 5–7 also begins with an equilibrium level of income of $875 billion, as given by the intersection of the $S + T$ line with the $I + G_0$ line. Then an increase in government expenditure (ΔG) of $215 billion is introduced, raising the total of investment and government expenditure to the line $I + G_1$. This line intersects the $S + T$ line at the full employment income level of $1,250 billion. Thus, the increased government expenditure can also succeed in increasing aggregate demand enough to raise equilibrium income to the full employment level.

The Government Multiplier

Figure 5–7 is useful in indicating how much equilibrium income has increased in response to an increase in government expenditure. In the process we can obtain an expression for an equilibrium multiplier for government expenditure corresponding to the equilibrium *Investment Multiplier* (see pp. 135–43). Note from the figure that, as we move from one equilibrium income to another, the change in government expenditure (ΔG) must be matched by an equal change in the sum of saving and net taxes

($\Delta S + \Delta T$). Thus, we have:

$$\Delta G = \Delta S + \Delta T$$

We are interested in an expression for the government multiplier, which is the ratio of a change in income to the change in government expenditure ($\Delta Y \div \Delta G$).

To obtain this, we must divide ΔY by both sides of our equation:

$$\frac{\Delta Y}{\Delta G} = \frac{\Delta Y}{\Delta S + \Delta T}$$

The right-hand side of this equation can be simplified if we divide all terms in it by ΔY, giving us

$$\frac{\Delta Y}{\Delta G} = \frac{1}{\dfrac{\Delta S}{\Delta Y} + \dfrac{\Delta T}{\Delta Y}}$$

The term $\Delta S \div \Delta Y$ is the ratio of the change in saving to the change in income, or the marginal propensity to save (MPS). (See *Propensity to Consume,* especially pp. 121–22). Similarly, the term $\Delta T \div \Delta Y$—the ratio of the change in taxes to the change in income—may be referred to as the marginal propensity to pay taxes (MPT). The government equilibrium multiplier can now be expressed as:

$$\text{Equilibrium multiplier} = \frac{\Delta Y}{\Delta G} = \frac{1}{\text{MPS} + \text{MPT}}$$

In a model of the economy without government we derived an *Investment Multiplier* (see pp. 135–43) of $1 \div \text{MPS}$. Note that in a model of the economy that includes government, this value for the multiplier would no longer hold; rather, the equilibrium multiplier described above would apply to changes in investment expenditure as well as to changes in government expenditure. This is because such changes would affect the $I + G$ line in exactly the same way. Note, too, that the equilibrium multiplier is considerably smaller in a model that includes government than in one that does not. By including the marginal propensity to pay taxes (MPT) as well as the marginal propensity to save (MPS), the size of the denominator has increased, thus reducing the value of the multiplier ratio. The logic of this is easily seen. The multiplier has a value larger than 1 only because of the additional consumption that occurs when increased investment or government expenditure raises income levels. When it is recognized that much of additional income must be paid out in taxes rather than for consumption, our estimate of the multiplier is necessarily lowered. The role of the equilibrium multiplier is considered further in our discussion of *Built-in Stabilizers* (see pp. 200–202).

Like our earlier discussion of the investment multiplier, this discussion of the government multiplier implies that the money supply fully expands to meet the indicated increase in aggregate demand. In our discussion of *Equilibrium Income with Money* (see especially pp. 215–17), we show how—if the money supply does not expand in this way—the stimulating effect of increased government expenditure may be partially offset by declines in other categories of expenditure, notably investment.

The Role of the Deficit

Fiscal actions to increase or retard the growth of aggregate demand are most effective if they are undertaken without regard to the balance in the government's budget. For example, if the government spends $10 billion more to help restore full employment, this can raise equilibrium income by considerably more than $10 billion. If, however, the government at the same time increases taxes by $10 billion in order to avoid running a deficit, much of the expansionary impact of the expenditure will be lost. The expenditure increase will raise the government component of total expenditure by $10 billion, but the tax increase will reduce the consumption component by nearly as much.

Consider a case in which households consume 80 percent of any additional income they receive. This is another way of saying that the marginal propensity to consume (MPC) is 80 percent. Then the tax increase of $10 billion will cause consumption to be reduced by $8 billion—while the remaining $2 billion will be reflected in reduced saving and tax payments. In general, expenditure increases will stimulate the economy more when they are not accompanied by increases in taxes or reductions in transfer payments. Likewise, increases in transfer payments or reductions in taxes will provide more stimulation when they are not accompanied by reductions in government expenditures.

Doctrines of the Deficit

A balanced government budget would be one in which government expenditures and transfer payments were just equal to taxes. There are differing points of view as to whether a budget in balance—or in surplus—should be a goal of fiscal policy. For many years economists and statesmen alike proclaimed the importance of balancing the budget every year. In the midst of the Great Depression—the largest collapse of aggregate demand in American history—President Herbert Hoover in 1931 called a balanced budget "indispensable to the restoration of confidence." Furthermore, in the campaign of 1932 his victorious opponent, Franklin D. Roosevelt, condemned Hoover for failing to meet that objective—although he later revised his views.

In 1958 President Dwight D. Eisenhower offered a different viewpoint. He said he was prepared to see the budget run deficits during a recession— but only if those deficits were matched by surpluses in times of prosperity. The budget need not be balanced annually, he argued, but it should be balanced in the long run—over the course of the *Business Cycle* (see pp. 82–86).

In the early 1960s President John F. Kennedy advocated a budget that would be balanced if the economy were operating at full employment; in 1971 President Richard Nixon tried to implement this idea. The idea is based on the fact that, if there is substantial unemployment in the economy, national income will be lower than it would be at full employment. As a result given tax rates will yield considerably less revenue than they would at full employment. This approach contends that government outlays need not be held down to match the lower level of current revenues. Rather, as President Nixon stated, "except in emergencies, expenditures should not exceed the revenues that the tax system would yield when the economy is operating at full employment."

Against all three of these views—annual balance, balance over the business cycle, and full employment balance—there is the view known as functional finance. Put simply, it is the view that the state of balance of the budget is not very important as a goal of fiscal policy. What is important, rather, is that the government actively use fiscal policy to counteract unacceptable levels of unemployment or inflation. If aggregate demand is too low, causing unemployment to be unacceptably high, then government expenditures and transfer payments should be increased or taxes reduced even if this means running a substantial deficit. If aggregate demand is too high, causing inflation to be unacceptably rapid, then government outlays should be reduced or taxes increased, even if this means running a substantial surplus. It is important that the economy be balanced—that aggregate demand be at appropriate levels—not that the budget be balanced. Franklin Roosevelt seemed to embrace the viewpoint of functional finance when he stated in 1936 that to have balanced the budget during the Depression years of 1933–35 "would have been a crime against the American people." Gerald Ford became the first Republican President to endorse this general approach when early in 1975 he asked Congress to cut taxes in an attempt to counteract a deepening recession. "When private spending is depressed," Ford argued, "government can properly absorb private savings and provide fiscal stimulus to the economy."

Comparing Viewpoints

Let us consider an economy in the condition described in Figure 5–8. Equilibrium occurs at an income level of $1,250 billion, at which the sum of saving plus net taxes $(S + T)$ equals the sum of investment plus government expenditure $(I + G)$. The economy is in a serious recession or de-

Figure 5–8   Budget Deficit at Less than Full Employment

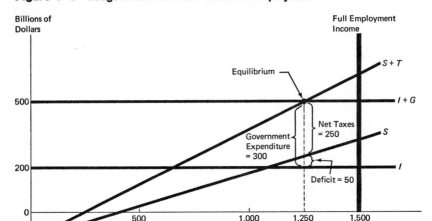

pression, since income is far short of the level ($1,500 billion) that would generate full employment. Note the condition of the government budget. Tax yields are low because they are so heavily dependent on the level of income, which is depressed. It is no surprise, then, that the level of government expenditure ($300 billion) is greater than the $250 billion in net taxes, resulting in a deficit of $50 billion.

We may compare viewpoints by considering how government expenditures might be adjusted to meet the demands of each one of our doctrines of the budget.

Annual Balance.   If the government seeks to balance the budget each year, it might reduce expenditures by at least the amount of the current deficit, $50 billion. Figure 9–9 shows the effect of such a reduction. When the level of government expenditure is reduced from $300 to $250 billion, so that the *I* + *G* line is reduced from $500 billion to $450 billion, the equilibrium level of income falls from $1,250 to $1,150 billion. Thus the economy moves even further away from full employment.

The reduction of government expenditures to $250 billion is only an attempt to balance the budget. In fact, it brings expenditures down only to the level of net taxes that were raised when income was at $1,250 billion. When income falls to the new equilibrium at $1,150 billion, however, net tax collections decline by an additional $20 billion, so that there is still a budget deficit of $20 billion. Further cuts in expenditure—sending the economy even further away from full employment—would be required to bring about an actual balance in the budget.

Balance over the Business Cycle.   If the budget must be balanced over

Figure 5–9   Attempt to Balance the Budget at Less than Full Employment

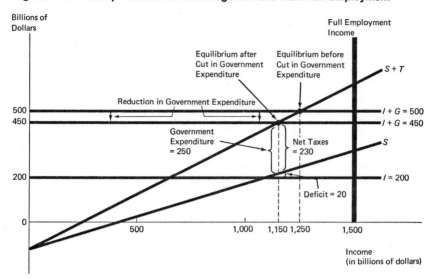

the business cycle, then Figure 5–8 does not provide us with enough information to decide what policy should be followed. It is permissible to run a deficit during the recession. But it is not permissible to increase the deficit in order to stimulate the economy, unless the current deficit happens to be less than the surplus the government expects to realize at full employment. Thus the policy could easily prevent the government from taking the full steps necessary for economic recovery.

Full Employment Balance.   If the policy of the full employment budget is to be followed, the government must keep current government expenditures at the level that tax revenues would reach at full employment. In Figure 5–10 government expenditures of $300 billion are exactly equal to full employ-ment net tax revenues. The policy would indicate that the government should stand pat, neither increasing nor decreasing its expenditures. This would certainly be more sensible than a policy of slashing expenditures in order to eliminate the current budget deficit. At the same time, however, the policy would preclude the government's taking any positive action to increase expenditures in order to stimulate aggregate demand and, thus, to move the economy out of the recession and toward full employment.

Functional Finance.   The policy of functional finance described in Figure 5–11 would involve increasing government expenditures to $425 billion. The $I + G$ line would be raised from $500 billion to $625 billion, the level required to restore the economy to full employment. This would certainly involve increasing the government deficit (from $50 to $125 billion). But note that the deficit would not increase nearly as much as the

Figure 5–10   Balancing the Full Employment Budget

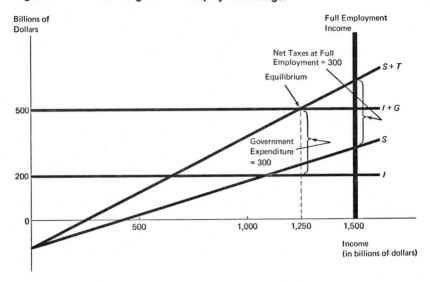

increase in government expenditures (from $300 to $425 billion). At higher levels of income, the government would realize much higher net tax revenues. The increased revenues would partly offset the effects of increased expenditure on the deficit.

In actual practice, the restoration of full employment is usually associ-

Figure 5–11   Using a Budget Deficit to Achieve Full Employment

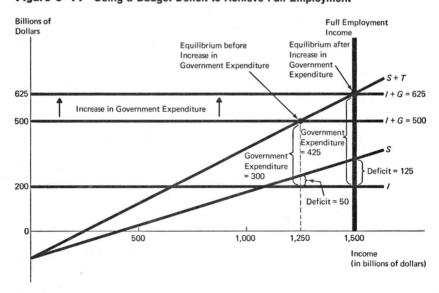

ated with a reduction in the government deficit. Net tax revenues rise sharply as the level of income grows. In addition, private investment expenditures typically increase enough so that increased government expenditures do not have to bear the full burden of shifting up the $I + G$ line. The increased investment may be a direct response to increased levels of expenditure in the economy—generating a greater demand for the capital goods needed to help produce higher levels of output (see *Investment Function,* pp. 157–59). Alternatively, it may be a response to an expansionary *Monetary Policy* (see pp. 204–9) pursued alongside the expansionary fiscal policy. The smaller the increase in government expenditures required to achieve a full employment level of income, the less likely it is that expansionary policies will increase the budget deficit.

Insofar as a policy of functional finance entails a government deficit, the government will have to borrow money and increase the national debt. The way in which the debt is financed—whether by borrowing from the public or from the Federal Reserve System—will determine whether or not the borrowing reinforces the expansion of aggregate demand and whether or not the debt can be increased without creating an additional burden on the public. We have assumed in our examples that the increased government expenditure is financed entirely by borrowing from the Federal Reserve System (see *Money Creation,* pp. 171–72) thus increasing the money supply and reinforcing the expansionary impact of the fiscal policy on aggregate demand. But this is not always the case. This issue is analyzed in our discussions of *Equilibrium Income with Money* (see pp. 210–17), *Monetarism* (see pp. 218–23) and *Public Debt* (see pp. 224–28).

It should be noted, too, that a policy of functional finance is not always a policy of government deficits and increased national debt. When the forces of private demand—consumption and investment—are strong, functional finance may imply that the government should run a substantial surplus to check inflation by holding aggregate demand down to the full employment level.

The conclusion of the analysis is clear. There is only one kind of fiscal policy that can hope to bring about desired changes in aggregate demand—a policy of functional finance designed explicitly to bring about such changes. The policy of the annually balanced budget represents a rigid straightjacket that can easily cause the government to aggravate rather than alleviate economic hardship. The policies of balance over the business cycle or the full employment balance are more flexible—but their goals are still to regulate the budget rather than to balance the economy.

BUILT-IN STABILIZERS

Built-in stabilizers are those standing policies or practices in the economy that automatically tend to partially offset changes in aggregate demand. Built-in, or automatic, stabilizers are contrasted with discretionary stabilizers, which are deliberate changes in government expenditures, tax rates, or the money supply made to counteract changes in aggregate demand. When economists speak of built-in stabilizers, they always include those mechanisms that cause the public sector to spend more and tax less when national income declines and to spend less and tax more when national income increases. Economists sometimes also define built-in stabilizers to include mechanisms in the private sector that cause households and corporations to save less when national income declines and to save more when national income increases. To some economists, a stable money supply is one of the most important built-in stabilizers.

The general effect of built-in stabilizers is to slow down swings in aggregate demand and hence to stabilize output, employment, and the price level. For example, if the economy is near full employment and there is a sudden housing boom that causes aggregate demand to go up by $20 billion, this might tend to create strong inflationary pressures. But the impact of the boom will be partially offset by automatic tendencies for lower government expenditures and for higher tax payments and higher savings out of the increased income. Built-in stabilizers can be seen as those elements in the economy that tend to reduce the multiplier (see *Investment Multiplier,* pp. 135–43 and *Fiscal Policy,* especially pp. 190–92) and hence to reduce the severity of the *Business Cycle* (see pp. 82–86).

Stabilizers in the Public Sector

There are a number of built-in stabilizers in the public sector. In the United States economy, the most common of these are programs of transfer payments to individuals to maintain their incomes whenever those incomes fall too low. Examples are unemployment compensation and welfare programs like Public Assistance and Aid to the Families of Dependent Children. If aggregate demand in the economy falls significantly below the full employment level, large numbers of men and women will qualify for unemployment compensation payments, and additional numbers may qualify for welfare payments. Thus, without the government passing any new laws or deciding on any new programs, the level of government transfer payments to individuals will necessarily go up. Likewise, when prosperity returns and aggregate demand approaches the full employment level, unemployment compensation and welfare payments can be expected to decrease.

The tax system is also likely to be sensitive to changes in the level of aggregate demand. This is especially true for the federal government, which relies heavily on a tax on corporate profits and a graduated tax on personal incomes. Corporate profits respond sharply to changes in aggregate demand, and the federal tax rate on these profits is nearly one-half. If the economy booms, corporate profits may go up by $10 billion, but corporations and their shareholders will be able to spend only an extra $5 billion, since the federal government will tax away the rest.

Personal income is not as responsive to changes in aggregate demand as are corporate profits, but taxes on personal income are paid at graduated rates. This means that additional income is often taxed at a higher rate than basic income. For example, a married couple with two children, earning $10,000 a year, may pay federal incomes taxes of $834, or less than 8.5 percent of their income. If the next year their earnings increase to $11,000, the additional $1,000 will be taxed at a rate of 19 percent. Thus, as the family's income rises, the share of income paid in taxes will also rise.

When all forms of tax income are considered, federal revenues will go up by about 35¢ for every dollar's increase in aggregate demand and will decline by about 35¢ for every dollar's decrease in aggregate demand. Together, the tax and transfer payment stabilizers that are built into the government budget can be quite important in reducing economic fluctuations.

Stabilizers in the Private Sector

The most important built-in stabilizer in the private sector is nothing more than the marginal propensity to save (see *Propensity to Consume,* especially pp. 121–24), which indicates that part of a change in income will be saved rather than transmitted into aggregate demand through an equal change in consumption. If individuals are tied to their habitual consumption standards, they will tend to consume a larger share of their incomes when income falls and to consume a smaller share when income rises. (See *Consumption Function,* especially pp. 149–50.)

Consider a family consuming $9,000 out of an after-tax income of $10,000—or .9 of the total. If the family's income falls by $1,000, it may try to maintain something close to its old consumption standard and still consume $8,500—a larger share (.944) of its lower income. Likewise, if income were instead to increase by $1,000, the family might be slow to increase its consumption standard and might spend only $9,500—a smaller share (.863) of its higher income.

The tendency for consumption behavior to stabilize the level of aggregate demand is accentuated by the ways corporations typically pay out part of their earnings to shareholders in the form of dividends. If corporate earnings have declined, the board of directors is reluctant to reduce dividends for fear that the company will appear to be on the decline, causing the price of its stock to fall. By the same token, if earnings have increased, the directors may be equally reluctant to raise the dividends the company is paying, since they would not be able to continue paying the higher dividends in future years unless earnings stayed high. For example, the XYZ Corporation may have a traditional dividend rate of 50¢ a share. If after-tax earnings are usually $1 a share, this enables the firm to save 50¢ a share. If the economy is booming, after-tax earnings may go up to $1.25, and maintaining the 50¢ dividend will enable corporate savings to go up to 75¢. If there is a recession, and after-tax earnings go down to 75¢, the corporation will save only 25¢. In general, corporations are likely to save a smaller share of their earnings when earnings are low and to save a larger share when earnings are high. There is likely to be considerable stability, then, in the consumption expenditures made by shareholders out of the dividends they receive.

Graphic Representations

We may gain a better idea of how the built-in stabilizers in the government budget operate to modify fluctuations in the economy by using the graphic tools introduced in the discussion of *Equilibrium Income with Government* (see pp. 179–87) and *Fiscal Policy* (see pp. 188–97). Recall that we defined net taxes (T) to include government tax revenues minus government transfer payments to individuals. We begin with the equilibrium condition that the sum of those activities that remove expenditure from the circular flow of aggregate demand, namely, private saving (S) and net taxes (T), must equal the sum of those activities that augment the circular flow, namely, private investment (I) and government expenditures (G):

$$S + T = I + G$$

Figure 5–12 shows how the response of the economy to changing conditions will depend on the strength of the built-in stabilizers. Both parts of the diagram—Figure 5–12a and Figure 5–12b—show an initial total for investment and government expenditures (I + G) of $500 billion. Both parts also show an initial equilibrium—where the sum of saving and net taxes (S + T) also equals $500 billion—at an income level of $1,000 billion. And in both parts of the diagram, the I + G line shifts up to $750 billion, representing, for example, an increase of $250 billion in private investment expenditures due to the discovery of some profitable investment opportunities.

Figure 5–12a represents an economy in which the built-in stabilizers are rather weak, as shown by an S + T line that slopes upward only very gradually. An increase of $6 in income is required to bring forth additional private saving and net tax revenues of $1. When private investment increases by $250 billion, no new equilibrium in the economy is realized until income has grown by a full $1,500 billion—from $1,000 billion to $2,500 billion. The income increase of $1,500 billion is needed to bring forth an additional $250 billion of saving and net taxes to match the additional $250 billion in private investment.

By contrast, Figure 5–12b represents an economy in which the built-in

Figure 5–12   Changing Equilibrium with Weak and Strong Stabilizers

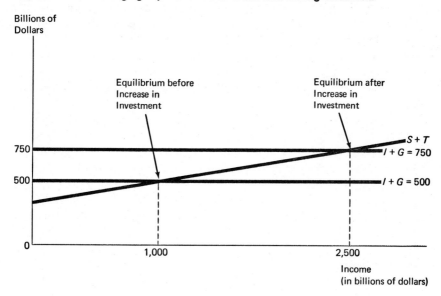

a   Changing Equilibrium with Weak Stabilizers

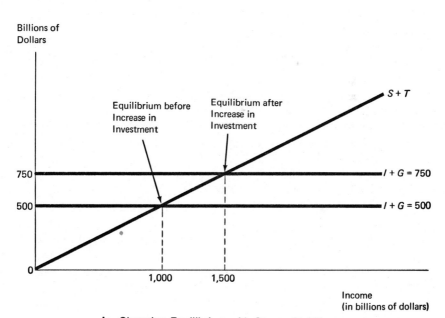

b   Changing Equilibrium with Strong Stabilizers

stabilizers are rather strong, as shown by an $S + T$ line that slopes upward rather steeply. An increase of only $2 in income is required to bring forth an additional $1 in additional saving and net tax payments. When private investment increases by $250 billion, the equilibrium level of income increases by only $500 billion—from $1,000 to $1,500 billion. That increased income of $500 billion is sufficient to bring forth the additional $250 billion in saving and net taxes needed to offset the $250 billion in increased investment.

Two general conclusions may be drawn from the analysis of Figure 5–12. First, built-in stabilizers may be seen as those characteristics of the economy that reduce the equilibrium multiplier (see *Fiscal Policy,* especially pp. 190–92). When built-in stabilizers are strong, then private savings and tax payments take a large share of each additional dollar that people earn, and people receive fewer transfer payments from the government as they earn more themselves. This means that an additional dollar of investment or government expenditure will not generate very large increases in consumption. Thus, in Figure 5–12a, in which the built-in stabilizers were weak, the equilibrium multiplier was high—$1,500 billion of additional income resulting from $250 billion of increased investment. By contrast, Figure 5–12b showed strong built-in stabilizers and a low equilibrium multiplier, so that the same increase in investment raised the equilibrium level of income by only $500 billion.

Second, built-in stabilizers can reduce instability in the economy, but they can never eliminate it. Both examples in Figure 5–12 show the equilibrium level of income increasing in response to the higher levels of investment spending. Indeed, some increase in income was necessary in order to bring forth the increased saving and net taxes which characterize the built-in stabilizers. Even if additional income brought forth no increased consumption—if any additional income were entirely allocated to higher saving and net taxes—then a dollar of increased investment or government expenditure would still raise equilibrium expenditure and income by a dollar. There would simply be no increased consumption to raise expenditure and income beyond that dollar.

Money as an Automatic Stabilizer

It is also possible to see the money supply as an automatic stabilizer in the economy. As was noted in the section on *Equilibrium Income* (see pp. 125–26), a model of the economy like that described in Figure 5–12 implicitly assumes that the money supply expands or contracts to accommodate changes in the expenditure intentions of households, businesses, and governments. Consider, however, an alternative assumption. If the money supply is held constant, then a substantial increase in investment demand—like that described above in Figure 5–12—cannot be realized so simply. In order to borrow the money required to carry out their new investment plans, firms will have to bid loan money away from others. This is often called crowding out other potential borrowers—including other firms seeking to invest, households seeking to finance consumption purchases, and governmental bodies seeking to cover deficits or to finance capital improvements (like roads, sewers, or schools). Interest rates will be bid up, and some borrowers will be driven out of the market for funds. As a result, the increase in aggregate demand from new investment will be at least partially offset by declines in demand from other sources.

Note, however, that the money supply may not be a fully automatic stabilizer. The Treasury Department can sit back passively and watch tax collections rise as national income increases. But the Federal Reserve System, which is the government agency in charge of monetary policy in the U.S. economy, cannot pursue a passive policy and expect to maintain the money supply at a fixed level. Private agencies—namely the commercial banks—can themselves play a very active role in the process of *Money Creation* (see pp. 167–72). If new investment demand causes interest rates to rise, the private banks will be eager to lend out more money, within the limits permitted by their existing reserves. The banks will also wish to borrow more money from the Federal Reserve System in order to increase their reserves. Only through an active *Monetary Policy* (see pp. 204–9)—by example, by discouraging banks from using the discounting mechanism to increase reserves—can the Federal Reserve System prevent the money supply from growing in the face of increased investment demand.

Implications of Built-in Stabilizers

There are two sides to the role of built-in stabilizers in the economy. If the level of aggregate demand in the economy is at a satisfactory level—high enough to provide high levels of employment but not so high as to cause severe inflation—then the stabilizers make fiscal policy much easier to manage. Changes in demand that originate in the private economy—for example, a rapid increase in the rate of inventory accumulation or a sharp decline in the rate of housing starts—will not have strong destabilizing effects on the level of aggregate demand.

But if the level of aggregate demand is not satisfactory, the built-in stabilizers may partially offset any efforts to improve the situation. For example, if the level of aggregate demand is too low to sustain full employment, the government might seek to stimulate housing construction by undertaking a more expansionary monetary policy. The level of aggregate demand would increase, but the increase might not be sufficient if government transfer payments were automatically falling off and tax collections were sharply rising in response to that increase. By reducing the size of the multiplier in the economy, built-in stabilizers tend to reduce the impact of discretionary government policies designed to change the level of aggregate demand.

MONETARY POLICY

Monetary policy consists of actions by the federal government to manage the supply of money and to influence interest rates and the availability of credit in the economy. Monetary policy may be either expansionary or restrictive.

An expansionary monetary policy is designed to stimulate the growth of aggregate demand through increases in the rate of growth of the money supply, thus making credit more available and interest rates lower. An expansionary monetary policy is therefore most appropriate when aggregate demand is low in relation to the capacity of the economy to produce—that is, when unemployment of resources, especially labor, is high. A restrictive monetary policy is designed to curtail the growth of aggregate demand through reductions in the rate of growth of the money supply, thus making credit less available and interest rates higher. A restrictive monetary policy would therefore be more appropriate in times of severe inflation.

The impact of monetary variables on aggregate demand may be illustrated by considering an expansionary policy. Assume that the Federal Reserve System directly increases the supply of money and also makes it easier for banks to lend out money. As a result, households, businesses, and governmental bodies all find it easier to borrow money, either by taking out bank loans or by issuing bonds. Banks and other lenders have more money available to lend at the prevailing interest rates, and the increased supply of money may drive interest rates down. Businesses find it cheaper and easier to raise funds for investments in plant and equipment. Builders and families find it easier to finance investments in new homes. Consumers find it easier to borrow in order to purchase automobiles and appliances. Even state and local governments find it easier to finance the construction of roads, sewers, and schools. Thus a broadly expansive monetary policy should have some impact in stimulating all categories of aggregate demand—investment, consumption, and government purchases. By the same token, a restrictive monetary policy can make it harder to borrow money and thus can discourage aggregate demand.

However, many months after a significant monetary expansion, there may be a tendency for interest rates to rise again. If the expansion succeeds in stimulating the economy, it will cause an increase in the *Demand for Money* (see pp. 161–66)—especially if the expansion itself encourages further investment by producers who are trying to meet an increased demand. Furthermore, if the public comes to expect an increased rate of inflation, lenders may insist on receiving higher interest rates, so that they can continue to earn a positive real return on their money. (For a more systematic analysis, see *Equilibrium Income with Money,* especially pp. 212–15.)

The Instruments of Monetary Policy

In considering the instruments of monetary policy, it is necessary to recall that the supply of money in the economy includes not only cash (currency and coins) in the hands of the public but also all the demand deposits (checking accounts) held by the public in commercial banks (see *Money*, pp. 39–40). It is also necessary to recall that the Board of Governors of the Federal Reserve System (FRS) is the government agency responsible for monetary policy in the United States. It requires each commercial bank belonging to the FRS to hold some portion of its deposits as reserves—either as cash in the bank's own vault or as a deposit in the bank's account with the regional Federal Reserve Bank. (See *Money Creation*, pp. 167–72.)

The three major instruments of monetary policy available to the Federal Reserve System are: reserve requirements, discount policy, and open market operations. Each of these will be described below.

Reserve Requirements. Congress has set broad limits on the amount that each kind of bank must hold as reserves to back up its deposits. Within those limits, the Board of Governors of the Federal Reserve System must set the specific reserve requirements. For example, the law says that the reserve requirement set for major city banks must be no lower than 10 percent of demand deposits (checking accounts) and no greater than 22 percent of those deposits. The Federal Reserve System has tended in the 1960s and early 1970s to set the specific requirement for large banks somewhere between 16 and 19 percent.

By changing reserve requirements, the FRS does not directly alter the quantity of money in the economy or even the quantity of bank reserves. It does, however, alter the power of a given level of bank reserves to support demand deposits. To see this effect, consider a bank with the following simplified balance sheet:

First National Bank

Assets	Liabilities
Cash Reserves: $1,000,000 Loans Outstanding: $4,000,000	Demand Deposits: $5,000,000

If reserve requirements were initially 20 percent of demand deposits, the First National Bank would need every penny of its $1 million in cash reserves to back up its $5 million in demand deposits. If, however, the FRS were to lower the reserve requirement to 15 percent, this would encourage monetary expansion. The First National Bank would then need only $750,000 in reserves to back up its $5 million in demand deposits, leaving it with $250,000 in excess reserves—reserves beyond its legal requirements—that could be lent out to earn interest. If the money were lent out but returned to the banking system in the form of new demand deposits—and if this process continued indefinitely—the bank reserves of $1 million could ultimately support $6⅔ million in demand deposits ($1 million = 15 percent of $6⅔ million) rather than the original $5 million. Thus, lowering reserve requirements increases the ability of the banking system to expand demand deposits—and hence to expand the supply of money. By the same token, for the FRS to raise reserve requirements is to curtail the ability of the banks to expand the money supply.

Discount Policy. Each commercial bank that is a member of the Federal Reserve System can use the process known as <u>discounting</u> to receive its own loans from the Federal Reserve Bank in its region. The commercial bank receives cash or an increase in its own account at the Federal Reserve Bank—either of which can serve as bank reserves—in return for its promise to repay the loan. The commercial bank may back up that promise to repay by pledging some of its own earning assets (U.S. government bonds or loan obligations from the bank's customers) to support the loan.

By changing its discount policy, the Federal Reserve System does not directly affect the supply of money or even the quantity of reserves held by commercial banks. It does, however, make it easier or harder for the commercial banks themselves to use the discounting mechanism to increase their own reserves. If the FRS wants to stimulate discounting, it can lower the interest rate it charges—the <u>discount rate</u>. Alternatively, it can simply encourage the commercial banks to use the discount privilege more freely by letting them know that the powerful FRS approves of their increasing their borrowings. Discount rates have typically been lower than the interest rates that banks could charge on their loans. Thus banks with good loan prospects and no excess reserves can turn a tidy profit by borrowing from the FRS and lending the funds to their customers. Historically, then, it has been FRS discouragement of excessive borrowing—rather than the level of the discount rate—that has kept member bank borrowing in check.

To see the effect of a change in discount policy, assume that the First National Bank would like to lend out $1 million more to a corporation that is prepared to pay 6 percent interest, but the bank needs all its existing cash to meet its reserve requirements. The First National turns to the FRS for funds, but the Board of Governors is discouraging discounting and charging 6 percent for the privilege, at which rate it would not be profitable for the bank to borrow and relend the money. Assume, however, that the FRS soon shifts to a more expansionary discount policy—cutting the discount rate to 4 percent and encouraging banks to exercise the privilege. First National might then apply for and receive a loan of $1 million from the FRS, using $1 million of its holdings of U.S. government bonds to back up the loan. The bank would pay 4 percent on this loan but could lend the money out to the corporation at 6 percent, thus increasing the money supply by $1 million. If the $1 million in extra reserves were returned to the banking system in the form of demand deposits and the excess reserves were then re-lent to the public, the ultimate expansion of the money supply could be much larger than $1 million. Thus, by pursuing an expansionary discount policy—by encouraging discounting and by lowering the discount rate—the FRS makes it easier for the banks to increase their reserves and hence to expand the money supply. By the same token, the FRS can retard the growth of bank reserves and the money supply by pursuing a restrictive discount policy—discouraging the use of the discount privilege and raising the discount rate.

Open Market Operations.   Under law the federal government must issue bonds whenever its runs a deficit—that is, whenever its expenditures outrun its tax revenues. The most common form of government bond has a face value of $1,000. It represents a promise by the government to pay $1,000 at some specified future date, at which time the bond is said to <u>mature</u>. A buyer may earn interest on the bond not only by receiving regular interest payments from the government but possibly àlso by buying the bond for less than $1,000 and holding it until it matures—or until it can be sold for more on the open market as the time of maturity draws closer. For example, if a bond is bought for $909 and in a year can be cashed for $1,000, the $91 gain corresponds to an interest rate of almost exactly 10 percent ($91 ÷ $909 ≈ 1 ÷ 10 = 10%).

The Federal Reserve System is the country's largest buyer and seller of government bonds. It often conducts its purchases and sales on the "open market"—that is, on the organized bond markets in New York City. When the FRS buys bonds on the open market, it may be directly increasing not only the reserves of commercial banks but also the money supply itself.

Consider the case of an open market purchase of $1 million in government bonds from a New York financier. The financier receives a check for the bonds from the FRS, which he promptly deposits in his account at the Chase Manhattan Bank. The bank in turn deposits the check in its own account at the Federal Reserve Bank of New York, and this adds $1 million to its legal reserves. The impact on the balance sheet of the bank is as follows:

Chase Manhattan Bank

Assets		Liabilities	
Deposit at FRB	+$1,000,000	Demand deposits: Financier	+$1,000,000

Thus, two things have happened. First, the money supply has been increased by $1 million—by virtue of the increase in the checking account of the financier. If the American Telephone and Telegraph Company should come along with an attractive bond issue, the financier would be in a position to buy $1 million of those bonds, thus facilitating AT&T's expenditure program and bolstering aggregate demand in the economy. Second, the reserves of the Chase bank are increased by $1 million. If the bank must observe a reserve requirement of 20 percent, then it can lend out funds or buy bonds with $800,000 and still maintain the reserves of $200,000 required to back up the financier's checking account of $1 million. If the funds lent out are kept within the banking system and continue to remain within it after successive lendings by different banks, those new reserves could eventually support $5 million in new demand deposits. (See *Money Creation,* pp. 167–72.) Thus, open market purchases of bonds from the public can be doubly effective by increasing the supply of money immediately and by increasing the potential of the banking system to expand the money supply even further.

Consider now the opposite case—in which the Federal Reserve Bank (FRB) of New York *sells* government securities on the open market. If a charitable foundation buys the bonds, it will issue a check to the FRB for $1 million on its account at the National City Bank. The FRB of New York will then use that check to reduce the National City Bank's account with the FRB. The effect on National City Bank's balance sheet would be as follows:

National City Bank

Assets		Liabilities	
Deposit at FRB	−$1,000,000	Demand deposits: Charitable foundation	−$1,000,000

Note the two effects of this open market sale of bonds. First, the money supply has been reduced by $1 million, represented by the reduction in the foundation's checking account with the National City Bank. Thus, the foundation now has less money with which to buy alternative securities. For example, if American Telephone and Telegraph Company comes along with an attractive bond issue, the foundation does not have $1 million with which to buy those bonds. If the foundation *had* bought AT&T's bonds, the funds would have been invested by the company and pumped into the economy. Instead, the Federal Reserve System got the $1 million, and it can sit on the money for as long as it wishes to maintain a restrictive monetary policy.

Second, the reserves of the National City Bank have been reduced by $1 million, as represented by the reduction in its account with the FRB. If reserve requirements were 20 percent, the open market sale has served not only to reduce the money supply directly by $1 million but also to reduce by $4 million more the ability of the banking system to expand the money supply.

In viewing open market operations by the Federal Reserve System, it is useful to recall that these operations consist of exchanging money for other assets—bonds—that are not money. Thus, when the FRS *purchases* bonds it gives money in return, and thereby helps to expand the public's supply of money. Likewise, when the FRS *sells* bonds it receives money in return, and thereby helps to contract the public's supply of money.

The FRS not only buys and sells bonds on the open market; it also can buy bonds directly from the U.S. Treasury. Consider the case in which the FRS acquires $1 million in government bonds as an asset, and in turn it credits the Treasury's account at the FRS with $1 million. The FRS balance sheet would be changed in the following ways:

Federal Reserve System

Assets		Liabilities	
U.S. government bonds	+$1,000,000	U.S. Treasury deposits	+$1,000,000

The Treasury is then free to write checks on its account at the FRS. If the recipients of those checks want cash for them, the FRS has the full legal power to print money (Federal Reserve Notes) in order to back up those checks.

Note that the U.S. Treasury is financing its deficit by selling bonds rather than by printing money. But it is selling those bonds to the FRS, which is creating money in order to buy them. In this case the government is creating the money to cover the deficit, and in effect monetary expansion is reinforcing the expansionary effects of *Fiscal Policy* (see pp. 188–97). If the FRS did not purchase the government bonds, the Treasury would have had to sell them on the open market. In the process, it would have acquired funds (from financiers, foundations, and others) that might otherwise have been used to purchase the bonds of private companies, like AT&T, or state and local governments. For the Treasury to mop up private funds in this way would be to offset—at least partly—the expansionary effects of fiscal policy. Thus government expenditure would have gone up, but Treasury bond sales on the open market would have caused private investment to go down. When the Treasury sells bonds to the FRS, however, there is no comparable dampening of investment expenditure. For a further discussion of these issues, see *Equilibrium Income with Money* (pp. 210–17), *Monetarism* (pp. 218–23) and *Public Debt* (pp. 224–28).

EQUILIBRIUM INCOME WITH MONEY

Equilibrium Income (see pp. 125–34) is that level at which aggregate demand just tends to perpetuate itself. By including money as well as government in our model of the economy, we are able to obtain a more complete understanding of the roles of *Monetary Policy* (see pp. 204–9) and *Fiscal Policy* (see pp. 188–97) in altering the level of equilibrium income.

We begin with the same assumptions concerning income determination as we used in discussing *Equilibrium Income with Government* (see especially p. 179) but with one very important exception. We no longer assume that the money supply responds passively to the forces of aggregate demand. Rather, we assume that the government can independently determine the supply of money in the economy and that this will influence some components of aggregate demand. The model will show the supply and demand for money influencing the interest rate, which in turn will influence the level of investment in the economy.

The level of investment—along with the level of government expenditure and the relationship between consumption and income—will determine the level of income in the economy, which in turn will influence the demand for money. This model ignores two other real possibilities. First, investment will be influenced by the availability of money as well as the interest rate. Second, money and the interest rate may also influence the borrowing decisions of consumers and of state and local governments. But by showing the influence of money on investment, the model will indicate the direction in which money may also influence the other components of aggregate demand.

Initial Equilibrium

We show an initial equilibrium in Figure 5–13. The bottom portion—Figure 5–13c—corresponds to a diagram like Figure 5–12 in *Equilibrium Income with Government* (see p. 181). The 45° line ($E = Y$) shows all the possible points at which the equilibrium condition—expenditure equals income— might be met. The total expenditure line ($E = C + I + G$) is based on the consumption line plus an investment expenditure of $300 billion and a government expenditure of $300 billion. Equilibrium occurs at an income and expenditure of $1,500 billion. This is indicated by the intersection of the total expenditure line ($E = C + I + G$) with the line that shows all points at which expenditure equals income ($E = Y$). In this model, however, the level of investment ($300 billion) must be consistent with monetary conditions in the economy. This depends on the other parts of the diagram.

In Figure 5–13a we show an equilibrium in the money market. The demand curve for money corresponds to one of the curves in Figure 4–17 in *The Demand for Money* (see p. 164). This curve represents the demand for money (at different rates of interest) that would occur at an income level of

Figure 5-13 Initial Equilibrium

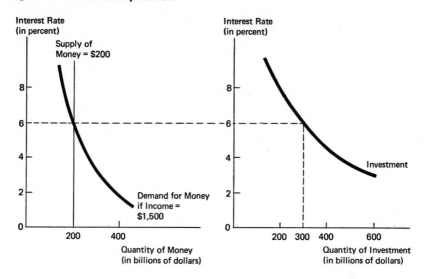

a Money Supply and Demand

b Investment Demand

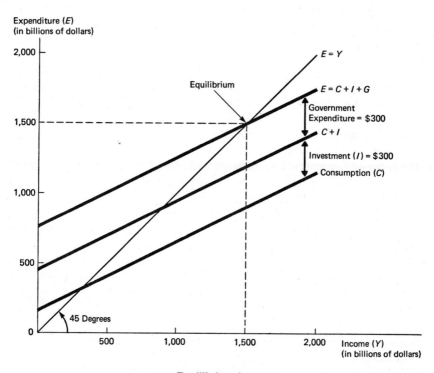

c Equilibrium Income

$1,500 billion. If the government sets the supply of money at $200 billion, the diagram shows that the quantity of money demanded will equal the supply at an interest rate of 6 percent.

In Figure 5–13b we show an investment demand curve that corresponds to Figure 4–16 in our discussion of the *Investment Function* (see p. 157). At an interest rate of 6 percent the curve shows that investors will want to invest $300 billion. This, then, is consistent with Figure 5–13c, where the $300 billion of investment combines with the consumption line and a government expenditure of $300 billion to produce an equilibrium income of $1,500 billion.

So far, so good. All parts of the picture are consistent with the equilibrium level of income of $1,500 billion. The problem is, if any part of the picture changes, so will several other parts. We will now look at the new equilibrium position that might be established if the government were to seek to stimulate the economy by increasing the money supply.

New Equilibrium with an Increased Money Supply

Figure 5–14 shows a new equilibrium income of $1,800 billion after the government has increased the money supply.

It is important to be clear as to how this does—and does not—come about. We can begin by looking at Figure 5–14a, where we see a drastic increase in the money supply—from $200 to $300 billion. If we look only at our original demand curve for money—the one that applied when total income in the economy was $1,500 billion—we might expect a decline in the rate of interest to 3 percent. Indeed, the rate of interest must decline somewhat to persuade members of the public to hold so large an increase in the quantity of money. But a lower interest rate implies a higher level of investment. A higher level of investment implies a higher level of income. And a higher level of income implies a shift to the right in the demand curve for money. At that higher income level the public will need more money to conduct transactions. It will therefore be willing to hold more money at any interest rate than it was willing to hold before at that same interest rate.

The new equilibrium in the money market is shown in Figure 5–14a. The new demand curve for money reflects the greater need for money to conduct $1,800 billion worth of final transactions—rather than the $1,500 billion worth indicated at the old equilibrium. It intersects the new supply of money at an interest rate of 4 percent. Given that greater need for money, the public would be willing to hold $300 billion dollars at a new interest rate of 4 percent. This is lower than the original 6 percent but not as low as the 3 percent that might have prevailed if the increased level of income had not caused a shift in the demand curve for money.

Figure 5–14b shows that investors will want to undertake much more investment than the $300 billion indicated at the old rate of 6 percent. The

Figure 5-14 Equilibrium with Increased Money Supply

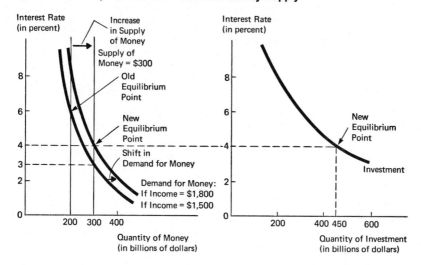

a **Money Supply and Demand**

b **Investment Demand**

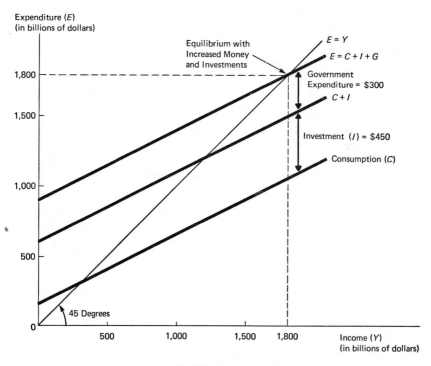

c **Equilibrium Income**

same investment demand curve indicates that, at the new interest rate of 4 percent, there will be some $450 billion of investment demand.

As Figure 5–14c shows, this increased level of investment is consistent with the higher level of equilibrium income in the economy. Together with the original consumption line and the original level ($300 billion) of government expenditure, the increase of investment from $300 billion to $450 billion generates an equilibrium income and expenditure of $1,800 billion. Some $150 billion of the increase in expenditure is the increase in investment induced by the lower rate of interest, and another $150 billion is the higher level of consumption induced by the higher level of income. Thus all three portions of our diagram are consistent with the new equilibrium in the economy.

Note that the velocity of money (see *Quantity Theory of Money,* pp. 173–76) has changed as between these two equilibrium positions. Initially we had $200 billion of money supporting an income level of $1,500 billion—for an average velocity of 7.5 ($1,500 ÷ $200 = 7.5). With the increase in the money supply and the lower interest rate, we now have $300 billion in money supporting an income level of $1,800 billion—for an average velocity of 6 ($1,800 ÷ $300 = 6). One way of seeing this is to recognize that the cost of holding money—the interest rate—has declined. Thus households and businesses are less concerned about economizing on their use of money—since it now costs less to have money sit idle for a while.

When we consider the dynamics of monetary expansion, it is clear that an increase in the growth rate of the money supply should—other things equal—have the immediate effect of pushing down the rate of interest. It would be several months—perhaps even a year or so—before income and expenditure would be stimulated enough to bolster the transactions demand for money, with its tendency to raise interest rates part of the way back to their original levels.

Under some circumstances, however, the monetary expansion could eventually result in interest rates higher than they were before. First of all, if monetary expansion stimulates a recovery of aggregate demand, the investment demand curve may not stand still—as we have shown it doing in Figure 5–14. Investment demand responds not only to rates of interest but also to the pressures of demand against the productive capacity of individual industries—as we have seen in our discussion of the accelerator principle (see *Investment Function,* especially pp. 157–59). General economic recovery could stimulate investment demand sufficiently that there would be a larger increase in income and expenditure than shown in Figure 5–14. This might shift the demand for money curve even further to the right than is shown in Figure 5–14a and bid interest rates up above their initial levels. But once underway, the economic recovery might have developed enough momentum that not even higher interest rates could turn it around immediately.

Secondly—as a result of the monetary expansion, the economic recovery, or both—the public might come to expect an increase in the rate of inflation. As we have seen in our discussion of *The Demand for Money* (see especially pp. 165–66), lenders of money tend to insist that the nominal rate of interest on a new loan be at least as great as the expected rate of inflation. Otherwise, they will be repaid with money that—even with interest added—can buy less than the money they lent out. Investors are typically willing to pay nominal interest rates at least that large, since increased inflation will usually mean that their investment projects will earn a larger number of dollars. Thus, an increase in inflationary expectations could also cause an eventual upward shift in the investment demand curve. This would leave the economy with higher nominal interest rates than before the monetary expansion began.

New Equilibrium with Increased Government Expenditure

Our earlier discussion of *Fiscal Policy* (see pp. 188–97) assumed that the money supply passively increased with an increase in government expenditure. We can now examine how fiscal policy will operate if the supply of money does not increase but instead remains fixed. Let us go back to our initial equilibrium, as described in Figure 5–13—with an interest rate of 6 percent, investment of $300 billion, and an income level of $1,500 billion. Now let us assume that the government attempts to stimulate aggregate demand in the economy by increasing government expenditure from $300 billion to $550 billion. Assume further that this is not financed by a tax increase, which might reduce consumption, or by selling bonds to the Federal Reserve System, which would increase the money supply. Rather, it is financed by selling bonds to the public, which would not directly affect either consumption or the money supply.

Figure 5–15 shows the kind of new equilibrium that might result. The equilibrium level of income has gone up from $1,500 to $1,800 billion, which has strengthened the need for money to carry out the higher level of transactions. Thus, Figure 5–15a shows that the demand for money curve has shifted to the right. With no increase in the supply of money, equilibrium in the money market occurs at a higher rate of interest—8 percent.

At this higher rate of interest, borrowing is more expensive and the level of investment declines. Thus, in Figure 5–15b the investment demand curve indicates a level of investment of $200 billion rather than the $300 billion that prevailed before the increase in government expenditure.

Figure 5–15c shows a new equilibrium level of income at $1,800 billion. The consumption line has not moved, but the higher level of equilibrium income has induced an increase in consumption of $150 billion. Government expenditure has increased by $250 billion to $550 billion. As a result of the higher interest rate, investment has declined by $100 billion to $200 billion. Thus, in the new equilibrium the $250 billion increase in government

Figure 5–15   Equilibrium with Increased Government Expenditure

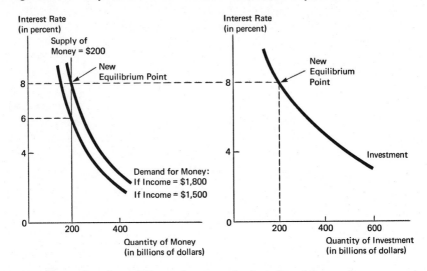

a   Money Supply and Demand

b   Investment Demand

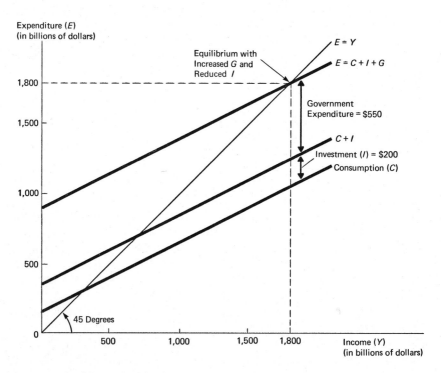

c   Equilibrium Income

expenditure has been partially—but only partially—offset by a $100 billion reduction in investment.

This illustrates how—with no change in the supply of money—an increase in one form of expenditure can "crowd out" some other form of expenditure. (See *Built-In Stabilizers,* especially pp. 202–3, and *Monetarism,* pp. 219–23.)

Note that again we have a change in the velocity of money. In our initial equilibrium, a money supply of $200 billion supported an income level of $1,500 billion—for an average velocity of 7.5. The increased government expenditure has increased the pressure on the money supply, making it more expensive to borrow but also making the velocity of money increase. In our new equilibrium the same $200 billion of money is supporting an income level of $1,800 billion for an average velocity of 9 ($1,800 ÷ $200 = 9).

Conclusion

This model is more sophisticated than the simple Keynesian models we developed earlier. By incorporating an active role for the rate of interest and the money supply, however, the model comes closer to capturing the view of macroeconomics that Keynes put forward in his book, *The General Theory of Employment, Interest, and Money.*

MONETARISM

Monetarism is a school of thought that uses the *Quantity Theory of Money* equation (*M* × *V* = *P* × *Q*) as its basic framework for analysis (see pp. 173–76) and argues that monetary policy is the only effective way to regulate aggregate demand. The monetarist school is led by Milton Friedman who for many years taught at the University of Chicago.

Offering an alternative analysis are the neo-Keynesians, who draw their major inspiration from the ideas put forward by John Maynard Keynes in 1936. They are led today by such economists as Paul Samuelson of M.I.T. and Walter Heller of the University of Minnesota. The neo-Keynesians use as their basic framework the expenditure equation of the equilibrium income model (*C* + *I* + *G* = *E*). (See *Equilibrium Income with Government,* pp. 179–87.) They also see *Fiscal Policy* (see pp. 188–97) as being fully as effective as monetary policy in managing aggregate demand.

The Alternative Frameworks

It is futile to think of the alternative frameworks for analyzing the problem of aggregate demand as "correct" or "incorrect." Both of them are true by definition. The neo-Keynesian expenditure equation:

$$C + I + G = E$$

is simply a definitional breakdown of expenditure into its three categories. Likewise, the Quantity Theory of Money equation used by monetarists:

$$M \times V = P \times Q$$

is also true by definition, since the velocity of money (*V*) is defined as the ratio of total expenditure (*P* × *Q*) to the money stock (*M*). Note, too, that both equations are expressions for Gross National Product (GNP). (See *National Income Accounts,* pp. 78.) GNP can be seen either as the level of total expenditure (*E*) or as the total quantity of goods and services (*Q*) times the average price level (*P*).

The difference between the two approaches can be compared with two ways of looking at the flow of water through a sewer pipe—say, at the rate of 6,000 gallons per hour. A neo-Keynesian investigator might say that the flow of 6,000 gallons an hour consisted of 3,000 gallons an hour from a paper mill, 2,000 gallons an hour from an auto plant, and 1,000 gallons an hour from a shopping center. A monetarist investigator might say that the sewer flow of 6,000 gallons an hour consisted of an average of 200 gallons in the sewer at any one time with a complete turnover of the water 30 times every hour. An expert in waste disposal would not take it seriously if two sewage engineers fought for very long over the difference between their two descriptions, but economists might seem to have been fighting over a comparable difference for years.

In fact, the differences between the monetarists and the neo-Keynesians go well beyond their preferences for one or another of two equally valid frameworks for analysis. The monetarists see a much more important role for money in determining aggregate demand, and they see monetary policy as much more important than fiscal policy in influencing that demand. Here we will consider only one of these points of difference.

Impact of New Government Expenditure

The monetarists and the neo-Keynesians differ sharply on the issue of whether fiscal policy can systematically influence the level of aggregate demand in the economy. Let us illustrate the argument with a specific case: Will a decision by the federal government to spend $5 billion more on the interstate highway program in fact stimulate the economy?

The neo-Keynesians are the first to point out that, if the spending is offset by raising personal income taxes enough to reduce private consumption by $5 billion, there would be no impact on aggregate demand from the spending and taxes combined. The composition of demand would simply shift from the consumption sector to the government sector. They argue that expansionary fiscal policy will ordinarily reduce the surplus or increase the deficit in the government budget (see *Fiscal Policy,* pp. 188–97). Unfortunately, the neo-Keynesians are not always careful to distinguish between two different ways of financing the deficit. To the monetarists, the effect on aggregate demand depends on how the deficit is financed. To understand this point, let us assume that the $5 billion in federal highway expenditure creates a budget deficit of $5 billion.

One way the Treasury may finance the highway construction is by selling $5 billion in government bonds to the Federal Reserve System (see *Monetary Policy,* especially pp. 207–9). This will cause a $5 billion increase in the money supply. In order to buy the bonds, the FRS will either increase the Treasury's checking account by $5 billion or print $5 billion in currency (Federal Reserve Notes) for the Treasury to spend that money. In this case, the monetarists say, there will be an increase in aggregate demand, not because of expansionary fiscal policy but because of monetary expansion.

Alternatively, the Treasury can finance the deficit without causing an increase in the money supply by borrowing the funds it needs directly from the public. It could offer $5 billion in bonds for sale on the New York bond markets and use the money received from that sale to pay the road builders for their work. In this case, the monetarists say, because the money supply has not expanded there may be no increase in aggregate demand—despite the creation of a $5 billion federal deficit. Instead, they argue, there will be crowding out of other potential borrowers in the bond market.

To understand this argument, we need to look at the New York bond market before the Treasury attempted to sell its bonds.

On the demand side, individual savers and savings institutions (like banks, insurance companies, pension funds and investment funds) will all be interested in buying bonds to earn a return on their money. On the supply side, a number of groups besides the federal government will be interested in selling bonds. American Telephone and Telegraph (AT&T) may be interested in borrowing money to finance the installation of videophones. Household Finance Company (HFC) may be interested in borrowing money on a large scale at low interest rates so that it can relend that money to its individual customers at a higher rate of interest. The city of Toledo, Ohio, may be interested in selling bonds in order to finance the expansion of its sewage treatment plant.

Let us assume that if the Treasury Department did not try to sell $5 billion worth of bonds, the market would establish a basic equilibrium interest rate of 6 percent—at which rate AT&T, HFC, and Toledo would all be willing and able to sell their bonds. Assume also, for the moment, that bond buyers have only a fixed amount of money available for the purchase of bonds. Then, if the Treasury Department enters into the market attempting to sell $5 billion in bonds, it must offer an interest rate high enough—say 8 percent—to bid the funds away from AT&T, HFC, and Toledo. It would take a substantially higher interest rate to force these potential borrowers to cancel or postpone their expenditures rather than pay such high interest charges. Thus, the increased $5 billion of federal expenditure can take place only by crowding out $5 billion of expenditure by businesses, consumers, and state and local governments. It is by assuming a fixed supply of funds on the bond markets that Friedman and other monetarists can argue that expansionary fiscal policy will not increase aggregate demand without expansionary monetary policy.

Moreover, the monetarists argue that monetary expansion can be fully effective in increasing aggregate demand even if it is not accompanied by fiscal expansion. For example, if bond dealers in New York are holding large amounts of U.S. government bonds, the Federal Reserve System may engage in open market operations (see *Monetary Policy,* especially pp. 207–9) and buy up $5 billion of those bonds in exchange for money. The increased $5 billion of money in the hands of the bond dealers enables them to buy more bonds from AT&T, HFC, and the city of Toledo—and may even make them willing to accept lower interest rates on such bonds. The eventual result will be more business investment, more consumer spending, and more public works projects by state and local governments. Thus the monetarists conclude: (1) that fiscal expansion works only if accompanied by monetary expansion; and (2) that monetary expansion works even without fiscal expansion. Monetary policy counts, they say, but fiscal policy does not. Increased government spending by itself can change the pattern of total expenditure by drawing resources into the hands of the federal government and out of the hands of private investors, consumers, and state and local governments. But, they argue, it cannot increase the total level of expenditure in the economy.

The Neo-Keynesian Response

Sophisticated neo-Keynesian economists do not attempt to dispute the monetarists on every point. They accept the equation for the quantity theory of money, $M \times V = P \times Q$, as true by definition, and they accept the argument that fiscal expansion can be far more potent if it is accompanied by monetary expansion. They would concede that simple models of *Equilibrium Income* (see pp. 125–34) and the *Investment Multiplier* (see pp. 135–43) are only valid on the assumption that changes in the money supply directly accompany changes in the spending plans of consumers, investors, and government. Such models, which omit any explicit role for either interest rates or money, cannot do full justice to the theory that Keynes put forward in his book, *The General Theory of Employment, Interest, and Money*. That theory is better represented by a model in which money and interest rates also influence the level of aggregate demand (see *Equilibrium Income with Money*, pp. 210–17).

At the same time, the neo-Keynesians would deny that fiscal expansion is completely ineffective without monetary expansion or that monetary expansion can always be fully effective without fiscal expansion.

Consider first the case of the increased government expenditure of $5 billion financed by selling bonds to the public. The money supply was not increased, but the interest rate was bid up from 6 percent to 8 percent, and this resulted in reductions in investment, consumption, and state and local government expenditures. Aggregate demand could have increased only if these reductions were not as great as the $5 billion increase in federal expenditures. Looked at another way, it could be said that if the money supply (M) did not increase, then aggregate demand could have increased only if the velocity of money (V) did increase. In fact, say the neo-Keynesians, it is perfectly reasonable to expect both these conditions to be met. One need only assume that the rate of interest has a significant influence on the *Demand for Money* (see pp. 210–17). Indeed, virtually every serious study of the subject finds that high interest rates are associated with a decrease in the quantity of money demanded to be held. This relationship makes sense. A financier may have $1 million in a checking account waiting to purchase some attractive stocks. Or an automobile company might have $50 million in a checking account waiting for a payroll that must be met in two weeks. If the federal government comes into the bond market and bids up the rate of interest, the financier and the auto company may both be persuaded to put their money to work earning interest, and the effect would be to draw idle money into the bond market. We can look at this effect in two ways. In the first place, it means that increased federal government borrowing of $5 billion need not force reductions of a full $5 billion in other borrowing—since more money is coming into the bond market. In the second place, even though the money supply is no larger, money that was formerly idle is now active, so the velocity of the total money supply is increased. Thus fiscal expansion can have some effect in stimulating aggregate demand even without monetary expansion. A case of fiscal expansion without monetary expansion is shown graphically in our discussion of *Equilibrium Income with Money* (see pp. 215–17).

The neo-Keynesians are also skeptical of the claim that monetary policy alone will always be capable of stimulating the economy. An expansive *Monetary Policy* (see pp. 204–9) does not directly increase anyone's expenditures. Rather, such a policy merely makes it easier for some persons or businesses to spend. Lower discount rates, lower reserve requirements, and open market bond purchases from the banks serve to increase commercial bank reserves or the ability of those reserves to support monetary expansion. But only open market purchases from the public actually increase the money supply—placing money directly in the hands of speculators, securities dealers, and financial institutions that formerly held U.S. government bonds.

It may, however, be easier to get reserves in the hands of the banks and money in the hands of the securities dealers than to convert this into actual spending. First, there may be a considerable delay, or lag, between the time the bank receives the reserves or the dealer receives the money and the time that the businessman obtaining a bank loan or selling new bonds actually spends the money on plant and equipment. (Indeed, the monetarists are among the first to admit that long and uneven lags create uncertainty as to the timeliness of monetary policy.) Second, in times of severe recession or depression, it may be very difficult to find a business that wants to take out a bank loan or to issue bonds in order to finance a capital investment. If aggregate demand is low, a lot of capital equipment is usually standing idle, and there is no point in installing more plant and equipment when the present facilities are not being fully utilized. Third, if interest rates are very low, then banks will have little incentive to make loans. Monetary policy to expand bank reserves would not be successful in expanding bank loans and the money supply.

In recent decades the U.S. economy has come closest to meeting this last circumstance during the Great Depression of the 1930s. Aggregate demand had fallen by nearly one-half, large parts of the capital stock were idle, and the demand for new investment funds had fallen virtually to zero. With so little demand for bank loans, interest rates were as low as 1 percent, and there was little incentive for banks to lend out money even when they had sufficient reserves to do so. In such circumstances it is difficult to dispute the neo-Keynesian contention that an expansionary fiscal policy—including direct government expenditure for such purposes as highway construction—could do more to increase aggregate demand than could efforts at monetary expansion alone.

It is possible, then, to learn something from both sides in the controversy between the monetarists and the neo-Keynesians without adopting an extreme position. The monetarists are correct in stressing that an expansionary fiscal policy can be reinforced by an expansionary monetary policy or that it can be offset—at least partly—by a policy of maintaining the size of the money supply. But the neo-Keynesians are correct in stressing that fiscal policy can be an important means for creating a demand for new money—and hence for stimulating the level of aggregate demand in the economy. Most economists, when actually given the job of recommending measures to expand or contract aggregate demand, will prescribe a combination of monetary and fiscal policies.

PUBLIC DEBT

The public debt is the amount of money owed by the government, usually to the holders of government bonds. The most discussed portion of the public debt is that held by the federal government—sometimes known as the National Debt—which amounted to $577 billion by the end of 1975. It also includes the debt of state and local governments, estimated at more than $200 billion.

There are three reasons why governmental bodies sometimes incur debt rather than levy taxes to cover their expenditures.

1. A political reluctance to raise taxes, especially in periods of extraordinary increases in expenditures, including wartime. Thus approximately $200 billion of the U.S. National Debt was built up during World War II.
2. A sense that certain capital improvements sponsored by the government ought to be paid for gradually, over the life of the investment, by those who will be taxpayers while the improvements are providing benefits. Thus state or local governments often sell bonds to pay for highways or schools rather than place the whole cost burden on those who happen to be taxpayers during the year the project is built.
3. The deliberate use of a federal budget to stimulate the economy. As we have seen in our discussion of *Fiscal Policy* (see pp. 188–97), the federal government may deliberately run a deficit in order to stimulate aggregate demand and restore full employment of labor.

The growth of the public debt—and particularly the National Debt—has caused considerable controversy over the years. Critics of government policy have generally argued that government cannot let the debt continue to grow forever and that the debt places an unfair burden on future generations. Let us examine each of these concerns in turn.

The Perpetually Growing Debt

A typical concern over the National Debt was expressed in the early 1960s by Congressman Clarence Cannon, then chairman of the Appropriations Committee of the House of Representatives. He declared: "Our government—like individuals and families—cannot spend and continue to spend more than they take in without inviting disaster."

It is true that the National Debt has continued to grow over the years. It was approximately $260 billion in 1946, and $577 billion by the end of 1975. This more-than-doubling in twenty-nine years has to be considered, however, in conjunction with some other statistics. First, the Gross National Product, which measures the market value of the commodities and services produced by the nation's economy, was seven times greater in 1975 than it was in 1946. Second, a growing percentage of the National Debt is held not by private individuals and businesses but by agencies of the federal government, notably including the Federal Reserve System and the Social Security Trust Fund. (For a description of how and why the Federal Reserve System buys government bonds, see *Monetary Policy,* especially pp. 207–9 and *Monetarism,* especially pp. 219–21.) Thus, the amount of National Debt in private hands was $350 billion—against the total debt of $577 billion—at the end of 1975. Privately held National Debt was equal to 100 percent of the Gross National Product in 1946—following the large accumulations of debt during World War II—but by 1975 it had dwindled to 23 percent of GNP. Interest costs as a share of GNP declined from 2.4 percent in 1946 to 2.1 percent in 1975.

Criticism of the National Debt often questions why government should be permitted to "live beyond its means," when families and businesses do not. The most immediate response is that families and businesses do. Recall that the National Debt doubled between 1946 and 1975. Over the same period, however, corporate debt went up more than 14 times, home mortgage debt went up 17 times, and consumer debt went up more than 23 times. Thus, by the standards of the other sectors of the economy, the federal government has been most restrained in its borrowing practices.

For most of the corporations and individuals involved in this vast accumulation of debt, borrowing was a perfectly responsible way to finance major expenditures. Businesses typically used the funds to build plants and to install capital equipment that would enhance their earning power. The households typically borrowed to buy a new house or new car, and in most cases they were able to look forward to many years of earning power to permit them to pay off the debt they had incurred.

In the case of the federal government, its earning power is the power to tax, and this is virtually unlimited. The rapid growth of the U.S. economy is the best guarantee of the government's ability to manage its vast debt. Ordinarily, however, the government does not have to raise taxes in order to buy back the bonds that it has sold to the public over the years. In a normal year the government pays off the holders of old bonds with funds raised by selling new bonds. New buyers are available because U.S. government bonds are an attractive asset—that is, they pay a good interest return for securities that entail so little risk.

The Burden on Future Generations

In 1960 President Eisenhower called for a reduction in the National Debt, which he characterized as "our children's inherited mortgage" and a burden "on our grandchildren." Some pessimistic observers have even translated this concern into an argument for birth control, wondering whether it is fair to bring a baby into the world already "owing" $2,000 as his or her share of the National Debt.

It is useful to begin thinking about the burden of the public debt by assuming that the level of government expenditure is given by the needs of the government in a particular year. The issue, then, is whether the government should cover some portion of those expenditures by borrowing money rather than by levying taxes. It is also useful to distinguish between an internal debt—one owed by the government to its own citizens—and an external debt—one owed to foreign governments and individuals. Let us consider three cases: (1) an internal debt acquired to dampen the economy, (2) an internal debt acquired in the course of stimulating the economy, and (3) an external debt.

An Internal Debt Acquired to Dampen the Economy.   On occasion—especially in wartime—the federal government does not want to bear the political consequences of raising enough taxes to cover its total expenditures. At the same time aggregate demand may be high enough that the government is concerned about the inflationary impact of a substantial deficit. In this situation the government may try to borrow enough money from the American public to dampen the inflationary pressures (see *Monetarism,* pp. 219–21).

There are two senses in which one generation cannot pass the burden of this kind of internal debt onto the next generation. First, government expenditures take real resources away from other current uses. For example, virtually no civilian automobiles were produced in the United States during World War II because the labor and capital of the automobile industry were used to produce tanks and bombers. The burden of that shift in resource use could only be borne by the generation that lived through the war.

Second, as the old generation dies out, it passes onto the next generation not only the National Debt but also its existing stock of U.S. government bonds. In this case, the children and grandchildren collectively inherit the debt but individually inherit the means to pay it off.

There are, however, three ways in which future generations might indeed be burdened by the decision to pay for government expenditures by selling bonds to the American public rather than by levying more taxes. First, the size of the capital stock passed on to future generations could be lower. This is because the bulk of government taxes—had they been levied—would have served to dampen private consumption expenditure. Borrowing money from the public, however, may bid away funds from private businesses seeking money to invest. As a result, there might be less investment in building up the capital stock of the economy.

Second, taxes in the future must be higher to cover interest payments on the debt. The higher taxes may create some small disincentives for work effort among taxpayers—and some incentives to spend time finding new ways to avoid paying taxes. Bondholders, by contrast, need exert no additional effort to receive the interest payments that the government owes them.

Third, some transfer of the burden can come about because, as members of the older generation retire from active economic life, they still survive. Thus, many of the men and women who bought U.S. savings bonds during World War II are now living in retirement and spending some of the savings they had accumulated in the form of government bonds. The current generation of working men and women—those who pay the major share of the personal income tax—may today have to pay taxes that are slightly higher because the older generation is living off this accumulated wealth. There is, however, some justification in letting members of the older generation live a little better today because they hold government bonds rather than tax receipts—in recognition of the economic sacrifices they made for the defense of the country in World War II.

Internal Debt Acquired in the Course of Stimulating the Economy. When aggregate demand is low and the government is concerned about high rates of unemployment, it may deliberately run a deficit in order to stimulate the economy. The stimulating effect will be partly offset if the government covers its deficit by borrowing money from the public, since this will tend to mop up funds that might otherwise be spent. The stimulating effect will be reinforced, however, if the government borrows from the Federal Reserve System, since the FRS will increase the money supply in order to buy the bonds. (See our discussion of *Monetary Policy* and *Monetarism,* especially pp. 207–9 and pp. 219–21.) In fact, well over half of the additions to the National Debt between 1946 and 1975 were acquired by the FRS and other government agencies.

Bonds sold to government bodies like the FRS carry none of the burdens associated with bonds sold to the public. First, there is no reduction in the size of the capital stock because the government does not enter the money markets competing with private businesses for investment funds. Instead, it obtains newly created money from the Federal Reserve. Indeed, by stimulating aggregate demand the government may be encouraging business to invest more in order to expand plant and equipment to meet the increased demand. Second, taxes do not need to be higher in order to meet interest payments, since it is the Federal Reserve System—a government agency—which is receiving the interest payments. Ultimately, the earnings of the FRS are returned to the federal government, and the taxpayer is none the worse for the experience. Third, there is no issue of redistribution of income between the generations by virtue of the redemption of the bonds. If the bonds are ever redeemed, it would be by the Federal Reserve System, and the exchange of money for bonds would go from one government agency to another. Thus, National Debt incurred to stimulate the economy carries *none* of the burdens and difficulties for future generations that can be associated with debt incurred as a substitute for tax increases.

An External Debt. By 1975 about $66 billion of the U.S. National Debt—nearly one-fifth of that privately held—was held by foreign individuals, companies, and governments. An external debt operates differently from an internally held debt, both when it is incurred and when it is paid back. When foreigners buy U.S. government bonds, they pay in dollars or other currencies that this country can use to help cover its purchases of imports from abroad. Other things equal, the $66 billion of externally held debt represents a real transfer of resources from foreign countries to this country. Indeed, the fact that foreigners had purchased $66 billion of U.S. government bonds in the U.S. money markets meant that roughly $66 billion more in funds was available for investment within the United States.

There is no reason to think that foreigners will want to hold that debt indefinitely. Insofar as they decide to sell back their bonds on the U.S. money markets, they will be able to obtain dollars with which to import goods from the United States. This could contribute to inflationary pressures on many of the goods—including farm products—that the United States sells abroad.

For the United States the process of borrowing abroad and repaying later could be wise or foolish depending on the circumstances. If the borrowed resources were invested wisely, and if the rate of interest paid on the bonds was not exorbitant, the incurring of external debt could be a prudent decision. It would be comparable, for example, to American Telephone and Telegraph Company borrowing money from outsiders in order to expand or modernize its equipment. If, however, the borrowed resources were squandered and the interest rates were high, the country might be worse off for having borrowed the money and being obliged to pay it back with interest.

Conclusions

The accumulation of National Debt over the past generation has not left a "crushing burden" for the future that we need view with alarm. Under normal conditions it is not the danger of a burgeoning National Debt that should be cited to curb any tendency toward recklessness in government spending. Rather, such spending should be checked if it represents a wasteful or less desirable use of resources. Necessary government expenditure should be paid for by borrowing from the Federal Reserve System whenever aggregate demand is too low to sustain high levels of employment. It should be paid for out of taxes or borrowing from the public if government deficits threaten to cause intolerable rates of inflation. In short, it is not the imagined hazards to the future of a growing National Debt that should govern the course of the government budget. Rather, it is how we can meet present-day needs through the most efficient use of resources, and how we can meet present-day dangers of high unemployment or intolerable inflation.

PLANNING FOR FULL EMPLOYMENT

Planning for full employment means establishing a long-run policy framework designed to bring—and to keep—the level of unemployment down to some minimal level. Planning implies much more than daily reactions to the course of economic events. It implies setting specific goals or targets and preparing in advance policies to prevent major deviations from those targets.

Full employment may be defined objectively, for example, as that level at which total job seekers do not outnumber total job vacancies. Alternatively, it may be defined subjectively as the highest level that can be obtained without generating unacceptable inflationary pressures. (See *Unemployment of Labor,* especially pp. 94.) Whatever specific employment target is established, planning for full employment implies some commitment to reaching that target within a limited period of time.

If full employment were the only goal of economic policy, it would be relatively easy to achieve. All that would be required would be sufficient *Aggregate Demand* (see pp. 71–76) for goods—commodities and services—so that every available worker would be needed to help produce those goods. For example, with the onset of World War II in the United States, aggregate demand increased by 91 percent from 1940 to 1943. In those three years the unemployment rate declined from 14.6 percent to 1.9 percent. The real problem is how to achieve the important goal of full employment without unduly sacrificing two other goals of macroeconomic policy—price stability and economic growth.

The Policy Mix

If the level of aggregate demand is too low to generate full employment, there are three broad policy tools that the federal government can use to stimulate that demand—monetary expansion, tax reductions, and increases government expenditures (see *Monetary Policy,* pp. 204–9, and *Fiscal Policy,* pp. 188–97). Each of these tools can be used to stimulate a different major component of aggregate demand. Thus monetary expansion is most likely to stimulate private investment, including investment in housing. Reductions in the individual income tax or increases in transfer payments are most likely to stimulate consumption expenditures. Increases in government expenditures add directly to that component of aggregate demand. Thus, by its decision on the policy mix—the choice of policy tools to influence aggregate demand—the government can greatly influence the composition of demand and, hence, the composition of output. (See Table 9–1 for a summary of these relationships.)

The choice of policy mix can be critical for the question of *Economic Growth* (see pp. 113–18). To see this more clearly, consider just two ways in which a government might stimulate aggregate demand to the level required

Table 5-1   The Policy Mix

Policy Tool For Expanding Aggregate Demand	Component of Aggregate Demand Most Heavily Affected
Lower Taxes on Personal Income ⟶ Higher Transfer Payments ⟶	Consumption (C)
Monetary Expansion ⟶	Investment (I)
Increased Government Expenditure ⟶	Government (G)

for full employment. In the first case the government might increase the money supply. This would lower the interest rate and cause investment to go up. As a result there would be a higher equilibrium level of income, which would cause consumption also to go up. Together, the increases in investment and consumption expenditures might bring aggregate demand up to the level required.

In the second case the government might increase its own expenditures. The higher level of income would also cause consumption to go up, but in the absence of any monetary expansion, the increased expenditure would also serve to crowd out some investment. The net effect—a large increase in government and consumption expenditures and a smaller decrease in investment expenditure—might also be an increase in aggregate demand sufficient to generate full employment. (For a graphical description of these two policies, see our discussion of *Equilibrium Income with Money,* especially pp. 212–17.)

In both cases the desired level of current aggregate demand could have been achieved. But in the case of monetary expansion, the economy would have realized an increased level of investment and therefore a greater capacity to produce in the future. In the case of increased government expenditures, the economy might have realized a decreased level of investment and therefore a lesser capacity to produce in the future. Insofar as investment contributes to growth, the policy mix that is used to achieve a particular level of aggregate demand can be vital in determining the growth rate of the economy.

Several times during the first half of the 1970s, the Federal Reserve System attempted to restrain the growth of the money supply when it perceived the fiscal policy of the President and Congress to be too expansionary. The net result may have been less investment—and less economic growth—than if the same levels of aggregate demand had been achieved through more monetary expansion combined with less fiscal expansion. For example, the same levels of government expenditures might have been combined with higher taxes and more rapid monetary expansion. The result would have been less consumption and more investment in the economy as a whole.

Attaining Full Employment

The best approach to attaining full employment will largely depend on the nature of the unemployment. Much long-term unemployment is due to a deficiency in demand—a level of aggregate demand that is too low to provide jobs for all those who are willing and able to work. But there may also be structural unemployment, resulting from a long-term mismatching between the demand for labor and the supply of it—a difference between the kinds of persons whom employers want to hire and the kinds of persons who are seeking jobs. For example, during the 1970s unemployment has tended to be higher among teenagers, nonwhites, women, and unskilled workers than among adults, whites, men, and skilled workers (see *Unemployment of Labor,* especially pp. 90–92). It has also tended to be higher in the central cities than in the suburbs, and higher in the older industrial states of the Northeast than in the newly industrializing states of the South and Southwest. High unemployment has tended to affect some industries (like construction) more heavily than others (like health care).

If aggregate demand is strong enough, then there are enough jobs to go around for everyone—not just for the kinds of persons whom companies would most like to hire. A tool company in Cincinnati may prefer to hire a white man from southern Ohio. But if the company has a large enough backlog of orders, it may be willing to go looking for a black woman from Alabama—and even to pay the costs of moving her up north and training her to do an unfamiliar job. If the demand for tools is strong enough, such costs can easily be passed on in the form of a higher price for tools. As Charles Schultze of the Brookings Institution has put it, if there is enough competition among firms for workers, "the unemployable become employable and the untrainable trainable; discrimination against blacks and women becomes unprofitable." He points out that the rapid decline of unemployment with the onset of World War II raised black incomes upward toward the level of whites faster than during any subsequent period.

The achievement of full employment entirely through the expansion of aggregate demand is typically accompanied by strong inflationary pressures. For example, during the three years in which spending for World War II restored full employment to the United States, the price level also increased by nearly one-third. The wartime inflation would have been even greater, except that some of the inflationary pressure was postponed until after the war through the imposition of stringent wartime price controls and the rationing of goods. While a planned effort to attain full employment must include the expansion of aggregate demand, it must also go beyond that approach.

Assume that the government is faced with a high level of unemployment—say, 7 or 8 percent of the labor force. If the government sought to reduce unemployment only to 5 percent, then it might be able to rely entirely on increases in aggregate demand. It would simply choose a mix of monetary and fiscal policies that reflected its priorities among consumption, investment, and government spending. With so many persons out of work, every sector of the economy would probably be able to absorb some of the unemployed. However, as employment grew, much of the remaining unemployment might be structural, and further increases in aggregate demand might not be equally effective in reaching those categories of workers with high rates of unemployment. Higher government expenditures for medical research might only tend to bid up the price of a limited number of research physicians and biochemists. Likewise, cutting everyone's personal income tax might cause increased demand in all consumption sectors and geographic areas—not just those in which unemployment was the highest. Therefore, two other approaches to attaining full employment would also be necessary. The first would be to reshape aggregate demand—to bring the character of the demand for labor closer to the character of the supply of labor. The second would be to reshape the supply of labor so that it could eventually produce those goods that consumers and taxpayers most desire.

To reshape aggregate demand is to stimulate the creation of jobs that can be done by those groups that are most heavily unemployed. The federal government might undertake job programs in those parts of the country, and for those kinds of workers, with the highest rates of unemployment. Alternatively, it might subsidize private firms, nonprofit organizations, or state and local governments to undertake such job programs—either through direct payments or through tax credits. In either case, the jobs provided should be geared to the skills—and potential skills—of those who are unemployed. The jobs should also be as productive as possible. A program of full employment will be more useful—and more politically attractive—if the jobs produce commodities and services that people value. Some of the value may be to individual purchasers—for example, buyers of the baseball bats that have been manufactured by a nonprofit corporation in the Los Angeles ghetto of Watts. Some of the value may be to collective consumers—for example, those who travel the highways built by unemployed workers in Appalachia. Likewise, there are many other jobs in such fields as health care, environmental protection, education, and care for the elderly that can be performed even by relatively unskilled workers.

Job programs for specific groups of workers can focus a portion of aggregate demand on those with the highest rates of unemployment. But those workers, once they are employed, will themselves begin to spend more money. To a limited extent they will spend it in ways that also stimulate employment among the hardcore unemployed. For example, a construction worker helping to build a new office building in an inner city may spend most of his grocery money within that same area. His spending will help provide jobs—as supermarket checkers and stock clerks—for inner city youths. But that spending will also increase demand for the services of canners, meat packers, and farmers far away from the city. If it is not easy to hire unemployed workers to provide these services, the result may simply be more upward pressure on the prices of canned goods, meats, and raw vegetables. If most of the remaining unemployment in the economy is concentrated among specific groups and regions, then the government may find it necessary to raise taxes to cover some of the costs of job programs for the hard-to-employ. Expenditures on those programs would provide specific demand for the services of the hard-to-employ, while the taxes would offset the inflationary impact of the increased general demand for consumption goods by the newly employed workers.

In the short run, programs to reshape aggregate demand to provide jobs to the hard-to-employ can contribute both to *Efficiency* (see pp. 18–23) and to *Equity* (see pp. 24–29). A large pool of idle workers often represents the greatest inefficiency in a modern economy. To the extent that those workers can be employed without raising taxes or increasing the rate of inflation—through monetary expansion or deficit spending—then the efficiency of the economy will be increased. The previously unemployed workers can be made better off without anyone else being made worse off. To the extent that it is necessary to raise taxes to offset inflationary pressures from job programs, then these programs will not increase efficiency—but they will probably improve the equity of the economy. After all, those who have been unemployed a long time are typically far needier than those who pay the largest share of taxes to the federal government.

But simply reshaping aggregate demand to meet the job needs of the unemployed can create some long-run inefficiencies. The particular commodities and services provided may not be the ones that consumers individually—or taxpayers collectively—would consider most useful. A total plan for full employment should also seek to reshape the supply of labor so that it can eventually serve the highest-priority needs of consumers and taxpayers. This can be done through programs to increase the mobility of unemployed workers and to upgrade or adapt their job skills. For example, the government can provide more information about job opportunities around the country—or even provide grants to help individual families to relocate in areas in which jobs are more plentiful. Since the early 1960s the federal government has spent billions of dollars for job-training programs to help unemployed workers acquire new skills. The best results seem to have come when aggregate demand was high enough for the economy to absorb newly trained workers and when their training was aimed at specific jobs that were available locally.

Maintaining Full Employment

Assume that the government has succeeded in achieving full employment in the economy. Let us now examine the kinds of policies that may be necessary to maintain low levels of unemployment.

Overall monetary and fiscal policies are the government's most powerful weapons to maintain—as well as to attain—full employment. These policies must be designed so that aggregate demand grows fast enough to permit the sale of the growing volume of output that can be produced by an increasing—and increasingly productive—labor force. If the economy is experiencing cost-push inflation from within, or inflation that originates in the world economy, then aggregate demand must also grow fast enough to permit the sale of that output at higher prices. Such a policy—often called ratifying the inflation—may make it somewhat easier for inflation to persist (see *Inflation,* especially pp. 97–99). But the failure to ratify an inflation may undermine full employment. For example, during 1974 the U.S. economy experienced a rate of inflation as high as 11 percent—largely due to higher world food prices and the quadrupling of the world price of oil by the Organization of Petroleum Exporting Countries. By contrast, aggregate demand increased at a rate of only 5.0 percent so that the real demand for goods fell by nearly 6.0 percent. As a result, unemployment shot up—from 5.0 percent of the labor force in early 1974 to 8.9 percent in May 1975—the highest rate since the end of the Great Depression of the 1930s.

Flexible monetary and fiscal policies are needed to achieve a steady growth of real aggregate demand. Monetary policy is, by its nature, highly flexible. In particular, decisions on open market operations—the purchases and sales of bonds by the Federal Reserve System—can be made on a week-to-week basis (see *Monetary Policy,* especially pp. 207–9). Government expenditure policy is largely determined on an annual basis, but there is some flexibility. Congress sometimes acts during a budgetary year to supplement the appropriations it has previously made. Furthermore, Presidents have sometimes ordered the slowing down or speeding up of the expenditure of funds for the construction of highways or sewage-treatment plants. Any major changes in tax policy, however, can take a long time to implement because they must be passed by both houses of Congress and signed into law by the President. For example, it took the Congress a full nineteen months to enact the tax cut first proposed in 1962 by President John Kennedy. However, it took the Congress only two months to cut taxes once President Gerald Ford requested such action to deal with the recession in 1975.

Economists have sometimes suggested that the Congress should adopt a formula by which tax rates would be adjusted automatically in response to changing economic conditions. For example, tax rates would shift downward to a limited extent whenever there were major increases in unemployment. When President Kennedy made such a proposal, the Congress was too jealous of its powers to consider the idea seriously. Such an approach could, however, be an important part of planning to maintain full employment.

But maintaining full employment will require more than increased flexibility in the enactment of overall fiscal and monetary policies. It will also require policies that deal more directly with increases in unemployment when and where those increases occur.

Area Stabilization

The geographic dimensions of the unemployment problem have become increasingly important. For example, once the unemployment rate had skyrocketed in 1975, the president and Congress acted to cut personal income taxes, to extend the duration of unemployment benefits, and to increase other federal government expenditures. But, at the same time, the downturn in the economy meant that many state and local governments experienced a sharp decline in the growth of their tax revenues.

Many of these governments were legally unable to run deficits and were forced to increase tax rates and to cut back expenditures. Thus, while the federal government was pursuing an expansionary fiscal policy, state and local governments were offsetting one-third of its expansionary impact through their own restrictive policies. Even worse, the state and local governments that pursued the most restrictive policies were necessarily those in the parts of the country that were hardest hit by the recession.

In 1976 Congress recognized this problem by enacting—over President Ford's veto—a temporary program designed to aid state and local governments in areas of high unemployment. One part of the program provided general budgetary support in order to make it less necessary for those governments to raise taxes and to lay off their own employees. Another part provided additional funds for those governmental units to provide new jobs for unemployed workers in their areas. Any comprehensive plan for full employment would have to include a permanent program of this sort, in which high rates of local unemployment would automatically trigger an infusion of federal funds to bolster government budgets and to help counteract local unemployment.

Sectoral Stabilization

Planning for full employment must also take into account the tendency for economic downturns to be concentrated in four sectors of the economy—business investment in plant and equipment, business investment in inventories, housing construction, and consumer durable goods (including automobiles and home appliances).

These four sectors have one thing in common. In each case high levels of demand cause an accumulation of stocks of goods, whether they be machinery, steel tubing, apartment buildings, or washing machines. The higher the level of stocks on hand as a result of one year's purchases, the less likely is a business or consumer to purchase as much the next year. A shoe company that built a new factory last year—like the family that bought a new color television set—is less likely to need another one this year.

If all four of these sectors are moving together, they can create a large boom or a large slump in the total economy. For example, in early 1974 these four sectors accounted for only one-fourth of total output in the economy—but over the next year they accounted for all of the decline in output that increased unemployment from 5 percent to nearly 9 percent. If economic planning could eliminate fluctuations in these four sectors, it could largely eliminate those downturns in the total economy that create high unemployment.

When these four sectors are not all moving together, an upturn in one sector typically does not cancel out a downturn in another. If there is a boom in sales of home freezers made in Iowa, and there is also a slump in sales of electrical generators made in Massachusetts, very few Massachusetts workers will actually move to Iowa to find work. Rather, generator workers remain unemployed in Massachusetts, while freezer workers work overtime in Iowa.

Economic planning for full employment, then, may have to go one giant step beyond overall fiscal and monetary policy. It may also have to aim to create sectoral stability—a smooth growth for sales and production in several major sectors of the economy. This would first entail setting a series of targets that would represent a steady, long-run growth path for each of these sectors. It would then mean using specific policy tools to keep demand in each sector closer to the long-run path. For example, the demand for new housing—and thus the demand for construction workers—would be stimulated during periods of abnormally low sales. But the demand for new housing would also be restricted whenever sales threatened to become abnormally high, because high sales would build up a stock of new housing that would eventually depress sales to abnormally low levels.

Experience since World War II has clearly shown that overall monetary and fiscal policy alone is not adequate to maintain stable growth in these four sectors. Policies to influence sales in each of the sectors might include:

1. Specific taxes in times of high demand and subsidies in times of low demand. The purpose would not be to increase or decrease sales in the long run but merely to even out their timing.
2. Selective credit controls—over interest rates, down payments, and the length of loans—that could be relaxed to stimulate sales and tightened to curtail them.
3. The systematic timing of government purchases—including purchases to stockpile basic commodities that would be needed later—in order to stabilize the growth of sales.

In addition, there might be other specific policies that could be tailored to the needs of specific sectors. For example, Sweden has established a system called an investment reserve. During periods in which business investment is high, firms must set aside a portion of their profits in a reserve fund. Firms may then spend the money on new investment projects during periods in which investment would otherwise be low.

Such policies for sectoral stabilization need not be applied to every sector of the economy. They need only be developed for those four sectors—consisting of about one-fourth of total output—that are most unstable when left to themselves. Such an approach would permit the stimulation of a depressed sector without setting off general inflationary pressures. It would also permit the curtailment of unsustainable—and possibly inflationary—growth of demand in a sector without setting off massive unemployment. Furthermore, it would not interfere with freedom of choice and the long-run efficiency of market mechanisms. Rather, it would set a climate in which the market mechanism could be rendered more compatible with the goals of full employment and price stability.

6
Public Finance

The field of public finance is concerned with the government budget—how the money is raised and how it is spent. In 1975, governmental bodies laid out $535 billion—enough money to buy nearly 36 percent of the nation's total production. More than a third of these outlays were directly returned to the people in the form of transfer payments—payments to bolster income rather than to compensate persons for current productive services. The remaining two-thirds were available for the purchase by the government of commodities and services, including the services of government employees. Far more of the transfer payments were laid out by the federal government ($173 billion) than by state and local governments ($20 billion). But many more of the actual purchases were made by state and local governments ($213 billion) than by the federal government ($130 billion). By any definition, government is a major part of the American economy.

The discussion of **Taxation** provides an overview of the way government revenues are raised and indicates some of the principles that govern the choice of taxes. The burden of taxes may actually be borne by different persons than those who simply turn the money over to the government, as described in **Tax Incidence**.

An important justification for government taxation and expenditure is the existence of **Externalities**—those effects of production and consumption that are not felt by the producers and consumers themselves. **Public Goods** are an extreme case of externalities, in which all the effects of an activity are external to the producers. An important way to decide if a particular expenditure is worthwhile is to evaluate both its total costs and its total benefits, a technique known as **Cost-Benefit Analysis**. A good deal of expenditure by state and local governments is from tax revenues raised at the federal level of government and distributed through a system of **Revenue Sharing**.

TAXATION

Taxation is the system of payments that individuals and firms are legally required to make to the government. Taxation is the major source, although not the only source, of income to most governments. Fees for the use of government services—obtaining a marriage license, for instance, or driving on a toll road—can be an important source of revenue. For local governments, substantial amounts of money can be raised from fines—for returning books late to the library, for illegal parking, or for criminal offenses. Governments usually also have the option of borrowing money to support their activities, and some governments—including the U.S. federal government—have the capability of raising money simply by printing more of it (see *Money Creation,* pp. 171–72). Nonetheless, while these are several ways in which the government can gain command over resources, taxation remains the cornerstone of most government finance in the United States.

Principles of Taxation

Over the years economists have described two main principles, or criteria, according to which taxes might be levied. The first is the benefit principle. It holds that, as nearly as possible, the persons who benefit from a particular government service should pay the taxes to support that service. The benefit principle is often roughly applied when motorists pay many of the costs of highway construction and maintenance out of taxes on gasoline. But the benefit principle is much harder to apply for expenditures like defense or foreign policy. These are sometimes called *Public Goods* (see pp. 259–61). Does everyone benefit equally from such expenditures? Should everyone pay the $400 or so that these activities cost per capita? Or do some Americans benefit more than others, so that they should pay more and others less? Furthermore, are some Americans positively damaged by these activities, so that they should be paid by the government rather than taxed? The benefit principle yields no useful answers to these questions. The discussion of public goods also deals with the problems of paying for such programs as national defense.

The second major principle of taxation that is often advocated is the ability to pay. This principle holds that the amount a family is taxed ought to take into account the income and size of the family—and possibly other factors, too, like its wealth or situation in life. The ability-to-pay principle is most readily realized through a tax on income itself, with some allowance for family size and such special circumstances as medical expenses.

The ability-to-pay principle is based simply on the idea that to tax a poor family $5 may keep meat off their table all week, while to tax a rich family $5 may only prevent them from enjoying an extra tidbit of caviar. We can formalize this approach in the theory of diminishing marginal utility. This theory holds that the larger a person's consumption, the less additional satisfaction he obtains from each dollar's worth of additional consumption. The principle is often used to justify <u>progressive</u> taxes—those taxes taking a larger share of the incomes of families with higher incomes. An upper-income family, it is argued, does not give up urgently needed goods if it pays 25 percent of its income in federal taxes, but such a tax rate would force a lower-income family to give up basic necessities.

It is useful to go beyond these two traditional principles in order to gain a comprehensive view of the objectives of taxation. In Chapter 1 of this book, three criteria are advanced for judging the performance of an economy—*Efficiency* (see pp. 18–23), *Equity* (see pp. 24–29), and growth (see *Efficiency,* especially pp. 22–23). A system of taxation, like any other form of government intervention in the economy, must be judged according to these three criteria. Thus some of the taxes that follow the benefit principle may promote efficiency in the use of resources. For example, a gasoline tax used for highway maintenance might insure that each car using a highway would pay for any additional highway costs it caused. But sometimes a tax is justified by considerations of efficiency going far beyond the principle of paying for the benefits received from government services. For example, in our discussion of *Externalities* (see pp. 254–58), one of the proposals described is that businesses pay special taxes based on the social costs of the air and water pollution they generate. Such taxes might well encourage the more efficient use of our scarce environmental resources.

Government can promote equity in the distribution of income through taxes consistent with the ability-to-pay principle—a steeply graduated income tax, for example. Many economists would argue that equity requires that public goods—like national defense—be supported through taxes based on the ability to pay. But the goal of equity can be extended beyond actual taxation to suggest that some families have incomes so low that they ought not to be forced to support the government at all, but ought to be partially supported by it.

Some features of the tax laws may not conform to either the benefit or the ability-to-pay principle but may be defended on the grounds that they contribute to economic growth. For example, the <u>accelerated depreciation</u> section of the federal corporation income tax law permits businesses to deduct the depreciation costs of their capital equipment much faster than the actual physical or economic depreciation. This is defended as giving a tax incentive to those firms that are most rapidly increasing their productive capacity by undertaking investment projects.

Thus the problem of taxation—like so many economic problems—can be described as one of trying to reconcile the multiple goals of efficiency, equity, and growth. Here, as elsewhere, it is necessary to recognize that there may be a tradeoff among the various goals being pursued. For example, a heavy corporate income tax may be defended on grounds of equity, since corporations tend to be owned by wealthier persons, who are in a better position to pay a larger share of the tax burden. A tax of 100 percent on the excess profits of a corporation—profits above some level defined as normal in the tax law—might seem more equitable. But it could seriously undermine efficiency, since corporate managers would be encouraged to spend frivolously any income that might threaten to raise profits above the level defined as normal.

Types of Taxation

At each level of government in the United States, one kind of tax seems to predominate. The major source of revenue for the federal government is the income tax on persons and corporations. (In addition, an increasingly important part of the federal tax structure is the payroll tax used to finance the Social Security program of old-age and other forms of assistance.) At the state level, the sales tax is generally most important. In 1975, this tax ranged from 2 percent to 7 percent on the dollar amount of retail sales, sometimes with exemptions for food, drugs, books or services. At the local level—cities, townships, and counties—the tax on property is by far the most important. The property tax generally covers the value of land and buildings (real property) but is sometimes extended to include equipment used by businesses and furnishings in private residences (personal property).

Each of these taxes is, of course, used at more than one level of government. Thus some state governments use income as well as property taxes to bring in some of their revenues. Likewise, some local governments levy their own sales taxes and income taxes. The federal government has sometimes levied taxes—usually called excise taxes—on the sales of particular goods that were considered luxuries or nonessentials—including theater admissions, jewelry, furs, and telephone calls.

There are additional taxes that contribute less to government revenues but are important nonetheless. Tariffs—or taxes on imported commodities—can significantly alter the trade patterns of a country. Several states and the federal government levy inheritance taxes designed to reduce the ability of families to perpetuate great fortunes from one generation to the next. (These inheritance taxes are usually supplemented by gift taxes on any wealth that the older generation transfers to the younger generation before death.) Most states and the federal government also impose a very heavy tax on the purchase of items characterized as "vices," such as liquor and cigarettes.

A form of taxation widely used in Europe is the value added tax, or VAT. The VAT is a tax paid by businesses, not on the total volume of their sales, but on how much they have added to the value of the product they are selling. Thus a flour mill might buy $75 worth of wheat, grind it into flour, and then sell the flour for $100. A sales tax would be based on the full $100 that the flour was worth, while a VAT would be based solely on the $25 that the mill added to the value of the wheat by converting it to flour.

Many of the taxes levied in the United States are paid by businesses rather than individuals. Ultimately, however, it is only individuals who own wealth and receive income. Therefore, individuals wind up paying all of the taxes that a government levies. In some cases, a tax paid by a business may reduce the incomes of the owners or shareholders of that business. In other cases, a tax on a business may result in lower wages for its employees or higher prices for its customers. The process by which a tax may be "shifted" from the taxpayer to other individuals in the society is described in our discussion of *Tax Incidence* (see pp. 247–53).

Progressive and Regressive Taxation

In describing the ways in which taxes affect families at different income levels, economists say that such taxes may be proportional, progressive, or regressive. A proportional tax takes the same share of a family's income regardless of the level of that income. For example, consider a flat-rate income tax of 6 percent with no exemptions or deductions. A family earning $1,000 a year would pay $60 in tax; a family earning $10,000 a year would pay $600; and a family earning $1,000,000 a year would pay $60,000. A progressive tax takes a larger share of the income of upper-income families than of lower-income families. Thus, a 10 percent tax on sales of yachts would be a progressive tax, because it would take nothing from low-income and middle-income families but might take a substantial portion of the incomes of high-income families. A regressive tax is one that takes a larger share of the incomes of lower-income families than of upper-income families. A sales tax on food and beverages is regressive, because a family earning $2,000 a year typically spends more than one-third of its income on food and drink, while a family earning $20,000 a year spends less than one-fifth of its income for those items. Consider a 5 percent sales tax on food and beverages. If a family earning $2,000 spends $700 a year on these goods, it would pay $35 a year in tax, or 1.75 percent of its income. If a family earning $20,000 spends $4,000 on these goods, it would pay $200 a year in tax, or only 1 percent of its income.

A general sales tax is also a regressive tax. This is so because high-income families typically save rather than spend a substantial portion of their incomes, while low-income families spend as much as—or more than— they earn. Consider the impact of a 5 percent sales tax on two different families: One family earns $100,000 and spends only $80,000 of that income. It would pay $4,000—or 4 percent of its income—in sales tax. By contrast, another family earns only $1,000 in a year but keeps alive by spending $400 from its savings. It would have to pay $70—or 7 percent of its income—in sales tax. Obviously, a sales tax is less regressive if it excludes some items (like groceries) that represent a large part of the expenditures of low-income families.

A tax on income itself can be proportional, progressive, or regressive depending on whether its marginal tax rates stay the same, increase, or decrease as income rises. The marginal tax rate is the rate paid on the marginal, or additional, dollar of income. The flat-rate income tax described above is proportional because it contains only one rate—6 percent. The marginal rate of taxation is 6 percent on the first dollar of income earned and on the millionth dollar of income earned.

The federal payroll tax that supports the Social Security program is a regressive tax because there is a dollar limit on the amount of income subject to the tax. For example, in 1976 the employee contribution to the Social Security and Medicare programs was a tax of 5.85 percent of the first $15,300 of income. To see the regressive nature of this kind of structure, consider a simpler case: a 6 percent payroll tax covering only the first $10,000 of worker income. The marginal tax rate would drop from 6 percent on the first $10,000 of income to zero on all income above that figure. Thus a worker earning exactly $10,000 would pay $600—or 6 percent of his income—to the payroll tax. A worker earning $20,000 would still be paying 6 percent on the first $10,000 of income, for the same total of $600—but this would come to only 3 percent of his income. The higher the income above $10,000, the smaller the share of income that would be represented by the $600 in payroll tax.

By contrast, consider a state income tax that exempts the first $5,000 of family income, taxes the next $5,000 at a rate of 2 percent, and taxes all income above that at the rate of 4 percent. Here the marginal rates are graduated upward from zero to 2 percent to 4 percent, suggesting that the tax would be progressive. Thus, a family earning $5,000 would pay no tax. A second family, earning $10,000, would pay nothing on its first $5,000 income but 2 percent ($100) on its next $5,000 of income. The total tax of $100 would represent 1 percent of family income. A third family, earning $20,000, would pay the same $100 on its first $10,000 of income but would pay 4 percent on its next $10,000 of income. Its total tax of $500 would represent 2.5 percent of family income.

This kind of graduation of marginal tax rates is necessary if an income tax is to be progressive. However, it is possible to undermine the progressiveness of even a graduated income tax by offering a number of loopholes—special ways to legally avoid taxes—that are more readily available to upper-income than to lower-income taxpayers. For example, the U.S. federal income tax law says that income from "long-term capital gains" will be taxed at no more than one-half the rate that applies to ordinary income. A capital gain is income from the sale of a piece of property (including a share of stock) for more money than it cost. In 1976 the tax law was changed so that, as of 1978, a capital gain would be considered long-term if the property were held one year or longer (the previous time period had been six months). Thus, $25,000 of income realized through speculation on the stock market may be taxed only one-half as much as $25,000 of income earned as a construction foreman. Low-income taxpayers typically receive very little of their income in the form of capital gains. This loophole, then, permits many upper-income taxpayers to pay a good deal less in federal income tax than the schedule of tax rates itself might suggest. For example, in one recent year the special treatment of capital gains cost the U.S. Treasury more than $6 billion—and more than 60 percent of the benefits were enjoyed by the 1.2 percent of the taxpayers whose incomes were more than $50,000. There are other controversial loopholes in the federal income tax. In calculating how much of his income is subject to tax, an individual may deduct any contributions made to charity. Any interest income from bonds issued by states or cities in the United States is exempt from the federal income tax. Furthermore, landlords are able to use artificially high allowance for the depreciation of the value of the buildings they own and rent out. While they may actually be making good money on the property, they are able to show—on paper—a loss that can be used to reduce the taxes they pay on their other sources of income.

The federal income tax is potentially a very progressive tax. Consider a family of four filling out a tax form in 1976. If they earned $7,000 in wage income, they would have had to pay $310 in federal income tax, or 4.4 percent of their income. But if that family had earned several hundred dollars more, the additional income would have been taxed at the rate of 16 percent. And a family receiving several hundred thousand dollars in stock dividends might have had to pay as much as 70 percent on each additional dollar received. However, when we look to the taxes that families actually pay, we see that the progressiveness of the federal income tax only extends up to income levels of about $50,000. For higher income levels, tax deductions and other loopholes completely offset the progressive impact of higher marginal tax rates.

TAX INCIDENCE

The incidence of a tax refers to who actually bears the ultimate burden of paying it. In the case of the income tax on individuals, the person who pays the tax generally bears the burden. For most taxes, however, the person or business firm that pays out the tax dollars may be able to <u>shift</u> some of that burden onto others. Consider the case of a tax paid by a business firm based on its inventories, its sales, or its profits. If the firm is able to pass the burden of that tax onto its customers in the form of higher prices, this is known as <u>forward shifting</u>. If the firm is able to pass the burden back to its workers or its suppliers, in the form of lower wages or lower costs, this is known as <u>backward shifting</u>. The full analysis of a particular business tax may find some of the burden shifted forward, some of the burden shifted backward, and some of the burden borne by the owners of the business.

The study of tax incidence typically compares the equilibrium position of the economy before the tax was imposed with the equilibrium position after the tax was imposed. In this manner an estimate can be obtained of whose real income or wealth has been reduced—and by how much—as a result of the tax.

The Shifting of a Sales Tax

To see how shifting can work, let us examine the case of a sales tax. Assume that South Carolina decides to levy a new 100 percent sales tax on walnuts. A customer buys a bag of walnuts that is listed as selling for 50¢, but at the cash register she must pay $1. The store will send the 50¢ of the tax to the state treasury, but who actually pays? A quick guess might be that the customer invariably bears the burden, because the 50¢ is directly extracted from her, even though the store turns over the revenues to the state. Actually, the issue is more complicated, and the full answer depends on the nature of supply and demand for the particular good being taxed. We can see this by examining several different situations in which a sales tax of 100 percent might result in an after-tax price of $1.00.

One possible supply and demand situation for walnuts is represented in Figure 6–1, which shows a downward sloping demand curve and an upward sloping supply curve. The downward sloping demand curve represents the varying quantities of walnuts that customers are prepared to buy at various prices. The supply curve represents the varying prices that a supplier of walnuts would have to receive in order to provide various numbers of bags of walnuts. Just above the supply curve—by a distance of 100 percent—is another curve representing supply plus tax. The supply-plus-tax curve describes the varying after-tax prices that a consumer would have to pay and still provide the suppliers with what they must receive in order to supply a bag of walnuts. For any particular number of bags this curve always indicates an after-tax price just 100 percent above the price that the supplier

Figure 6-1   Shifting of a Sales Tax

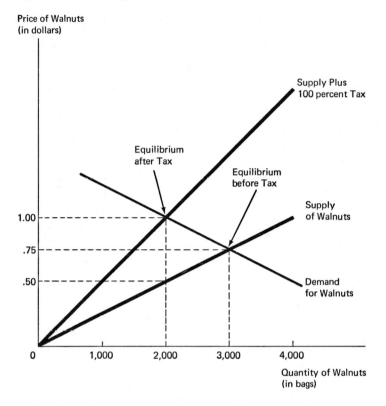

Price of Walnuts
(in dollars)

would have to receive. Before the imposition of the tax, market equilibrium occurs where the demand curve intersects the supply curve, indicating a quantity bought and sold of 3,000 bags and a price of 75¢ a bag. After the imposition of the tax, market equilibrium occurs where the demand curve intersects the supply-plus-tax curve—indicating what the buyer must pay both to the store and to the government of South Carolina. The new after-tax equilibrium gives us a quantity of 2,000 bags bought and sold at a before-tax price of 50¢, to which the tax of 100 percent, or another 50¢, is added.

Note from the example that the customer has not borne the full burden of the tax. The tax is 50¢, but the price the customer must pay goes up by only 25¢ as a result of the tax—from 75¢ to $1. On the other hand, walnut sellers are realizing 25¢ less a bag—50¢ rather than 75¢. Thus the incidence of this particular tax is shared equally by customers and sellers. We would, of course, need more information to tell how the burden on walnut sellers is shared among retail stores, wholesalers, and walnut growers.

Influences on the Shifting of the Sales Tax

The nature of supply and demand for a particular good will determine the incidence of a sales tax on the good—that is, how much of the tax is borne by the buyers or the sellers. We can see this by examining some other cases in which a 100 percent sales tax also results in a price of $1 and a quantity sold of 2,000 but in which buyers and sellers bear very different shares of the tax.

If the supply of the good were considerably more elastic—more nearly horizontal—then a much greater share of the sales tax would be borne by the buyers. This could occur, for example, if walnut growers were able to sell their product on a national market, of which South Carolina represented only a small part. Then, if the sales tax forced a reduction in the quantity sold in South Carolina, little impact would be felt on the price that South Carolina stores would have to pay for walnuts. Figure 6–2a illustrates the case in which the supply is perfectly elastic (horizontal). Here the national market price of walnuts is 50¢, both before and after the South Carolina sales tax, so that all 50¢ of the tax is shifted to the consumer.

Figure 6–2b shows the opposite case. Here the supply curve is considerably more inelastic—more nearly vertical—and a much greater share of the burden of the sales tax is borne by the seller. Figure 6–2b might represent the situation for a good like an orchid, which can only be produced after many years of cultivation but is perishable once it is ready to be harvested. For example, the supply of orchids in South Carolina this year might be rather inelastic if local growers had already committed themselves to growing a particular quantity of orchids, and if the costs of refrigeration and transportation put serious limits on how many orchids they could afford to ship out of the state. Orchid sellers would pay for their inflexibility by having to bear, as Figure 6–2b suggests, the major burden of a new sales tax on orchids, 40¢ of the full 50¢ paid. Over a longer run, however, orchid growers could take the tax into consideration and decide to cultivate fewer new orchid plants, tending to force up the price. Thus, in the long run, the supply of orchids in South Carolina would be considerably more elastic, and over the years consumers could expect to bear an increasing share of the burden of the orchid tax.

It is also possible to describe how demand conditions affect the shifting of a sales tax. In general, the more inelastic the demand for a good—the more vertical the demand curve, because consumers insist on buying walnuts regardless of price—the greater the share of the sales tax they will bear. Likewise, the more elastic the demand—the more consumers are willing to eat almonds and pecans if the price of walnuts goes up—the greater the sales tax burden that will fall on the suppliers. Figures 6–3a and 6–3b illustrate these two cases.

The after-tax situation is the same in both cases. Figure 6–3a shows

Figure 6-2 Shifting of a Sales Tax with Elastic and Inelastic Supply

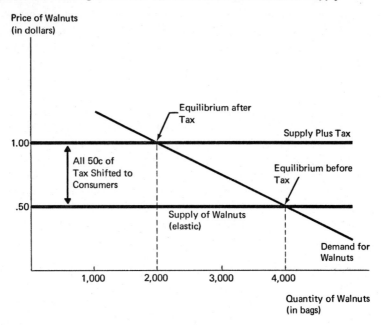

Price of Walnuts
(in dollars)

Equilibrium after
Tax

Supply Plus Tax

1.00

All 50c of
Tax Shifted to
Consumers

Equilibrium before
Tax

.50

Supply of Walnuts
(elastic)

Demand for
Walnuts

1,000   2,000   3,000   4,000

Quantity of Walnuts
(in bags)

a   Perfectly Elastic Supply

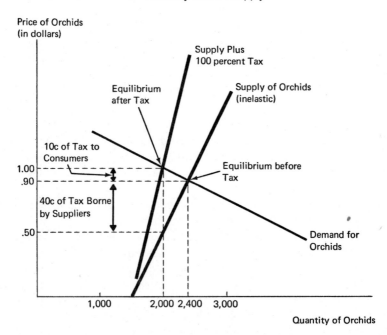

Price of Orchids
(in dollars)

Supply Plus
100 percent Tax

Equilibrium
after Tax

Supply of Orchids
(inelastic)

10c of Tax to
Consumers

1.00
.90

Equilibrium before
Tax

40c of Tax Borne
by Suppliers

.50

Demand for
Orchids

1,000   2,000 2,400   3,000

Quantity of Orchids

b   Inelastic Supply

Figure 6–3   Shifting of a Sales Tax with Inelastic and Elastic Demand

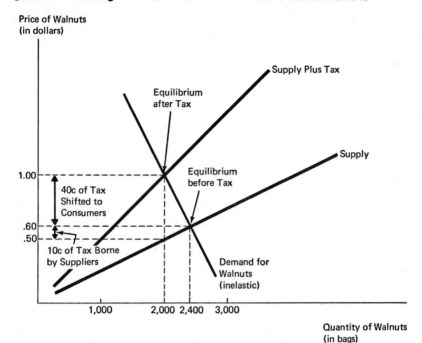

Price of Walnuts
(in dollars)

Supply Plus Tax

Equilibrium
after Tax

Supply

1.00

40c of Tax
Shifted to
Consumers

Equilibrium
before Tax

.60
.50

10c of Tax Borne
by Suppliers

Demand for
Walnuts
(inelastic)

1,000   2,000 2,400   3,000

Quantity of Walnuts
(in bags)

a   Inelastic Demand

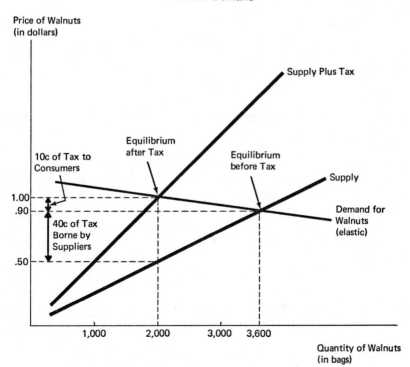

Price of Walnuts
(in dollars)

Supply Plus Tax

Equilibrium
after Tax

10c of Tax to
Consumers

Equilibrium
before Tax

Supply

1.00
.90

Demand for
Walnuts
(elastic)

40c of Tax
Borne by
Suppliers

.50

1,000   2,000   3,000   3,600

Quantity of Walnuts
(in bags)

b   Elastic Demand

how, with a relatively inelastic demand, the tax resulted in a substantial increase in price paid by the consumer but almost no decrease in the price received by the supplier. Figure 6–3b describes the case in which, with a relatively elastic demand, the tax resulted in very little increase in the price paid by the consumer but a substantial decrease in the price received by the supplier.

Looking back at all three figures, it is possible to see a range of results. In each case the price after the 100 percent sales tax was $1, so that the amount of tax paid was 50¢. But the amount of tax actually borne by the customer varied from the whole 50¢ in Figure 6–2a, in which supply was perfectly elastic, to 10¢ in Figures 6–2b and 6–3b, in which demand was more elastic than supply.

Running through our discussion of the sales tax is the notion that those whose market behavior is the least flexible—those with inelastic demand or supply behavior—are most likely to bear the burden of the tax. Those who can rapidly adjust their behavior to the tax by selling more walnuts outside of South Carolina, or by buying pecans instead of walnuts, are likely to be able to avoid the direct burden of the tax.

The Shifting of the Personal Income Tax

A tax that is much harder to shift than a state sales tax is the federal personal income tax, which makes up a large share of the revenues of the U.S. government. Businesses are in the middle, between their suppliers and their customers. They have some opportunity to shift taxes away from themselves (that is, away from their owners) by raising the prices they charge their customers or by lowering the prices they offer to their suppliers. But individuals paying a tax on their personal incomes are not so fortunate. The vast majority of working men or women are not in a position either to demand a raise or to cease working just because income taxes have increased. For most Americans, then, it is a good first approximation to say that the burden of the federal individual income tax is not shifted but is borne by those who pay it.

There are times, however, when individuals are in a position to alter their working behavior somewhat in the face of changes in the income tax. For example, consider the case of the Madison Helicopter, a very popular group of rock performers. By playing the same cities several times a year, they might be in a position to get 100 bookings a year at $10,000 each, bringing them an annual income of $1 million. If the tax rate on each additional dollar earned is 50 percent, this means that each additional concert nets them $5,000. Assume that the tax rate then goes up to 70 percent. The members of the group now decide that they are rich enough not to be bothered with so many concerts if each one will only bring in $3,000 after taxes. They therefore decide to cut back on the number of appearances. With fewer chances to see Madison Helicopter concerts, the group's fans will be willing to pay a higher price to attend each one, and the yield from each one may rise from $10,000 to $15,000. Thus, the performers are able to shift some of the burden of the higher income tax forward onto their fans, who love them anyway. It is the unusual ability to raise the wage by withdrawing some labor services that enables the Madison Helicopter to shift the income tax forward.

Some other highly paid professionals—like doctors and lawyers—may also respond to high tax rates on their additional income by taking on less work than they would at a lower tax rate. If this were to become widespread enough, there is some possibility that the reduced supply of the services of professionals could permit them to drive up their fees. In this case, too, there might be some shifting of the burden of the individual income tax.

EXTERNALITIES

Externalities are side-effects of production or consumption that the market permits producers or consumers to ignore in making their decisions. They are benefits for which the market does not reward the originator or costs for which the market does not penalize the originator.

Externalities constitute the difference between the social effects of an action and the private effects. For example, the private costs of driving a car include the payments the driver must make for gasoline, oil, repairs, insurance, and the depreciation of the vehicle. Costs external to the driver include the air pollution generated by the exhaust fumes, the traffic congestion to which the car may contribute, and any special inconvenience to other drivers that may be caused by road-hogging or reckless driving. The social costs include both the private costs that the driver must bear, and the external costs that the market permits the driver to ignore.

Types of Externalities

Two important distinctions must be made in discussing externalities. They can accompany acts of either production or consumption, and they can be either positive (benefits) or negative (costs). From these two distinctions it is possible to describe four basic types of externalities.

Positive production externalities are experienced by anyone who passes a bakery and inhales the aroma of freshly baked bread or pastry. A special case of double externalities has long intrigued economists: the honey farm located next to the apple orchard. The bees could not produce honey without the nectar from the apple blossoms, and the apple blossoms could not develop into fruit without the bees spreading their pollen. Thus neither form of production could take place without the other.

Negative production externalities are more common and more important. Economists of the nineteenth century often illustrated this type by describing a railway engine that might emit sparks capable of igniting a forest along the tracks. In recent years the problems of air and water pollution have been recognized as the most important kind of negative production externalities. The blackening of the air over industrial centers and the fouling of streams that run alongside factories have today become dramatically evident. Economists no longer treat externalities as theoretical curiosities but rather recognize them as one of the major problems of modern society.

Positive consumption externalities are not always obvious but can be very real nonetheless. Beautiful flowers in one family's front yard can benefit the whole neighborhood. Few people would have as much fun going to a baseball game, a rock festival, or a beach if no one else showed up. Being there with the crowd is—at least up to a point—a major part of the enjoyment.

Negative consumption externalities are sometimes more obvious. If there are so many people at the ball game, the rock festival, or the beach that movement is impossible, then one clearly has too much of a good thing. Other persons generating negative consumption externalities include the camper who throws a beer can into the trout stream, the moviegoer who chews popcorn too loudly, and the music lover in the rooming house who practices on the saxophone for five hours a day.

Implications of Externalities

Externalities are sometimes described as a case of <u>market failure</u>. In the face of externalities, even the most perfect market with the purest competition will be unable to allocate resources with *Efficiency* (see pp. 18–23). If beekeepers are unable to appropriate to themselves all of the benefits generated by their bees, there will be inadequate market incentives to raise bees. Likewise, if "bathing beauties" are unable to appropriate to themselves the full psychic benefits of their presence, there will be an inadequate supply of them at the beaches. On the other side, the presence of negative externalities or external costs may create overincentives for certain activities. If paper manufacturers are not forced to bear the costs of the water pollution they generate, the economy may well produce too much paper for its own good. Likewise, if popcorn munchers are not penalized in any way for keeping everyone else from enjoying the movie, there will be too much loud popcorn consumption in theaters.

A simple extension of *Supply and Demand Analysis* (see pp. 63–68) can be used to show the effect of a negative production externality. Figure 6–4 shows a downward sloping curve representing the market demand for paper at varying prices. Also shown is an upward sloping supply curve based on private marginal costs of producing paper; these are costs that producers themselves incur in producing another ton. The market is in equilibrium when 150 tons of paper are bought and sold at a price of $200 per ton. Let us assume, however, that the market fails to take into account an external cost of $75 per ton. This might represent the fact that water pollution from each ton of paper produced kills some trout and destroys some natural beauty. The social marginal cost of producing paper thus includes not only the private (or internal) marginal cost realized by the paper manufacturer but also these external costs. For this reason, the social marginal cost curve is parallel to the private cost line but above it by a uniform distance of $75. If the full social cost of producing paper were taken into account, less paper would be produced, and it would be sold at a higher price. The optimal solution would occur where the price that consumers would be just willing to pay at the margin—as described by the demand curve—is just equal to the social marginal cost of production. Thus Figure 10–4 shows that the optimal solution would be 100 rather than 150 tons of paper, sold at a price of $250 rather than $200 a ton.

Note that the optimal price of paper is not a full $75 per ton above the

Figure 6-4   Private and Social Costs in the Paper Industry

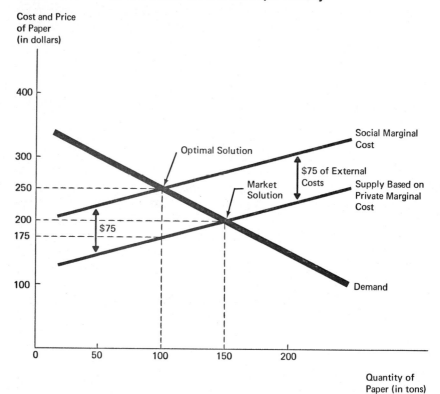

market price. If the actual price of paper were $250 per ton, only 100 tons of it would be demanded. At that level of production the marginal private cost of production would be only $175 per ton, $25 less than at the higher level of production indicated by the market solution. When the external cost of $75 is added to the private cost of $175, we have the optimal price of $250 per ton.

Unfortunately, there are precious few ways in which individual neighbors of a paper mill, acting alone, can bring about an optimal solution. They cannot force the manufacturer to cut production to the point where the social marginal cost equals what consumers are prepared to pay for an additional ton of paper. If they could act, they might prefer an end to all production rather than merely a cutback to 100 tons. The presence of externalities, then, creates a natural role for government to alter the market solution.

The Role of Government

One important role of government is to force producers and consumers to internalize—meaning to bear themselves—the costs of any externalities they generate. This is sometimes done through direct regulation of business. For example, zoning laws might be imposed to minimize the negative externalities of putting a slaughterhouse in the middle of a residential neighborhood. Sometimes firms are nationalized—that is, taken over by the government—in an effort to force them to recognize the social costs of their decisions. In actual practice, however, this is seldom a very effective way of eliminating externalities. Managers of government enterprises often operate with as little regard for external costs as do managers of private firms. For instance, it was a British government corporation—the National Coal Board—that allowed a giant heap of slag from a coal mine in Wales to pile up dangerously. One day in 1966 the heap collapsed, and more than one hundred persons were buried alive. Likewise, state-owned paper and pulp mills in the Soviet Union were the first to introduce pollution into the waters of Lake Baikal in 1966, thereby threatening its unique collection of marine plants and animals.

Economists generally see taxes and subsidies as the best solution to the problem of externalities. The idea is a simple one. If every ton of paper produced creates pollution costs of $75 for the neighbors of the paper mill, the government should tax the company $75 for the pollution associated with each ton of paper. The effect would be to raise the private marginal cost of producing paper to equal the social marginal costs. Thus the external cost would be internalized, and the manufacturer would be forced to cut back production in recognition of the full social costs. The tax would yield enough revenue so that the government could grant subsidies—as high as $75 per ton of paper produced—to clean up the pollution, to restock the waters with trout, or to compensate the neighbors for the costs of the pollution.

Figure 6–4 indicates that the response of the paper mill to the pollution tax would be to cut back production to 100 tons per year. The tax would have the effect of increasing the private marginal cost to the level of the social marginal cost, thus forcing the producer to internalize the externality. What the diagram does not show is the long-run response of the manufacturer, which could be very important from the standpoint of pollution control. The ideal tax would not be on paper production as such, but on the pollution associated with that production. Paper makers would not only have an incentive to cut back on production; they would also have a strong incentive to change the technology they employ in order to reduce the amount of pollution associated with each ton of paper. In the long run, pollution might be reduced far more—and production be reduced far less—than is implied in Figure 6–4.

A tax on an external cost like pollution is not designed to eliminate it completely. This could only be done by making the pollution illegal and subjecting the producers involved to severe penalties and rigorous enforcement. Such action is certainly appropriate for some of the most lethal and damaging forms of air and water pollution. For example, it should be illegal to pollute important fishing waters with certain mercury compounds that can render fish poisonous. But many economists are suspicious of a "zero" pollution standard applied broadly to everything described as environmental pollution, whether it be radioactive fallout or merely bad breath in a movie theater. They suggest that the marginal social cost of each form of pollution be carefully assessed. Dangerous forms of pollution should then be outlawed. More tolerable forms should be taxed in a manner commensurate with their costs, and those who bear the remaining costs should be compensated at the expense of the polluter. This approach would be a far cry from arresting anyone who spits in a lake or who walks down the street smoking a cigar. But it would also be a far cry from leaving polluters scot-free to ignore the external costs of their actions.

PUBLIC GOODS

Goods can be classified as public goods if their consumption is necessarily shared by all members of a community. The existence of public goods is an important justification for governments to engage in some forms of economic activity.

A principle of nonexclusion applies to public goods, in two senses: (1) because one person's use of the good does not interfere with or exclude another person's use, so that it costs nothing to add another user; and (2) because it is impossible to exclude any member of the community from benefitting from the good.

Public goods may be of two sorts: those that can be produced—like battleships or lighthouses—and those that are gifts of nature or of the past—like clean air or the Liberty Bell. Both sorts are subject to the principle of nonexclusion. Battleships and other elements of national defense act on behalf of all citizens simultaneously. A lighthouse protects all ships in the vicinity from crashing into a rocky coast. All the people of a city can breathe its air without detracting from the ability of others to do so. Everyone can simultaneously derive some satisfaction by knowing of the continued existence of the Liberty Bell.

By contrast, goods are private goods to the extent that an exclusion principle applies: (1) the consumption of the good by some persons excludes its consumption by others, and (2) the agency providing the good can exclude someone from the benefits of the good—such as someone who has not paid for it. Most of the commodities and services commonly bought and sold can be considered pure private goods. An ear of corn is a pure private good, even though it can be cut in half and shared equally by two persons, because each individual kernel of corn can be eaten by one person only to the exclusion of the other.

In the real world there are few pure public goods—those that are by their nature fully and equally shared by all members of a community. Police and fire protection, radio and television signals, city streets, and clean rivers are examples of goods that approach, but do not fully meet, the definition of a pure public good. It is difficult to confine the benefits of these goods to selected members of the community, but those who live closer to the source of the benefits may enjoy them more fully than others. All law-abiding citizens are safe if the police are doing their jobs, but those who live across the street from the police station may be safer than others.

Some goods seem to be public using one criterion of nonexclusion, but not the other. If a whole town has been built above a vast underground pool of oil, there is no easy way for the discoverer of the oil to exclude all his neighbors from drilling for it, but every barrel of oil that one person pumps out is a barrel less for his neighbors. An opposite case occurs whenever there are empty seats in a concert hall. More individuals can enjoy a concert at no additional costs of production and without detracting from the enjoyment of others—but it is a simple matter to exclude anyone from the hall.

The concert hall example suggests that a public good may take on more of the characteristics of a private good if its use increases to the point of congestion, so that one additional person's use can only take place at the expense of another person's use. Goods that have the characteristics of public goods up to the point of congestion—like parks, streets, or bridges—are sometimes called limited public goods.

Policy Problems

Pure private goods can often be efficiently produced and consumed privately. If markets are competitive, each producer can decide how much to produce by comparing his costs of production with the market price, and each consumer can decide how much to purchase by comparing that price with the satisfaction provided by the good. No good will be produced for such a market unless there is a consumer who will benefit by at least as much as it costs producers to bring that good into being.

There is no comparable mechanism to govern the production and consumption of public goods. The problem has two sides, corresponding to our two senses of the principle of nonexclusion. First, if it is impossible to exclude users from the benefits of a good, there is often little incentive for private firms to provide that good because potential buyers could refuse to pay and still enjoy its services. Economists call this the problem of the free rider—the person who listens to the open-air concert, or watches the baseball game through the fence, or tunes in the noncommercial television channel but contributes nothing to the costs of providing these services. In this sense, the public good may be seen as an extreme case of positive production *Externalities* (see pp. 254–58). If a lighthouse keeper is unable to exclude free riders and therefore unable to charge for his services, he cannot be rewarded in the marketplace for any of the benefits he provides. Second, since the cost of adding a user is zero, total welfare would be reduced if a citizen were somehow excluded from enjoying the good simply because he was unwilling to pay for it. For example, it costs nothing for a battleship to protect one more citizen in the homeland. The citizen who enjoys the protection of the battleship is presumably better off, and no one is worse off for the fact that he shares in that protection, even though he may not contribute a penny toward its costs. The logic, then, of the pure public good is that it should typically be paid for out of compulsory taxes (so that there are no free riders) and provided to users free of charge (so that its use is maximized).

Voluntary purchases or contributions will typically cause too few public goods to be used or will result in the costs of their use being spread unfairly. Consider the case of police officers patrolling a block in a crime-ridden neighborhood. Many of the neighbors might willingly contribute enough to have this service provided privately. Once it was sure to be provided, however, other neighbors might seek a free ride—knowing that the patrols would generally discourage muggers and that the police could not tell in advance whether or not the potential victim of a particular mugging had actually contributed.

This problem does not arise when public goods are paid for by taxes raised by governments responsive to the people. Consider the case of a referendum to decide whether a sidewalk patrol shall be established and paid for by an income tax on all regular users of the sidewalk. A voter might decide that the benefits of the patrol were worth more to him than the additional tax would cost him. He could then vote for the program with the knowledge that, if it passed with the required number of votes, all of those benefitting from the patrols would also be helping to pay for them.

In practice, there are several reasons why this procedure would not be perfect. A safe sidewalk is not likely to be a pure public good in the sense of being shared equally by all members of a particular political community: some users might live too far away to be taxed, and habitual strollers would benefit more heavily than shut-ins. An income tax might not be the most equitable way to pay for the patrols. In addition, there is no magic majority (one more than half, two-thirds, or nine-tenths) that would clearly justify forcing the minority to pay taxes for a service it did not greatly desire. Furthermore, representative government (let alone oligarchy, monarchy or dictatorship) removes the actual decision one step further from the people actually paying taxes and benefitting from services. It is difficult, however, to escape the logic that only government taxing powers can adequately finance the provision of public goods. Voluntary financing would work only if each citizen were completely honest about paying for those services he actually wanted and used.

Sometimes nongovernmental agencies, like charities, help supply some of the public goods a society needs. In a few cases, business firms may sponsor public goods—like television programs or free baseball games—as a means of advertising or of obtaining favorable publicity. Sometimes small neighborhoods are cohesive enough to organize voluntarily to provide public services without a significant number of free riders. Few public goods, however, can be adequately supplied in this way, and it is difficult to imagine charities, advertisers, or neighborhoods ever getting together sufficiently to support the U.S. Navy.

COST-BENEFIT ANALYSIS

Cost-benefit analysis is the technique of assigning a dollar value to all of the costs and all of the benefits of a particular project—often a government project. The comparison of costs and benefits can be used to help decide whether or not the project is worth undertaking.

The formal technique of cost-benefit analysis originated with the U.S. Army Corps of Engineers as it evaluated various projects to improve navigation on American rivers. Congress made the practice mandatory in the Flood Control Act of 1936, which specified that the Corps should only build projects for which the expected benefits—to whomever they might accrue—were greater than the costs. The benefits could be purely private—to boat owners using a harbor or to farmers enjoying protection from the flooding of a river. For the project to be justified, those benefits would have to be at least as great as the costs to the government of dredging the harbor or damming the river.

During the early 1960s the cost-benefit approach was adopted by the Department of Defense and spread quickly to other agencies. It often took the form of <u>cost-effectiveness</u> analysis. In this case no serious effort was made to place a dollar value on the benefits of a government program—be it defending Guam or providing preschool training for underprivileged children. Rather, the analysis starts with the objective taken for granted and asks what method of achieving it would be the least expensive—or the most cost-effective. Several methods of defending Guam, for example, might be simulated in a computer—using submarines, ground troops, and aircraft carriers—and the least expensive method selected. Or, different kinds of preschool programs might be tried out in different parts of the country to find the least expensive way of giving children a "head start."

In 1965 the federal government formally adopted a system of combining cost-benefit and cost-effectiveness analysis with long-range planning and the regular evaluation of existing government programs. Known as PPBS (for Planning-Programming-Budgeting System), it was actually applied only to a limited range of programs. It did, however, force government agencies to be more concerned with measuring and evaluating the impact of government programs.

An Illustration of Cost-Benefit Analysis

To describe some of the elements of cost-benefit analysis, let us assume that the Dullsville city government is considering spending $1 million in 1979 to build a new outdoor swimming pool on the east side of town. The plan is to charge swimmers only 25¢ each, or just enough to cover the operating costs of the pool—for lifeguards, chlorination, and locker room maintenance. To cover the costs of building the pool, new taxes must be levied.

The main benefit of the pool is the enjoyment of an estimated 40,000 swimmers per year. One measure of the benefit to them is the $10,000 they will pay each year in order to use the pool. But if this is the full extent of the benefit, the project is not justified because this money will only cover the costs of operating the pool, not of building it. The city government might then want to go further and estimate how much each swimmer would benefit—as revealed by how much each swimmer would actually be willing to pay for the use of the pool. Some might be willing to pay $2, others $1, others 50¢, others only 25¢. By adding up all the money that swimmers would be willing to pay over and above the 25¢ each they actually pay, we would get a measure of the extra benefits derived from building the pool. This measure is sometimes known as the consumers' surplus. As a first approximation, we might use these extra benefits to represent the benefit to the public from the decision to build the pool. However, we would have to bear in mind that low-income swimmers might enjoy the pool as much as high-income swimmers but that they would not be willing to pay as much above 25¢ for the use of the pool.

At this point a major problem surfaces for most cost-benefit analysis: how to relate costs and benefits that occur at different times. The pool will cost $1 million to build in 1979, while the benefits to the swimmers may be spread out over forty years. The simplest approach would be to lump together all the benefits, regardless of the year in which they were expected. Under this approach, if the pool generated $25,000 worth of consumers' surplus for each of forty years, then the benefits would total $1 million—and hence they would equal the costs. This would not be satisfactory, however, since it would ignore the *Opportunity Cost* (see pp. 11–17) of using the $1 million in other ways. For example, if the city government simply lent out the $1 million at 8 percent interest, it could earn $80,000 each year in interest payments alone and still have the $1 million left over at the end of the forty years.

The opportunity cost of the funds over time can be included in one of two ways. The simplest would be for city government to sell bonds to pay for the swimming pool and to pay them off in equal installments over forty years— comparable to the way a family pays off its home mortgage. At an interest rate of 8 percent, it would take 40 annual payments of $81,743 each to pay off the $1 million in construction costs. Alternatively, the city government might decide to pay for the pool construction all at once, out of 1979 revenues. It could still evaluate the future benefits of the pool through a process of discounting each of those benefits back to the present. (See *Discounting the Future,* pp. 44–47.) For example, if the interest rate of 8 percent were used to discount returns, the benefits in any year would be divided by a factor representing the amount that money lent in 1979 at 8 percent would be worth in that year. For benefits realized in 1980 it would be necessary to divide by a discount factor of 1.08, representing the fact that a dollar lent in 1979 would realize $1.08 by 1980. Similarly, the discount factor for 1981 would be 1.08 $\times$ 1.08, or 1.1664, since a dollar lent in 1979 would be worth $1.1664 by 1981. Through this process of discounting future benefits—giving them a lesser weight the later they were to be realized—it would be possible to compare the future benefits with the present costs. The result would be the same as under the annual payment method. That is, if the discount rate were 8 percent, then the 40 annual benefits would have to be $81,743 each in order to have a total discounted value of $1 million. In this case, then, the cost-benefit ratio for the project would be 1—that is, the future benefits, discounted to 1979, would just equal costs in 1979.

A number of side-effects of the pool might be included in a cost-benefit calculation—besides the direct benefit to the swimmers. By providing summer recreation, Dullsville might be keeping the swimmers "off the streets"—preventing them from incurring costly injuries or committing costly crimes. On the other hand, the pool might make life very noisy and unpleasant for those who live in neighboring homes and might lower the value of their property. By locating the pool on the east side of Dullsville, the city is making it more accessible for those who live in that particular area. As a result, the swimmers who benefit from the pool may come from families that are considerably poorer—or considerably richer—than the taxpayers who are paying for the construction. A city government interested in redistributing income from rich to poor might want to give extra weight to each dollar of benefits if the swimmers are predominantly poor. Each of these side-effects of the pool is difficult to measure and to assign a specific dollar value.

Cost-Benefit Analysis in Government Budgeting

Cost-benefit analysis lends itself neatly to the task of drawing up a government budget—deciding which projects to include and which to exclude. There are some rules of thumb that can guide this process.

The clearest rule is that a project, or part of a project, should never be undertaken unless it has a cost-benefit ratio of at least 1—that is, unless its benefits are at least as great as its costs. To do otherwise would be a waste of the taxpayers' money. It does not follow, however, that all projects with a cost-benefit ratio of 1 or more ought to be undertaken. For one thing, several of the projects studied may be attempting to do similar things. For example, the Dullsville city government might be evaluating plans for a swimming pool on the east side of town, a swimming pool in the center of town, and a recreational park on the east side of town. Each project, if built by itself, would provide more benefits—because it would receive more use—than each would if all three projects were built together. Second, it might never be appropriate to undertake a project for which the cost-benefit ratio was only 1. Taxes cost money to collect, and sometimes the levying of additional taxes can create waste as taxpayers spend effort trying to avoid them. The real cost of $1 worth of taxes, then, may be something more than $1, and government should insure that the benefits are at least as great.

Third, the government may not have enough money to undertake all of the projects with cost-benefit ratios greater than 1. For example, the Dullsville city government as a whole may be unable to raise taxes or borrow money beyond the $1 million, or the city council may have authorized the recreation department to spend no more than $1 million on new projects in 1979. The problem for the recreation department, then, would be to find the best single use of the $1 million, rather than to find out how many times it could spend $1 million beneficially.

What cost-benefit analysis can do is to give government a way of determining which projects should receive the highest priority. If funds are limited, or if several projects are designed to do the same job, governments should choose those that yield the highest net benefits—those in which benefits exceed costs by the widest margin.

It is not always easy to undertake a cost-benefit analysis, or even a cost-effectiveness analysis, of a government program. It is hard to determine all the indirect effects of a governmental action, and it is even harder to assign a specific dollar value to those effects. But governments can use cost-benefit tools to better understand the implications of expenditure proposals and to make more effective use of the taxpayers' money.

REVENUE SHARING

Revenue sharing is a process by which tax revenues are collected at one level of government and distributed to governmental units at lower levels. Within the United States two forms of revenue sharing are common: the sharing of federal revenues with the states, and the sharing of state revenues with the localities. In 1973 some 24 percent of the income of the states came from various federal grants. Some 31 percent of the income of local governments came from state grants and 6 percent from federal grants.

Revenue sharing in some form is an almost universal practice in the world today, characterizing the relations among governmental levels in communist and noncommunist countries alike. What has become an important issue within the United States is not whether there should be revenue sharing but how much there should be and how the shared funds should be distributed and administered.

Reasons for Revenue Sharing

There are three broad reasons for various programs of revenue sharing: (1) to overcome any disparities between the tax base of a unit of government and its expenditure needs; (2) to permit more government activities to be financed through taxes that minimize distortions and inequities; and (3) to insure that certain overriding goals and policies are implemented throughout the country or the state.

Disparities Between the Tax Base and Expenditure Needs. Income, sales, and property—the bases for most government taxation—are distributed quite unevenly among all the states of the Union. They are also unevenly distributed within those states. One study sought to determine what would happen if every state in the Union used the same tax structure, one that was fairly typical of the states as a whole. The finding was that Nevada would be able to bring in two and a half times as much revenue per capita as Mississippi. Thus, in order to provide the same level of governmental expenditures per capita, Mississippi would have to levy taxes at rates two and a half times those in Nevada.

Disparities can be just as great in terms of expenditure needs, although these are harder to measure. Areas with large concentrations of poor people have greater needs to provide welfare programs, medical assistance, and compensatory education programs. Areas with large concentrations of older people have greater needs to provide public transportation services and medical assistance. Areas with large concentrations of young people have greater needs to provide schools.

Expenditure needs can become acute whenever these sources of need converge. This has happened in some major central cities, from which many middle- and upper-class families have fled to the suburbs. At the same time, these cities are often experiencing a slow growth of their tax bases—from income, sales, and property. The combination can be a massive disparity between the tax base and expenditure needs. By the 1970s that disparity had grown so great that one city—Newark, New Jersey—was forced to tax homes and apartments at a rate of 10 percent of their market value—or five times the average property tax rate for the United States as a whole.

Financing through taxes that minimize distortions and inequities. Tax collection at higher levels of government is a useful device for minimizing distortions and inequities. It is often very difficult for one small unit of government—say, a city or town—to levy local taxes high enough to meet its own needs and fair enough to improve the distribution of income. If Minneapolis were to levy a sales tax 2 percent higher than that in its twin city of St. Paul, people who live in Minneapolis would do much more of their shopping in St. Paul. The city government of Minneapolis might permit pressing city needs to go unmet, rather than drive a great deal of business out of the city. If, however, the state of Minnesota raised the sales tax for the state as a whole, the funds could be used to support municipal services in both cities without nearly as much distortion of the pattern of economic activity. Likewise, the state of Illinois might want to levy a very progressive income tax that would "soak the rich." In all likelihood, however, many of the wealthy people who work in Chicago would move to nearby suburbs in Wisconsin and Indiana and commute to work from there. The wider the jurisdiction of a governmental unit, the less concern it need have that higher taxes will be massively avoided by people merely moving their money to where it will be taxed less heavily.

Implementation of overriding goals and policies. Grants from higher levels to lower levels of government can be an important way to carry out the goals and policies of the higher level of government. A state may give education grants to local school districts in order to insure a minimum level of education throughout the state. The federal government may finance a nationwide school lunch program in order to insure that no schoolchild goes without lunch. In some cases grant programs are justified because conditions in one area directly affect the welfare of people in another area. For example, the people of Indiana and Pennsylvania would be seriously inconvenienced if there were no four-lane highways in Ohio. In other cases there is a sense of community to consider—a sense of being an American that makes people in Oregon care if children starve in Mississippi, and a sense of being an Iowan that makes people in Des Moines care if children do not receive an adequate education in Keokuk.

Goals that can be particularly difficult to implement purely through local initiative are concern for minorities and redistribution of income to the poor. The Congress of the United States is sometimes responsive to these concerns when it appropriates money for federally financed programs. Local city councils and township boards tend to be more exclusively concerned with delivering services to the majorities that elected them.

Federal Revenue Sharing in the United States

Federal grants to the states existed only on a small scale until the 1930s and the New Deal administration of President Franklin Roosevelt. But by 1960 such grants had grown to $19 billion. Many of the Great Society programs fostered by President Lyndon Johnson in the late 1960s operated through grants to the states and localities. By the mid-1970s such grants accounted for well over $50 billion, or about a fifth of the federal government's total civilian expenditures.

Grants-in-aid, the form of most of this revenue sharing until 1972, had three characteristics. First, the grants were earmarked for some particular project or category of expenditure—most often in the fields of highway construction, welfare, and education. Second, the grants were often subject to federal performance standards. Third, the states and localities were often required to provide some matching funds of their own. Some of the grants-in-aid were distributed according to a formula that spelled out exactly how much a particular state or locality would receive. For example, funds to support elementary and secondary education would be distributed according to the number of pupils in different categories. Other grants were distributed only to support specific projects that would be designed at the state or local level and submitted to a federal agency for approval. For instance, urban renewal funds would be available only to support specific programs of slum clearance or rehabilitation.

In the mid-1960s Walter Heller, who had been chairman of the Council of Economic Advisors under Presidents Kennedy and Johnson, proposed a more general approach to revenue sharing. He suggested that the federal government begin distributing some portion of its tax revenues to the states and localities on an unconditional basis—no "strings" attached. President Johnson never endorsed the idea, but President Nixon did, and Congress adopted a program of general revenue sharing in 1972. The program consisted of completely unrestricted grants to the states of from $5 to $7 billion, two-thirds of which was to be passed through the states to local units of general government—cities, townships, and counties. Funds were mainly distributed under a threefold formula; states received more if they had more people, were making a greater tax effort, and had lower per capita incomes.

This general revenue-sharing plan was intended to make additional funds available to the states and localities, enabling them to increase expenditures or to reduce taxes. Many cities used the first funds for new construction projects, while others—like Newark—used all of their first-year allocation to reduce high property taxes. By the end of 1976 the program had provided state and local governments with $30.2 billion over five years.

In addition, President Nixon in 1971 advocated a program of special revenue sharing. The intent was for more than four hundred specific grant-in-aid programs to be combined into six areas—education, law enforcement, manpower, rural development, transportation, and urban development. The federal government would no longer specify how the funds should be used within these broad categories, and no matching funds would be required. Although Congress responded slowly and without enthusiasm, it did take some actions along these lines. For example, it eliminated specific grant programs in such fields as urban renewal and Model Cities—programs to rebuild or rehabilitate poor neighborhoods—and created a single bloc grant for "community development" activities.

Arguments over Federal Revenue Sharing

There are two major arguments in favor of expanding general revenue sharing and consolidating federal grants-in-aid into broad categories of special revenue sharing. It would eliminate some of the bureaucratic "red tape" that often impedes the administration of the programs, especially under project grants. Thus it would relieve the local governments of the trouble and expense of filling out voluminous federal application forms, of waiting through long periods of negotiations with federal representatives, and of being subjected to minute federal supervision of the way local projects are executed. Also, it would permit a choice and design of projects closer to local preferences. If the city council of Denver puts the highest priority on improving the city's bus system, it would not be forced to choose between federal money for highway expansion or for airport improvement.

There is, however, one major argument against the consolidation of all federal grant programs; it would eliminate one of the strongest means of implementing national goals and policies. For example, if pollution reduction is a serious national goal, the federal government may want to influence the form of transportation that the Denver city government seeks to subsidize with federal funds. If reduction of income disparities is a national goal, the federal government may wish to continue concentrating federal funds on educational programs for the disadvantaged rather than permitting the states to redistribute such funds to the wealthy suburbs. If federal funds can be freely used for such purposes as building tennis courts and buying band uniforms—as some general revenue-sharing funds have indeed been used—it will be all the more difficult for the federal government to effectuate broad national purposes.

7

International Trade

International trade can be described statistically as a small share of the U.S. economy. For example, less than 9 percent of the goods and services used by Americans in 1975 were imported. But these imports came to nearly $127 billion, and they included much of the oil and many of the metals and raw materials needed to run our economy. They also included many of the foods (bananas, coffee, chocolate, and tea) that we take for granted and many of the cheaper consumer goods (from toys and shirts to motorcycles, electronic equipment, and small cars) needed to keep the cost of living under control. The ability to export also means that American farms and factories can be more fully utilized in producing those things—from soybeans to computers—that they are best suited to produce because they can sell these goods beyond the limits of the American market.

This sort of trade is based on international specialization—one country producing more of a commodity than it uses itself and selling the remainder to other countries. The basis for this international specialization is considered in our discussion of the competing concepts of **Absolute and Comparative Advantage**. The **Exchange Rate** is the price at which a country's currency sells on international money markets. The system by which exchange rates are determined and balance of payments surpluses and deficits are adjusted is known as the **World Monetary System**. All of the international transactions between one country and the rest of the world, including financial transactions as well as sales of commodities and services, are added up in a balance sheet known as the **Balance of Payments**.

Often governments are not willing to let the forces of the market dictate the character and quantity of international trade, and they impose **Trade Restrictions**, the most important of which are import tariffs, export taxes, and trade quotas. Sometimes—most dramatically in the case of the European Common Market—a number of neighboring nations will join together to eliminate trade restrictions among themselves. Such a development is known as **Regional Economic Integration**.

ABSOLUTE AND COMPARATIVE ADVANTAGE

Absolute advantage and comparative advantage are two alternative theories of international specialization. Both theories attempt to determine which goods a country should produce for itself and export to other countries and which goods it should import from other countries.

The theory of absolute advantage holds that a good will be produced in that country where it costs least in terms of real resources. If Mali exports peanuts, the theory suggests, it is because the resource costs of producing peanuts (capital, land and labor) are lower in Mali than in the countries with which Mali trades.

The theory of comparative advantage challenges this idea. It states that a good will be produced in that country where its cost is least in terms of the other goods that might have been produced with the same resources. Given the poor quality of much of its soil, little capital, and the low technical skills of its agricultural works, Mali may actually not be very good at growing peanuts by current world standards. But Mali may have almost no capability at all in making plows, so that it must give up the production of only a small number of plows in order to grow lots of peanuts. Under these circumstances, it makes sense for Mali to export peanuts and to use the earnings to import plows. Mali produces peanuts rather than plows not because the country is more productive than the rest of the world in growing peanuts (absolute advantage), but because it is relatively more productive in growing peanuts than in making plows (comparative advantage).

Comparative advantage can be applied to economic relations within a smaller framework as well—even within an individual town. For example, a town's leading brain surgeon may also be its most skilled automobile mechanic. Yet, when his car breaks down, he takes it to a garage to be repaired by the garage mechanic, because the time it would take the surgeon to repair the car might better be spent in performing several delicate operations. The garage mechanic gets the job not because he is the best person in town to do it, but because he is far better at auto repairs than he is at brain surgery. The mechanic does not have an absolute advantage, but he does have a strong comparative advantage.

The idea of absolute advantage as the basis for economic specialization has a strong intuitive appeal. But on reflection the idea of comparative advantage—introduced by the English economist David Ricardo in 1817—makes more sense. Indeed, it has come to be the cornerstone of modern thinking on international trade.

The Presence of Comparative Advantage

The principle of comparative advantage can be most easily understood by describing a model of a simplified international economy. Assume, for example, that there are only two countries in the world, Germany and the

United States, and that they produce only two goods that are portable enough to be traded between them—computers and automobiles. Assume that all the autos are identical and all the computers are identical. Assume also that productive resources do not move freely between the two countries, so that goods must be traded if each country is to take advantage of the other's particular capabilities in production. To simplify even further, let us assume—as Ricardo did—that labor is the sole productive resource in the economy, that all workers within a country are equally productive, and that labor within a country can be transferred freely between production of the two goods.

Table 7–1 describes the hypothetical resource (labor) costs of producing goods in the United States and Germany before any trade occurs. We assume that these costs will be constant, at least over small changes in the quantities of goods produced.

Table 7–1 indicates that in the United States it takes 20 labor days to produce a computer and only 10 labor days to produce an auto. By contrast, in Germany it will take 60 labor days to produce a computer and 15 labor days to produce an auto. Thus the United States clearly has an absolute advantage in both computers and automobiles. That is, the United States can produce both goods at lower resource costs per unit of output. Despite this absolute advantage, trade can occur between the two countries. Its direction will depend on the nature of comparative advantage.

We can best think of comparative advantage in terms of *Opportunity Cost* (see pp. 11–17)—the amount of one good that has to be given up in order to produce the other good. For example, what are the opportunity costs of making a computer in each country? Table 7–1 says that producing a computer in the United States takes 20 labor days, while producing a car takes only 10. This means that each computer produced takes away enough labor (20 labor days) to produce two autos (at 10 labor days each). The opportunity cost of producing a computer in the United States—the alternative production that must be foregone—is 2 cars. In Germany the situation is different. Each computer requires 60 labor days, and each auto 15 labor days. This means that each computer produced takes away enough labor (60 labor days) to produce 4 autos (at 15 labor days each). The opportunity cost of producing a computer, therefore, is only 2 autos in the United States but is 4 autos in Germany. By the same token, the opportunity

Table 7–1   Resource Costs of Production in Two Countries

Labor days required per unit of output	U.S.	Germany
Computers	20	60
Automobiles	10	15

cost of producing an automobile is only one-fourth of a computer in Germany, but one-half of a computer in the United States. Hence, the opportunity cost of computers is lower in the United States, while the opportunity cost of autos is lower in Germany. This hypothetical example suggests that it may be to the advantage of both countries if more computers are produced in the United States and more autos are produced in Germany.

To follow through on this suggestion: If the United States is going to produce more computers and trade them for German automobiles, it is going to want something more than two autos for every computer it produces for export. After all, it could get two autos for a computer without bothering to trade, merely by shifting 20 workers from computer production into automobile production. Likewise, if Germany is to produce more cars for export to the United States, it is going to want something more than a fourth of a computer per auto. It could obtain one-fourth of a computer without trading, merely by shifting 15 workers from auto to computer production.

Trade would be possible, then, on any basis that would permit the United States to gain more than 2 autos per computer but would force the Germans to give up less than 4 autos per computer. For example, the trading ratio might be 3 to 1. (This would be the case, for example, if each auto sold for $3,000 in world markets and each computer for $9,000.) The United States could then export 4 computers and receive 12 autos in exchange. The impact of such a trade is outlined in Table 7–2.

To produce the 4 additional computers for export, the United States would have to shift 80 workers from automobile production to computer production (since 20 workers are required to produce each computer). This would reduce auto production by 8 units (since 10 workers are required per unit). The United States, however, would be importing 12 autos, so that it would be able to consume 4 more than was possible without trade. Automobile consumption would go up by 4 units in the United States, but computer consumption would not decline, since the 4 computers exported would all be produced by the 80 workers shifted into the computer industry.

As for Germany, producing the 12 extra autos to be exported to the United States will require adding 180 workers to its auto production (since

Table 7–2   Changes Due to the Trade of Four U.S. Computers for Twelve German Autos

	United States				Germany			
	Labor Days	Pro- duction	Trade	Con- sumption	Labor Days	Pro- duction	Trade	Con- sumption
Computers	+80	+4	−4	0	−180	−3	+4	+1
Automobiles	−80	−8	+12	+4	+180	+12	−12	0

15 workers are required per auto). By taking these 180 workers out of computer production, Germany must reduce its computer output by 3 units (since 60 workers are required per unit). At the same time, Germany will import 4 computers. Thus Germany will be able to consume one more computer than was possible without trade and will not have to reduce its car consumption at all.

The foregoing example illustrates a general rule of international trade. Where comparative advantage exists, two trading partners are both able to share in the gains from trade. That is, there will always exist some ratio of exchange between two products that will permit both countries to consume more of one commodity without having to consume less of the other. The exact ratio at which trade will actually occur depends on many factors—the full range of production conditions, demand conditions, and the knowledge and bargaining power of the traders in both countries. But trade is such a dominant feature of economic life—among individuals and firms as well as among nations—largely because comparative advantage creates so many opportunities for mutual benefit.

Voluntary trade to exploit comparative advantage promotes *Efficiency* (see pp. 18–23) among nations, since it makes the U.S. better off—by being able to increase its consumption of real goods—without making Germany worse off.

Inside the United States, however, the kinds of shifts we have described are not painless, especially in the short run. At best—in times of full employment—causing workers to shift from one form of production to another may force families to find new homes and force workers to learn new skills and adjust to new routines. At worst—in times of high *Unemployment of Labor* (see pp. 87–94)—the worker who loses his job to imports may find small comfort in the thought that somewhere else another worker is finding a new job producing exports. But in the long run, the economy will be more productive—and workers as a whole will be better off—if the country shifts its pattern of production to exploit its comparative advantage.

The Absence of Comparative Advantage

In some circumstances the resource costs of production will not indicate any comparative advantage. For example, Table 7–3 assumes a different set of pretrade labor requirements for computers and autos. In this example,

Table 7–3   Alternative Resource Costs of Production

Labor days required per unit of output	U.S.	Germany
Computers	20	60
Automobiles	10	30

the United States again has an absolute advantage in both products, since both may be produced in the United States using less labor than in Germany. But what about comparative advantage? In the United States, 2 autos must be given up to obtain the 20 workers required to produce one computer. Likewise, in Germany, 2 autos must be given up to obtain the 60 workers required to produce one computer. The opportunity cost of autos in terms of computers is identical in both countries. To export computers, the United States would have to be offered more than two cars per computer, and to export automobiles, Germany would have to be offered more than half of a computer per car. But these two offers are inconsistent with each other. Thus the pretrade cost ratios will offer no basis for trade to occur. Comparative advantage does not exist.

Other Possible Bases for Trade

Where there are no differences among countries in the basic capabilities at producing goods, two bases for trade among them may still exist. First, patterns of demand may differ among countries. For example, most consumers in one country may consider dog meat a delicacy, while in a neighboring country the consumption of dog meat is abhorrent. In the first country, dog meat lovers may grab up all the stray dogs in the alleys and still demand so many more dogs that farmers are prepared to go to the trouble and expense of raising dogs commercially. As the cost goes up, "dog-nappers" will be raiding the alleys of the second country and shipping the poor creatures over the border to be eaten. The number of alleys in which dogs breed and live may be the same in both countries. Trade will be based not on differences in the production capabilities of the two countries but on different consumption preferences.

Second, a basis for trade can grow out of economies of scale—the cost advantages of large-scale production. For example, Germany and the United States may have the same labor requirements for autos and computers, but both commodities will require less labor per unit if produced on a larger scale. There may be substantial setup costs in both industries—the costs of obtaining the basic production machinery, or the costs of creating a production line. Both countries might find it advantageous if each were to specialize completely in the production of one good and import the other. For instance, the United States might produce all the automobiles for both itself and Germany, while Germany might produce all the computers for both itself and the United States. There might be no difference in production conditions between the countries and, hence, no economic basis for deciding which country should specialize in which product. Even so, they might be wise to decide—if only by the toss of a coin—that one of them would set up a computer industry and the other one an auto industry.

To summarize, the theory of international specialization seeks to answer the question of which countries will produce what goods, with what trade patterns among them. Differences in production conditions—the element highlighted by the theory of comparative advantage—provide the most important part of the answer. But a complete answer must also take into account differences in demand conditions and the advantage of using trade to fully exploit the economies of large-scale production.

Sources of Comparative Advantage

Ricardo illustrated his discussion of comparative advantage with examples—similar to those used here—of labor requirements per unit of production that differed from country to country. He did not attempt to look systematically at *why* it might take more labor days to produce cars in Germany than in the United States. Modern treatments follow the lead of the twentieth-century Swedish economist Eli Heckscher in describing the fundamental source of comparative advantage as differences in factor proportions—relative endowments of various factors of production among countries. If a country has large quantities of the factors of production—land, labor, and capital—suited to producing coffee and very little of the factors suited to producing aluminum, then the country will probably export coffee and import aluminum. Natural resource endowments, climate, soil conditions, availability of labor, labor skills, availability of capital, and specific types of capital equipment—all these contribute to determining where a country's comparative advantage will lie. As the theory of comparative advantage suggests, sometimes a country will import a good not because it is unable to produce that good domestically, but because it is so well endowed to produce other goods for export. For example, several South American countries import milk, not because they are unable to raise dairy herds but because the abundance of their mineral resources makes it cheaper for them to export oil or copper and to use the proceeds to buy milk from abroad.

Comparative advantage is not a static concept. Indeed, a country may develop a particular comparative advantage purely through its own actions, independent of the endowments of nature. Switzerland, for example, has to import most of the raw materials from which timepieces are made, but centuries of experience in watchmaking have given Switzerland a comparative advantage (based on acquired labor skills) that is independent of natural resources. Likewise, the United States—through the continuing research and development expenditures of its government and businesses—has acquired a unique comparative advantage in many lines (like computers) that use the most up-to-date technology.

EXCHANGE RATE

The exchange rate is the price of one currency expressed in the terms of another currency. Exchange rates tell us how much we will have to pay in dollars if we want to purchase a British pound, a Japanese yen, a West German mark, or an Indian rupee.

Exchange rates are the central focus of international transactions, because the prices of many goods are originally expressed in the prices of the country producing the goods. A night in a London hotel room may cost 9 pounds, a Japanese radio 2,500 yen, a year's food for an American soldier stationed in Germany 3,000 marks, and a bolt of Madras cloth 100 rupees. What these goods cost the American consumer or the American government will depend on the exchange rate—the dollar price of the particular foreign currency.

The exchange rate can be expressed in one of two ways. When we are speaking of transactions between the United States and West Germany, it is possible to say that the exchange rate is, say, 3 marks for a dollar. But it would be equally accurate to say that the exchange rate is $\frac{1}{3}$ of a dollar, or $33\frac{1}{3}$¢, for a mark.

For the individual buyer or seller—consumer, tourist, businessman, or government—the exchange rate will largely determine the direction of international transactions. For example, assume that a Japanese radio sells for 3,000 yen, while the same radio can be produced in the United States for $25. The exchange rate will determine whether U.S. radio companies will try to produce radios in the United States or buy them in Japan. If the exchange rate is 300 yen per dollar (so that the yen is worth $\frac{1}{300}$ of a dollar), then the company can buy 3,000 yen for $10 and use the 3,000 yen to buy a radio. Even after shipping costs, this would probably make more sense than producing the radio for $25 in the United States. On the other hand, if the exchange rate is 50 yen per dollar (so that the yen is worth $\frac{1}{50}$ of a dollar) it will take $60 to buy the 3,000 yen with which to buy a radio. In this case it would be cheaper to make radios in the United States—and it would probably be worthwhile trying to sell some of them to Japan.

Equilibrium Exchange Rate

The exchange rate is a price for a currency and has many similarities to other prices—the price of apples, for example. The price of apples has an equilibrium value determined in the apple market by the intersection of the demand for apples and the supply of apples. The exchange rate is also determined in a market—the foreign exchange market—by the intersection of the demand for a currency and the supply of that currency.

There is a difference, however, that can lead to considerable confusion. In the apple market, like most markets, a good is being exchanged for money. Those who have the money and want the good—in this case, the consumers of apples—are conventionally described as the source of the demand. Similarly, those who have the goods and want the money—in this case, the apple growers—are described as the source of supply. But, to step away from convention for a moment, this could just as well be seen as a case in which growers are demanding dollars and are willing to pay in apples to the consumers who are supplying dollars.

In the case of the foreign exchange markets—in which one currency is traded for another—this kind of flexible perspective is needed. After all, both sides are supplying one currency and demanding the other. For example, consider a market in which dollars are traded for marks. Germans are supplying marks and demanding dollars, and Americans are supplying dollars and demanding marks. Which side we call supply and which we call demand depends entirely on the *name* we give the market. If we call it the market for marks, then we should say that Germans are supplying marks and Americans are demanding them. If we call it the market for dollars, then we should say that Americans are supplying dollars and Germans are demanding them. But it is only one market we are describing—just as there is only one market for apples, whether we call it a market for apples to be purchased with dollars or a market for dollars to be purchased with apples.

The basic demand for a currency on the foreign exchange markets is derived from foreign demand for the things that the currency can buy. For example, the basic U.S. demand for German marks stems from many sources. American consumers demand German cars and wines; American companies demand German shipping and insurance services; American tourists demand German hotel rooms and nightclub entertainment; American investors demand German stocks and bonds; and American companies operating in Germany demand new factory buildings and locally built machinery. The American government demands military equipment and housing for its soldiers stationed in Germany, and those soldiers themselves demand groceries and an occasional night "on the town." All these demands can be met only if Americans are able to use their dollars to buy marks. This is the basic source of the American demand for marks. Together with the German willingness to supply these commodities and services at various prices, this provides the supply of dollars to Germany.

Likewise, German consumers, investors, tourists, businesses, and government agencies all want to buy things from the United States. This—together with the willingness of Americans to supply these commodities and services at various prices—creates the basic German demand for dollars.

Figure 7–1 shows the foreign exchange market for these two currencies as a market for dollars priced in terms of marks. We use the standard tools for understanding markets introduced in our discussion of *Supply and Demand Analysis* (see pp. 63–68). The horizontal axis represents the quantity of dollars demanded and supplied. The vertical axis represents the price in marks at which varying amounts of dollars would be supplied and

Figure 7–1   Market for Dollars in Terms of Marks

Price of Dollars
(in marks)

demanded. The demand for dollars is based on the German demand for
American commodities and services. The supply of dollars is based on the
American demand for German commodities and services, since that is what
causes American buyers to offer dollars in exchange for marks. The market
is in equilibrium at a price of 3 marks per dollar, at which price Germany
both demands and supplies $5 billion. This price can also be expressed by
saying that the mark would be worth $33\frac{1}{3}$¢.

The demand curve for dollars slopes downward to the right. To see the
reason for this, assume that the dollar prices of U.S. goods are not significantly affected by variations in American sales to Germany. Therefore, the
prices that Germans have to pay for American goods are in direct proportion
to the price that Germans have to pay for dollars. If the dollar costs 2 marks,
then a $5,000 American Buick will cost Germans 10,000 marks. If the dollar
costs 3 marks, then the Buick will cost 15,000 marks. If the dollar costs 4
marks, then the Buick will cost 20,000 marks. As dollars cost more, Germans
will be able to afford fewer American goods and will demand fewer dollars
with which to buy those goods.

The supply curve for dollars slopes upward to the right. This is the
normal case (although it may not hold under all conditions). It will clearly be

true if we assume that the dollar prices of the goods Germany sells are not significantly affected by variations in German sales to the United States. For example, the United States may be prepared to buy varying amounts of German Rhine wine at a standard price of $3 a bottle. If the price of a dollar is 2 marks, then a German wine dealer will only get 6 marks for each bottle he sells to the United States, and he may be inclined to try to sell more on the German market or on other foreign markets. If the price of a dollar is 3 marks, then the wine dealer will get 9 marks for a bottle, and selling to the United States will have greater appeal. If the price of a dollar is 4 marks, then the dealer will realize 12 marks per bottle, and he will try to sell a major part of his stock in the United States. Thus, German dollar earnings from wine—one component of the supply of dollars to Germany—will increase as the price of a dollar goes higher.

Appreciation and Depreciation

The term appreciation describes an increase in the value of one currency in terms of another currency. Likewise, the term depreciation describes a decline in the value of one currency in terms of another.

Figure 7–2 shows two ways in which the value of the dollar might appreciate in terms of marks if the exchange rate is responsive to changes in supply and demand. Figure 7–2a shows an upward shift in the German demand for dollars—from D_1 to D_2. This might represent, for example, increased German demand for American computers following the demise of a French computer company that had been selling many machines to Germany. Figure 7–2b shows a backward shift in the German supply of dollars—from S_1 to S_2. This might represent, for example, a late frost killing off German wine grapes or a long strike at a German Volkswagen plant. In either case, the effect is to raise the equilibrium price of the dollar to Germans from 3 marks to 4 marks. Note that this appreciation in the value of the dollar is the same thing as a depreciation in the value of the mark from $33\frac{1}{3}$¢ to 25¢. The depreciation of one currency is the logical counterpart of the appreciation of the other.

Figure 7–3 shows two ways in which the value of the dollar might depreciate in terms of the mark. Figure 7–3a shows a downward shift in the German demand for dollars—from D_1 to D_2. This might be due, for example, to an increase in the dollar price of American farm products, making them less attractive to German customers. Figure 7–3b shows an increase in the supply of dollars to Germany—from S_1 to S_2. This might be due to Germany's development of a new camera line to compete more effectively with Japanese cameras or to a decision by General Motors to invest in a major expansion of its Opel plant in Germany. In either case, the effect is to lower the equilibrium price of the dollar from 3 marks to 2 marks. This represents an appreciation of the mark from $33\frac{1}{3}$¢ to 50¢.

Care must be taken in describing changes in the exchange rate. In the case above, it makes no sense to say that the exchange rate as such has

Figure 7-2   **Appreciation of the Dollar**

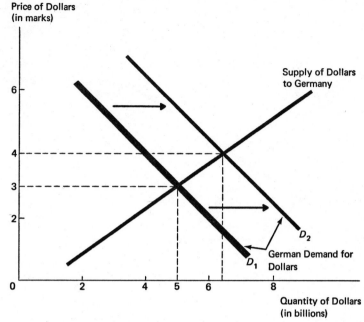

Price of Dollars
(in marks)

Supply of Dollars
to Germany

D_2

German Demand for
Dollars

D_1

0

Quantity of Dollars
(in billions)

a   Upward Shift in Demand for Dollars

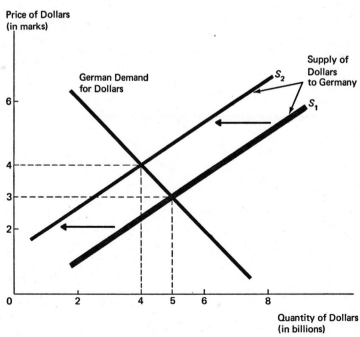

Price of Dollars
(in marks)

German Demand
for Dollars

Supply of
Dollars
to Germany

S_2

S_1

0

Quantity of Dollars
(in billions)

b   Reduction in Supply of Dollars

Figure 7-3   Depreciation of the Dollar

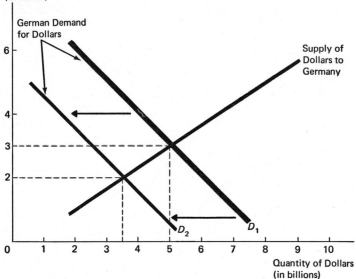

a   Downward Shift in Demand for Dollars

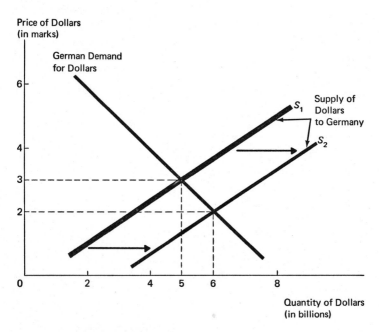

b   Increase in Supply of Dollars

risen or fallen. To be accurate, we say that the price of the mark—the exchange rate for marks in terms of dollars—has risen. Or that the price of the dollar—the exchange rate for dollars in terms of marks—has fallen. The exchange rate has risen or fallen depending on how we have chosen to express it.

In a world of many currencies, appreciation and depreciation are not always clear-cut terms. At one time the dollar price of the British pound may be $2.00 and the dollar price of the German mark may be 40¢. A year later the dollar value of the pound may have fallen to $1.50, while the dollar value of the mark has risen to 50¢. In this case, the dollar will have appreciated with respect to the pound (worth $\frac{2}{3}$ of a pound rather than $\frac{1}{2}$), but the dollar will have depreciated with respect to the mark (worth only 2 marks rather than $2\frac{1}{2}$ marks).

Devaluation and Revaluation

Two other concepts related to the value of a currency are devaluation or revaluation. These describe decreases or increases in the official value of the currency in terms of gold. From 1934 to 1971 the U.S. government had a policy of buying and selling gold at the fixed official price of $35 an ounce—which meant that the official value of the dollar was $\frac{1}{35}$ of an ounce of gold. Throughout the 1960s the United States found itself selling more gold than it was buying, and its gold stock decreased sharply. As a result, President Nixon abandoned the policy of buying and selling gold in 1971, and the official price of gold was subsequently raised. Raising the official dollar price of gold can be described as devaluation of the dollar, although the price lost any real meaning as soon as the United States ceased to buy or sell gold at that price. Indeed, early in 1975 the official price of gold was $42.22, but the U.S. auctioned off some of its gold holdings at roughly four times that price.

There are only two meaningful kinds of changes in the value of the dollar: changes in its domestic purchasing power brought about by inflation or deflation (see *Inflation,* pp. 95–104) and changes in its international purchasing power brought about by depreciation or appreciation in terms of other currencies.

Fixed vs. Flexible Exchange Rates

Up to this point we have described exchange rates as though they were fully flexible and responsive to shifts in supply and demand. From the end of World War II to 1973, most governments—usually through their central banks—attempted to maintain a fixed value for their currencies in terms of some other widely used currency, usually the dollar. Some governments still make this attempt. (See *World Monetary System,* especially pp. 291–94). To see how this system operates, let us consider the case of the German central bank trying to maintain a fixed exchange rate of 3 marks to the dollar.

The central bank can maintain that fixed exchange rate only if it stands willing to buy and sell dollars to all takers at 3 marks to the dollar. As long as the bank pursues this policy, then no German who wants to buy dollars need pay more than 3 marks, and no American who wants to sell dollars need accept fewer than 3 marks. The central bank can continue this policy, however, only if it has substantial international reserves—holdings of dollars, other currencies, or other assets, like gold or U.S. government bonds, that can be readily sold to obtain dollars. The bank accumulates reserves or pays them out as it becomes necessary in order to stabilize the dollar value of the mark.

To illustrate this process, consider Figure 7–4, which describes the German central bank trying to maintain a fixed exchange rate of 3 marks to the dollar. Germany receives $5 billion from Americans wishing to buy German goods and pays out $3 billion to Germans who want to buy American goods. Thus the quantity of dollars supplied exceeds the quantity of dollars demanded by $2 billion. In order to prevent the dollar surplus from driving down the price of the dollar (driving up the price of the mark), the central bank must intervene in the private market and pay out 6 billion marks

Figure 7–4   Fixed Exchange Rate for the Dollar—Excess Supply

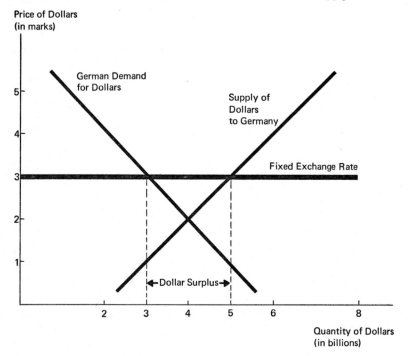

Price of Dollars
(in marks)

Figure 7–5   Fixed Exchange Rate for the Dollar—Excess Demand

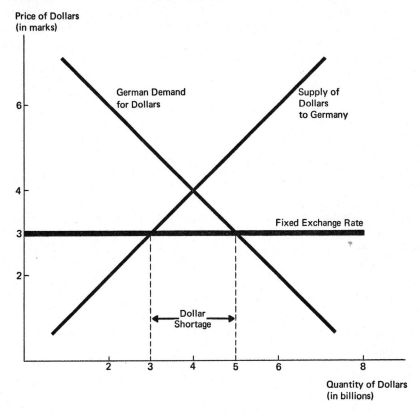

to buy up the surplus of $2 billion. In the process, the central bank adds $2 billion to its reserves of foreign currency.

Figure 7–5 shows a fixed exchange rate of 3 marks to the dollar after there have been shifts in the supply and demand schedules. Here the German demand for dollars to buy American goods comes to $5 billion, or $2 billion higher than the $3 billion that Americans are supplying in order to buy German goods. The central bank must use $2 billion in reserves to buy up 6 billion marks in order to prevent the price of the dollar from rising (to prevent the price of the mark from falling).

The German central bank may well find itself alternating between these two forms of activity. One month it may have to sell marks to buy dollars; another month it may have to sell dollars to buy marks. If it is able to maintain a fairly stable level of reserves over the months, the fixed exchange rate is probably fairly close to its equilibrium level. On the other hand, the German central bank may have to buy dollars month after month, and year after year (as in Figure 7–4) to meet the regular commercial demand for marks. In this case, the mark is <u>undervalued</u> in terms of dollars and the dollar is overvalued in terms of marks. That is, the equilibrium price of the mark in terms of dollars is above the fixed price that the central bank is trying to maintain. Alternatively, it may be (as in Figure 7–5) that the regular commercial demand for dollars is so great that the central bank is repeatedly paying out dollars and depleting its reserves in order to support the price of the mark. This would be a good indication that the mark is <u>overvalued</u>—that the equilibrium price of the mark in terms of dollars is lower than the price the central bank is trying to maintain.

The central bank may decide that the mark is undervalued, and that it does not want to go on accumulating dollar reserves. It may then attempt to correct the situation by fixing a new exchange rate at (what it guesses to be) the equilibrium level. In this case, the bank will suddenly announce a substantial appreciation of the mark in terms of the dollar. Alternatively, a decision that the mark is overvalued—often forced by the sense that dollar reserves cannot last much longer—can lead to a sudden and substantial depreciation of the mark in terms of the dollar.

Adjusting the exchange rate can help to correct the disequilibrium in the foreign exchange market. For example, if Germany is taking in more dollars than it is spending, an appreciation of the mark in terms of dollars should help to reduce the dollar surplus in two ways. First, it will make a wide range of German commodities and services more expensive to Americans and thus reduce the tendency for Americans to sell dollars to buy marks. Second, it will make a wide range of American commodities and services cheaper to Germans and thus increase the tendency for Germans to sell marks and buy dollars to spend on U.S. goods. The appreciation of the mark and corresponding depreciation of the dollar may take time to affect spending patterns. It may be too small to eliminate the whole German dollar surplus, or it may be so large that it converts the dollar surplus into a dollar shortage. But if the underlying supply and demand curves remain the same, the appreciation of the mark should have some effect in causing movement along those curves—reducing the quantity of dollars supplied by the U.S. and increasing the quantity of dollars demanded by Germany.

WORLD MONETARY SYSTEM

The world monetary system is the set of relationships among the major trading nations of the world. It determines how they set the values of their currencies and how they settle any financial imbalances among themselves.

If trading among nations takes the form of barter agreements, there is no real need for a world monetary system. For example, the representatives of two governments might meet and decide to exchange a ton of chickens for seven tons of corn. However, most foreign trade today takes place among individuals and firms, with goods being exchanged for different currencies. To facilitate this kind of trade it is useful if there is a known ratio—the *Exchange Rate* (see pp. 279–88)—at which one currency may be exchanged for another. It is also useful if there is some mechanism for dealing with financial imbalances among nations. These arise if some countries tend to buy more abroad than they sell, while other nations are selling more than they buy. The world monetary system describes the ways in which these two problems are handled.

We shall consider three general patterns for a world monetary system: a gold standard, a system of flexible exchange rates, and a system of fixed exchange rates among paper currencies. The latter is represented by the "Bretton Woods system" that prevailed for the first twenty-five years after World War II.

The Gold Standard

Under a pure gold standard, every country's money is either made of gold or can be directly converted into gold. For example, the little country of Yano may have a currency called the ducat. The people of Yano may carry paper ducats around for convenience, but the government of Yano stands ready to trade one ounce of gold for every 35 paper ducats that are presented to it. If the American government makes a similar promise with respect to the dollar, then one dollar is worth one ducat in international trade, because both currencies are backed by $\frac{1}{35}$ of an ounce of gold.

Assume, however, that under an exchange rate of one dollar for one ducat, Yanoians find American and other foreign goods very cheap, while foreigners find Yanoian goods very expensive. As a result, Yano will find itself buying abroad more than it is selling—that is, running a *Balance of Payments* deficit (see pp. 295–99). Yano can begin by paying out ducats to cover the deficit. If the deficit persists, however, people in other countries may become reluctant to hold ducats. They can then immediately turn them in at Yano's central bank and redeem each of them for $\frac{1}{35}$ of an ounce of gold. In effect, then, Yano will end up paying for the balance of payments deficit by exporting some of its gold holdings.

The outflow of gold can temporarily finance the balance of payments deficit, but the problem of eliminating that deficit would remain. Recall, however, that Yano's whole money supply is convertible into gold. The government of Yano knows from experience that it must keep on hand enough gold to meet the demands of anyone who presents paper money for conversion into gold. As its gold stock dwindles, the government must reduce the domestic money supply in order to maintain a healthy ratio between the paper money outstanding and the gold stock. This might be done by raising taxes or by reducing government expenditures, since either policy—or both in tandem—would mean that the government was taking in more money as taxes in relation to the money it was paying out in expenditures. As a result *Aggregate Demand* (see pp. 71–76) would tend to be reduced in the economy. A direct effect on Yano's trade position would be a reduction in demand for imported goods as well as for domestic goods—thus improving the balance of payments. An indirect effect of the curtailment of aggregate demand would be a reduction in the pace of price *Inflation* (see pp. 95–104) or even the creation of a price deflation. Yano's goods would then be cheaper on the world market, thus making the country's exports more attractive to other nations and further reducing the deficit on the balance of payments. Eventually, the payments deficit would be ended, the loss of gold would cease, and the reductions in the domestic money supply could stop.

The adjustment mechanism under the gold standard can work effectively if the government of Yano is responsive to changes in its gold supply. Balance of payments deficits can be eliminated and exchange rates can be maintained at constant levels. The implication of the gold standard, however, is that the level of aggregate demand in the domestic economy must be constantly manipulated to meet the changing demands of the balance of payments. Reducing the money supply and aggregate demand may bring not only reductions in the domestic price level but also increases in the unemployment of labor and capital and, hence, substantial losses of real income.

The gold standard was the dominant world monetary system in the decades before World War I, and it provided a fair degree of international economic stability. However, few countries in the second half of the twentieth century have been prepared to accept the domestic economic instability that is entailed by adherence to the gold standard.

Flexible Exchange Rates

At the opposite end of the scale from the gold standard would be a world monetary system based on flexible *Exchange Rates* (see pp. 285–88). Under such a system the rates of exchange among currencies are allowed to fluctuate freely with changing supply and demand conditions.

To see how this might work, assume that the money supply of Yano is made up entirely of paper money and bank deposits with no guarantee that they can be converted into gold. Assume further that the <u>foreign exchange</u>

markets—where currencies are traded—value the Yanoian ducat equally with the American dollar. Assume as before, however, that at this exchange rate Yanoians will be spending more ducats on foreign goods than Americans and others are spending dollars on Yanoian goods. As a result, foreigners begin to accumulate more ducats than they desire for buying Yanoian goods. An excess supply of ducats on the foreign exchange markets can have only one effect—driving down the dollar value of the ducat.

As a result of this depreciation of the value of the ducat, foreigners will be able to buy Yanoian ducats—and hence, a ducat's worth of Yanoian goods—for less than a dollar, and they will tend to want more of them. On the other hand, dollars will now cost Yanoians more than a ducat, so that foreign goods will become more expensive to Yanoians. The depreciation of the ducat will cause Yano to export more and to import less and thus will tend automatically to correct the deficit in Yano's balance of payments.

Thus, under flexible exchange rates, it is not necessary to undertake a sharp contraction of the domestic money supply and aggregate demand in order to correct a deficit. The decline in the value of the ducat will itself bring about the correction. This is not to say that the process will be painless. Imported goods will cost more to Yanoians, and the more vigorous export demand may bid up the domestic prices of some exportable goods. But making tradable goods more expensive is the system's way of inducing Yano to use fewer of them and to end a situation in which Yano is buying more from the rest of the world than it is selling.

Under the gold standard, exchange rates were fixed, but changes in a country's trade position could cause serious domestic economic instability. Under flexible exchange rates international economic stability suffers, because the value of the ducat (and other currencies) is subject to change from day to day, but there is no need to induce massive deflation and unemployment merely to correct a deficit on the balance of payments.

Fixed Exchange Rates—the Bretton Woods System

Toward the end of World War II most of the Allied nations sought to devise a new world monetary system that would combine the international stability of the gold standard with the domestic stability of flexible exchange rates. Returning to the gold standard was impossible, since most of the world's monetary gold supply was owned by one country, the United States. The new system grew out of the major international monetary agreements reached in 1944 at a conference in Bretton Woods, New Hampshire.

The basis of the Bretton Woods system was a network of fixed—but adjustable—exchange rates. Of the world's major currencies, only the American dollar was tied directly to gold, and only for international purposes. The U.S. government reaffirmed its promise to other governments—first made in 1934—to buy gold from them or to sell gold to them at

$35 an ounce. This meant that a dollar acquired in international trade could be exchanged for $\frac{1}{35}$ of an ounce of gold and that $\frac{1}{35}$ of an ounce of gold could be exchanged for a dollar. The dollar became the key currency in the new world monetary system.

Most of the other noncommunist countries of the world, including Great Britain and France, fixed the values of their currencies directly in terms of the dollar, allowing no more than a 1 percent deviation up or down. Some other countries did this indirectly, by fixing the values of their currencies in terms of the British pound or the French franc.

Thus, if our fictitious country, Yano, were a part of this system, the Yanoian government might have assigned a value to the ducat of $1. The Yanoian national bank would then need to hold international reserves— gold, dollars, and currencies or bonds issued by other important foreign governments. The bank could use these reserves on the foreign exchange markets to buy up Yanoian ducats whenever their value seemed to be falling below 99¢. Reserves could be acquired by the bank selling ducats whenever their value tended to rise above $1.01. In this way, the Yanoian bank could insure that the value of the ducat would never fluctuate by more than 1 percent around its official value.

For its part, the United States was not formally committed to maintaining the dollar value of any of the world's currencies. Its job was to maintain the gold value of the dollar, so that every country could feel that the dollar reserves they were holding were "as good as gold."

To facilitate the workings of the new world monetary system, the Bretton Woods agreement established a new international organization, the International Monetary Fund (IMF). The IMF serves as a kind of international bank for central banks. For example, if Yano's central bank found that its international reserves were running too low to continue to maintain the dollar value of the ducat, it could turn to the IMF. On the basis of how much it had originally contributed to the funding of the IMF, Yano would have the right to withdraw a certain amount of dollars and other reserves in exchange for ducats. Beyond those rights, the IMF directors might agree to let Yano exchange additional ducats for dollars, although the ducats would have to be brought back within five years. Thus Yano could immediately bolster its reserve position and could afford to implement gradually any harsher remedies for the balance of payments deficit—depreciation of the ducat, trade restrictions, or reductions of domestic aggregate demand. On the other hand, Yano might decide that it actually wanted to depreciate the dollar value of the ducat. Under the IMF rules it would be required to obtain permission from the fund directors. If they found that Yano's balance of payments was in "fundamental disequilibrium," they would grant Yano permission to depreciate the ducat, though not by more than 10 percent. In this way, fixed exchange rates could in fact be adjusted to changing economic realities.

Beyond Bretton Woods

Two major problems of the Bretton Woods system surfaced during the 1960s and early 1970s. On the one hand, the United States began running substantial balance of payments deficits in the early 1950s, which meant that central banks in many parts of the world began accumulating several dozen billions of dollars. As some of them were turned in for gold (at $35 an ounce) the U.S. gold stock fell sharply—from $25 billion worth in 1949 to less than $10 bilion worth in 1971. By that year the dollars and dollar assets (like U.S. government bonds) that foreign central banks could potentially convert into gold were seven times the size of the remaining U.S. gold stock. American government officials made it plain to other governments that converting dollars for gold would be considered an unfriendly act, so the promise to sell gold became increasingly hollow.

On the other hand, the system of fixed exchange rates was proving too rigid in the face of shifts in supply and demand on the foreign exchange markets. If a country like Yano were running a deficit on its balance of payments, speculators would begin to suspect that it would eventually be forced to depreciate the ducat. They would borrow ducats in Yano—on a one-year loan, for example—and sell them on the world market for the official price of $1. This would increase the supply of ducats on the foreign exchange markets and tend to force down the price. The Yanoian central bank would attempt to intervene by buying up ducats, which would further deplete its reserves.The Yanoian bank might then turn to the IMF, or to a friendly government, to borrow more reserves to bolster its position. But the harder the Yanoians tried, the more convinced the speculators would become that the value of the ducat could not be maintained. Billions of dollars in speculative, or "hot," funds might flow from country to country within a single week in the course of a foreign exchange crisis. Its reserves exhausted, the Yanoian bank might finally relent and lower the value of the ducat to 90¢. The speculators could then buy up ducats for 90¢ to pay off debts for ducats they had borrowed and sold for a dollar.

The Bretton Woods system broke down in two stages. In August 1971, President Nixon bowed to the inevitable and "closed the gold window." That is, he announced that the United States would no longer buy or sell gold at any price. Over the next two years more and more of the major trading countries of the world abandoned the attempt to maintain a fixed dollar value for their currencies. By March 1973, the major trading nations were letting their currencies "float" in value on the foreign exchange markets, although there was still some buying and selling by central banks to prevent major fluctuations.

In the years immediately after 1971, many government officials and bankers complained that the international monetary system was in chaos. The price of gold fluctuated on world markets just like any other commodity—first shooting up to the neighborhood of $200 an ounce, and by the mid-1970s settling down to less than two-thirds of that level. The widespread floating of exchange rates was in direct violation of the rules of the IMF, but no one really wanted to enforce those rules. There was an increasing realization that the new approach worked, permitting the world economy to adapt well to rapidly changing conditions. For example, the quadrupling of oil prices in late 1973 caused major shifts in world financial flows. Those shifts were achieved with changes in the market values of some currencies but without the traumatic foreign exchange crises that would have been inevitable under the Bretton Woods system.

In 1976 the members of the IMF agreed to formalize the new approach. They began to phase out any remaining ties between gold and currency values. They also agreed to amend the rules of the IMF to let each member country choose one of three approaches: (1) a floating exchange rate; (2) a fixed exchange rate; or (3) an exchange rate tied to the value of a few other currencies, which would float together in dollar value.

Once it had been broken, the Bretton Woods system—like Humpty Dumpty—could not be put back together again.

BALANCE OF PAYMENTS

The term *balance of payments* is used in two senses. In one sense, it is the system of accounts used to summarize all the international transactions of a country during a given period of time. It is an accounting table that includes totals for such items as imports and exports, government purchases abroad, investments across international boundaries, and changes in the government's holdings of gold and foreign currencies.

In another sense, the balance of payments describes the net balance between supply and demand for a country's currency on some portion of the transactions recorded in the system of accounts. Thus the United States might be said to have a deficit in its balance of payments if it must pay out more money than it receives in some segment of its international transactions. Likewise, the United States might be said to have a surplus if it is taking in more than it must pay out in some segment of its international transactions.

To understand these concepts better, it is useful to look first at the structure of the balance of payments accounts and then to examine the particular portions that are used to describe the balance between the dollars taken in and the dollars paid out.

The Structure of the U.S. Balance of Payments

The U.S. balance of payments accounts—since 1976 called the Summary of U.S. International Transactions—are divided into two broad segments: the current account and what we may call the asset account.

The current account summarizes the flows of commodities and services between the United States and the rest of the world. The current account includes five kinds of items: (1) private exports and imports of commodities, or "merchandise;" (2) exports and imports of other goods and services, including shipping and insurance services and expenditures abroad by tourists; (3) payments of income on assets held in other countries; (4) net grants by the U.S. government to other governments; and (5) U.S. government transfer payments to persons living abroad, including those receiving government pensions or Social Security payments.

The asset account describes changes in the assets of Americans that are held abroad and in foreign assets held in the U.S. The changes in private assets include the results of direct investment (like the building and equipping of a factory in another country) and financial investment (like the purchase of stocks and bonds in another country). They also include loans taken by private individuals and changes in bank deposits held in other countries. The changes in government assets include changes in the amounts of foreign currencies and government bonds that may be held by government treasuries. They sometimes include also the ability to draw on the country's account with the International Monetary Fund, the agency that serves as a kind of international bank for government central banks (see *World Monetary System,* pp. 292–94).

Concepts of the Balance

The traditional purpose of describing a balance of payments account is to indicate the pressures on a country's international reserves—its official holdings of gold and foreign currencies and bonds. If, for example, the goods that a country is importing are worth more than the goods it is exporting, then—other things equal—the country may have to dip into its reserves to pay for the extra goods it has bought. In the U.S. international accounts, a debit is any item that increases the foreign claim on American holdings of dollars on foreign currencies. Debits would include imports of merchandise, tourist expenditures abroad, or American use of dollars to invest abroad in plant and equipment. Debits are traditionally denoted by a minus sign (−). By contrast, a credit is any item that increases the American claim on foreign holdings of dollars or other currencies. For example, any export of goods from the United States creates an obligation on the part of foreigners to pay money to Americans; consequently it is listed as a credit. Credits are denoted by a plus sign (+).

The various concepts of a balance in international transactions are obtained by considering only some portions of those transactions and comparing the credits with the debits. If the credits exceed the debits, the difference between them is called a surplus—a positive balance. A surplus means that the net effect of transactions increases American claims on foreign holdings of dollars or other currencies and thus strengthens the reserve position of the United States. If the debits exceed the credits, the difference between them is called a deficit—a negative balance. A deficit means that the net effect of transactions increases pressure on U.S. reserves by generating an excess of foreign claims on American reserve holdings.

In Table 7–4 we present a simplified version of the current account transactions of the United States for 1975—using the presentation introduced by the U.S. Department of Commerce in 1976. We have rearranged the table somewhat to show clearly the three most important balance concepts now being used.

The Balance on Merchandise Trade.　This sense of the balance includes only one kind of item—exports and imports of commodities, or "merchandise." It is an ancient concept for analyzing trade flows that began when merchandise trade was almost the only form of international commerce. The 1975 balance shows a surplus of $8,983 million—the amount by which merchandise exports exceeded merchandise imports that year.

The Balance on Goods and Services.　This sense of the balance includes not only merchandise trade but also other goods and services—like shipping, insurance, and tourism—and income from assets held abroad. The

Table 7-4   U.S. International Transactions—Current Account—1975 Data (millions of dollars)

	Exports (or other credits)	Imports (or other debits)	Net for Item	Net for Table Thus Far
Merchandise trade	+107,133	−98,150		
Balance on merchandise trade				+ 8,983
Other goods and services	+ 23,059	−21,779		
Income from assets abroad	+ 18,219	−12,212		
Balance on goods and services				+16,270
U.S. government grants			−2,893	
U.S. government transfers			−1,727	
Balance on current account				+11,650

SOURCE: U.S. Department of Commerce, "Summary of U.S. International Transactions" (June 16, 1976).

1975 data show that the U.S. exported more of these other goods and services than it imported and that American individuals and firms earned more on their assets abroad than foreigners earned on their assets in the U.S. As a result, the balance on goods and services showed a surplus in 1975—$16,270 million—that was even larger than the surplus on merchandise trade.

The Balance on Current Account.   The balance on current account includes all of international transactions in the current account section. These include the merchandise, the other goods and services, and the income from assets abroad that make up the balance on goods and services. But they also include two items reflecting money sent abroad by the U.S. government—grants to other governments (including many forms of nonmilitary foreign aid) and transfer payments to persons living abroad (including government pensions and Social Security payments). Both items showed a net debit in 1975. Thus the surplus on the balance on current account of $11,650 million—while still considerable—was somewhat less than the positive balance on goods and services.

A positive or negative balance on current account must be paid for by someone. If the balance shows a deficit, this means that the U.S. has paid out more than it has taken in and that foreigners must have increased their net holdings of U.S. assets—dollars or other assets that might have been purchased with dollars, including bonds, stocks, or real estate. If the balance shows a deficit, this means that the U.S. has taken in more than it has paid out and that Americans must have increased their net holdings of foreign assets, including currencies and bank deposits. The 1975 current account surplus of $11,650 was accounted for in three ways, as shown in Table 7-5. U.S. assets held abroad were known to increase by $31,131 million, while foreign assets held in the U.S. increased by only $14,879 million—for a net increase in U.S. assets of $16,252 million. This is, of

**Table 7–5   U.S. International Transactions—Asset Account—1975 Data
(millions of dollars)**

Increase in U.S. assets abroad	31,131
Increase in foreign assets in the U.S.	14,879
Net increase in U.S. assets	16,252
Statistical discrepancy	4,602

Source: U.S. Department of Commerce, "Summary of U.S. International Transactions" (June 16, 1976).

course, considerably larger than the current account surplus of $11,650 million. Such disparities are handled in the international accounts by a "balancing item"—more accurately called a fudge factor—known as the statistical discrepancy. This entry may largely represent hidden capital transactions, like the shifting of money to or from secret Swiss bank accounts.

The three balances we have described are poor measures of the pressures on the international reserves held by the U.S. government. Many of the changes in assets included in the asset account can alter those pressures. For example, a payment of an additional $5 billion for imports of petroleum will reduce the surplus or increase the deficit shown on the balance on current account. But if the oil-exporting nations immediately use the $5 billion to buy shares of stock in American companies, then those dollars may never leave the country—and they will exert no short-term pressure on the U.S. to run down its holdings of international reserves. Thus the most inclusive balance now being calculated by the Department of Commerce—the balance on current account—only tells a part of the picture. Other balances that were calculated up until 1976 were more comprehensive and gave a better picture of the pressures on U.S. holdings of international reserves.

The Significance of the Balance of Payments

The significance of the balance of payments can best be understood if we examine the cost to a country of running a persistent deficit in its trade accounts. In a broad sense, the international position of a country's currency will be weaker if it is persistently losing reserves. How this manifests itself will depend largely on the nature of the World Monetary System (see pp. 289–94) and whether the country is operating under a system of fixed or flexible Exchange Rates (see pp. 285–88).

Under a system of flexible exchange rates, the simplest way to view a loss of reserves by the United States is to say that other countries are acquiring more dollars and that the United States is losing its supply of foreign currencies with which to buy back those dollars. In effect, the world's supply of dollars is increasing faster than the world's demand for those commodities, services, and capital assets than can be directly purchased with dollars. This will tend to drive down the value of the dollar in terms of other currencies. This result could be immediate under a system of fully flexible exchange rates. Indeed, the mere expectation of a significant deficit on the U.S. balance of payments might cause speculators to sell dollars and to buy other currencies—thus driving down the international value of the dollar.

The decline in the international value of the dollar would tend to correct the deficit. With the dollar cheaper for foreigners to buy, U.S. export goods priced in dollars will be more attractive on the world market. And with foreign currencies more expensive to Americans, imports from abroad will be less attractive on the American market. Even though the deficit will not persist indefinitely, the adjustment may be somewhat painful, since it will mean devoting more of the country's production to export goods and enjoying fewer imports from the rest of the world. But it may be the least painful way of ending a situation in which a country is, in effect, spending abroad more than it is earning abroad.

Under a system of fixed exchange rates, the significance of a deficit is somewhat different. For a foreign country that has fixed the value of its currency in terms of dollars, a loss of reserves means a lessened ability to use dollars to buy up its own currency and, hence, to support the international value of its currency. If the country ever runs out of reserves—or comes close—it will be unable to prevent the value of its currency from falling. For the United States the situation has been unique. From 1934 to 1971 the U.S. government guaranteed the value of the dollar not in relation to other currencies but in terms of gold—by standing prepared in its relations with many other governments to buy and sell gold at a fixed price of $35 an ounce. This was equivalent to standing ready to buy and sell dollars for $\frac{1}{35}$ of an ounce of gold.

Such a guarantee was only as good as the ability of the U.S. gold stock to back up this promise. Using concepts of the balance of payments that included many private capital movements, the U.S. balance was in deficit over much of the 1960s, and this meant that there was a large accumulation of dollars in other countries. The deficit was partly financed by reductions in the U.S. gold stock, but largely by a massive accumulation of dollars and U.S. government bonds abroad. By 1971, foreign central banks had acquired the ability to buy the remaining U.S. gold stock many times over, and President Nixon was forced to end any sales of the gold that remained.

Within a few years, most of the world's important trading nations shifted over from fixed to flexible exchange rates. As a result, the importance of a U.S. deficit shifted. The concern was no longer to prevent an outflow of the remaining U.S. gold stock but rather to prevent too great an erosion in the international value of the dollar.

TRADE RESTRICTIONS

Trade restrictions are any policies or practices that interfere with the free flow of trade among nations.

Restrictions often take the form of taxes on goods imported from other countries or exported to them. Import taxes—usually called <u>tariffs</u>—are commonly levied in one of two ways, *ad valorem* or specific. <u>Ad valorem tariffs</u> are taxes of a fixed percentage on the value of an imported good. Thus, an *ad valorem* tariff of 15 percent on television sets would come to $15 on a set that costs $100 to import and would come to $30 on a set that costs $200 to import. By contrast, <u>specific tariffs</u> are expressed as particular dollar amounts. Thus a specific tariff of $15 would be applied whether the TV set cost $100 or $200 to import.

Trade restrictions can also take the form of <u>quotas</u> on imports or exports. A government may require that no more than 250,000 tons of soybeans be exported abroad or that no more than 3 billion barrels of oil be imported during a particular year. Usually quotas are compulsory, with specific legal penalties for any trade beyond the quotas. Sometimes, however, voluntary quotas may be negotiated. For example, a government might be persuaded to restrict its own producers from exporting more than a million tons of steel or $500 million worth of textiles to another country.

Other kinds of trade restrictions can be invoked as well. Sometimes health, safety, or pollution laws prevent the importation of goods made in other countries. Sometimes government agencies are required to buy domestically produced goods even when foreign goods can be obtained at a lower price. Sometimes cumbersome procedures at customs offices create delays and "red tape" that discourage the importation of goods. But the most important restrictions are taxes and quotas, and these need to be examined in more detail.

Import Tariffs

To understand the impact of an import tariff, look first at an unrestricted market for one imported good—portable television sets of a given size and quality. Assume that transportation costs are low enough that they can be ignored. Assume also that there are no restrictions on imports of TV sets into the United States. Then these sets will be imported if the prevailing world price, expressed in dollars, generates more demand than supply within the United States. Figure 7-6 shows such a situation.

The horizontal line in Figure 7-6 shows a world price for portable television sets that is assumed to be constant at $100 over the range of sales to the United States. The world price line is, in effect, a supply curve to the United States from the rest of the world. At the same time, the upward sloping line represents a supply curve for the United States from domestic producers. The heavier portions of the two lines show the lowest possible

Figure 7–6 U.S. Market for TV Sets

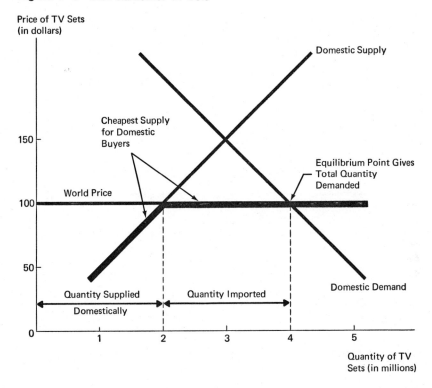

price at which different quantities can be bought. For small quantities of output (up to 2 million sets), it will be cheaper to obtain TV sets from domestic suppliers, and that portion of the domestic supply curve will be operative. For any larger quantities of output, however, the world price is lower than the price that would be charged by domestic producers, and the remaining portion of the world supply curve becomes operative. The diagram shows that market equilibrium (see *Supply and Demand Analysis,* pp. 63–68) will be achieved where the world price line intersects the domestic demand line. The world price of $100 will be the domestic price. The total quantity demanded will be 4 million sets. Since the world price is also the domestic price, the quantity supplied domestically will be given by the intersection of the domestic supply curve and the world price line, indicating a quantity of 2 million. The remaining demand (2 million sets) will be supplied by imports.

If we introduce a tariff into this market, the first effect will be to raise the domestic price of portable TVs. As Figure 7–7 shows, the domestic supply curve is not directly affected by the tariff, but the world supply curve is affected. If American consumers can only buy a foreign TV by paying the

Figure 7–7   Effect of a Tariff on TV Sets

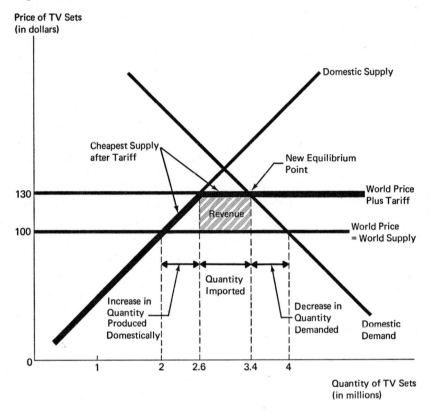

Price of TV Sets
(in dollars)

world market price of $100 plus the tariff of $30, then the domestic price of imported TVs will be $130. The supply curve that is operative to American consumers will now consist of the domestic supply curve up to the height of $130 and the horizontal world supply line for any additional sets that might be demanded. The new market equilibrium indicates a reduction in the quantity demanded (from 4 million to 3.4 million sets) and a domestic market price of $130. Thus the new price of imported TVs is not so high that importation ceases, and the new domestic market price is simply the world price plus the tariff.

The higher price induced by the tariff not only reduces the quantity of TV sets that consumers can afford to buy. It also induces domestic suppliers to produce more TV sets for the domestic market (from 2 million to 2.6 million sets). Imports are thus reduced from two directions: (1) because consumers are now demanding a smaller number of TV sets and (2) because domestic producers are now providing a larger number of them. Total imports are now reduced to 0.8 million sets—the difference between domestic demand of 3.4 million and domestic supply of 2.6 million.

Figure 7-7 also shows that the tariff, since it is not high enough to cut off imports, generates $24 million in tax revenue for the government. This is represented by the shaded rectangle in the figure, the width of which is the quantity of imports, 0.8 million, and the height of which is the amount of tax, $30, charged on each set imported.

For some countries—including the United States in the early days of the republic—the tariff can be a major source of tax revenue. But for the United States in the last third of the twentieth century, other sources of revenue—particularly the personal and corporate income taxes—have dwarfed the importance of tariff revenues.

A tariff has other important effects on consumers and producers. For consumers, a tariff raises the price that must be paid, not only for imported goods but also for their domestic counterparts. In Figure 7-7, the tariff raised the price of domestically produced TV sets as well as imported ones, because it meant that domestic producers no longer had to meet the competition of the world price of $100. They needed only to meet it at the world price plus the tariff, or $130. For domestic producers, a tariff has two consequences. It encourages firms to increase production, even to the point at which the resources used to produce the good cost more than the world price of the good. It also increases profits in the industry, since firms can charge the new, higher price on all units of output they sell—not just on those that cost more to produce.

The tariff in our example may create additional domestic employment in the television industry. But at what cost? The consumers who continue to buy TV sets despite the higher price now have less income with which to buy other goods. The consumers who are priced out of the TV market must spend another year of deprivation, staring at their radios. In these two ways, therefore, consumers bear the cost of the decision to deny them the right to buy foreign goods at the world price. Producers of other goods may be hurt as well, since the foreign countries that would have earned dollars selling TV sets to the United States are now able to buy fewer American export goods like automobiles, computers, wheat, and soybeans.

Import Quotas

An alternative device for restricting imports is the import quota. Under some circumstances, an import quota will have the same effect on domestic prices, production, and consumption as an import tariff. For example, if there are lots of U.S. producers of TV sets and if each producer simply responds to a given market price, then there is an import quota that would create a market equilibrium at the same domestic price as a tariff. Look again at Figure 7-7. There an import tariff of $30 cuts imports of TV sets to 0.8 million units (the 3.4 million sets sold at home minus the 2.6 million sets imported) and results in a domestic price of $130 per set. Instead of the tariff of $30 dollars, the government might have imposed a limit of 0.8 million on the number of TV sets that could be brought into the country. This could result in the same market equilibrium as in Figure 7-7. At a domestic price of $130, the many U.S. companies would together be willing to produce 2.6 million sets. This, when added to the imports of 0.8 million, would satisfy the U.S. demand at $130 of 3.4 million sets.

But TV set producers might not respond that way. To take an extreme case, assume that only one U.S. company, the Nadir Electronics Company, makes portable TV sets. If, on top of the world price of $100, the government adds a tariff of $30, then the Nadir Company could not charge much more than $130 for a set. At any higher price, U.S. consumers would simply start buying foreign TV sets for $130—and they could legally import from abroad all the 3.4 million sets that they want to buy at $130. If, on the other hand, the government limits imports to 0.8 million sets, the Nadir Company can charge much more than $130 for a TV set. American buyers might grab up all 0.8 million sets that they could legally import from abroad, but beyond those sets, the Nadir Company would have a captive market. It could not charge so high a price that it would lose all its customers. But it might well be able to make more profit by selling, say, 2.2 million sets for $160 each than by selling 2.6 million sets for $130 each. The loser would be American consumers, who would have to forego the enjoyment of .4 million TV sets and would have to pay $30 more for each domestic set.

There is another reason why some groups prefer quotas over tariffs. Under a quota, a government typically does not receive the tax revenues that it would have received under a comparable tariff. Often it assigns licenses permitting various importers to import a particular quantity of goods. Those importers thereby gain the right to buy TV sets on the world market for $100 each and sell them on the U.S. market at $130 each. The profit of $30 per set goes into the pocket of the importer who is fortunate enough—or influential enough—to receive the import license. The quota benefits producers and hurts consumers at least as much as the tariff. In addition, however, the quota benefits the importer at the expense of the government and, ultimately, of the taxpayer.

Export Restrictions

Taxes or quotas on the export of goods are in some ways the opposite of import restrictions; they hurt the producer and benefit the consumer. Their overall effect, however, is to reduce further the mutual gains from trade among nations. In the United States, export taxes are forbidden by the Constitution, but quotas are sometimes used to restrict exports.

Assume that the world price of soybeans is $100 a ton. Any farmer who could sell abroad for $100 would not sell at home for less, so in the absence of an export quota, the domestic price will also be about $100 a ton. An export quota on soybeans would cause less to be sold abroad and more to be sold at home. American consumers would be able to enjoy soybean products (including meat grown on soybean feeds) at a domestic price lower than the world price—say, $70 a ton. At the same time, soybean farmers would receive less for their crops—only $70 on the portion sold within the United States but $100 on that portion that they would still be permitted to sell abroad.

Evaluation of the Restrictions

It may be tempting to see the export restrictions on soybeans and the import restrictions on TV sets as canceling each other out. As far as producers are concerned, there is a sense in which this is true. TV set manufacturers are better off as a result of the import restrictions, while soybean growers are worse off as a result of the export restrictions. Income is redistributed from one group of producers to the other, but there would appear to be no overall loss of real income. The case of consumers is different, however. At first glance the canceling might appear to be even more direct. That is, as a result of the import restrictions, consumers have to pay $130 for TV sets that sell on world markets for $100. As a result of export restrictions, however, they are able to enjoy soybean products on the basis of $70 a ton rather than the world price of $100 a ton. Is there any sense in which consumers are helped or hurt?

To understand the situation, think of two consumers—George Beaneater and Herman Tubewatcher. Assume that Beaneater would be willing to pay only $71 for the products made from one more ton of soybeans but that he buys them because their price is only $70. Tubewatcher, on the other hand, would be willing to pay as much as $129 for a new TV set but does not buy one because it would cost $130. Assume that a middleman comes into the situation who is able to work around the trade restrictions. He offers Beaneater $100 for the ton of soybeans, then sells them on the world market at the world price of $100. He uses the money to buy a foreign TV set at its world market price of $100. He then offers the TV set to Tubewatcher for $100 and thus recoups his initial expenditure for the soybeans. Note that both consumers are better off. Beaneater has received $100 for a ton of soybeans that he valued at only $71, and Tubewatcher has been able to buy a TV set for $100 that he valued at fully $129. The situation before the middleman intervened was clearly inefficient (see *Efficiency,* pp. 18–23), since both men could be made better off without anyone else being made worse off.

This example suggests that the import and export restrictions tended to deny the economy an important supplement to its domestic production capability—the ability to exchange one good for another at world prices. The middleman in our example was simply performing the classic role of free trade in the world market, exchanging one good for another on terms that are favorable to both parties. In the example, the United States has a comparative advantage (see *Absolute and Comparative Advantage,* pp. 273–78) in soybeans as compared to TV sets. Another country, say Japan, may have a comparative advantage in TV sets as compared to soybeans. Trade restrictions could cause Japan and the United States to produce both soybeans and TV sets primarily for their own domestic markets. Thus they would prevent the full consumer welfare that is possible through the exploitation of comparative advantage.

REGIONAL ECONOMIC INTEGRATION

Regional economic integration refers to a set of coordinated actions designed to draw the economies of two or more countries closer together. Such actions may include: reducing barriers to the free flow of commodities or factors of production among the countries; creating common trade barriers to the outside world; or coordinating policies on taxation, government expenditure, monetary expansion, and the regulation of business.

Once the parties to an integration agreement decide what kind of integration they would like eventually to achieve, they usually establish a schedule for gradually eliminating the barriers and differences in economic policy that have divided them. Ten- or fifteen-year programs of transition have been common in the efforts at economic integration undertaken since World War II.

Types of Economic Integration

There are three distinct approaches to the integration of markets among countries—free trade area, customs unions, and common market. Each brings a different degree of unification.

A free trade area represents a group of countries that have eliminated all trade barriers—tariffs and quotas—on commodities produced within the area, although each country may retain its own separate barriers to trade outside the area. In the early 1960s seven European nations, including the United Kingdom, joined together in the short-lived European Free Trade Area (EFTA). In addition, most of the South American countries have been slowly working toward the creation of a Latin American Free Trade Area (LAFTA).

A customs union carries the process of integration one step further. Not only are trade barriers eliminated for goods produced within the region, but the countries adjust their own tariffs and quotas to establish a common set of barriers against goods produced outside the region. There is free trade within the "wall" of tariffs (or "customs"), but there is a common tariff wall against trade with the outside world. A customs union, or *Zollverein,* was the first step toward the unification of the various German states in the mid-nineteenth century. Following World War II, Belgium, the Netherlands, and Luxembourg joined together in a customs union known as Benelux.

A common market carries economic integration yet another step. Not only is there free trade in goods within the region and a common set of barriers against imports from outside the region, but there is also free movement of the mobile factors of production—capital and labor—within the region. Any restrictions against the migration of labor from one country to another are removed, as are any restrictions against citizens or companies of one country building plants or buying up companies in another country. The European Economic Community (EEC)—often called the European

Common Market—is the most prominent example of a common market in modern times. Created by the Treaty of Rome in 1957, it originally united the three Benelux countries with Italy, France and West Germany. Over the next fifteen years the six countries moved to eliminate completely all tariff and quota barriers on nonfarm products. In 1973, three more nations—United Kingdom, Ireland, and Denmark—joined the EEC and let the EFTA die on the vine. During the 1960s most of the Central American countries also joined together in a Central American Common Market. Although it has been plagued by political problems among some of the members, it has gradually strengthened its common economic policies.

Even a common market falls far short of a fully integrated economy. Such an economy would share a common currency and monetary policy, a common set of tax laws, and common policies for the regulation of business. Full economic integration is difficult to realize without a high degree of political integration as well. Indeed, Jean Monnet—the French economic statesman who was the guiding spirit of the EEC—always described the Common Market as an important first step toward a common European government.

The Impact of Regional Economic Integration

The creation of a customs union or common market from a group of countries with disparate trade policies has two immediate objectives: the lowering of trade barriers within the region (ultimately to zero) and the unification of trade barriers between the individual countries and the rest of the world. As a result, barriers to trade with the outside world will be increased in some cases and reduced in others.

Lowering trade barriers within the region can lead to important gains from increased specialization. It will permit some companies to expand their sales—partly at the expense of other less efficient companies in other countries. For example, Germany may have been producing some typewriters itself but also importing similar machines from Italy. A high tariff against Italian machines may have served to keep the price of imported typewriters high and thus permitted German producers to sell their machines at the same high price. If Germany and Italy join together in a common market, then the German tariff on Italian goods will be eliminated, and Italian typewriter manufacturers will be able to sell many more machines in Germany. With the elimination of the tariff the price of Italian typewriters within Germany will fall, forcing German manufacturers to cut their prices as well. German consumers will benefit from being able to buy more typewriters. German manufacturers, however, may not be able to make so many typewriters at the lower price. They may be forced to cut back production or even to go out of business. Thus the adjustment may be painful for German typewriter companies and workers. However, German consumers will enjoy cheaper typewriters and Italian firms may be able to enjoy benefits of large-scale production that will lower the price of typewriters for Germans even further. And, with the elimination of Italian tariffs on German automobiles or electronic equipment, these industries may begin to capture more of the Italian market. German typewriter workers will then have little trouble finding new work. Thus lower barriers can mean increasing international specialization and *Efficiency* (see pp. 18–23). Both countries will produce more along the lines of their comparative advantages (see *Absolute and Comparative Advantage,* pp. 273–78), and many producers will be able to exploit the economies of large-scale production.

The elimination of trade barriers within the region can boost productivity even if trade patterns are not changed. Producers may respond to the challenge of greater foreign competition and cut their costs and prices. For example, the elimination of the German tariff on typewriters will lower the price of typewriters in Germany. German manufacturers may respond by installing more modern production methods and by cutting waste so that they can continue to compete with the Italians at the lower price. As a result, fewer resources will have to be used in providing German consumers with typewriters.

By contrast, the creation of a common wall of trade barriers between the common market and the outside world may or may not increase the efficiency of world production. If a country began with high tariffs against foreign products and if the common tariff wall consists of much lower tariffs, then the change could be beneficial. Consumers within the country will be able to obtain goods from outside the common market at a lower price than they had to pay when the country's tariffs were higher. Inefficient producers within the country, who survived because of high tariff barriers, will now be forced to increase their productivity or to release resources to other, more productive, industries. The same kinds of benefits that resulted from eliminating tariffs within the common market will be extended to trade outside the market.

The case will be different, however, if a country begins with low tariffs and is forced to accept a common tariff wall that is much higher. For example, a country that has been giving high tariff protection to an industry may join in a common market and seek to have those tariffs included in the common tariff wall surrounding the whole market. This can impose substantial hardships on consumers in other countries who had been enjoying cheap imports. For example, before Britain joined the European Economic Community, it had imposed very low—or zero—tariffs on a wide range of agricultural commodities and had imported foodstuffs from every part of the world. France, on the other hand, insisted on continuing to protect inefficient French agriculture from foreign competition by maintaining high trade barriers on the entry of foods from outside the market. Britain, by joining the EEC, was forced to accept higher agricultural prices in order to obtain the benefits of the free entry of British manufactured goods to the large European market.

Economists, then, offer a mixed verdict on regional economic integration. It is useful insofar as it lowers trade tariff barriers among the countries within a common market and between the countries inside the market and the outside world. But it can be harmful insofar as it forces all the countries within the market to accept the high trade barriers that were previously imposed only by some of the members. The lower the external wall surrounding the new market, the more beneficial regional economic integration is likely to be.

8

Economic Development

By the mid-1970s the United States' economy was producing an average of more than $7,500 worth of commodities and services for every American. At the same time more than a billion people lived in countries—such as India, Zaire, and Indonesia—that produced an average of less than $200 per person. The success or failure of efforts at economic development in poor countries can mean the difference between prosperity and starvation for hundreds of millions of human beings.

One popular explanation of the causes of underdevelopment is analyzed in our discussion of the **Vicious Circle of Poverty**. Several economic historians have attempted to summarize the process of development by describing **Stages of Growth**.

Economists offer a variety of prescriptions for achieving rapid economic development. Some stress the rate of **Capital Formation**, the buildup of the productive assets of the economy. Some stress the necessity for **Balanced Growth**, in which the pattern of production grows in accord with the pattern

311

of growing demand for goods. Some stress **Land Reform**, steps to bring about a more equal distribution of land ownership. While each of these prescriptions has its pitfalls, we can learn from the successes and failures of recent efforts at development and see how economics as a discipline can provide useful guidance to nations attempting to rise out of poverty.

VICIOUS CIRCLE OF POVERTY

The vicious circle theory describes the less developed country as trapped in its own poverty. Some activity, like capital formation, is seen as necessary for development, but the very fact of poverty prevents that activity from flourishing. Through a circular chain of causation, the low-income economy is seen as unable to increase output significantly faster than population is growing; consequently, income per capita stagnates.

Examples of the Vicious Circle Theory

The most common example of the theory is the <u>vicious circle of saving</u>, applied to a country that is experiencing a low income per capita and a high rate of population growth. The theory traces a causal chain of five links: (1) the low per capita income determines a low rate of domestic saving; (2) the low rate of saving means that most current output is being consumed and little is used for investment; this in turn means a low rate of growth of the capital stock; (3) if an increase in output requires a fixed amount of additional capital, the growth of the capital stock directly determines the growth of output: (4) if the output growth rate is no greater than the population growth rate, output per capita does not grow; (5) the level of income per capita remains at its initial low level. This circular chain is depicted in Figure 8–1, which shows each cause and effect connected by arrows.

Figure 8–1 **The Vicious Circle of Saving**

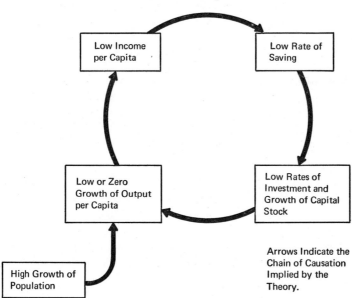

Another commonly discussed vicious circle of poverty relates to health and nutrition. Low incomes generate poor health care and low nutrition levels, and these keep the labor productivity low, insuring that output and income will also remain low.

In the same manner economists have proposed many other vicious circle theories. The only requirement is that some deficiency be seen both as a cause and a consequence of poverty. The following are a few other activities or attributes that are sometimes described both as necessary to development and as deficient due to poverty: literacy, basic education, labor skills. entrepreneurship, effective developmental planning, investment in social overhead capital (transportation and communications networks), large domestic markets, labor mobility, agricultural production for market rather than for home consumption, land reform, improved income distribution, and political stability.

A particularly dismal addition to the vicious circle argument is the theory of the low-level equilibrium trap. The theory assumes that the rate of population growth is highly sensitive to the level of per capita income, because poverty serves to keep death rates high. Any tendency for income to grow faster than population will soon cut death rates and stimulate a faster growth of population until income per capita again ceases to grow and a new equilibrium is restored. A substantial critical minimum effort—a widespread development program, typically involving massive foreign aid—would be required to break out of the vicious circle and to get income growing faster than population can grow.

There can be an optimistic side to the theory, however—the notion that once a vicious circle of poverty is broken, it is transformed into a virtuous circle of growth. Gunnar Myrdal, the Swedish economist and sociologist, argues that, if stagnation has circular causes, then growth may be a cumulative process. For example, if higher income per capita could somehow be initiated, then that higher income would generate higher rates of saving and investment. The capital stock would then grow faster, and this would generate a faster growth of income. Thus the economy would have completed the first round of an upward spiral of accelerating growth.

Evaluation of the Vicious Circle Theory

The theory is subject to two major objections, one theoretical and the other empirical. From a theoretical standpoint, a vicious (or a virtuous) circle, like any chain, is no stronger than its weakest link, and most of the vicious circles described have some very weak links indeed. In general, the theory assumes that important economic variables have only one determinant—that the level of nutrition, for example, is determined solely by the level of income. But economic phenomena typically have many causes, and there are relatively inexpensive educational programs and low-cost food supplements that can substantially enrich dietary practices in a poor country.

Every time a variable in a vicious circle chain has determinants that are not part of the circle, an opportunity exists to break into the circle and to begin lifting the country out of poverty.

Consider again the links of the savings circle: (1) Among the less developed countries, there is no strong tendency for the poorest countries to have the lowest saving rates. Higher export earnings and higher interest rates seem to stimulate saving even in very poor countries. (2) If a substantial portion of domestic savings is fleeing the country—into Swiss bank accounts, for example—then measures to reduce the capital flight could stimulate investment even without increasing the amount of domestic saving. (3) Faster technological progress and better utilization of resources can generate a faster growth of output even if the capital stock does not grow any faster. (4) Dissemination of birth control information and devices can reduce the birth rate even in a poor country. The ability to break into the chain of causation at any one of these links means that even a low-income country can break out of a vicious circle of poverty and begin to grow. Conversely, it means that even a fast-growing country can break out of a virtuous circle of development and begin to stagnate.

Viewed empirically, the vicious circle theory does not really fit the facts of recent growth experience. The theory would seem to predict low growth of output and zero growth of per capita output for many low-income countries. By contrast, during the 1960s and early 1970s, growth of output for the less developed countries as a whole was somewhat greater than for the developed countries as a whole.

The less developed countries did not grow as fast in output per capita, but only because their rates of population growth were significantly higher. Very few of the less developed countries for which we have statistics show a stagnating or declining per capita output—and those that do are not clustered among the poorest. Rather, moderate growth is the typical experience, and in a few cases (like Taiwan and South Korea) growth has been truly impressive. If the vicious circle of poverty is a real trap, it can only be for those few remaining areas of the world (like New Guinea) that are too poor even to produce statistics.

The vicious circle concept describes some of the real difficulties of breaking out of poverty. But rapid development is far from impossible. It has been experienced by many poor countries in the past, and it is being experienced today. Likewise, several of the most developed countries— including the United States and Canada—have had difficulty in matching the growth performances of some of the poorer countries. Neither theoretical considerations nor actual experience seems to justify either the extreme pessimism of the vicious circle theory or the extreme optimism of the virtuous circle theory.

STAGES OF GROWTH

Theories of the stages of growth attempt to describe a series of distinct and definable periods through which all economies—or a special group of economies—must pass in the course of economic development.

Stage theories of development were common among the German economic historians of the nineteenth century. Some described the evolution of the scope of the market—from trade only within a household or clan to trade within an entire nation. Others described stages in the dominant form of production—from a primitive economy with hunting and fishing to a modern economy with agriculture, manufacturing, and international commerce. Still others described the evolution of the means of exchanging goods—from simple barter through the use of money and into modern systems of credit. Karl Marx traced past development through stages of primitive culture, feudalism, and capitalism, and he looked forward to capitalism developing into socialism and eventually into communism. All of the stage theorists shared Marx's belief that "the industrially more developed country presents to the less developed country a picture of the latter's future."

This belief generated a new interest in stage theories of economic history among the new group of development economists who emerged following World War II. Walt W. Rostow, one of the most prominent of these, presents such a theory in his book, *The Stages of Economic Growth*.

Rostow's Five Stages

Rostow describes five stages that he claims are relevant to the development of most countries—including Great Britain, Germany, Japan, Turkey, and India. He argues, however, that special variations of the theory would be required to handle some special cases—like the United States, Canada, Australia, and New Zealand. These countries were essentially overseas offshoots of Great Britain at a time when it was already in a relatively advanced stage of development. Therefore, Rostow says, they were "born free" of the obstacles to development in a traditional society. What will be described here, then, is the main body of his theory rather than its extension to these special cases.

Rostow sees a developing economy going through at least five stages: traditional society, preconditions for takeoff, takeoff, drive to maturity, and age of high mass consumption.

Traditional Society. The traditional society is marked by limited production possibilities. It is a world in which modern science and technology are not yet known—or at least not yet systematically applied to the economy. Indeed, it is a society that does not believe that the world can be systematically manipulated for productive purposes. The economy is heavily agricultural, organized in small, self-sufficient regions, with political power based largely on land ownership. Income is at too low a level to do much more than support minimum levels of consumption.

Preconditions for Takeoff. According to Rostow, the preconditions for takeoff first developed in Great Britain, where the discoveries of modern science were applied to industry and agriculture. More usually, he argues, it requires some external shock—the threat of invasion or the fear of humiliation by foreigners—to undermine the values of the traditional society and to cause its members to seek alternatives. For the first time economic growth is seen as being both possible and desirable. New and enterprising leaders assume command of government and private economic activity. They broaden the scope of education. They begin to stimulate saving and to channel resources away from consumption by landowners and into productive investment. They seek to unify and to modernize the national economy, applying new technology initially to agriculture and raw material extraction but eventually to transportation and communications as well.

Takeoff. The takeoff to self-sustained growth is, in effect, an Industrial Revolution. Rostow describes it as a period of twenty to thirty years in which the traditional social structures, values, and vested interests that have resisted steady economic growth are "finally overcome." Economically progressive forces become dominant in the society, and growth is integrated into the habits and institutions of the economy. The stimulus for the takeoff may take several forms. It may be a political revolution, like the Meiji Revolution in Japan in 1868. It may be a series of economic innovations, like the development of textile technology in Britain toward the end of the eighteenth century. Or, it may be the opening of new markets, like the burgeoning of European demand for Swedish timber in the 1860s.

Rostow describes three specific characteristics of the takeoff period: (1) an increase in the rate of net investment; (2) the development of one or more leading sectors—usually in manufacturing, raw material processing, or railroad expansion—whose rapid growth stimulates the growth of the entire economy; and (3) the "existence or quick emergence of a political, social and institutional framework which exploits the impulses to expansion."

Drive to Maturity. Following the successful completion of the takeoff, Rostow sees the economy as going through about forty years in which modern technology is extended beyond the leading sectors to cover the whole range of economic activity. Investment increases to about 20 percent of national income, the economy adopts a more refined technology and more complex manufacturing processes.

Age of High Mass Consumption. This stage begins when the leading sectors of the economy begin to shift to the production of durable consumer goods—sewing machines, vacuum cleaners, washing machines, and automobiles. The economy can produce an income substantially above that needed for basic food, shelter, and clothing, and increasing attention is given to providing programs of social welfare and security.

Rostow envisions that economies may evolve beyond the stage of high mass consumption. He limits his basic description, however, to those five stages that he feels can be clearly read from history.

Criticisms of the Five Stage Theory

The most trenchant criticism of the Rostow theory is that presented by Simon Kuznets of Harvard, one of the first Nobel Prize winners in economics. To Kuznets, the Rostow description of economic development fails to delineate distinct stages, each with its own common and unique characteristics. For example, the preconditions and takeoff stages overlap at many points. Rostow describes both stages as involving an increase in the rate of investment to the point where total output increases more rapidly than population. He places the development of a transportation and communications network as part of the precondition stage but then lists railroad development as one of the more common leading sectors of the takeoff.

Kuznets argues that all the stages from preconditions onward seem to be part of a continuous process in which leading sectors emerge and stimulate the overall growth of the economy. Kuznets perceives this process as a single experience, which he calls "modern economic growth."

Kuznets also doubts the validity of the notion of "self-sustaining growth" initiated in the takeoff stage. He concedes that past economic growth can make future growth easier by providing the economy with a surplus of income above that required for basic consumption. At the same time, however, past economic growth may make future growth more difficult. Severe pressure may have been put on natural resources. People may have grown fat and lazy and less interested in increasing production. Entrenched economic interests may have arisen that will oppose the introduction of new areas of development that threaten their established position. "Economic growth," Kuznets concludes, "is always a struggle." It cannot be taken for granted once the economy has passed through some point of no return like a takeoff stage.

Two other important lines of criticism of the Rostow thesis have been voiced. Several "radical" economic historians have questioned Rostow's view of traditional society. They argue, for example, that Peru or India in the nineteenth century were not "traditional" societies but rather societies that had been demoralized and impoverished by colonial exploitation. Certainly Rostow fails to recognize the flourishing—and often highly prosperous—civilizations that existed in many parts of Asia, Africa, and Latin America before the colonial and imperial incursions of the Western powers.

Other more traditional economic historians have questioned whether any stage theory can hope to generalize about stages which take place in different countries at different points in historical time. For example, the age of high mass consumption—with its conspicuous sales of consumer durable goods—came into being in many countries at the time these goods were invented and developed. These historians suggest that Great Britain was late in experiencing such an age because most consumer durable goods had not yet been invented when Britain was completing its drive for maturity. At the same time, this age may come early in the development of some of the poorer countries simply because such goods can now be cheaply and plentifully produced.

Conclusions

Rostow's writings on the stages of economic growth can be read profitably. They contain some useful insights into the ways that habits, values, and political systems can impede or promote economic development. His stage theory, however, has little value as an analytical tool. It is difficult to quarrel with Kuznets' conclusion that Rostow has failed to show that modern economic growth is anything more than a continuous process beginning in the preconditions period and continuing through the period of high mass consumption.

CAPITAL FORMATION

Capital formation is the process of building up the capital stock of a country through investing in productive plant and equipment. Gross investment—the total expenditure on plant, equipment and inventories—is not the best measure of capital formation. It includes a certain amount of investment undertaken merely to replace old capital that has depreciated by wearing out or becoming obsolete. Net investment—gross investment minus an allowance for the depreciation of old capital—better reflects the rate of capital formation.

Emphasis on Capital Formation

Development economics came into its own as a new field of study in the years following World War II, as more and more economically underdeveloped areas became politically independent and undertook development programs of their own. The first group of new development economists put great emphasis on the importance of capital formation. For example, in a book entitled *Problems of Capital Formation in Underdeveloped Countries,* the late Ragnar Nurkse—a Norwegian economist who taught at Columbia University—asserted that the process "lies at the center of the problem of development in economically backward countries." These economists were greatly impressed with the plentiful and sophisticated capital equipment of the developed countries as contrasted with the meager and relatively primitive tools and machinery available in the less developed countries.

Some simple arithmetic also lends credence to the importance of capital formation—comparing the net investment rate with the incremental capital-output ratio. The net investment rate is the ratio of net investment in the economy to total production. For example, if an economy produces $1 billion in commodities and services, while devoting $150 million to net investment, it has a net investment rate of 15 percent. The incremental capital-output ratio, or ICOR, is the ratio of the change in the capital stock to the change in output. For example, if every $3 in plant and equipment added to the capital stock is associated with $1 in additional output per year, the ICOR would be 3. Put another way, if the $150 million devoted to net investment in our economy is associated with an increase of $50 million in the annual flow of output, then the ICOR would be 3. Note that an increase in output of $50 million would be 5 percent of the initial product of $1 billion. Thus the growth rate of the economy—in this case, 5 percent—would be ⋅ equal to the net investment rate divided by the ICOR—in this case, 15 percent divided by 3.

This logic suggested to Nurkse and others the great importance of increasing the rate of capital formation. Assume, for example, that the observed ICOR actually describes the capital requirements for increased output and that it will remain constant at 3 in the face of an increase in investment. Then, if the net investment rate in an underdeveloped economy could be increased from 15 percent to 24 percent, the rate of growth of that economy could be increased from 5 percent to 8 percent. To development economists this suggested a clear role for the government. If private savings were not enough to finance increased investment, and if foreign aid could not be obtained on an adequate scale, then the government must increase taxes in order to finance capital formation. The government could either lend the tax money to the private sector (say, through development banks) or use the tax monies to undertake investment projects of its own. In either case, the all-important rate of capital formation would be increased.

Two decades of experience with these kinds of development policies have caused some disillusionment. First of all, as tax revenues have grown, government expenditures have tended to keep pace, leaving less of a surplus for investment purposes than might have been imagined. Second, some very impressive investment programs have not had the desired impact on output. Much of the capital has been invested wastefully, sometimes on projects that serve better as monuments to their builders than as contributions to the nation's production. Inefficient projects obviously increase the incremental capital-output ratio, and if the ICOR increases along with the rate of net investment, then the rate of growth of output will not increase at all. In practice, less developed countries show a wide range of ICORs, ranging from as low as 2 to as high as 6 or more. For many countries, then, reducing the ICOR—making capital more productive—is as important as increasing the rate of capital formation.

The Role of the Interest Rate

As part of the effort to encourage capital formation, many of the less developed countries deliberately kept interest rates low. Governments lent foreign aid funds or domestic tax revenues to private firms—or made funds available to government agencies—at interest rates much lower than those prevailing on the open market. At the same time, banks were encouraged to lend funds at low interest rates and were often forbidden to pay more than a ceiling interest rate to their depositors. The idea was that the low interest rates would stimulate capital formation. Furthermore, it was assumed that the low rates of private saving in the economy were due to low incomes and would not be very responsive to higher interest rates.

This kind of reasoning ignored two important factors in the economy. (1) When governments offered loans at low interest rates, investors as a whole were typically interested in borrowing much more money than the government had available. If governments had raised interest rates, then loan funds would have gone to the projects that were able to earn the highest return and hence were able to pay the highest rate. Instead, governments generally used other standards for allocating scarce investment funds. Sometimes funds were allocated to the projects that the government felt were most worthy, sometimes they went to investors who were friends or relatives of government officials, and sometimes they were given as a result of outright bribery. Allocating scarce investment funds in this way contributed to the inefficiency of investment projects and a high incremental capital-output ratio. The actual rate of investment was not stimulated, since the available investment funds were limited. All that was stimulated by this allocation method was a demand for the funds greater than the supply.

(2) Governments also ignored the fact that ceilings on interest rates to savers were often being enforced in times of moderate or high inflation. This meant that the purchasing power of savings—even after interest payments were added in—often diminished. For example, if the banks were restricted to paying no more than 12 percent to their depositors and the rate of inflation were 20 percent, then the real value of a depositor's savings would go down by 8 percent a year. The negative real return on savings deposits often discouraged families from saving at all, or it encouraged them to hold their savings in an idle form, such as precious metals that might be smuggled into the country. Every dollar of savings used to buy precious metals from abroad was a dollar that could not be used to buy machinery for the country's development.

Several countries have tried to reform this system of artificially low interest rates, often with marked success. In 1965, for example, banks in South Korea were paying a ceiling interest rate of 15 percent, while the rate of inflation was 20 percent. This meant that bank depositors were losing 5 percent a year in purchasing power. The Korean government acted to raise interest rates to 30 percent and then consistently held them substantially above the rate of inflation. As a result, the savings rate in the country doubled within three years. At the same time, the higher interest rates did not discourage investment, because the demand for investment funds was already much greater than the supply. Rather, the greater supply of investment funds permitted a higher net investment rate in the economy. The efficient use of investment funds also kept the ICOR at one of the lowest levels in the world.

The Role of Trade Policies

In many countries government trade policies—especially *Trade Restrictions* (see pp. 300–306) designed to promote *Balanced Growth* (see pp. 324–27)—have also interfered with the efficient use of investment resources. High tariff walls often provided extraordinary levels of protection for domestic industry, regardless of its efficiency. Many governments have tried to ration imports, which often meant that large amounts of capital equipment stood idle while firms waited for licenses to import the raw materials they needed to operate. Reductions in trade restrictions were another important part of South Korea's economic reforms. These actions helped to increase the rate of growth of production from 6 percent before 1965 to 11 percent afterwards.

An Evaluation of Capital Formation

Today, development economists as a whole are less enthusiastic than they were in the 1950s about the central role of capital formation. They are much more inclined to stress the efficient use as well as the quantity of investment resources.

Nonetheless, capital formation is still recognized as important. It can increase productivity in existing lines of production, it can enable the economy to enter new lines of production, and it can embody new technological developments in production. But policies to increase the efficiency of the use of the capital stock are as important as policies to increase its rate of growth.

BALANCED GROWTH

Balanced growth is a pattern of economic development in which each sector of production grows as demand for its output grows. Thus the pattern of supply in the economy changes in balance with the pattern of demand.

The concept of balanced growth was introduced into the development literature by the Norwegian economist, Ragnar Nurkse. It is often associated with the concept of the big push, developed by Paul N. Rosenstein-Rodan of M.I.T. This controversial theory holds that development can occur only if it is initiated by a widespread program of investment simultaneously taking place in many sectors of the economy.

The Case for Balanced Growth and the Big Push

The case for balanced growth and the big push is rooted in a logic that Rosenstein-Rodan first advanced in the example of a shoe factory. Assume that a less developed country tries to initiate development by building a modern, large-scale shoe factory. It hires workers who had been unemployed or helping on their families' farms but making very little contribution to production. All that changed after the first year of factory production is that the country now has a good many shoes available, and the shoe workers now have an income they had not previously received. If these workers would simply use their new incomes to buy the shoes, there would be no problem. The difficulty arises because the workers want to spend only a fraction of their incomes on shoes but want to spend most of their incomes on other goods—food, clothing, and shelter. If shoe workers are the only ones who increase their incomes, the shoe factory would only be able to sell a fraction of its output, and the investment in that factory would not prove profitable.

The more general form of the argument holds that economic development in the modern world requires large-scale factories in order to capture important economies of scale. However, the income generated by one or two such factories will be expressed as a balanced demand for a variety of goods. Thus, the pattern of supply created by the building of one or two factories will not be appropriate to the pattern of demand of the new factory workers. As Nurkse put it, "the need for a balanced diet" gives rise to the need for balanced growth.

If we must have large-scale units of production and if we must immediately create a balanced pattern of new production, then clearly the need is for a widespread program of large-scale investments, or a big push. As Rosenstein-Rodan put it, "proceeding bit by bit will not add up in its effects to the sum total of the single bits." The big push calls for balanced growth in the short run, on a year-to-year basis, not just as a long-run policy goal. This line of thinking stresses massive investment programs, often guided by the government and aimed at widespread industrialization for the domestic market.

An Evaluation of Balanced Growth

The logic of the balanced growth argument is appealing, and many governments have attempted to pursue development policies along these lines. Upon reflection, however, it becomes clear that a balanced growth-big push program is not feasible, is not necessary, and is not desirable.

(1) The program is not feasible, because many factors of production are scarce, even if the country has a plentiful supply of unskilled labor. A big push to achieve balanced growth would require vast amounts of capital—beyond the saving and borrowing capacity of most poor countries. It would require extensive skills in engineering, organization, and industrial management. It would require large amounts of foreign exchange—dollars and other foreign currencies—to buy the capital goods needed to build the factories and the raw materials needed to supply them. Thus it would not be possible for less developed countries to build in a single year large-scale shoe factories, pants factories, tomato canneries, bicycle factories, and all the others needed to provide a "balanced diet" of consumer goods. Large-scale production in one industry can often only be achieved at the expense of large-scale production in the others.

(2) The program of balanced growth is not necessary because it is possible for a less developed country to sell its increased output of specific goods even without experiencing a large increase in its own purchasing power. In the first place, the building of a shoe factory in a country may make shoes widely available for the first time at reasonable prices. This may cause all kinds of other workers to buy more shoes and fewer of the other goods that the newly employed shoe workers can now buy. Second, the building of the shoe factory may cause a change in world trade patterns. The country may stop importing as many foreign shoes once the shoe factory is built within its borders, or it may export a large quantity of the shoes it is now producing. Since world trade patterns are not fixed, these are two very real prospects for selling the output of the shoe factory.

(3) The program of balanced growth is not desirable, because it flies in the face of the principle of comparative advantage (see *Absolute and Comparative Advantage,* pp. 273–78). The country may have large cattle resources that it is exporting in the form of beef and hides while simultaneously importing shoes made abroad with those same hides. Such a country might benefit much more by using its hides to produce shoes for the world market, and then importing canned tomatoes, bicycles, pants, and all the rest with the money earned from the sale of shoes. By specializing along the lines of its comparative advantage, a country might be able to develop considerable skills at shoe making and to concentrate its limited research

capabilities on improved manufacture of shoes under local conditions. These advantages of specialization are not possible under a program of balanced growth.

Thus, we can conclude that the program of short-run balanced growth—simultaneous development of production capability in a wide range of industries—is not a useful guideline for economic development.

Alternatives to Short-Run Balanced Growth

Two alternatives can be advanced to the program of short-run balanced growth implied in the big push policy: unbalanced growth or balanced growth over time. Which approach is desirable and feasible may depend on the circumstances of the individual country.

Unbalanced growth occurs when a country attempts to pursue its comparative advantage by specializing in certain agricultural or manufacturing industries largely for the export market. For example, one of the leading sectors of Japan's remarkable development in the late nineteenth century was the production of silk for the world market—first raw silk and later silk textiles. Today, a small country like Singapore—little more than a single city on an island—cannot achieve large-scale production on a balanced range of goods. It does, however, refine petroleum on a very large scale by processing the crude oil produced by its neighbors and selling the refined products throughout Asia.

Balanced growth over time is a strategy more feasible for a country with a large domestic market and a wide range of natural resources. It can evolve one step at a time. In one year the country might build a large-scale shoe factory to substitute for its existing imports of shoes. The next year it might replace imports by building a pants factory, with a tomato cannery the third year, and a bicycle factory the fourth. Over time a large country like India or Brazil could hope to achieve large-scale production of a wide variety of goods produced for the domestic market. Indeed, throughout the 1950s and the early 1960s, both India and Brazil pursued these kinds of policies. India came to produce such goods as steam locomotives, typewriters, air conditioners, and jet aircraft. Brazil came to produce railroad cars, adding machines, freezers, and buses. Even a country as large as Brazil could grow only at moderate rates when it ignored comparative advantage. In the mid-1960s it turned away from its policies of balanced growth over time and stopped artificially discouraging export production. From 1968 to 1975 exports went from $1.9 billion to $8.7 billion, representing a sustained growth rate of nearly 25 percent a year. At the same time the growth of total production increased sharply to 10 percent a year, one of the fastest rates in the world. By the 1970s, Brazil was earning more through the sales of manufactured goods than through its traditional export, coffee. It exports watches to Switzerland, shoes to Italy, soybeans to Japan, and automobile engines to the United States. Thus, even a large country with diverse resources and a large internal market can profit by moving away from a policy of balanced growth. Brazil has enjoyed a new prosperity by following its comparative advantage to fit into a pattern of world economic specialization.

LAND REFORM

Land reform is the redistribution of land ownership from large landlords to those who have been working the land as tenants, paid agricultural workers, or serfs. Sometimes land reform is defined more broadly to include other forms of changing land ownership, such as the consolidation of very small parcels of land, the creation of cooperative or collective farms, or the division of lands previously held in common by the inhabitants of a village. Here we will discuss land reform only in the narrower sense of the redistribution of the ownership of large estates.

The need for land reform is suggested by the following statistics for Latin America in the mid-1960s: In Brazil some 4.7 percent of the farms used 59 percent of the country's land devoted to agriculture. In Guatemala a mere 0.1 percent of the farms held 41 percent of the land.

Land reform typically has two major objectives. The first is a more equal distribution of the income from agriculture and of the social and political power associated with land ownership. The second is increased agricultural production from better use of the land. A land reform program almost automatically helps to achieve the first objective of more equal income distribution. The success or failure of a program, however, often hinges on whether it increases—or at least maintains—the level of agricultural production. This in turn may depend on the original system of land tenure—the pattern of land holdings—as well as the precise character of the land reform.

Agricultural economists have described three broad patterns of large land holdings in less developed countries: (1) the collection of small plots that a landlord leases to individual tenant farmers, (2) the integrated plantation, and (3) the traditional landed estate. Land reform has different implications in each type of holding.

Collection of Small Plots

In some parts of the world—including India—large land holdings are merely collections of many small plots of land that a single landlord leases to individual tenants. The tenants may pay a rent that is fixed in terms of money, or they may engage in sharecropping. Sharecroppers agree to pay the landlord some share of the crop that they harvest or of the money it brings. The share is often as high as one-half or two-thirds.

Often the plots are too small for families to do more than eke out a subsistence level of living—especially after they have paid the landlord. From the standpoint of production, the tenant farmer has very little incentive to invest in improvements of the land, such as fences, storage sheds, tree crops, or irrigation wells. For one thing, he cannot be sure that he will be able to lease the land the following year. But above all he is afraid that once he improves his plot the landlord will evict him or raise his rent.

The landlord makes no contribution to production. Thus land reform that displaces him and distributes land ownership to the tenants cannot hurt production—and may even improve it substantially. The new owners of the plots may now be able to improve their lands, secure in the knowledge that they are the ones who will enjoy the benefits.

The Integrated Plantation

The opposite extreme is represented by the integrated plantation, like the tea plantations of South Asia or the banana plantations of Central America. Typically, many kinds of specialized workers are joined together for the growing—and sometimes the elementary processing—of a single export crop. The most productive of the plantations employ modern capital equipment and skilled management, both of which may sometimes be supplied by foreigners. Many functions—like marketing, purchasing, and training—are handled by the central management. Typically, the laborers work for wages and have no stake in the land beyond what they are paid for working it. Often the land is worked very intensively in growing crops like sugar, coffee, and rubber. In some cases, the large size of the plantation may reflect not only the economic power of its owner but also economies of scale. For example, if expensive capital equipment is used in the growing and harvesting of the crop, it will pay for itself only if it can be used over a large area of land.

In some cases it is possible to divide up a large plantation among the families that work it without any loss of production. Plantation workers, however, seldom exhibit the "land hunger" of the small tenant farmer. Rather, they have grown accustomed to working for wages, and their demands are typically for higher wages and benefits and better working conditions. This can be useful because in many cases the plantation needs the central management and specialized capital equipment that the owners have been providing. If the nationalization of a foreign-owned plantation causes the withdrawal of top management and the removal of capital equipment, this can result in serious losses of production—at least until the country has had time to train new management and to replace the equipment. Some countries that have nationalized large plantations have attempted to maintain them as integrated production units, operating them either as state enterprises or as worker-run cooperative farms.

The Traditional Landed Estate

The traditional landed estate is most commonly found in Latin America, where it is known as the *latifundium*. It lies somewhere between our two other cases of the collection of small tenant farms and the integrated plantation; it typically represents a combination of uses. Some lands are worked on a large scale, entirely for the benefit of the owner, and some small plots are worked part-time by the families of the workers for their own benefit. Often the owner lives away from the estate, leaving its management to salaried officials. The estate lands are worked by laborers and tenants, many of whom may have been tied to the land by inherited rights and duties. For example, the father of the family may be obliged to work three days a week on the estate lands; his wife and daughters may be required to work as domestic servants in the house of the owner. In exchange, they may receive the use of a plot of land. In addition, some of their labor may be interest payment on family debts to the owner accumulated over the generations.

Often the Latin American *latifundium* is so vast that no serious effort is made to conserve or economize the use of land. Large parts of it may be used for cattle grazing, while other parts may be left idle. Often the *latifundia* are surrounded by privately-owned small plots, or *minifundia*. These lands are either owned individually by small farmers or sometimes owned collectively by Indian villages but tilled by individual families.

The combination of vast estate lands alongside small plots represents a blatantly inefficient use of land resources. Production could be increased if some of the lands used wastefully on the large estate could be added to the *minifundia* or to the small plots of the estate workers. At the same time, the landlord and his agents sometimes play a role in stimulating production. Not only do they manage the work on the lands operated for the owner, but they sometimes provide seed and equipment for the working of the small plots. A thorough program of land reform would have to insure that a state agency or a cooperative body took over these economic roles. Otherwise, the new owners of the estate lands would be forced to sink or swim by themselves.

An Evaluation of Land Reform

In many countries—including Japan, Mexico, and Taiwan—land reform has been an important instrument for the redistribution of income. It has created an independent group of small farmers able to support themselves and better able to demand their share of social and educational services from the government.

In many instances, however, land redistribution by itself is not enough to maintain and stimulate agricultural production. Often it is necessary to provide access to credit at reasonable rates of interest, to provide agricultural extension workers to train farmers in the newest production techniques, and to make it possible for small farmers to share in the use of agricultural implements.

Land reform will work best if it leaves families securely in control of their own lands. Ideally, a program of land reform will be carried out shortly after it is announced. The land will then be quickly transferred to its new owners, who will be able to improve that land with some confidence. By contrast, disputes over compensation and technical details may postpone the execution of a land reform program for many years. Then neither the existing owners nor the future owners will be able to undertake improvements with the confidence that they will be around to enjoy their benefits. Thus, the announcement of a land reform program can reduce production, although the carrying out of a well-planned program can stimulate production.

Land reform should never be seen as a substitute for price incentives to encourage agricultural production. During the 1950s and early 1960s many less developed countries pursued economic policies that discouraged rather than stimulated such production. For example, they often imposed very high tariffs on manufactured goods, while imposing low tariffs on agricultural goods. This had the effect of creating a high price for the goods that farmers needed to buy but a low price for the goods that farmers sold. In addition, governments sometimes severely restricted the export of agricultural commodities, thus denying farmers the advantage of the higher prices that they might have enjoyed on the world market. Together, these policies created a "price squeeze" that often held back agricultural development. In addition, many of the larger less developed countries put the great bulk of their investment funds into industrialization. They neglected investments in those things that could have made agriculture more productive and more profitable—roads, irrigation facilities, fertilizer, storage facilities, and research.

These policies can be corrected even without land reform. But unless they are corrected, programs of land reform will not make a maximum contribution to increased agricultural production.

INDEX